Dmytro Stus

Vasyl Stus
Life in Creativity

Translated from the Ukrainian by Ludmila Bachurina

UKRAINIAN VOICES

Collected by Andreas Umland

19 *Olesya Yaremchuk*
    Unsere Anderen
    Geschichten ukrainischer Vielfalt
    Aus dem Ukrainischen übersetzt von Christian Weise
    ISBN 978-3-8382-1635-5

20 *Oleksandr Mykhed*
    „Dein Blut wird die Kohle tränken"
    Über die Ostukraine
    Aus dem Ukrainischen übersetzt von Simon Muschick
    und Dario Planert
    ISBN 978-3-8382-1648-5

21 *Vakhtang Kipiani (Hg.)*
    Der Zweite Weltkrieg in der Ukraine
    Geschichte und Lebensgeschichten
    Aus dem Ukrainischen übersetzt von Margarita Grinko
    ISBN 978-3-8382-1622-5

22 *Vakhtang Kipiani (ed.)*
    World War II, Uncontrived and Unredacted
    Testimonies from Ukraine
    Translated from the Ukrainian by Zenia Tompkins and Daisy Gibbons
    ISBN 978-3-8382-1621-8

The book series "Ukrainian Voices" publishes English- and German-language monographs, edited volumes, document collections, and anthologies of articles authored and composed by Ukrainian politicians, intellectuals, activists, officials, researchers, and diplomats. The series' aim is to introduce Western and other audiences to Ukrainian explorations, deliberations and interpretations of historic and current, domestic, and international affairs. The purpose of these books is to make non-Ukrainian readers familiar with how some prominent Ukrainians approach, view and assess their country's development and position in the world. The series was founded and the volumes are collected by Andreas Umland, Dr. phil. (FU Berlin), Ph. D. (Cambridge), Associate Professor of Politics at the Kyiv-Mohyla Academy and Senior Expert at the Ukrainian Institute for the Future in Kyiv.

Dmytro Stus

VASYL STUS
Life in Creativity

Translated from the Ukrainian by Ludmila Bachurina

Bibliografische Information der Deutschen Nationalbibliothek

Die Deutsche Nationalbibliothek verzeichnet diese Publikation in der Deutschen Nationalbibliografie; detaillierte bibliografische Daten sind im Internet über http://dnb.d-nb.de abrufbar.

Bibliographic information published by the Deutsche Nationalbibliothek
Die Deutsche Nationalbibliothek lists this publication in the Deutsche Nationalbibliografie; detailed bibliographic data are available in the Internet at http://dnb.d-nb.de.

УКРАЇНСЬКИЙ ІНСТИТУТ //ІІІКНИГИ

Dieses Buch wurde mit Unterstützung des Translate Ukraine Translation Program veröffentlicht.
This book has been published with the support of the Translate Ukraine Translation Program.

Cover images: Cover of the KGB criminal case file of Vasyl Stus (1972), Branch State Archives of the Security Service of Ukraine (HDA SBU) 6/67298/1; Photos of Vasyl Stus from the 1972 criminal case file, HDA SBU 6/67298/1/6 zv. Public Domain.

ISBN-13: 978-3-8382-1631-7
© *ibidem*-Verlag, Stuttgart 2021
First published in Ukrainian by Dukh i Litera Publishing House

Alle Rechte vorbehalten

Das Werk einschließlich aller seiner Teile ist urheberrechtlich geschützt. Jede Verwertung außerhalb der engen Grenzen des Urheberrechtsgesetzes ist ohne Zustimmung des Verlages unzulässig und strafbar. Dies gilt insbesondere für Vervielfältigungen, Übersetzungen, Mikroverfilmungen und elektronische Speicherformen sowie die Einspeicherung und Verarbeitung in elektronischen Systemen.

All rights reserved. No part of this publication may be reproduced, stored in or introduced into a retrieval system, or transmitted, in any form, or by any means (electronic, mechanical, photocopying, recording or otherwise) without the prior written permission of the publisher. Any person who does any unauthorized act in relation to this publication may be liable to criminal prosecution and civil claims for damages.

Printed in the EU

Dedicated to all who keep the faith
against "objective" circumstances
The Author

Either the world will accept me as I am, as birthed by my mother, or it will kill me, destroy me. But I will not give up! And from every one of my moments, from every feeling and thought I will draw my portrait, that is, a portrait of the whole world ...
Vasyl Stus

Contents

Preliminary Remarks 9

Life after Death: Reburial and Struggle for Heritage (Year 1989) ... 17

Vasyl Stus' Ancestry and Childhood 63

The Poet's Youth 113

Meetings and Leave-Takings (1961–1963) 131

The Bastion of Your Own Self (1963–1965) 155

"And All That Is Like the Gifts of the Lord" (1966–1972) 197

"Creativity Time / Dichterzeit" 257

Epilogue: A Chronicle of Resistance 331

Preliminary Remarks

Vasyl Stus.
Poet.
Human rights activist.
Man.
Friend. Husband. Father. Prisoner. Philosopher. Acquaintance. Beloved. Known and unknown. Politician and anti-politician at the same time. Alive and long dead — from the viewpoint of human life, but not in historical perspective.

Who are You? Why, for several decades after Your death, has Your figure been attracting attention, provoking resistance from some and true admiration from others? Why are You clambering up and falling down at the same time?

Why, despite such a significant interest in You, do the following words by Mykola Ryabchuk seem both so close to the truth and at the same time unrelated to Your texts: "*Vasyl Stus, demythologized by young critics, has much less of a chance of becoming a Ukrainian popular cultural hero than his mythologized populist hypostasis may suggest*"?[1]

And what made almost 100,000 people pour into the frosty streets of Kyiv on November 19, 1989, to pay their last respects to You, who had remained unknown even to many writers. (People have often confessed to me that they learned about Vasyl Stus on that day. But no famous person, as far as I know, dared to write about it).

For some reason, the *fate* of Vasyl Stus has strengthened with time and still serves as a litmus test of authenticity, proving once again that a person, against all odds, is still able to overcome fear and become worthy of his calling. I am sure that if the officials of the Ukrainian Communist Party Central Committee and KGB, who

---

[1] Mykola Riabchuk, "'Nebizh Rilke, syn Tarasa' (Vasyl Stus)," in *Heroi ta znamenytosti v ukrainskii kulturi*, ed. and compil. Oleksandr Hrytsenko (Kyiv: UTsKD, 1999), 231.

decided in 1972 to charge the poet, had realized that they were creating a national myth of the indomitable Ukrainian spirit, they would never have brought the case, which was completely made up and "tied" to the confrontation between Petro Shelest and Leonid Brezhnev,[2] to court.

But that's exactly what happened ...

At that time, the same Fate—combining the instinct of self-preservation and the desire for self-immolation, providence, and faith, everyday life and holiday—led Stus' parents to move from starving and despairing Rakhnivka to working Stalino. And the same Fate drove Vasyl from there to Kyiv, a city that repeatedly rejected him as a foreign body before honoring him as a hero after his death. Fate tested the poet in new ways and by new trials, but he, divining its commands, found in himself the strength and will to proudly accept the challenge. This is how the mystery of Vasyl Stus' life was created, according to whose internal logic, against all odds, he had to self-actualize to the very maximum, to "expend" himself. A constant readiness to maximally fill the moment of life, whatever the circumstances, makes it possible to speak today of the phenomenon of Vasyl Stus—a man, a poet, a husband, a father, a son, known and unknown, good and ...

Yet this book is not only about Vasyl Stus. After all, whoever he was, whatever he created of himself, his dependence on the socio-cultural and political conditions under which he happened to live was so great that to understand the true motives of the poet's actions, it would be necessary to encompass his social history. Then what could we say about Vasyl Stus, whose personality would thus be subordinated to the *"common, to social life, in all its concrete historical connections and indirectness"*?[3]

In some of his manifestations, this *"esthete, aristocrat, Westerner, this admirer of the esoteric Rilke and anyone hostile to what is*

---

[2]   For more details see Mikhail Kheifets, *Izbrannoe*, Vol. 3: *Ukrainskiie siluety. Voennoplennyi sekretar'* (Kharkiv: Folio, 2000), 26–28.

[3]   Dmitry Blagoi, "Problemy postroeniia nauchnoi biografii Pushkina," *Literaturnoe nasledstvo*, Vol. 16/18 (Moscow, 1934): 270. See also I. Ya. Losievskii, "Nauchnaia biografiia pisatelia: problemy interpretatsii i tipologii" (Kharkiv: Krok, 1998), 22.

'*ours,*' *this foreign spirit*"⁴ paradoxically proved much closer to the established tradition of subordinating the Ukrainian artist to the pains and problems of his people than to any high aesthetic detachment from political discourse (the latter, however, does occupy an extremely important place in Stus' poetic world). The poet voluntarily consigned the Word to the struggle for the preservation of Ukraine's national dignity and tradition. "*If life were better, I would not write poetry, but would work on the land,*"⁵ he wrote in the preface to the collection *Zymovi Dereva* (*Winter Trees*). And this was not a pose. It was rather a conscious choice and the expression of a readiness to form part of a great national tree.⁶

In these circumstances, the trends and tendencies of literary fashion, which occupy an important place in the formal aspect of the poet's work, are always assigned a secondary, subordinate function.⁷ "*The main thing is not to betray the truth of life,*" Vasyl Stus used to say.

---

4   Riabchuk, "'Nebizh Rilke, syn Tarasa' (Vasyl Stus)," 232.
5   Vasyl Stus, "Dvoie sliv chytachevi," in his *Tvory*, 4 vols, 6 books (Lviv: Prosvita, 1994-1999), Vol. 1, Book 1: 42.
6   It is with the living tree that the poet most often associated the nation, the people, and tradition. See, in particular, his programmatic works: *The Broken Evening Branch Is Swaying…*, *We Are Circling Around the Trunk…*, etc.
7   In a way this confirms the formation of the traditional, rather than modern, discourse around Stus' work. See, in particular, "'Stusivs'ki chytannia'," *Slovo i chas*, No. 7 (1998): 17-28 (papers by Mykhailyna Kotsiubynska, Yevhen Sverstiuk, Eleonora Solovei, and Mykhailo Naienko; No. 8 (1998): 62-70 (papers by Mykola Bondar, Halyna Burlaka, Mykola Kodak, Viktoriia Plaksina, and Dmytro Stus); as well as the following articles: Mykhailyna Kotsiubynska, "Poet," in Vasyl Stus, *Tvory*, Vol. 1, Book 1: 7-38; Kotsiubynska, "Fenomen Stusa," *Suchasnist'*, No. 9 (1991): 26-35; Mykola Zhulynsky, "Vasyl Stus, 1938-1985," *Literaturna Ukraina*, April 19, 1990; Yuri Shevelyov, "Trunok i trutyzna: Pro *Palimpsesty* Vasylia Stusa," *Vasyl Stus u zhytti, tvorchosti, spohadakh ta otsinkakh suchasnykiv*, compil. and ed. Osyp Zinkevych and Mykola Frantsuzhenko (Baltimore and Toronto: Smoloskyp, 1987), 368-401, etc. All of these authors in one way or another comprehend the figure of Vasyl Stus primarily in the traditional Ukrainian context, barely indicating a direction of possible intertextual and comparative studies. They are opposed by a small group of researchers of a more modern cast, as it were, whose texts are mostly collected in the book *Stus yak tekst*, ed. Marko Pavlyshyn (Melburn: Department of Slavic Studies, Monash University, 1992) (articles by Tamara Hundorova, "Fenomen Stusovoho 'zhertvoslova'," pp 1-29, and Marko Pavlyshyn, "Kvadratura kruha: prolehomeny do otsinky Vasylia Stusa," 31-52). The figure and works of Vasyl Stus are perceived through a largely non-traditional discourse in the articles by

Given this choice (today is the pathetic cliché is that of "serving the interests of the people"), it is not surprising that Vasyl Stus entered the history of Ukrainian literature and culture not thanks to his poems, but, as it were, only with their substantial support. And when, in the mid-1970s, his poems, as insightfully recited by Nadiia Svitlychna, started to be heard quite often on Radio Liberty, behind them there was the image of a fighter against the system, a man who for many listeners was an example of inviolability.

In this way, complementing and opposing each other, the works and biography of Vasyl Stus continue to exist today. The writer, whose works organically combine elements of populism, and of the modern and postmodern,[8] in real life appears to be a post-sixtier,[9] a dissident who, "*guided by personal responsibility ... for the fate of the whole nation*," decided that it was not only possible but necessary "*to oppose the authorities' violence by adopting a position of civil disobedience.*"[10] Strict adherence to this position through his whole life paradoxically brought him closer to and, at the same time, distanced him from the sixtiers' movement and its ideas. Vasyl Stus was well aware that his path guaranteed neither career success nor material benefits. It was a path to nowhere; nevertheless, he recklessly offered himself for the defense of national and human dignity: "*Fate has given me a sign – I bravely follow its call. For I want to be worthy of the native people, who will be born tomorrow, having thrown off the shame of age-old languishing. And in that nation, I will achieve immortality!*"[11]

To follow this path with dignity, it was necessary not only to learn to endure moral and physical torture and humiliation, to multiply the copies of his works, which were destroyed by civil servants at the first opportunity; it was necessary not just to harden and

---

Vasyl Ivashko, "Mif pro Vasylia Stusa yak dzerkalo shistdesiatnykiv," *Svitovyd*, No. 3 (1994): 104–120; Kost Moskalets, "Strasti po Vitchyzni: Lyst do mandrivnyka na Skhid," in his *Liudyna na kryzhyni* (Kyiv: Krytyka, 1999), 209–254.

[8] See Mykhailo Naienko, "Vystup na pershykh Stusivs'kykh chytanniakh," *Slovo i Chas*, No. 6 (1998): 26–28; Dmytro Stus, "*Palimpsesty* Vasylia Stusa: tvorcha istoriia ta problema tekstu," in Vasyl Stus, *Tvory*, Vol. 3, Book 1: 13.

[9] Naienko, "Vystup na pershykh Stusivs'kykh chytanniakh", 28.

[10] Vasyl Stus, "Holos z Ukrainy," in his *Tvory*, Vol. 4: 482.

[11] Idem, "Lyst do druziv vid 30.07.1978," ibid., 468.

accept separation from family and friends; but also to create an inner world that would allow him to feel confidence and not despair under any circumstances. Mykhailyna Kotsiubynska describes this as "*self-exploration*," a quote (or is it a term?) borrowed from Vasyl Stus himself.[12]

The ability to balance the demands of his inner world and his actions—"with/without dignity"—at a sky-high height, in the historical conditions of the second half of the twentieth century, allowed the poet to withstand all the trials that befell him.

How was his inner world formed, out of which not only poems and works, but—perhaps even more significantly—Stus' style of life grew, a style described by the poet's contemporaries as an inability to pass by someone else in pain and despair?

It would seem that it is this openness to pain and suffering that makes the poet's figure either all-admirable or all-repulsive: no one is indifferent—there is either full recognition and esteem or else utter rejection and denial of this way of life. Given such polarization, it seems possible to see Vasyl Stus' personality at the intersection of those lines of force that transform a man of the crowd (an ordinary man) into a "*man with a biography.*" In this regard, Yuri Lotman says that "*not everyone who lives in this society has the right to a biography.*" After all, each type of culture "*forms its own models of 'people with biographies' and 'people without biographies' ... each culture creates in its ideal model a type of person whose behavior is entirely determined by the system of cultural codes and a person who has a certain freedom of choice for his own behavior model.*"[13]

A striking biography is always a "breaking out" of the ordinary, a violation of given canons, the creation of one's own honor code, and atypical behavioral conduct, recognized to be socially significant to the extent that the latter serves as an example for other people to define their life strategies. The creation and formation of a person with a proud and independent profile is a much more

---

[12] Mykhailyna Kotsiubynska, "Stusove 'samosoboiunapovnennia' (iz rozdumiv nad poeziieiu Vasylia Stusa)," *Suchasnist'*, No. 6 (1995): 137–144.

[13] Yurii Lotman, "Literaturnaia biografiia v istoriko-kul'turnom kontekste," *Uchenye zapiski Tartuskogo universiteta: Trudy po russkoi i slavianskoi filologii*, No. 683 (1986): 106.

complicated affair than any literary work. After all, literature is, in the first place, an attempt to comprehend the world by artistic means. Instead, life creation is the creation of oneself, one's destiny, and thus the world around oneself. And this struggle of the individual to have the right to -actualize, in some cases, actually affects the existing state of society, causing a greater or lesser reaction (transformation, modification) of the latter. And here, in this preface, we use lofty words, but only by using such high registers of contradiction can we speak about Vasyl Stus.

The poet's inner desire for self-actualization naturally coincided with the clear fixation by the Soviet and Ukrainian intelligentsia, in the first decades of the postwar period, on the philosophical ideas of existentialism, which were perceived by many unbelieving intellectuals as the only possible alternative to the doctrine of Marxism-Leninism.

Only a few people were lucky enough to buy, in the original, the theoretical works even of those authors relatively loyal to the USSR, like Karl Jaspers, Maurice Merleau-Ponty, Gabriel Marcel, Jean-Paul Sartre, and Albert Camus (translations were not even contemplated). Therefore, the fundamental understanding of this philosophical trend was formed by "husking" the grains of meaning from the groundless criticism of the existentialists by Marxist philosophers. Admittedly, this did not provide the opportunity to form a clear idea of existentialism as a philosophical trend; instead, it allowed anyone interested to add his own individual ideas about what existentialism might be. And the fact that existentialism proclaimed human individuality as the highest value, and connected the existence of the world with everyone's self-actualization, made this philosophical doctrine the most influential in the formation of not only the young Vasyl Stus but of many people who entered upon life in the late 1950s and early 1960s.

To a certain extent, it was his imagined and individually supplemented existentialism that helped Vasyl Stus start a concentrated effort to create an inner, real self, one of whom he would not be ashamed. In addition, the idea of living every day "on the edge," between life and death, "at the maximum," was very close to Stus' psychological type. That is why the poet finally managed to rid himself of the dominating influence of existentialist ideas only in the early 1970s. As Ivan Dziuba rightly remarks, Vasyl Stus outgrows his existential worldview, opening it *"into experiencing the fate of his people and belonging to them, into a feat for them."*[14]

The process of the formation of Vasyl Stus' personality actually finished on the eve of his arrest in 1972. The rest was simple and clear. Only one thing remained unclear: will you, Vasyl Stus, like millions of your predecessors, be able to pay the inhuman price? A decade-long fee for the right to be the one he wished, to complement the unfolding horizontal with a rapidly growing vertical.

Working on this book, I often caught myself thinking that the poet felt his destiny too early, and some of his actions before 1972 strangely resonated with the future. Having no rational explanation for this temporal rupture ("nonlinearity"), I decided to start the book with his reburial, when Vasyl Stus returned to Ukraine both as a creator and as a man with a biography. This was the beginning of his "life after death," the point that drew attention to his figure in his homeland. For him, this meant achieving absolute success, because all his life he sought to be interesting to his people.

I hope that *Vasyl Stus: Life in Creativity* will be only the first attempt to comprehend the mystery of Vasyl Stus' life. And that more thorough and interesting works in this direction will appear after its release. I have simply tried to collect and systematize what I regard as the most important material. And if it helps someone open the "door" to the secret of the life and work of Vasyl Stus, then my ten-year labor is not in vain.

---

[14] Ivan Dziuba, "Rizbiar vlasnoho dukhu," in Vasyl Stus, *Pid tiaharem khresta: Poezii* (Lviv: Kameniar, 1991), 19–20.

Life after Death: Reburial and Struggle for Heritage (Year 1989)

> Every star has its time — to rise and to go down ...
> Vasyl Stus

He had to return. Not to Rakhnivka, which suffered for hundreds of humiliating years, not even to Yuzivka–Stalino–Donetsk, under its skies swiftly filling with the smoke from gob piles, but to a city as hostile to strangers as Kyiv. This city still had to bow to us, the Ukrainians. And it did not matter that after the funeral of Lesia Ukrainka in July 1913,[1] it showed respect and fear only to the military forces of the Whites-Reds-Browns-Reds-Again, or filed to deceitfully bow in proudly flunkyish columns of demonstrations, thousands of people strong, selected and controlled by the KGB and MVD. We are coming back. So, you, flattering and ugly frog of internationalism, still have to bow to the nationalists: Yurii Lytvyn, Oleksa Tykhy, and Vasyl Stus ...

* * *

November 1989. Borisovo. Here and there in the cemetery there were markers without surnames. The world seemed to stop. I perceived only untrodden virgin snow, and divined rather than saw a seldom beaten path, which seemed to record the traces of a crime — infrequent visits to still fresh graves, filled by the newly deceased prisoners from the nearby prisons of the Perm region and tended by those providing services for the political camps VS-389/36 (strict and special regime units). It was not surprising. They were well paid. Unlike the criminal camps it was a quiet job and you could let

---

[1] For more details about Lesia Ukrainka's burial, attended by thousands of people, see M. O. Moroz, *Litopys zhyttia ta tvorchosti Lesi Ukrainky* (Kyiv: Naukova dumka, 1992), 514–515.

it slide that a significant number of the detainees did not show proper respect to the staff: money, as you know, does not smell.

For some reason, it was here, in the cemetery, as Slavko Chernilevsky (the director of the film *Vasyl Stus: The Road of Thorns*) too anxiously asked to wait to film the "historic" moment of my approach to the grave, that for the first time since my father's death my eyes filled with tears and my frame was racked by the dry spasms of internal sobbing. Taking my hat off my head, I tried to hide this unmanly moment, but the cameraman, Bohdan Pidhirny, had already set up the camera and followed me through the deep cemetery snow, forcing me to hasten into the forest to avoid his capturing my tear-stained face.

None of us knew for sure what would happen in a few hours, whether we would have to go on a hunger strike, as agreed with Oleh Pokalchuk, to gain permission to rebury Vasyl Stus and Yurii Lytvyn in Ukraine. I had to stay in the cemetery, and Oleh had to go to Chusovoy, suffering the first police blows. This thought flashed in my mind but did nothing to contain either the sobs or the tears.

Having jumped over the fence, I almost hid in the woods, leaving the indignant Bohdan with nothing. He could not follow with an old camera in his hands, realizing that any similar movement could harm the equipment, which would mean no chronicle.

After a while, after approaching the already familiar marker bearing a can on which the humiliating number "9" was carved, I was still not able immediately to soothe the internal spasm. But doing so strangely gave me confidence that everything would be fine.

"We will not go on a hunger strike," I told Oleh. "I will only go away with my dad."

He was not surprised, still being under the influence of nightly Bible readings. He, I and ... a mystical voice that sounded so distinctly that Oleh almost physically felt the presence of someone else with us.

"Strangely, I'm talking to my father," I told him.

And it was not important whether he believed me then or attributed my strange behavior to the considerable nervousness of a 23-year-old man, but he and I still remember the festive atmosphere of the Chusovoy hostel, which in the morning was filled with a pure disembodied calm and a readiness for everything. I have not felt anything like this before or since. It is likely through such an experience that monks bring themselves closer to the pure service of God, taming the flesh and tempering the spirit. It was easier for us (me?) as, other than Vasyl Stus, our spirits were tempered by the deaths of thousands of fighters against the Soviet regime and the millions of its wordless victims, who went to Perm, in particular, with obedient as sheep, hoping for incredible things. Someone had to be the first, to become a symbol of victory at least over forgetfulness, the myth of the indomitability of the Ukrainian spirit. And these were the first: Volodymyr Shovkoshytny, Vasyl Ovsienko, Stanislav Chernilevsky, Oleh Pokalchuk, Bohdan Pidhirny, Vasyl Hurdzan, Valerii Pavlov, Serhii Vachi, Volodymyr and Mykola Tykhy, the Perm/Chusovoy poet Yurii Belikov, the director of the Ogonyok ("Flicker") international mountain skiing center Leonard Postnikov, as well as dozens of other people who happened to be next to us, instead of in safety, having stepping aside, helped by the necessary acquaintance, advice or even by an almost illegal action. In particular, the driver of our truck, the father of six children, Valeryi Sidorov, drove the Ural off-road almost six hundred kilometers, having two flat tires, to pick up the bodies of Lytvyn and Stus. Police officers, on Moscow's orders, vilely accused him of killing a boy because it was necessary to somehow disrupt the reburial. But our determination and that of thousands of Kyivites was so obvious that even the regime gave in and the "all clear" came from both Kyiv and Moscow.

* * *

I had dreamed of reburial for four years, since the death of Vasyl Stus on the night of September 3/4, 1985.[2] However, when my

---

[2] All documents indicate the night of September 4 to 5, or simply September 4. However, after collecting a large number of testimonies and recollections, I think we can say that Vasyl Stus died on the night of September 3/4. And the next night, as Vasyl Ovsiienko writes in his memoirs, the body of Vasyl Stus was taken out of the dungeon in a "villainous" way.

mother, her sister Shura (Oleksandra Loveiko) and I, together with a close friend of our family, Margarita Dovhan, flew to Perm (via Moscow, because they had to pick me up, a member of a construction battalion, who had returned to his unit only a few days after surgery in Ivanovo), we could do nothing but stand over the grave on our arrival at the settlement of Kuchino.

"Cho zh vy tak dolga yekhali?" ("Why did it take you so long to get here?" [Russian]), Major Dolmatov asked my mother, glad that I was wearing a soldier's uniform and that the military commandant's office could be used on the first unpleasant occasions.

"I sent you a telegram, I asked you to wait, I...," Valentina Popelyukh[3] desperately whispered rather than said.

"Vy shto, nie panimaietie, shto schas nie zima, tieplo, tielo nachinaiet razlagatstsa. A khaladilnikav u nas nietu" ("Don't you realize that it is not winter? It is warm and the body is decomposing. And we have no refrigerators" [Russian]), another officer gave evidence of his care ...

"Killers,": the word just flew out of my mother's mouth, and we traveled the 10 kilometres to the village of Borisovo, where a freshly dug grave was located on its edge just near the swamp.

"Vot yesli by vy vchiera priiekhali... ("If you had come yesterday ..." [Russian]), a man in a civilian jacket stated ...

"I beg you, step away, let us be alone," my mother said with a restraint she could barely muster to the contented and frightened faces of the KGB officers. And we were left at the grave alone with them watching us only 20–50 steps away.

I felt a strange bitter taste in my mouth and the need to become a kind of support to my mother. She stooped to the lumps of a foreign land, which now put pressure on the chest of her husband Vasyl Stus, an obscure poet in Ukraine, whose stubborn letters had convinced her that they already belonged to history.

This black cross of women crucified on the grave made me promise to myself that the body of my dad, to whom we were not even allowed to say goodbye, would be pulled out of this almost eternal frozen earth. It was in April 1981 that we saw Vasyl Stus

---

[3] Valentyna Popelyukh (born 1938) was Vasyl Stus' wife.

alive for the last time.[4] Three years later, in 1984, we came to my father, but he would not consent to the "pre-rendezvous" humiliation and refused to meet. This was understandable ... But how could I forgive my mother's bitter tears, welling in her eyes along the jolting road on our way back from Kuchino camp to Chusovoy?

However, after my father's death, I had first to try to return Vasyl Stus' personal belongings and his manuscripts. In one of the letters that disappeared from our apartment during an unauthorized search, my father wrote that he was at work on a collection of poems and translations titled *The Bird of the Soul*. However, my mother's requests were not met.

"Poslie neabkhadimai pravierki lichnyie vieshchi vam vyshliut" ("Personal belongings will be sent to you on completion of the necessary check" [Russian]).

I could not obtain any other answer, and after returning from the construction battalion, I primarily concerned myself with this unreturned blue notebook containing Goethe, Rilke, Rimbaud and other "anti-Soviet" people whose works undermined the Soviet system. At that time, reburial seemed less important to me than the return of this inheritance, but the accelerating process of the USSR's partial disintegration and decentralization brought political issues to the forefront. The reburial, which seemed unlikely to happen only a year earlier, suddenly became a real prospect, and the newly created Galfilm studio's interest in making a film meant that it would tackle a lot of the organizational problems that were too complicated for a 23-year-old man.

So, when after a long correspondence the necessary permission from the Chusovsky district authorities was obtained, Vasyl

---

[4]   Paradoxically, in this very Chusovoy, whose river runs along lands made tragic by the fate of thousands and thousands of Ukrainians, from time to time frightening the eye with a glimpse of white (earth? bones?). The director of the Ogonyok Olympic mountain skiing center, Leonard Postnikov, opened a museum of the Chusovaya river. His first exhibits were the Ermak Chapel saved by Postnikov and a large memorial stone, the first monument to the victims of repression in the USSR. It was in 1981 that Vasyl Stus was still alive and had just arrived at VS-389/36, located at a distance of 40 km from Postnikov's future museum.

Gurdzan actively proceeded with collecting documents and permits for the transportation of Yurii Lytvyn's ashes. Volodymyr Tykhy did the same for his father Oleksa.

Reburials were originally planned for August 1989, but a telegram arrived the day before their departure about the dangerous epidemiological situation in the Perm region and a prohibition on exhumation. There was nothing for it but to postpone the reburial, and the shooting team had anyway flown to the Urals to film material about the already half-ruined camp:[5] the Soviet authorities were actively destroying the Gulag sites to hide at least in this way their crimes' locations and the machinery of their commission. The Soviet and fascist systems are very similar in this and many other respects: in 1944–1945, the SS men also destroyed death camps, driving the emaciated, nearly transparent skeletons of once healthy people and killing the exhausted by the side of the road.

"*On August 24, I was already in Perm,*" the film director Volodymyr Shovkoshytny recalls. "*Being the director of the film* Vasyl Stus: The Road of Thorns, *I was due to organize the reburial of the mortal remains of V. Stus, Y. Lytvyn, and O. Tykhy and, of course, to ensure the work of the film crew.*

There was no reason to worry about it. As late as June 15, Dmytro Stus, the poet's son, received an official response from the head of the multi-branch production association of housing and communal services (MPO ZhKKh) of the Chusovoy City Executive Committee of the Perm region, V. V. Kazantsev. It said: "In response to your application, MPO ZhKKh informs you that the permission for the reburial of the citizen Stus V. S. has been granted. Transportation of the remains is due to be performed in a zinc coffin. The necessary documents for exhumation and transportation of the remains will be issued upon your arrival in the town of Chusovoy."[6]

Albeit with a slight delay, the same documents were received for Yurii Lytvyn. The necessary documents for the reburial of

---

5   Mart Niklus, who managed to visit the site with Estonian TV, which was making a film about him, repeatedly mentioned this in his letters to me and Vasyl Ovsienko.
6   Volodymyr Shovkoshytny, "'Narode mii, do tebe ya shche vernu...'," *Ukraina*, No. 4 (1990): 7. The telegram is stored by the family in Vasyl Stus' archive.

Oleksa Tykhy were not prepared in time.⁷ There was an agreement for the reburial of Vasyl Stus and Oleksa Tykhy at the Lisove Cemetery. I didn't even think of the Baikove Cemetery: we would just be happy with reburial being allowed, and thankful for that.

The year of the reburial turned out to be too ambiguous. The vast majority of people were still caught in a web of fear and uncertainty. Society was still dominated by the belief that "perestroika" was initiated only to identify the newest freedom volunteers and to reap another bloody harvest. The intelligentsia grew more convinced that the regime did not have its former strength and character, but still continued to monitor events with fear, not daring open opposition.

The ideologues of the party system continued to take measures to "strengthen the international and patriotic education of the population," and the regime's newspaper *Pravda* published a summary of the CPSU Central Committee resolutions "*on additional measures to restore justice to victims of repression of the 1930s, 40s and early 50s. The Central Committee decided to submit for the consideration of the Presidium of the Supreme Soviet of the USSR a proposal for a legislative act to nullify the out-of-court decisions of "troikas" [three-member extrajudicial bodies that passed sentences during the Great Terror of 1937–1938] and "special" councils; and to consider all citizens who were repressed by the decisions of the specified bodies rehabilitated. This measure does not apply to traitors and punitive expeditioners of the Great Patriotic War period, Nazi criminals, etc.*"⁸

Fighters of the Organization of Ukrainian Nationalists (OUN) and the Ukrainian Insurgent Army (UPA) were considered traitors to the homeland. And the freedom volunteers and independence fighters of the 1960–1980s were not mentioned at all: the time had not yet come.

---

7   Shovkoshytny's statement in the above-mentioned article that the documents concerning Oleksa Tykhy were prepared is not correct. Their collection started in the last weeks before departure but not all the permits were obtained from the authorities. Had the reburial had taken place at that time, Oleksa Tykhy's ashes would most likely not have been transported.

8   V. F. Verstiuk, O. M. Dziuba, and V. F. Repryntsev, *Ukraina vid naidavnishykh chasiv do siohodennia: Khronolohichnyi dovidnyk* (Kyiv: Naukova dumka, 1995), 634–635.

However, the events of that year were accelerating with incredible speed. On February 11, 1989, the constituent conference of the Taras Shevchenko Ukrainian Language Society took place. That same year the withdrawal of Soviet troops from long-suffering Afghanistan finished and the media started a fraught debate on the draft program of the People's Movement of Ukraine for Reconstruction (i.e., Perestroika),[9] which involved the head of the ideological department of the CPU Central Committee, the future first President of Ukraine, Leonid Kravchuk. Although the latter defeated his not very courageous opponents with communist rhetoric, he objectively helped (*At least one can talk to him! And they show it on TV! And one isn't imprisoned for that, at least not right away!*) to overcome the panic fear of the USSR's state repressive machine.

At the same time, the government continued to conceal the truth about the consequences of the Chernobyl disaster. Many looked at the Armenian-Azerbaijani conflict in Nagorno-Karabakh with fear and hope for the eventual collapse of the Union. And it gradually turned into a banal massacre of civilians by the warring sides.

Society, divided into small interest groups, gathered in smoky kitchens. Closing the door tightly, turning on the water and covering the phone with a pillow (the simplest, though not very reliable protection against eavesdropping and interception), activists of newly formed public organizations as well as people simply involved in the recent repressions had intellectual conversations. Society was buzzing with excitement and the air seemed to thicken to such an extent that something was bound to happen. But what would it be?

However, this regards the, so to speak, "safe" official Ukrainian intelligentsia. There were also many Ukrainians who had returned from the camps and were actively involved in the process of legalizing the national political life of the republic. Thus, back in 1987, the Ukrainian Cultural Club (UCC) was established, which for a time held its meetings in the Rovesnyk ("Age Mate") club and was then the largest organized Ukrainian opposition structure in

---

[9] Ibid., 636–637.

Kyiv, and perhaps in the entire Ukrainian SSR. It was in the UCC that a core of active oppositionists was formed which included those who, quite in the spirit of the time, were active in the field of cultural studies. However, unlike official culture scholars (who, taking advantage of the moment, actively started filling in the "blank spots" of the Ukrainian literature of the Executed Renaissance period), Serhiy Naboka, Yevhen Sverstiuk, and other UCC members focused on the work of writers imprisoned or displaced from official creative life in the 1960s. After one of these meetings, which took place in early 1988, and was dedicated to the work of Vasyl Stus, the head of the ideological department of the CPU Central Committee, Leonid Kravchuk, directed that the Club be deprived of the right to hold its meetings in large halls, in which, despite the natural fear, a lot of people had always gathered.

At the beginning of 1988, the Ukrainian Group to Promote the Implementation of the Helsinki Accords was transformed into the Ukrainian Helsinki Union[10] (UHU), and the UCC joined it as a collective member.

The struggle of the Crimean Tatars for a return to their historical homeland also indirectly but significantly fueled the political situation in the republic. In July 1987, initiative groups in Uzbekistan alone collected about thirty thousand signatures under the text of the "Nationwide Appeal of the Crimean Tatars to M. S. Gorbachev."[11] They were supported by such iconic figures of Soviet culture as Yevgeny Yevtushenko, Bulat Okudzhava, Vladimir Dudintsev, and others.[12] For a number of reasons, this struggle did not find direct support among Ukrainians, who paid little attention to the problems of other peoples of the USSR and tended to focus

---

[10] Ibid., 628.
[11] Ibid., 626.
[12] Despite all the protests and appeals, on December 4, 1987, the USSR Council of Ministers passed a resolution "On restricting the registration of Crimean Tatars in a number of settlements of the Crimean Oblast and the Krasnodar Krai." See ibid., 627.

on the struggle against narrowing the sphere of use of the Ukrainian language.[13]

In Galicia in the late 1980s, there was a struggle for the legalization of the Ukrainian Greek Catholic Church, which was forced to go underground after the war. In November 1987, the Committee for the Defense of the Ukrainian Catholic Church was established in Lviv, headed by the long-term political prisoner and priest Ivan Hel.[14]

Such initial structuring of the national life, carried out by small groups of active citizens, took place in other republics as well. The leading role was played by people in the Baltic republics. The memory of their independent existence as national states had not been completely erased from their historical consciousness. In the midst of all these events, no one paid much attention to the increasingly noticeable pairing of the ideological education of Komsomol leaders with an economic one, embodied by the opening of the International Institute of Management in August 1989 in Kyiv.

1989 was to be a turning point, after which the Soviet government would either brutally crush the sprouts of new life, or the energy of the hatred accumulated during decades of fear would make social change irreversible. Mikhail Gorbachev used to repeat that "the process is already under way and there is no return to the past." However, the second component of this statement had yet to be proved.

The main event of 1989 was the first and last democratic election in the history of the USSR held on March 26. An important event of the election campaign was the inaugural conference of the Memorial Ukrainian Historical and Educational Society, which took place on March 4 at the Republican Cinema House. Wives,

---

[13] In particular, it is worth mentioning Oles Honchar's resonant letter to the Secretary General of the CPSU Central Committee, Mikhail Gorbachev, in which he expressed his concern about the narrowing of the sphere of use of Ukrainian and made proposals aimed at surmounting the shortcomings of the national and cultural policy of the USSR. It is also impossible to ignore Ivan Dziuba's series of articles, *Because It's Not Just Language, Sounds...*, which earned him the Taras Shevchenko State Prize in 1990.

[14] Verstiuk, Dziuba, and Repryntsev, *Ukraina vid naidavnishykh chasiv do siohodennia*, 627.

mothers and children of Valerii Marchenko, Vasyl Stus, Ivan Svitlychny, Oleksa Tykhy, Yuriy Lytvyn and other recent political prisoners who had either died in the camps or lost their health and ability to work there (like Ivan Svitlychny). During the break between meetings, an improvised information exhibition was held, the whose main purpose was to break the information blockade artificially imposed by the authorities on these names.

Although the act seemed quite illegal, the majority of the conference delegates still found the courage to read the materials that women hung on their persons (it was strictly forbidden by the directorate to hang anything on the walls).

This conference also showed the significant diversity in the perception of social processes (national, ideological,[15] tactical and strategic) by former convicts, which later led to the fragmentation and even mutual hostility of the once fellow prisoners.

Under the pressure of undeniable facts and evidence that did not threaten the then top Soviet and party leaders with direct discredit, the ban on the publication of crimes by the Soviet regime was raised, and on April 16, 1987 the official newspaper *Pravda Ukrainy* published the report of the Government-sponsored commission formed to study the circumstances and documents associated with the mass burial of Soviet citizens in the 19th quarter of

---

[15] Many of the debates at this conference were devoted to discussing such a seemingly insignificant terminological problem as what word should be used to describe the ideology of the repressions of the 1930s: *stalinizm* or *stalinshchyna*. Behind all this was the unwillingness of society to admit that the conveyor belt of death was not due so much the arbitrariness of one person (*stalinizm*) but fundamental to the basis of the existence and development of the state (*stalinshchyna*). In this context, they did not want to mention Lenin's name, which still remained beyond criticism, at least in public conversations and debates, or to focus on those repressed in the 1960s and 1970s. Although the persons repressed in those years were active participants in the founding congress, they were forced to accept the rules of the game proposed by the Central Committee and the KGB if they had any hope of public attention and mass media coverage. Information about the creation of the Memorial Society appeared in the official press, although it was significantly edited by censors.

the Dnipro forestry in Kyiv near Bykivnia. The commission's conclusions confirmed that mass executions had been carried out in this location by the NKVD in 1937-1941.[16]

However, the facts of the artificial famine in Ukraine and the closely connected movement of the Ukrainian sixties[17] continued to be concealed at the official level.

On July 1, 1989, the constituent conference of the People's Movement of Ukraine for Reconstruction[18] took place in Kyiv, and marked a fundamentally new stage in the government's confrontation with the people. Viacheslav Chornovil, who was actively supported by the Ukrainian poet Ivan Drach, and many other representatives of both the official and oppositional Ukrainian intelligentsia, should be recognized as the leader and main driving force of this process.

---

[16] See *Pravda Ukrainy*, April 16, 1989.

[17] In his study *Soviet Ukrainian Dissent*, Jaroslaw Bilocerkowycz provides interesting statistics of the social structure of the Ukrainian resistance movement in the second half of the 20th century: 58.9% of the dissidents, according to the researcher's incomplete and selective data, were from the peasantry; 30.4%, from the intelligentsia; 10.7%, were workers. For more details, see Jaroslaw Bilocerkowycz, *Soviet Ukrainian Dissent: A Study of Political Alienation* (Boulder and London: Westview, 1988), 67-68; see also Heorhii Kasyanov, *Nezhodni: Ukrains'ka intelihentsiia v rusi oporu 1960-80-kh rokiv* (Kyiv: Lybid', 1995), 190. Yet allow me to disagree with these eloquent figures (to my knowledge objective data is not available). Based on my personal communication with different people from these segments, at least 2/3 of those called "intellectuals" by Bilocerkowycz and Kasianov were of peasant origin, because the absolute majority of them belonged to the first (and not even the second) generation of the intelligentsia and, therefore, had no support from influential parents, friends, etc. Indirectly, the lack of such support and advice "helped" them find themselves behind bars in the KGB pre-trial detention facilities without any hope of escaping by great or small compromises with the authorities. Without an influential public "rearguard," those "peasants," who through great efforts made their way to the capital, had either to repent atrociously and sling the maximum amount of mud at their fellows or endure the maximum term of imprisonment. A smaller part of the "intelligentsia" consisted mainly of Russified dissidents of Jewish descent, who, although united with the Ukrainians by their struggle against the regime, defended not so much national as universal democratic values. These groups differed culturally and mentally to a large extent but were on mostly friendly terms.

[18] Verstiuk, Dziuba, and Repryntsev, *Ukraina vid naidavnishykh chasiv do siohodennia*, 640.

The name of Ivan Drach was notably repeated the most, as his resilience and steadfastness attracted the general attention. In the public mind, this was primarily due to the serious illness of his son, who was exposed to excessive radiation working as a doctor in the Chernobyl zone.

It is not surprising that Ivan Drach became the first leader of the People's Movement of Ukraine for Reconstruction (Rukh), whose constituent congress took place on September 8-10, 1989.[19] The hot summer of 1989 saw televised debates between Kravchuk, Drach, Popovych, and other initiators of the creation of this national public organization. There were also frequent meetings between the Chairman of the USSR Council of Ministers Nikolai Ryzhkov and representatives of the Donbas strike committees, as well as the consistent and constant demands, less noticeable in the Ukrainian environment, by the Crimean Tatars to return to their homeland.[20]

Add to this the numerous rallies that took place almost every day and it was clear that the authorities were gradually losing authority over a hitherto controlled society and openly feared the reburial of people whose very names were banned.

At the same time, there was a confrontation at the top: on the one hand, the TV debates between Leonid Kravchuk—Ivan Drach—Myroslav Popovych seemed to mark the moral defeat of the latter two; and, on the other hand, the very fact of such public televised debates was a remarkable achievement in the overcoming of seventy years of fear of the system. At the same time, letters condemning Leonid Kravchuk's behavior were sent for internal review to the ideological departments of the CPSU at the local level. Kravchuk was opposed by Volodymyr Ivashko, whom the Plenum of the Central Committee of the Communist Party of Ukraine (CC

---

[19] Verstiuk, Dziuba, and Repryntsev, *Ukraina vid naidavnishykh chasiv do siohodennia*, 642 At that time, the first recordings of Taras Petrynenko's song appeared. It contained the line: "even the birth of a child requires movement" (*rukh*).

[20] Despite the persecution and strict ban on the return of Crimean Tatars by police in Crimea, there was no concealing the obvious fact: contrary to official policy, Crimean Tatars were returning home. On July 7, 1989, the first issue of the Crimean Tatar *Dostluk* (*Friendship*) weekly supplement to the official newspaper *Krymskaia pravda* (*Crimean Truth*) was published in Simferopol, which was a first small victory.

CPU) on September 28, 1989, elected First Secretary of the CC CPU.[21] Ivashko replaced the seriously ill Volodymyr Shcherbytsky, under whose "reign" the reburial of Vasyl Stus was impossible.[22]

Ramifying tendencies in the country intensified: constant rallies in the Baltic republics turned into armed confrontation with the authorities, bloody conflict in Nagorno-Karabakh, a volcano of emotions in Crimea and Lviv. Such gradually laid the groundwork for the idea of reburial. And it was clear to all involved that this idea would become a national rather than family affair: both the authorities and Vasyl Stus' relatives lost the chance to keep reburial as an intimate family affair.

Since mid-1989, the direct pressure of the KGB on the family had also relaxed: the authorities temporarily acknowledged their defeat to conceal their ugly faces in the new era and the new states.

The events connected with politics and the reburial created a kind of power-psychological vacuum in which some could no longer prevent, while others did not yet have the audacity to act with confident responsibility in the absence of permission. Eventually, all meant that the burial, which was planned for August 1989, did not take place.

At the end of the summer, only a film crew went to Perm to film the hastily destroyed VS-389/36 camp, where Vasyl Stus' life journey was cut off.

The film crew, which was expected by Volodymyr Shovkoshytny in Perm, arrived there on August 28. From August 29 to September 1,[23] the camp was filmed in consultation with Vasyl Ovsienko, a former prisoner who had been held in the same ward as Vasyl Stus for several months.

At such a time we had to be limited to this.

---

[21] Verstiuk, Dziuba, and Repryntsev, *Ukraina vid naidavnishykh chasiv do siohodennia*, 643.

[22] I suspect the real reason for Volodymyr Shcherbytsky's personal (according to "informed" sources) hatred of Stus will not be known for a very long time. In any event, no official documents revealing his "direct" interference in the fate of Vasyl Stus have been found. However, at the level of "unofficial" conversations, there is much indirect evidence that, in 1972, Stus was convicted on the instructions of Shcherbytsky or of someone acting on his behalf.

[23] Shovkoshytny, "'Narode mii, do tebe ya shche vernu...'," 7

The tension continued to rise into October.

I was then convinced that reburial was a secondary matter. The main thing was to return my father's last collection *Bird of the Soul*, written during his second imprisonment, from exile. However, no results were gained through the correspondence carried out with the support of Henrikh Dvorko. Yet the original wording of the answer—"*all materials were destroyed after death*"—was softened after my strong reply and gave me some hope. However, the Writers' Union, the general situation, and the Ukrainian Helsinki Union, which had not yet been transformed into a political party, proved to be the catalyst that changed priorities: when an opportunity for reburial arises, it should be seized.

Slavko Chernilevsky[24] and I decided to depart in mid-November. A second official permit was obtained. Only confrontation in the press was cause for concern. It was in 1989 that the thick veil of silence around the name of Vasyl Stus was torn. *Prapor* (*Banner*), *Literaturna Ukraina* (*Literary Ukraine*), *Molod' Ukrainy* (*Youth of Ukraine*), *Ukraina*, *Literaturnaya Rossiya* (*Literary Russia*), *Zhovten'* (*October*), and *Kyiv* published small selections of poems with different commentary, which, despite the ugly preface-afterword, seemed to insistently introduce the name of Vasyl Stus into the Ukrainian literary context.[25]

---

[24] Stanislav Chernilevsky was a director of the three-part documentary film *Black Candle of the Enlightened Road*. Together with Volodynyr Shovkoshytny he did the bulk of the organizational work on reburial.

[25] The first materials appeared in the newspaper *Literaturna Ukraina* accompanied by a long and irresolute article of Mykola Zhulinsky, director of the Institute of Literature of the Academy of Sciences of Ukrainian SSR (see his *Iz zabuttia – v bezsmertia (Storinky pryzabutoi spadshchyny)* [Kyiv: Dnipro, 1990], 416–439). If a certain abstractness and uncertainty in the article did not remove the ban on the poet's name in the Soviet Ukrainian press, at least it served as permission for others to publish his poems. (It must be noted that the tone of the article could not have been different. The series of materials that made up the book *Iz zabuttia – v bezsmertia* [*From Oblivion to Immortality*] was based on diaspora materials and was designed to legalize the previously forbidden names of Ukrainian writers.) However, publication was done in several ways. Particularly disgusting was the article in the newspaper *Molod' Ukrainy*, published on the instructions of the Central Committee and, in an additional slight, in an issue signed not by the editor-in-chief but by his deputy. When I proposed publishing a response to the lampoon, the frightened deputy made excuses for himself, saying,

The behind-the-scenes conversations at that time, which were occasionally passed around in the press, were also eloquent. Dmytro Pavlychko, Pavlo Zahrebelny, and a few other Ukrainian writers said that was the first time that they heard the name of the poet Vasyl Stus.

It was high time to form a group for departure.

It was rather difficult to do, as the political maneuvering and actual recklessness of many national leaders who had only recently been released from prison forced them to take responsibility for the possible consequences.

After talking to my mother, Valentyna Popelyukh, Henrikh Dvorko,[26] and Ihor Bondar,[27] I decided to ask Ms. Iryna Kalynets[28] to take charge of the Kyiv part of the reburial. She agreed.

"we want to publish Stus' words and that is now possible only in this form." The magazine *Ukraina* (No. 23 [1989]: 6–7) called its material about the poet "We Missed Life." The materials in the magazines *Prapor* (No. 2), *Zhovten'* (No. 7) and *Kyiv* (No. 10) were completely different. The publication in the newspaper *Literaturnaya Rossiya* (November 17, 1989) was important, although the quality of the Russian translation left much to be desired.

[26] Henrikh Dvorko (1931–2012) was Doctor of Chemical Sciences, who in the late 1960s signed well-known protest letters against the arrests and military intervention in Czechoslovakia. As a result, he was fired from leading chemical institutes and had to work under the direction of a person who did not even hold a Candidate degree. After the arrest of Ivan Svitlychny, Dvorko helped his family financially. He was an organizer of the "Pripyat Republic," where the sixtiers gathered for summer vacations (after their arrests, their children gathered there). He was also the only person who did not destroy Vasyl Stus' self-published collection *Merry Cemetery* in 1972. At the time of the events described, he was Dmytro Stus' father-in-law.

[27] Ihor Bondar was a stoker who was engaged in the distribution of self-published Ukrainian materials. In the 1960s, he served three years in a criminal camp.

[28] Iryna Kalynets (Stasiv, 1940–2012) was a Ukrainian writer and activist in the Ukrainian resistance. She was arrested in 1972 and served her sentence in Mordovia separated by a few rows of barbed wire from Vasyl Stus. In 1975, when Stus was wounded in the camp by an awl, his life was saved only thanks to a hunger strike Kalynets organized together with Nadiia Svitlychna and Nijolė Sadūnaitė in the women's zone, demanding medical assistance for the victim.

The group departing for Perm included Oleh Pokalchuk,[29] who provided physical and organizational support, and Vasyl Hurdzan,[30] as we still needed to make a film. Valery Pavlov went as a videographer, and Bohdan Pidhirny as a cameraman. The sound director was Oleh Vachi. Oleksa Tykhy's sons, Volodymyr and Oleksandr, also went with us.

Volodya Shovkoshytny (the director of the film) left a week earlier than the rest to arrange all the necessary formalities on the spot. We were supposed to fly on November 15.

On November 13, a spontaneously formed funeral organizing committee, which I met through Ihor Bondar, gathered on Belorusskaya Street, in Mr. Ihor's apartment.

On one side, Levko Lukianenko, Mykhailo Horyn, Dmytro Korchynsky, Vasyl Ovsienko, Yevhen Pronyuk, and a few other people called to represent public organizations; on the other side, I as a representative of the family.

Attention was mainly paid to printing leaflets, sewing flags, and organizing a demonstration. I felt uneasy from the very beginning: everyone was convinced that the main thing was flags and leaflets. But what about the Ural unit, who were so often humiliated? ...

There was no talk about it.

When all the "recommendations" of the organizing committee were set out, I let them know that Iryna Kalynets would be in charge of Vasyl Stus' reburial in Kyiv and if the committee members had any plans to participate, they should coordinate all their actions with her. I also added that anyone who did not agree with such a decision could take part in the reburial of Yuri Lytvyn and Oleksa Tykhy. Where Vasyl Stus was concerned, I could not accept Levko Lukyanenko's proposal to carry the coffins from Boryspil airport to Kyiv or to turn the event into a political demonstration. Iryna Kalynets and I had agreed to push for maximum concessions

---

[29] Oleh Pokalchuk (born 1955) is a Ukrainian poet, translator, and bard. He has engaged in business and politics, and promoted the establishment of Plast (the National Scout Organization) in Ukraine.

[30] Vasyl Hurdzan (1926–2001) was an activist in the Ukrainian resistance and a political prisoner.

from the authorities, as we had not had any armed or militarized escort. And in general, the public resonance of this action had nothing to do with me as I was engaged in the reburial of my father ...

After my words, a terrible silence descended on the room for a few minutes. It seemed that even the always-bright aspect of Bondarev's cozy apartment darkened with the incredible tension and complete lack of understanding between the two sides. Neither Levko Lukyanenko nor Mykhailo Horyn, who in all candor had not expected such resistance to their plans, reacted, at least not until Dmytro Korchynsky exploded.

He spoke about the urgency and importance of these events for Ukraine, saying that nothing like this had happened since the reburial of Shevchenko and that this was not a family but a national matter. It had been easier a hundred years ago because "Shevchenko had no children."

That gave me serenity and determination.

Rising to my feet, I spoke in the direction of Korchynsky:

"I don't care much about your opinion of me, Mr. Dmytro, or the opinion of all your organizations. However, the family and I took care of all these arrangements. And it does not matter how sorry you are that Stus has a son. This is a simple fact and you will have to accept it. I will say further that this son considers everything that happens to be *exclusively* a family affair. I do not care if anyone likes it or not. Those who want to participate will coordinate their actions with Iryna Kalynets."

Korchynski flounced out of the apartment.

Of course, I overestimated my own strength and underestimated the support of the newly formed public structures, without whose intervention reburial in 1989 would have been impossible. However, this minor explosion helped me not only to create a future single nerve center headed by Iryna Kalynets, who proved to be a brilliant diplomat, under much more difficult conditions, in keeping events under control and not provoking the beatings that occurred in 1995, in then independent Ukraine, during the funeral ceremony of Patriarch Volodymyr (Romaniuk).[31]

We parted, without reaching a final agreement on any matter. Once I arrived at Henrikh Dvorko's apartment on Petrovsky St.,[32] I called Iryna Kalynets in Lviv and, informing her of everything that had happened, asked her to come to Kyiv as soon as possible. The next day, I together with Oleh Pokalchuk purchased rubber gloves, ropes, tarpaulins, and cloth for the mortal remains of Vasyl Stus and Yuriy Lytvyn if, as we somehow had little doubt, the exhumation process had to be performed by us.

Slavko Chernilevsky and Bohdan Pidhirny hunted for film stock and a camera. Fortunately, there was a video camera, but it was only fit for amateur filming.

On the evening of the same day, a message came from Moscow that Alexander Tykhy was sick with fever and, obviously, would not be able to fly to Perm. Given that Oleksa Tykhy was buried in the Perm cemetery, Volodya, his youngest son, had to take it upon himself alone.

It was previously agreed that the newly formed All-Ukrainian Association for Victims of Repression would send two people to fly with us. I telephoned the Head of the society, Yevhen Pronyuk, who says:

---

[31] On July 14, 1995, the Ukrainian patriotic forces, without securing the approval of the authorities, decided to bury Patriarch Volodymyr on the grounds of St. Sophia's Cathedral, which was surrounded by special police units ready for such an attempt. When people, instigated by the organizers, started digging a grave at the gates of St. Sophia's bell tower, force was used against them. The bloody events of that July were not only a deathless disgrace to the authorities, who were so bold as to carry out such a blasphemy, but also showed the irresponsibility and indifference to the people of those who organized the funeral. Neither the people nor the ashes of the lost person should become small counters in political games. And I intentionally refrain from mentioning here the name of the man who ordered the troops to beat people, because, having the experience of organizing such an event, I am convinced that those who planned all this are no less responsible for everything that happened.

[32] Dvorko's apartment was the headquarters for the reburial of Vasyl Stus, Yuriy Lytvyn, and Oleksa Tykhy.

- Vasyl Gurdzan and someone else will fly with you. I cannot be more precise as everyone is busy with leaflets, making flags and Kyiv action organizational arrangements.

- Don't you understand (I say irritably) that Volodya alone may not be able to resolve all the problems in Perm? After all, he is a son. If the exhumation has to be carried out without the support of the local authorities, is he supposed to dig the grave by himself?

- But you have so many going there.

- They are going to make a film. The studio has invested in the reburial and wants to film everything that will happen there. So, if you would like to participate and want all of the remains transported, please find a person who can help Volodya in Perm. We have a plane ticket already.

- Agreed, we will come up with something. Someone will fly with you.

I hung up, but the anxiety did not go away. I felt that the entire Perm part was under threat, and I could not change anything, because I had no leverage to influence the situation.

Then, for the first time in my life, I felt my father's support and decided to leave it all up to fate. We had to do everything we could and let fate decide.

We departed from Boryspil on November 15. It was my birthday. At the age of 23 it was too soon to take responsibility. Too soon to understand that on a frosty night, the nine people who were walking up the steps to board the "Kyiv–Perm–Novosibirsk" plane were flying not only to repatriate the bodies of Oleksa Tykhy, Yurii Lytvyn, and Vasyl Stus. First of all, we wanted to prove that we Ukrainians take care of something else besides our own philistine well-being. And, at least once in our lives, some of us are ready to risk everything we have to pay our last respects to those who managed to live not only for themselves and their families. There are millions of such people in Ukrainian history, but we remember the names of only a handful who, in addition to their feats in life, left behind a space of high love, which ensured that they would be remembered not only by their relatives. We flew to prove that the sense of self-respect, so organic to the small nations of the Armenians, Georgians, Estonians, Lithuanians, is no stranger to us.

And even though all the necessary documents were obtained, I doubted that we would achieve what we desired.

The previous prohibition was depressing, but the determination of the people (of whom only Vasyl Ovsienko, Vasyl Hurdz and I knew Vasyl Stus very well) was impressive. The others were flying to touch history.

This time the preparatory work for obtaining the documents was done to a high standard. On October 20, 1989, Volodymyr Shovkoshytny called Chusovoy again and hit a wall of "absence":

> "The chief doctor of the Sanitary Epidemiological Station V. V. Dyvdin is not available. His Deputy and the Head of the epidemiological department strongly insist that the situation is difficult. (Oh, we are remembered here!) They say, dysentery plus viral hepatitis.
> As agreed, I am sending a telegram on behalf of the First Secretary of the Union of Cinematographers of Ukraine, Mykhailo Belikov, to the Head of the Perm Regional Sanitary Epidemiological Station, Shaklein, and his Deputy, Luzin (the day before Luzin informed S. Chernilevsky by phone that all was calm in the region). And on October 24, we received the telegram: "The epidemiological situation in the Chusovskoy District this year is good. Perm Regional Sanitary Epidemiological Station. Deputy Chief Doctor Luzin."
> **The telegram is encouraging, but ... Just in case, we "arm" ourselves with a letter addressed to the same director of the BVO ZhKH V. V. Kazantsev:**
> "The Union of Cinematographers of the USSR has started work on filming Vasyl Stus: The Road of Thorns about the outstanding Ukrainian poet. As the family has decided to rebury the father and husband, the film crew has included this episode in their film.
> Please inform us regarding the possibility for reburial of the ashes of V. S. Stus and the provision for this action by the communal services of Chusove town on November 2-3 or on November 15-18 this year.
> First Secretary of the IC of the USSR, People's Deputy of the USSR M. O. Belikov.
> **Such a request to the Head of the District Communal Services! However, we did not dare to send this document by mail. It was decided that I would deliver it personally. We also decided not to make a fuss before the October holidays[33] and agreed to reburial on November 15-18.**

---

[33] In the USSR and for the first 10 years of independent Ukraine, November 7-8 was a public holiday and ritually celebrated. Parades, rallies and other festive events were designed to give the October coup in tsarist Russia a landmark significance. The celebrations were magnificent, with the obligatory noisy excessive drinking. A reburial on these days meant failure because *none* of the Soviet officials would help in its implementation under any circumstances, and would have thrown up every possible obstruction due to his official duties.

So, on November 7, I went to Moscow, hoping to gain the support of the Board of the Writers' Union. Vitaliy Krykunenko, a consultant on Ukrainian literature, treated me with respect and I flew to Perm with a letter from the Union addressed to the Executive Committee of the Chusovsky District Council of People's Deputies.

"The Secretariat of the Board of the Writers' Union of the USSR requests to assist the writer V. Shovkoshytny, the relatives of poets V. Stus and Yu. Lytvyn in resolving the issue of reburial of the writers' ashes in their homeland.
Secretary of the Board of the Writers' Union of the USSR
Yu. T. Gribov."[34]

Volodya Shovkoshytny was waiting for us at Perm airport.

We had ten tickets, but did not see the tenth member of the group come.

10–15 minutes before the end of check-in, I called Yevhen Pronyuk from Boryspil Airport:

- Good afternoon, Mr. Yevhen. This is Dmitry Stus. Passenger registration is nearly over, and there are no people from the Association for Victims of Repression. Wasn't it possible to ask a man not to be late here?

- Dmitry, you know, we are really short of people. And here we have leaflets, flags, and transport. Someone needs to organize the arrival of people from the regions. We decided that it would be better for you to just return the ticket for a refund and hire someone directly in Perm ...

I listened to this tirade as if in a fog. At a certain point, it seemed that the ground opened under my feet and there was nothing to keep me upright. I do not remember what I said then, I just cannot forget the stern eyes of the casual passengers and a sense of burning shame: How can I tell Volodya about it? How can I leave him alone in Perm? How?

---

[34] V. Shovkoshytnyi. "Narode mii, do tebe ya shche vernu ..." ("My people, I will come back to you ..."),7. An abridged variant of the article was published in the book: Ne vidliubyv svoiu tryvohu ranniu. Vasyl Stus – poet i liudyna. Spohady, statti, lysty, poezii. [I did not fall off my early anxiety. Vasyl Stus – poet and person. Memoirs, articles, letters, poems]. – K.: Ukrainskyi pysmennyk (Ukrainian writer), 1993, 365-371.

"Those beasts didn't send anyone," I muttered only to Oleh and Volodya, wo hid his shame for the people who should have taken care of the main thing. "I'm sorry."

Volodya rushed to call Moscow for Alexander to take medicine and fly the next day to Perm. It was good that there were no financial problems: something was provided by the Galfilm film studio, something was given by Nadezhda Svitlychna and something was collected by people in Ukraine, and we definitely had something.

The organization of the event in Kyiv was in full play and we were walking up the steps to board the plane which was to transfer us from November 15 to the 16th of November.

Volodya Shovkoshytny and ... an unexpected thaw were waiting for us in Perm. It was +2-3º C at night.

- If this weather lasts at least a day, we will not have to make a fire on the graves, Vasyl Ovsienko mentioned as we walked to the exit of the airfield.

I remembered my last visit here in September 1985, when we came to say goodbye to my dad and found only a freshly made earth mound. And my mother's desperate tears, shed in 1984 as well, when my father could not stand another humiliation — "Nagnis. Razdvin yagaditsi. Agali galovku" ("Bend over. Spread your buttocks. Expose head") — by pre-visitation "shmons" (inspections) that involved almost physically sensible hatred for my father. I remembered other tears — tears of guilt in the eyes of the dearest person, who emerged from behind the screen where the shmon took place, and my ears burned from the humiliation of the dearest person, a feeling of stupid disgusting fear and powerlessness to change anything ...

"What will our meeting be like now, Dad?" And will it happen? — I was tortured by doubts, as we trod the last meters of the airfield.

- It will happen, the sentence sounded as if from afar ...

- Who are you talking to sometimes? Oleh asked me when we climbed into the suburban train to Chusove.

"Yes, something is running through my head," I told him, not wanting to admit my incomprehensible weakness, and hastened to change the subject.

I did not call Irina Kalinets and my wife, Oksana Dvorko, from Perm. The group's complete lack of certainty did not facilitate night calls, which would only increase the anxiety of relatives. During the 4-hour suburban train ride to Chusove, where the Russian poet Yura Belikov and rooms in the local sports and working hostel were waiting for us, we discussed the details of the exhumation.

- When my friend filmed an exhumation a couple of years ago, he said that even despite fortifying themselves with alcohol, almost everyone vomited ...

- We need to fix vodka ...

"You have to pray beforehand," added one of the Vasyls (Ovsienko? Gurdzan? I do not remember).

Volodya Shovkoshytny remained in Perm. Coffins were prepared there. He did everything he could, and more. On the 17th he had to take the zinc coffins to the cemetery of the village of Borisovo in the Chusovsky District, where under markers with punched numbers rested the "boys." That is the term the members of the group in those days used for Yuriy Lytvyn, Oleksa Tykhy, and Vasyl Stus.

The preparatory work carried out by Volodya Shovkoshytny on the eve of our arrival was so essential for the final success that it must be recorded on its own.

> In Perm I got to know Yuriy Belikov - a poet, journalist, editor of the avant-garde literary supplement "Children of Strontium." He was preparing material about ... Vasyl Stus. Yuriy will help us until the very last minute, and in the meantime he gives me the phones of not-indifferent people in Chusove. There were many of them.
> On November 10, I sign a letter to the Deputy Head of the Perm United Air Detachment I. D. Grachev — the permission to transport home on November 18 by flight №7262 Novosibirsk - Perm - Kyiv three zinc coffins with the remains. Ihor Dmytrovych is a man who is not indifferent to the poet. He keeps wondering why he has never heard anything about the poet and is struggling to understand why a man is condemned for "Howls like a beast, drinks horilka [vodka] ..." even in Ukrainian ...
> Deputy for the regime at the airport prohibited filming ...

At the regional sanitary-epidemiological station, I show the telegram to the Union of Cinematographers of Ukraine and ask for a certificate (permission) to call the film crew.
"You are trying to fool me!" Chief Doctor G. V. Shaklein is hesitating. And calls Chusove by a selector. The Chief Doctor of the Chusovsky Sanitary Epidemiological Station V. V. Dyvdin[35] crosses his heart that the permission will be granted.
This is already a tiny ray of hope.
I go to a special trust to order zinc coffins. The Chief Engineer Valery Pavlovich Kartsev turned out to be a man no less vigilant and no less quick-witted than the one at the sanitary-epidemiological station:
"You're beating about the bush!" And he disappears without a trace.
The coffins were ordered without him for November 16.
Our first day in Chusove is Monday the 13th! And what do we have: Kazantsev is on vacation, the Chief Engineer Musykhin is at a meeting in the City Executive Committee. I have asked to inform the management of my arrival and I am back in half an hour. The secretary looks down, points at the man:
- Are you Musykhin? I ask.
- Kazantsev!
What attention! Even the manager has come back from vacation.
I show all my documents and explain everything. But he already knows all this and I know that he knows ... Then I submit Belikov's Deputy request and ask him to write: "Rejected. Kazantsev." or "Agreed. Kazantsev." The answer is the most unexpected one: "We have information (!) that at the governmental level of the USSR and Canada (!!) the issue of Stus' reburial in Canada is pending" ...
"If Stus wanted to go to Canada," I say, "he would not get to Kuchino!" And besides, here is his son's letter!
- Then, go there!
- To the KGB?!
- Well ... there ... And we ... will do everything.
That's perfectly fine. I will go there.
"What has brought you here?" Vladimir Ivanovich, the friendly young man, asks.[36]
- These are our responsibilities. Our debts. - I take out all my documents, letters, and certificates.
All this is laid on the table. He carefully records the numbers and most important details from my papers.

---

[35] Vasyl Ovsienko in his book *Svitlo liudei* (Light of the People) indicates that the correct spelling of the surname is Dyvdin, not Dyldin, as erroneously stated in the publication of V. Shovkoshytny. 66.
[36] Volodymyr Ivanovych Chentsov was the Head of the Chusovsky KGB regional department. From the end of 1981 to the end of 1984, he worked as a criminal investigator for the KGB in VS-389/36 camp and, according to V. Ovsienko (See: *Svitlo liudei* [Light of People], 66), *"was one of the people responsible for the deaths of political prisoners."*

- The information from your communal services about the reburial of Stus in Canada is nonsense, I explain. "You must know that even in their lifetime inmates of that prison were not in a rush to get to Canada ..."
I take out of my bag the tenth issue of Kyiv magazine and the thirty-ninth issue of Ogonek, where Stus' poems and the statements requiring his rehabilitation are published.
He is smiling reproachfully. And I continue:
- We came here not to settle accounts. We want our homeland to get back her sons. I have visited a legal adviser and know that there is no ban on it. Having treated me to tea with lemon Vladimir Ivanovych ... came out...
Then a conversation with the Director of communal services:
- Vladimir Ivanovich has promised us his support. So please write here: "Agreed. Kazantsev" or "Rejected. Kazantsev."
And at this stage the communal struck me dumb:
- I have neither the right to agree or reject! ...
- But you have given the official permission?!
- I have gone beyond my authority. Kopalno does not belong to the territory of the City Executive Committee! He smiled sourly. - Get permission from the Sanitary Epidemiological Station and dig.
- Without any papers?!
- Any.
The only support the communal services in the person of V. V. Kazantsev gave us was the address of the factory, where we agreed with the coppersmiths to seal up the coffins.
I am going to the City Sanitary Epidemiological Station. The Chief Doctor is on a business trip. The Head of the Department Anvar Ravilovich Sharipov does not provide information:
- I cannot do anything without the Chief. Besides, I will share my thoughts with him: it isn't winter yet.
The brown snow of the factory Ural town is falling outside the windows...[37]
From 4 to 6 p.m., I speak in the editorial office of the local newspaper Chusovskoy rabochii (Chusovoy Worker). We have friends and a forum. I write a statement to the Director of the printing house Oleksandr Mykolayovych Mykhalyov for a truck. The coffins should be taken from Perm to the plane already holding the remains and then be delivered back to Perm. One-way distance is approximately 230 kilometres. Thanks to Mikhalyov, we have found a bus to transport the group to the cemetery and back to the hotel, which is 20 kilometers away. This is more than opportune, because the Director and the Chief Engineer of PATO, the bus company, which last time even took "Tourist" freely, adamantly refused us.
On the evening of the 13th, I call V. V. Dyvdin's home number. He has promised to issue a certificate-permission on the morning of the 14th. Eventually, we get it. That's all. No more papers are needed. The Chusovoy Sanitary

---

[37] The town of Chusovoy was built around a metallurgical giant founded by French industrialists in the late 19th century. The Ogonyok tourist center is located on the outskirts, the largest and most modern ski center in the USSR.

Epidemiological Station allows exhumation and transportation in zinc coffins of ashes of the following persons:
1. Stus Vasil Semenovych, buried in the village of Kopalno.
... Grave Nr 9...
2. Lytvyn Yuri Timonovich, buried in the village of Kopalno.
... Grave Nr 7...
I went to the regional police department. I met the criminal investigation department chief, Anatoly Semenovych Mikryukov. He checked my documents again.
- From the legal point of view, everything is correct. The only thing is the District Inspector will join you to observe the formalities. And you will take someone from the village council in Kopalno as well ...
He summoned the district inspector, Faizul Abdulayevich Matyakubov. We agreed that on November 17, at 8:30, we would pick him up at Verkhneye Kalino, where he lived.
The newspaper editor promised to provide a car to take the coppersmiths to the cemetery. With the director of the Ogonyok school of the Olympic reserve, L. D. Postnikov, we went to the city cemetery (to the Ritual cooperative) to see about the gravediggers. And here it became clear that we would have to dig by ourselves ...
I was starting to believe that we would rebury Stus and his comrades. I called Yuri Belikov in Perm for him to look for a forensic expert because the local one had refused to go to the cemetery. I agreed with the Hotel Manager Lidia Ivanovna Alekseeva on group accommodation ...[38]

The group arrived at Chusove on the 16th, in the middle of the day. Volodya Shovkoshytny and Volodya Tykhy remained in Perm. The titanic work done by Shovkoshytny seemed to prevent any trouble. Little did we know that surprises were only just beginning.

After check-in at the hotel, I called home:

"It's all right." Settled. So far, no adventures.

"Why couldn't you call from Perm?" My wife and Iryna Kalinets were indignant at me in two voices. "We are resolving the issue regarding burial in the Baykove cemetery.[39] They called from the

---

[38] Shovkoshytny, "'Narode mii, do tebe ya shche vernu...'," 8–9.
[39] The idea to bury the bodies of Vasyl Stus, Yury Lytvyn and Oleksa Tykhy in the Baykove Cemetery in Kyiv first occurred to Volodymyr Holoborodko, because no one but him believed in the possibility of obtaining such a permit. And he ... made an unfortunate slip. He went to the Union, the Central Committee and ... he got the permission. Ironically, when they went to the cemetery to choose a location for the burial, Vasyl Stus' wife, Valentina Popelyukh, was without a seat in the car. Iryna Kalinets had to look for a seat for my mother. Holoborodko, who really wanted to personally choose a location, was left "without a place."

Pope's residence ...[40] They offered to hold a funeral service in the Catholic Church in Petropavlivska Borshchahivka,[41] but I refused," Ms. Iryna said. "The boys should be buried according to Orthodox ceremony. Even though all sorts of surprises are possible in the Orthodox Church. This is a matter of principle."

She did not suspect how much she would regret that decision on the day of the reburial.

"Well, everything is fine. Tomorrow at dawn, we are leaving for Kuchino. I will give you a call if something goes wrong," I said and hung up.

The long beeps seemed to magnify the emptiness that separates Chusovoy from Kyiv: we are here, they are there, but once again we all have to rely on fate because we cannot provide each other with any communication or material support. We all hope that each of us will do his best. However, even across the insurmountable abyss of uncertainty, there was the feeling that not only your enemies but also your friends were watching your every step, hoping that you would not make a mistake, that you simply had no right to make a mistake. I don't know why, but it seemed that this Kyiv support had become decisive: psychologically we were ready for everything except defeat...

Having agreed to meet in Chernilevsky's room at 8 p.m., Oleh Pokalchuk and I went to buy shovels and ropes. Despite our fears, none of the members of the group showed any negative emotions

---

[40] One episode well characterizes the tense situation of that. Oksana Dvorko, who was a kind of liaison between Perm and Kyiv, and therefore in intently anticipating news from the distant Urals, picked up the phone and heard something completely unexpected:
- You have a call from the Pope's residence ...
- From where? She did not understand. How, when under constant stress, could you digest information not directly related to the reburial?
- From the Pope.
- Excuse me, we have no "papa" (father in Russian), we only have "tato" (father in Ukrainian), she answered.
- From the Patriarch of Rome, she heard from the receiver and a pleasant voice began to ask about the problems and complications arising from reburial ...

[41] A suburban village that almost merged with the Ukrainian capital. Very close to Sviatoshyn, where Vasyl Stus' family lived.

when it became known that they would have to dig and exhume on their own.

The surprises started at 8 o'clock.

"Vasyl Ovsienko left for Perm to hand the death certificates over to Volodya Shovkoshytny because coffins would not be provided without it," Slavko Chernilevsky immediately informed us. He has to return tomorrow morning. We will have to go to the cemetery without him. Vasyl will arrive with local journalists a little bit later. The truck with the coffins will arrive at the cemetery. However, not in the morning, but around noon.

Well. Things happen.

We part. Someone had a pocket Bible. I asked to borrow it for the night. Oleh and I read aloud from randomly opened pages. It calmed and allowed you to concentrate and internally mobilize. Our reading was interrupted by a sudden knock on the door.

- Guys, this is awful! All my money was stolen! Slavko was almost crying.

"Don't worry," I say. "I have brought some with me just in case."

We decided that we would not involve the police, because an investigation could mess up the whole business. Today, a decade and a half after the event, I do not rule out the possibility that this "robbery" was one of the well-planned scenarios designed to complicate or ruin things.

Slavko went to his room slightly calmed, but still tense.

We set to the Bible again.

It is a strange thing. I still remember in detail the whole chronology of that night, when the words extended into implications, impressions, and visions of the next day as though preparing us for something extra material. I remember in detail my impressions of the conversation with Oleh and ... the parallel influence of the sound of my dad's voice. The words were transformed into emotions, incomprehensible and unspoken feelings, which produced the absolute certainty that we would succeed at the enterprise. Oleh also felt this presence, although we had never discussed this strange aura with him. To some extent, these night visions as we read the Bible explain the unexpected and almost unbelievable endurance of all of us the next day. Our certainty of success was almost absolute, which must have greatly astonished and irritated the civil servants.

We read the Bible almost until dawn.

On the morning of November 17, having pushed ourselves to eat something, we went to the cemetery in the village of Borisovo. It took 2 to 3 hours. On our way, we picked up the policeman Matyakubov who had to make sure we didn't do anything wrong. Then someone in civilian clothes approached us.

"If we are forbidden to carry out the exhumation, I will go on a hunger strike in the central square of Chusove," said Oleg, who knew about Stus only from the stories of his brother, Yurko Pokalchuk. The latter had been the best man at my parents' wedding. Yet in 1980, he had not dared meet Stus: he had had a trip to Latin America, and how could you appear after a ten-year absence to a person who was actually a stranger to you?

"And I will stay here," I answered Oleh. "I won't leave without my dad ..."

Let's move on.

In Perm, at the same time, a well-directed farce reached its climax.

Volodymyr Shovkoshytny managed to pick up the coffins from the special plant only at 9:15 a.m. on November 17. Only two were ready. The third had to be finished by Tykhy's sons because the master coffin maker had been brutally beaten by someone.

The truck with the precious cargo drove in the direction of the village of Borisovo, but its journey turned out to be too tortuous and nervous:

"About 10 o'clock, we were stopped at the checkpoint outside the city," Volodymyr Shovkoshytny recalls. *"This checkpoint was probably of strategic importance because there were three captains on duty (which of the drivers saw that?!), a sergeant-major, and even a man in blue tights sitting in a Zhiguli [a car based on the Fiat 124 manufactured in the Soviet Union] №78-85 PM.*

First, they checked the permit, then the steering box. They found that it was broken. Then they were forced to open the speedometer but the seals were in place. I got out of the cab. The driver pointed to the outer right rear wheel. It had a flat tire. While we were busy with the steering wheel, the other two wheels on the right got flat tires by "themselves." They put a spare wheel to replace the front one. The left rear wheels were divided between both sides. There was one good wheel and one with a flat on each side. The watch showed 11:40. There was another four and a half hours to drive. At 2 p.m. they would be waiting for us in the cemetery. Two captains check the steering box. There was a backlash, they said (who ever saw a Soviet truck without that backlash?). We go to the checkpoint again. (The one in the tights was there). Captain Chernyava asked on the radio what was going on in Chusove. He was told that the car left Perm yesterday for aviation fuel (the tank holding it is on the bodywork), the permit indicated different cargo and the driver had a certificate stating that the customer is the Writers' Union of the USSR. Again, I showed the three captains (and first of all, "blue tights") all my certificates and authorization documents. I repeat that the coffins are in the cemetery already, that tomorrow we have to take them to the plane, that the plane has been ordered, that relatives are waiting in Kyiv, that different services are waiting, that it is a sacred matter, that...

The driver wrote an explanatory note. Chernyava read it and approved.

- That's all. We are going! - I said.

Three captains and a sergeant-major looked at "blue tights" (such tights are memorable!) — There was no permission.

- "Do you know," one of the captains said suddenly, "that you are suspected of causing a road accident?"

- ?!!

- A boy was injured.

- Was there a boy?! - I ask gently. - By the way, where and when did it happen?

The captains frowned for a moment, and then the one who told us about the crime found the right words to say:

- On Heroyiv Hasan St.!

That was wise: there was no other way out of the city.

- "You will have to drive to the Sverdlovsk Regional Department of the DAI (the State Automobile Inspectorate)," the captain says, "there is an investigator already waiting there."

- Tell them, - I lost my temper, - that without a lawyer I will tell the investigator to stuff it ...

We got in the car. Eight out of twenty-four stars sat in the Zhiguli, next to them is "tights." They warmed up the car for a minute, three, five. On the seventh minute, I approached the car.

I told "tights" that the KGB promised to help me. Both kept silent.

It took a long time to go to the regional office. The captain and "tights" were behind us. It was a police escort ... I was getting ready to go on a hunger strike ...

We entered the office of the chief of the district department of the State Automobile Inspectorate.

- Comrade Captain! What's up with Chusovoy? - asks "our" captain.

- The command is the "All clear" - The team was "repulsed" - the honest eyes of the captain-leader assumed a shifty expression looking around, trying to gain a footing. - We have to apologize to you. An error occurred - the car number is the same, but the range is different ...

Well, there you are, everything has been solved successfully! - a happy smile lit up the face of "our" captain and he lifted up his arms.

- I told you this when we were at the checkpoint!

- Accept our apologies! – said the captain-leader again.[42]

Thus, in a truck with flat tires, the driver Sydorov and the writer Shovkoshytny went over roads full of holes to Perm and then to Borisovo, because, as the driver later said, "obviously they could not be bad people if those dirtbags bosses tried so hard to stop them being buried."

However, the group gathered in the cemetery knew nothing about it yet.

Despite a previous agreement, we failed to find the Head of the Village Council and our bus arrived at the cemetery without him.

I was blinded by the clean carpet of white snow, marked in many places by the tracks of birds and animals. A cemetery lay to the right of the road. My throat was constricted by a spasm of tears,

---

[42] Volodymyr Shovkoshytnyi. "Narode mii, do tebe ya shche vernu ...," 9.

which I could not hold back. Valery Pavlov's video camera was followed behind me as he wanted to capture a "historical" shot. And I choked up with tears. *Yesterday, only yesterday, I heard, Dad, your voice, and today, today we are waiting for a meeting. For some reason, I am sure that everything will turn out. I am not the best son. That is true, but you are not the best father either.* Pavlov ran ahead with the camera, and I was forced to hide in a small forest, not reaching the graves of my father and Lytvyn: strangers should not see my tears.

In about half an hour the spasms let up and with swollen eyes and ready for anything, I approached the graves. The knees softly sank into the wet, pleasantly soft snow We were lucky, that idea echoed in my head. It would be easy to dig, the ground was not frozen, and in Kyiv on the day of departure, the temperature reached minus fifteen degrees ...

The knees quickly got wet from the comfortable, almost warm snow. The barrel of the camera shoots close, and I do not want to see anyone else here, I need to be alone for a while ... I ask everyone to leave and stay at my father's grave alone for a moment.

Then everything resembled a slow-motion movie.

Matyakubov forbade us to start digging up the graves until the zinc coffins were brought and he had some paper from his management.

"Say it, say it," I thought, but said aloud:
– "Well, let's go back to Chusovoy to get the permit."

At noon, V. Chernilevsky, V. Gurdzan, V. Pavlov and I got on the bus to return to Chusovoy. Fate played another joke on us: Oleh stayed in the cemetery, I had to return.

In the district center, contrary to the worst forebodings and predictions, everything was solved simply. They allowed us to dig up the graves, but not to remove the caskets until the arrival of the zinc coffins.

When we returned to the cemetery, Oleh Pokalchuk had already started digging up his father's grave. I do not know what Matyakubov said and whether he told him anything, but the cop did not dare to physically interfere, given Oleg's physique.

The permit we brought relieved the tension, although some civilians joined the policeman who had gone to check if he had been deceived.

While Oleg, now joined by other members of the expedition, dug up the grave of Vasyl Stus, Vasyl Gurdzan and I began digging up the grave of Yurii Lytvyn. There was a short prayer. Rather than the ritual spitting on the hands, the shovel gently and easily penetrated the blanket of snow and entered the mysterious earth of the tomb. Despite internal fears, the digging was calm and easy, the frozen ground was no obstacle, and the physical work relieved us from psychological stress and the uncertainty of circumstances: "When will the coffins arrive? (will there be coffins?)"

From time to time some characters approached us:

- You have a good chance of spending tonight in prison - they muttered, however without lingering for long near any of us. We tried not to be left alone, the instinct of self-preservation asserting itself. Probably the only time in my life that a situation very clearly defined who was a friend and who was a foe.

At 2:30 p.m., Vasyl Ovsienko, Yuriy Belikov, the Director of the local printing house Mikhalyov, and Nikolai Gusev, a journalist from the *Chusovskoy rabochii* (*Chusovoy Worker*) newspaper, arrived.

Taking turns, we continued to sink into the ground layer by layer.

And only one thought from time to time came to mind: is this my father's grave? Is he buried here? Is not this yet another fabrication by the authorities, which I never trusted since my childhood? When this obsessive doubt (in Kyiv, my mother and I for some reason were very afraid that, in 1985, we were not shown the real grave of my father) became too persistent I set to work vigorously.

At 3 o'clock we heard Oleh Pokalchuk's joyful exclamation:

- Got it! Guys, there's something solid here! It seems we have reached the casket door!

Putting down the spades, we all gathered around the grave. Of course, this was our first victory. And what a victory! Despite everything, in spite of the whole world, in spite of the cops who immediately surrounded us on the sides of the grave, in spite of those indifferent Kyiv leaflets-printers and the heartlessly arbitrary bureaucracy, we still achieved our goal.[43] The feeling of love and gratitude for these people, in whose company I was lucky to be, overwhelmed me, and I went from one to the other like a sleepwalker thanking them, sometimes aloud, and –sometimes silently.

My father's grave turned out to be shallow—"between 100 and140 cm"[44]—and dry. At that moment, I did not attach much importance to this.

Oleh Pokalchuk and Vasyl Ovsienko brushed the earth off the casket and prepared it for raising: fastened the ropes under father's coffin at the head and feet. Each movement was recorded by Pavlov on videotape. Bohdan Pidhirny was running somewhere all the time to recharge his very old camera, and the lack of film forced him to shoot only what he deemed "special."

Yuriy Lytvyn's grave turned out to be deeper: "150-180 cm."[45] However, we finished digging it up before dusk as well.

The hole in which Lytvyn's casket was located, unlike Stus' grave, quickly filled with water. It was growing dark. Volodya Shovkoshytny had still not come with the zinc coffins. Chernilevsky slowly started a panic: Where are the trucks? Internally, I remained unnaturally calm and waited for only one thing—the moment when the casket lid would be lifted. "Is it him or not?"—the pre-departure fears and anxieties did not let go, gave me no peace.

---

[43] At that moment and in Perm in general, we were as if isolated from the rest of the world. Deciding that we should rely only on ourselves, we did not trust to any external assistance. Without the psychological guidance of all the members of the Perm expedition, we would not have been able to achieve the special unity that characterized the film crew in November 1989. However, it is now clear that without the help of all concerned people in the world, who put pressure on the Gorbachev's administration, the new composition of the Central Committee of Ukraine and the Ukrainian government to allow reburial, we would never have broken through the wall of "playing it safe" and the bans. Writing these lines a decade and a half after the event and trying to recreate the feelings and emotions of that time, against all odds, I express my gratitude to those who made considerable efforts to organize the Kyiv part of the reburial, and to those who put pressure on the governments of the USSR and the Ukrainian SSR. Without them, the reburial of Vasyl Stus, Yurii Lytvyn and Oleksa Tykhy in 1989 would have been impossible.

[44] Ovsienko, *Svitlo liudei*, 66.
[45] Ibidem.

Although I knew that if something were wrong, I would not be so calm, feeling even comfortable in this cemetery housing hundreds and hundreds of tragic and bloody human destinies generously showered with the "natural" and indifferent abuse of the empire's servants.

At 6 p.m., already in complete darkness, under the almost frankly joyful and mocking glances of our minders, we still remained calm and confident that nothing had happened. It was a long way to go to Perm. And on the road, as everyone knows, anything can happen. Despite trying to keep busy doing something, conversations failed to start, and everyone was looking for some kind of occupation for himself.

Yura Belikov with Bohdan Pidhirny and Vasyl Ovsienko even went to the nearest "izba" (a typical Russian house built from square frames of logs) to find out if there was a telephone there. It turned out that there was no telephone. Instead, they managed to agree with the owners, Nina Vasylivna and Serhiy Tymofiyovych Zherebtsovs,[46] to connect a powerful electric lantern (almost a searchlight) brought from Kyiv by Bohdan Pidhirny to their electrical network.

At 6:40 p.m., the upturned graves were flooded by artificial but still encouraging light. The policeman, the *oper* (police investigator), Dyvdin (the representative of the sanitary-epidemiological station), and Kazantsev (communal services) were shocked and one of them even went to the house to "talk" to the "disloyal" owners. However, he returned defeated. And it was encouraging to us that members of the "ordinary" Russian people had decided to help, neglecting the local authorities, on which, like all residents of small towns and villages they were quite dependent.

Well, we had done our best. The only thing was to wait. Having warmed ourselves for five minutes in the projector's light we were plunged into darkness again ...

A minute, two, three, four passed... From time to time I looked at my watch. The second hand seemed silent and unwilling to move at a regular pace. Having lit a cigarette I made my way through the

---

[46] Ibid., p. 67.

wet snow to a nearby strip of wood, leading into the deep darkness of a nearby swamp. The soil sinks beneath my shoes but does not cave in. For some reason, that was the moment that I came to understand one of my father's expressions, which came from his letters and conversations of 1979-1980: "Time is not a linear category." It all depends on how you, an individual, fill (expand/narrow) its boundaries. Sometimes, a single minute enriches you with a spiritual knowledge, such as cannot be gained by a lifetime's experience.

These were just such minutes.

The possibility that the truck would not arrive with the coffins was not thought of. It was a trial and you had to go through it, dropping the facade of everyday life ...

"Dmytro, Dmytro," I heard Oleh's distant voice. "They have arrived, the truck has arrived!"

I returned to the joyful excitement of friends and the officials' disappointment. The latter were not at all prepared for such a course of events. Volodya Shovkoshytny told us the story of his experiences in the circles of hell, and the driver Sidorov only grunted and worked on the truck:

"The wheel rims are completely bent. Never mind! We will get there and make the best of a bad job. It is a long night," he said, taking a drag on a cigarette with satisfaction. "Oh, I want to drink, but you must not. They will be all over us ... bitches ..."

At 7:30 p.m., my father's coffin was raised. I did not take part, watching the process from the side, trying to remember every detail. First, a wider part of the box appeared above the edge of the grave — that should be the head — then a narrower one: the legs. Wearing the rubber gloves brought from Kyiv by Oleh Pokalchuk, the participants carrying out the exhumation started to open the lid. A few nails came out easily.

It was darkened, but — fantastic! — untouched by corruption, it was the native face of my father, looking at me. Corruption had only marked the tip of his nose, which used to be so alive and almost mobile during conversation, especially when Dad was in a good mood. His eyes were closed — monsters, but not fully — it quietly sank in. Only then did I feel the eerie silence, which was not broken even by the close-standing minders around us.

There was a shoe with its sole "hanging out its tongue" just under his face, hiding a protruding Adam's apple. I imagined that one of the servant-supervisors, as he was burying Dad in a rush to prevent us from saying goodbye to him in 1985, threw that shoe at a random place on Dad's body before hammering down the casket lid. It struck him, as I figured to myself, on the face.

Below there was some unnatural damage to the left side of the chest.[47] Only two buttons were done up (in addition, one button was offset), the uniform had almost decomposed. The second shoe took refuge shyly at his feet as if hiding from the shame of his partner, which someone had forced to despise its former owner.

To restrain the powerful impulse to fall upon my father's neck after an eight-year separation, I turned away and involuntarily clenched my fists.

**Forgive me, Vasyl, that I saw your naught
while lifting the casket lid,
that oper Kovalevich was all eyes
(Well, turn away!), but operas are on the stakeout -
watching your son (son!) had turned away,
but oper will never turn away,
cemetery shaky gates
held arms out, and sunflower husk
is scattered by sullen cop
on pure snow of the doubling crosses,
and he is ready to stitch the son up
with abuse over his father's grave ...[48]**

---

[47] It was this damage that provided additional evidence in favor of the version of Vasyl Stus' violent death. This was commented also by Yurii Belikov, who went to the local clairvoyant with photos of my father. The picture we saw that November evening gives Yurii Belikov grounds to say that "*the circumstances of Stus' death have not been made clear yet*": Yury Belikov, "Vo imia ottsa i syna," *Za cheloveka*, No. 10 (44) (December 2001): 6.

[48] Ibid.

When Vasyl Ovsienko, Oleh Pokalchuk and others transferred Vasyl Stus' body to a cloth brought from home and then the cloth with the body to one of the zinc coffins, a bone crunched. It seemed to be the neck.

Vasyl Gurdzan placed church symbols inside. We stood and prayed. And lit a cigarette. The boys carried the coffin on their shoulders, not yet sealed and covered with a door, to the truck. They sealed it there. And I felt that this was my last and finest meeting with my dad ...

We were illuminated by the stars and the moon, whose light filled the space not only of the cemetery but also shone on the beautiful and proud river, against whose current Yermak once went to conquer Siberia. We also went against the current, and it did not take much effort for the current to become our companion.

Before 8 o'clock we returned to the upturned grave of Yurii Lytvyn: his casket was already covered with water up to the lid. The striking contrast to the grave of Vasyl Stus made us freeze with uncertainty. To raise the casket to the surface, one of us had to put a rope under the casket knee-deep in grave water.

Physical fear of the corpse's poison returned and pressed on the psyche. Imagination and the spine-chilling eeriness of the task threatened to become an insurmountable obstacle, made all the worse by painful fantasy. The eyes of our minders shone with malice as if they thought: "Are your knees shaking?" Oleh Pokalchuk took the initiative. Going down to the bottom (his pants did not dry before we got to Kyiv) without any ado he did what each of us subconsciously preferred to put on someone else's shoulders.

The lifting of Lytvyn's casket was a long and hard process. Vasyl Ovsienko, unable to keep his balance, started sliding into the hole, but someone's strong hand caught hold of him at the last moment. Finally, the casket was lifted out, torrents of dark water pouring down from it. When the casket lid was raised we saw an almost completely decomposed body, which for unknown reasons had no time even to expose the bones of the host. Contrary to the fears of the day before, it did not frighten or discourage anyone. Silently, some wearing gloves, some without them, we began to transfer the body to a white cloth. The skull cracked and Vasyl Ovsienko's bare hand received a drop of the brain which once strained, worked, and governed Yury Lytvyn's life. Now, at the whim of fate and by the evil will of self-satisfied criminals, it found itself on the hand of a former sworn brother, causing concern to the newly arrived local doctor. Yes, we violated all the rules of exhumation. However, was there a way not to violate them under those conditions?

Finally, the body was transferred to a zinc coffin. A memorial service was held. We bowed ... to the holes staring at us with black emptiness and a series of numbered markers. They had lain in a strange land.

Having removed the numbers from the markers and somehow filled the graves, we went back to Chusove. A long and extremely bright day was coming to an end so quickly that even the second hand regained its usual beat.

Around 11 o'clock at night, we arrived at the hotel. There we learned that the Tykhy brothers had not managed to exhume their father in Perm. Everything was postponed to the day of our departure. Volodymyr Shovkoshytny and the driver Valery Sidorov spent the whole night tinkering with the truck. It had to go in the morning and who knew what other surprises would lurk around the corner. And we had to get to the plane on the Ural off-road.

An hour and a half before departure, a zinc coffin with the ashes of Oleksa Tykhy was delivered to Perm airport. Unlike me, the Tykhy brothers had to carry out the exhumation themselves. But it worked!

We boarded the plane light-heartedly, soared into the dark sky of Perm to land in Kyiv after a few hours of flight ...

Kyiv greeted us with an unexpected glow of red-black and yellow-blue flags and several thousand people. Contrary to expectations, it did not cause any emotions, at least for me. Kyiv's cold after the slush of Perm seemed something unreal, free of internal tension. Everything that caught my eye seemed not worth noting as a special effect. The rally, the leaflets ... Some truck, where for some reason we stood together with my mother with candles in our hands. Her eyes — abysses of grief studded with the crystals of long-dried tears — wandered somewhere in the past.

Oleh Pokalchuk's trousers and shoes had still not dried out and were becoming stiff before our eyes. Attempts to get the organizers of the meeting, Mykhailo Horyn, Yevhen Pronyuk, and others, to arrange a car that would take Oleh home failed. They said there were more important things. And although the money was found without any problems, for some reason the "more important things" provoked a particularly sharp and even inadequate reaction.

The cargo was finally released. My mother and I stood under a shower of patriotic speeches and high-sounding words, and I didn't hear anything — I saw only Lytvyn's grave, where Oleh was standing, trying to put a rope under the casket and not soak his outer clothes ...

Candles ... many candles ... my mother's completely dry eyes. Fate did not allow her to see her husband for a last time or to stay alone with his coffin. The public torture continued.

Finally, everything was finished ... Ihor Bondar took the responsibility of getting the coffins to the Pokrovska (Intercession) Church, where the next day the funeral services were to take place ...

The next day was the coldest of the whole winter of 1989–1990. The temperature reached minus 25 degrees, but it seemed that people who had gradually extricated themselves from the clutches of fear, felt it not at all.

The funeral service in the church dragged out. Orthodox priests, at the authorities' behest, did everything possible to ensure that the service carried on indefinitely. Interrupting them, the Greek Catholic priests had to intervene and finish it. In addition, we had to drive to Chornobylska Street.[49] It was 2 p.m., the time that the motorcade was scheduled to arrive at Sofiivska Square, where a crowd of many thousands was already waiting to say

---

[49] In a sixteen-story building at 13A Chornobylska St., Apt. 94, Vasyl Stus lived in Kyiv between his two prison terms, from August 1979 to May 1980.

goodbye and to get acquainted with names unknown to the majority: Vasyl Stus, Yuriy Lytvyn, and Oleksa Tykhy.[50]

After 3 p.m., we arrived at Sofiivska Square, which greeted us with flying flags and tens of thousands of human faces, who, after waiting in the cold for several hours, were anxiously waiting, uncertain whether we would come or not.

The organizers of the action had not managed to reach an agreement: desperate people insisted that the coffins with the remains should be carried from St. Sofia, but Iryna Kalinets had already agreed with the authorities to take the bodies to the cemetery by bus.

---

[50] This statement is not in the least an exaggeration. Even the film's director, Stanislav Chernilevsky, knew almost nothing about Vasyl Stus before his reburial. When I met him, his knowledge of the future hero of the film was limited to a few poems heard on Radio Liberty, recited by Nadezhda Svitlichna. They did not know even that much about Lytvyn and Tykhy. Vasyl Ovsienko and Vasyl Hurdzan did their best to expand the participants' knowledge about these people. About the same, if not even less, was the knowledge of the people gathered on Sofiivska Square in Kyiv. However, another factor contributed to this mass reburial: people overcoming seventy years of fear for the first time filled the streets for something other than the celebrations of the first of May or the seventh of November. And as much as the Ministry of Internal Affairs and the KGB set out to "control" the reburial, much remained out of their control. Tykhy, Lytvyn, and Stus were the first to break free of "distant Siberia," to which millions of Ukrainians had been deported and from where only a few returned, with almost every Ukrainian family having their "internees." Therefore, consciously or not, when seeing off the last three Ukrainians who died in the camps, each of them accompanied by his relatives, peers, and childhood friends. It is likely that this psychological phenomenon made Vasyl Stus' name quite popular and well-known in Ukraine in what turned out to be a short time. I must admit that credit for that goes to Levko Lukyanenko, Vasyl Ovsieko, Yevhen Pronyuk, Dmytro Korchynsky, Mykola Horbal and many other people. They took a diametrically opposite position on the priority and necessity of certain actions. I considered the Perm reburial part to be the main affair and they stressed the Kyiv part. Because, in addition to the Christian content, it was important to help people overcome the long-standing fear of the authorities. Looking back on those days from a distance of 15 years, I must thank luck for assigning the governance of these two interconnected parts to Irina Stasiv-Kalynets who found the necessary compromise between family and national and political interests. This chapter provides a private view of the history of the reburial seen by relatives' eyes. Moreover, to preserve emotional truth, almost no time adjustments were made to "smooth" things over.

It took half an hour to sort out everything. The most active participants began to shake the bus carrying the coffin of Vasyl Stus, trying to force the removal of the coffin and the body of Vasyl Stus. In the bus, the coffin and the relatives of Vasyl Stus swayed in obedience to these strange, already inhuman swings. Mom cried. Oleh Pokalchuk, who was sitting next to me, only tightened his hold on my hand, but I still broke free and left. Oleh followed me. The young and grown men who a moment ago had been rocking the bus together, looked blackly at us, made a lane and no longer tried to play their games. Thus, in the heart of the funeral procession, a climate of confrontation and almost antagonism arose, and it was not dispelled.

In five minutes, the procession started moving: Iryna Kalynets managed to agree with the security services on a new scenario for the funeral procession. It is quite possible that Ms. Iryna's conversation with the police and the KGB about the need to change the scenario, rather than trying to dictate to the thoroughly intimidated secret services under the shelter of a crowd of thousands of people, helped prevent the worst.

A decision was made to stop at the monument to Taras Shevchenko, carry out the coffins and bow to Kobzar (Taras Shevchenko's nickname). We made three circles of honor and then the coffins were carried at shoulder height to the cemetery. We followed my father's coffin and did not recognize the city that only the day before was indifferent to everything. Now the streets to the Baykovo cemetery filled with thousands of different faces.

And here were the graves. There were short speeches by Ivan Drach, Mykhailyna Kotsyubynska, Levko Lukyanenko, Iryna Kalinets, Zenovy Krasivsky …

People kept coming. The suffering, weary faces of those who had walked the same path as my father and survived made their way to the graves. Around the frozen holes the dense wall of people was extremely tight: it was possible neither to move nor escape the pressure of the rows before and behind. Many ran past other graves to be present at the historic moment. As always, journalists were the most bothersome. The funeral procession was slowly turning into a banal crowd. People still kept coming. At one point, I even had to grab the hand of my mother, who was almost pushed down into one of the graves. The cold was growing fiercer. The sun dipped below the horizon 20 minutes earlier. Twilight was dying into the dark.

Finally, it was finished. The coffins were laid to rest and the gravediggers ... were kicked off.

"Let's fill the holes with earth using our hands," cried the reckless people, forgetting the cold.

The difference between Perm and Kyiv was unbearable. Having asked Ihor Bondar to stay until the grave was filled in,[51] I threw a few lumps torn from the ground on my father's coffin (I could not reach the others) and almost ran home.

Thus ended the four-day epic of the reburials of Vasyl Stus, Yurii Lytvyn, and Oleksa Tykhy, which helped Ukrainians break free of fear and at the same time revealed the gap that, throughout Ukrainian history, existed between Ukrainian man and those who claim to be his leaders. Everyone has his own interests.[52] Today, this thesis, unfortunately, remains as relevant as ever.

Thus, on November 19, 1989, the name of Vasyl Stus started to enter the minds of Ukrainians precisely as a fighter-martyr, an innocent killed for the truth and rights of the Ukrainian people. Mykola Ryabchuk, Kostiantyn Moskalets, Tamara Gundorova, Vasyl Ivashko, Marko Pavlyshyn and a few other researchers are trying to dismantle this populist stereotype, which was finally formed under the influence of reburial.

However, this stereotype is fully motivated. One might even say it was programmed by the fate of Vasyl Stus, which he, contrary

---

[51] Ihor Bondar, together with his guys and some Greek Catholic priests, were filling in the graves. In the darkness that suddenly filled the sky, the people, frightened by the hopeless attempt to fill in the graves using their hands and the responsibility for leaving the graves open, started quickly to break up or, as described by Ihor, to turn tail and run away. Igor Bondar and his boys filled in the graves, and the Greek Catholic priests brought by him "sealed" them.

[52] According to various sources, the number of people who accompanied Stus, Lytvyn and Tykhy on their last journey ranged from 75,000 to 105,000. Kyiv had not seen such a large number of people since 1917. That year, on April 1 (March 18 in the old style), a 100,000-strong demonstration of Ukrainian social and political forces took place in Kyiv, which ended with a rally on Sofiivska Square.

to numerous of his statements, was consciously and consistently forming. Someone had to become a "voice of resistance and protest," he wrote in his reflections. And this precept appears in Stus' work too often to be ignored.

However, and here I completely agree with the thesis of "modern" researchers, the formation of Stus-the-artist occurred in parallel with the formation of Stus-the-patriot, but under the influence of a reading far broader than the patriotic. Hence his worldview, his very way of perceiving the world, although it showed the signs of a European-educated intellectual, yet it was of one who, understanding and enamored of this cultural space, above all respected Ukrainian traditional rural culture, which he desperately tried to modernize or at least to present in the language of (to him) contemporary art.

Today, as this book is being written, there is no doubt that in Ukrainian history Vasyl Stus belongs to the too small "handful" of personalities whose moral authority is recognized in both the East and the West of Ukraine. However, today I am not at all sure that the *life creativity* of Vasyl Stus, which is often opposed to his works, is less important for the formation of the world in which we have to live today.

> And the Lord has not warned me again,
> and again the road has gone.
> So — goodbye — in space
> and — goodbye in time.[53]

Bibliography

Stus, Vasyl. *Tvory*, Vol. 5 and 6 (2 books) (Lviv: Prosvita, 1994–1999).

Belikov, Yurii. "Vo imia ottsa i syna," *Za cheloveka*, No. 10 (44) (December 2001).

---

[53] Vasyl Stus. *Tvory* [Works]. V. 6 (additional). Book 1, 355.

Bilocerkowycz, Jaroslaw. *Soviet Ukrainian Dissent: A Study of Political Alienation* (Boulder and London, 1988).

Kasyanov, Heorhii. *Nezhodni: Ukrains'ka intelihentsiia v rusi oporu 1960–80-kh rokiv* (Kyiv: Lybid', 1995).

Moroz, M. O. *Litopys zhyttia ta tvorchosti Lesi Ukrainky* (Kyiv: Naukova dumka, 1992).

Ne vidliubyv svoiu tryvohu ranniu: Vasyl Stus – poet i liudyna: Spohady, statti, lysty, poezii (Kyiv: Ukrainskyi pysmennyk, 1993).

Ovsienko, Vasyl. *Svitlo liudei: Spohady-narysy pro Vasylia Stusa, Yuriia Lytvyna, Oksanu Meshko* (Kyiv, 1996).

Permskie politlageria (Perm, 1995).

Shovkoshytny, Volodymyr. "'Narode mii, do tebe ya shche vernu...'," *Ukraina*, No. 4 (1990).

Verstiuk, V. F., O. M. Dziuba, and V. F. Repryntsev, *Ukraina vid naidavnishykh chasiv do siohodennia: Khronolohichnyi dovidnyk* (Kyiv: Naukova dumka, 1995).

Zhulynsky, Mykola. *Iz zabuttia – v bezsmertia (Storinky pryzabutoi spadshchyny)* (Kyiv: Dnipro, 1990).

Vasyl Stus' Ancestry and Childhood

> When giving birth to us, no one cares about our opinion, unfortunately.
> (Vasyl Stus)

In the first half of the twentieth century, the Ukrainian village, sung by Mykola Gogol and Velimir Khlebnikov, Taras Shevchenko and Panteleimon Kulish, Hryhir Tyutyunnyk and Oleksandr Dovzhenko, as well as many other writers and intellectuals, and not only those of Ukrainian origin, entered the period of its ultimate decline. Rapid industrial growth and the technological revolution were incessantly dragging its most active creative part into the cancerous tumors of the city, destroying not only its conventional way of life and customs but also putting a time bomb under its living base—tradition.

The peasants were in real danger of "falling out" of history. Every year, the cultural centers of agricultural Ukraine more and more acquired the features of urban culture, consigning the village to "live by memories," i.e., to preserve in its environs the facade of a cultural presence in the form of songs, rituals and customs that were quickly losing their sacred character. Under the pressure of the young and aggressive cultural field of the industrial city, the original traditional cultures were increasingly transformed into pasteboard pieces of scenery. Although they remained intrinsic and meaningful to the first generation of migrants who moved from the villages to the cities, these traditional cultures were completely alien to their children and grandchildren, who could not psychologically attune themselves a slow-rhythm culture, organically entwined with the natural environment and closely bound to the greatest peasant value—the land. And although on the eve of the First World War these processes had not yet taken a threatening form, but existed only as tendencies, mass escapes into "the hamlets" of the distant and foreign lands of the Russian Empire of Stolypin's time, as well as the desire of active youth to break free of the rural environment and join social groups which offered the above-mentioned dynamism and life prospects, gradually became more apparent in Ukraine's peasant cosmos.

The trouble lay not in the basic fact of the mass separation from the land by its former caring owners who knew and understood it. The trouble was the increasingly visible inconsistency of rural traditions and customs with the spirit of modern times. Yet this was the case not only in Ukraine: in Ireland, England, Italy, Austria-Hungary, Prussia and Spain, the status of the peasant gradually became synonymous with poverty and capriciousness. And this happened in those countries much earlier than in our own. This was a global trend, which bypassed the Ukrainian lands only because of the too long preservation of serfdom and a slowness characteristic of the Russian Empire.

The industrial and technological path of development chosen by Europe, the winner of the world civilization race, inevitably had to make itself felt in our country as well. These processes could not happen painlessly, and therefore Ukraine encountered all the cataclysms, pains and shortages that other European countries had experienced a little earlier, including those arising from their much poorer quality of soil. More or less hungry years, mass emigrations overseas, the emergence of an organized crime system: one way or another, these were the payment for the disintegration of the peasant class and the hollowing out of the content of modern man's traditional way of life.[1] In Ukraine, whose rich soil allowed a good

---

[1] It is worth pausing here to note the close connection between the rise of the communist and fascist regimes with the disintegration of the peasant class and the extremely difficult psychological adaptation of people from rural areas to urban life, which has a completely different model of human relations. Under the new living conditions, uncomfortable for former peasants, the number of people dissatisfied with their situation increased considerably. All the troubles and irritations caused by the "lost force," precisely noted by Panas Myrnyi, these deracinated peasants sought to "shift" onto other people's shoulders. Under such circumstances, the role of external random voluntaristic factors (such as a slightly lower living standard, war, instability, the appearance of a charismatic personality) increased significantly, and this, coupled with the psychological dissatisfaction with their own lives, created a fertile ground for the easy manipulation of crowd sentiment. The latter had grown considerably, as yesterday's caring owner became a cheap and unskilled working unit in the city, preoccupied with the problems of getting his daily bread. This dissatisfaction

master to subsist on his own, this process stretched over almost a century and generally ended in the early 1970s,[2] the last few decades being an agony.

All these tragic, and later tragically farcical processes, seethed inside the Ukrainian peasantry, to a certain extent becoming one of the important psychological reasons for the defeat of the Ukrainian revolution of 1917-1920. The split, uncertain position of the peasants (not in status, but in origin), who supported almost all the existing political forces in Ukraine, seemed to program in advance the defeat of the hetmanate (a Ukrainian Cossack state), the UPR (Ukrainian People's Republic) and the Greens. In the latter case, the defeat occurred despite the fact that Nestor Makhno managed to create (however marginal it may have been in historical terms) a real anarchist state, one that, despite being besieged and lacking an internally unified peasant consciousness, remains the only state formation of an anarchist type.

However, none of these formations was either sufficiently consistent in the destruction of the old world, or sufficiently cynical

---

was strengthened by the impossibility of returning to their previous lives, as most had to sell their small plots of land to move to the city. Thus, in order to structure and subdue this newly formed and rapidly growing crowd, it was necessary only to invent an idea that would justify aggression and direct the energy of the "new" force to destroy the world, a world which the former peasants hated because they could not find a place in it. It is not surprising, then, that all the fascist and communist regimes of the twentieth century had their base in low-skilled workers, most of these being former peasants.

2   Of course, we cannot say that today, at the beginning of the third millennium, rural social relations as such have been completely destroyed in Ukraine. However, today's Ukrainian village is growing increasingly similar to a town in terms of its type of social coexistence. As in the town, the law or the power of lawlessness in the countryside has long superseded traditional and customary law. And songs or rituals rooted in past generations no longer perform a function other than a decorative and ethnographic one, and have no connection with real life but begin and end on the stage (whether real or imaginary is of little importance), preserving the form but completely losing the sacred content. This process has gone so far that, since the turn of this century, even the poets have ceased to seek integrity in the folk, shifting their search to the individual word. Let us recall that in the early twentieth century, the creator of imperial futurism, Velimir Khlebnikov, traveled through Ukrainian villages looking for a not yet lost spiritual knowledge, which, according to him, had never existed in Russian villages.

to take the populist step of openly initiating a redistribution of property. None had constant support on its side. Therefore, the victory of the Bolsheviks seems quite natural, because they were the only ones not afraid to wager on the great power of dissatisfaction, even though its consequences could not be predicted.

And although there were differences between individual regions (for example, the Ukrainian South was significantly different from the central-western Podillia, the region where Vasyl Stus' ancestors lived), all the above-mentioned processes took place everywhere, forcing people to make a difficult choice and creating in the peasant community a complete uncertainty regarding its own forces.

Podillia had long held sacred the old traditions and well-established customs regarding the rich Zaporizka outlaws, though themselves devoid of traditions. Ever since the days of the Polish-Lithuanian Commonwealth, local adventurers were either recruited into the army or else pushed to join the ranks of the Cossack outlaws, thus freeing peasant communities from their excessive aggression, an aggression that Lev Gumilev called "passionarity." However, passionarity, given Podillia's geographical location on the border between the Polish-Lithuanian Commonwealth (in the northwest) and the Cossack outlaws (in the southeast), was not absent from this region. However, forcing the most aggressive people out of their communities provided relative stability and even some psychological comfort for a considerable period of time.

The region's boundary location did not allow men of no character to survive. It was necessary to know how to be decisive and courageous, to take responsibility, and not to be afraid to take risks. The choice allowed by the boundary made the master's oppression less unbearable and softened serfdom, forcing the master to become more caring, since he, although having some minimal safeguards for his position, was often forced to adapt to new circumstances. A large number of Poles, who settled in large numbers in the northwest of the Vinnytsia region, allowed the more or less organic combination of agricultural tradition with the dictates of the law.

Even industry, which was actively developed in the region from the end of the eighteenth century, was so closely connected with the land and with the process of agricultural production, that it was not perceived as hostile, but greeted with a certain relief. The number of dissatisfied people here was much smaller and the respect for the law (not least because of its proximity to Europe) was greater. Therefore, the national revolution of 1917, which degenerated into a social revolution, was perceived by the locals quite skeptically, as none of the existing political forces — not the UPR, not the hetmanate, not the Bolsheviks — defended the interests of the peasants, whom they considered an anarchic factor or (quite rightly) an anti-revolutionary element.

Of course, for their political apathy, the peasants had to pay. They were subject to almost constant looting by both the regular army and irregular military units. However, they also had to pay for "love" and support. To defeat Nestor Makhno, in 1921-1922 the Bolsheviks had to exterminate about a million peasants in the Ukrainian South by starvation.

Their love and feeling for the land, even under conditions of constant looting, allowed the peasants, accustomed for many years to all sorts of surprises, not only to survive but also to significantly strengthen their farms. So, when the Soviet authorities launched an open attack on the prosperous peasants (in Soviet terminology, the "kurkuls"), there were those in Podillia w h o could be plundered and, even more important, there was s o m e t h i n g to plunder.

This was not hindered even by a fairly homogeneous ethnic composition (85.1% of the population in 1926 identified themselves as Ukrainians[3]), which, however, had a significant admixture of Polish blood. Prolonged Polish rule brought with it a rather tangible influence of the Greek and Roman Catholic cultural traditions (more perceptible, however, in Western Podillia). The religious culture of the inhabitants of the region was quite high, and the institution of the Church held a significant place in their lives.

The establishment of Bolshevik rule in Podillia came about in the years of the new economic policy and was initially received quite calmly until it became clear that the announced beginning of

---

[3] According to the data given in the article "Podillia" in *Entsyklopediia Ukrainoznvstva* (Encyclopedia of Ukrainian Studies), V.6, 21-41.

industrialization would be at the cost of the plunder of the Ukrainian peasants and their complete enslavement within the collective farm system.

Given that the peasants constituted the majority of the population of Podillia, it is clear why Bolshevik terror in this region was so severe. It did not pose the threat of complete physical extermination (the first country in the service of the "workers and peasants" still needed slaves who would cultivate the land for nothing), but aimed at both the complete destruction of the psychology of the "master" and of certain economic interests. The industrialization proclaimed by Joseph Stalin required money, robbing the peasants was the easiest way of getting it. According to all the laws of physiology and psychology, a body in mortal danger throws all its effort into confronting it. Therefore, it was quite natural that during the twentieth century a number of personalities emerged from the peasant community who defended the natural habitat of their parents, their customs, and traditional way of life, increasingly entering into conflict with the industrialization of even ancient agricultural centers — Ireland, Ukraine, Italy, Bavaria, Spain. Throughout the past century, these clusters of contradictions erupted in fascist and communist regimes, became a location and formed the social base for terrorist organizations and militant anarchist groups, which posed a challenge, doomed from the beginning to failure, to the main course of the development of European civilization. Naturally, the vast majority of these movements originated in lands with ancient agrarian traditions, whose inhabitants sought to resist the dictates of the Law, the only idol possible in the existence and functioning of the "new" world, which openly rejected the peasant way of life based on customary law.

When the wave of world industrialization reached the Russian Empire, which maintained its stability precisely by adopting a slow path of development, conflict inevitably arose between the supporters of modernity and Eurocentrism (Communists, Socialist-Revolutionaries, and other progressives) and the traditionalists (running from supporters of tsarism at one extreme to autonomists at the

ANCESTRY AND CHILDHOOD 69

other). The latter, once drawn into the orbit of the dictatorial European civilization, were doomed, although they had the support of the vast majority of the population.

No wonder that the victory of the first (namely, the Bolsheviks) in a few years' time resulted in large-scale war against the peasantry and the psychology of the small land holder as a whole.

In this context, it appears quite natural that these problems were most acutely felt by those destined to change their small homeland: the Irishman Joyce, the emigrants Kafka and Camus. The latter, in response to accusations of being indifferent to Algeria, his birthplace, responded with sentence that has provoked massive commentary: *"I believe in justice, but I will defend my mother before justice."*[4].

It is this priority of the "mother" over justice that reveals ears that protrude too clearly to go unnoticed. The heretic Camus is the obvious bearer of the traditional way of life, which, despite all its challenges to public morality, reveals a typical peasant: the "self before all." Abstract truth, justice and the laws of historical development only increase the distance between man and the world.

All those words, however, with a much lower degree of generalization, can be applied also to Ukrainian writers who left despairing villages to try by all means to find success in the capital and in the other cities.

A small number of their descendants have achieved real recognition and success in life, but few of them have become part of urban culture. Unfortunately, their lives often mimicked the phrase attributed to Korotych: "In the first part of his life the Ukrainian writer tries to escape the village, and the second is spent glorifying the beautiful country life ..." This contradiction helps explain the fact that for most of today's bearers of urban culture (especially the children) the Ukrainian classics remain alien and abstruse and are held up to mockery by schoolchildren (*"I would rather*

---

[4] Quote from: *Zenkin Sergey*. Zhitiya velikih eretikov. Figuryi inogo v literaturnoy biografii // Inostrannaya literatura [Lives of the Great Heretics: Figures of difference in literary biography] // Ynostrannaia lyteratura.(Foreign Literature) 4, 136.

eat bricks than read Pavlo Tychyna," etc.), although academic literary studies diligently pretend that there is nothing to worry about.

There is. And how!

It is no secret that most descendants of peasant culture felt and realized all this perfectly well, but could not express the problem at the level of public rather than private discourse. *"In populist discourse, literature and writers were seen as one big family ... The populist myth envisaged that, in an ideal people's family, there is harmony between the generations, children respect their parents, the young respect the old, the old take care of the young, and the authority of parents and elders is indisputable."*[5]

This statement of the obvious, not yet articulated at the level of public discourse, is a kind of recognition of defeat, of weakness, of the clearly unnecessary efforts to achieve the goals declared by populism, i.e. popular education. It was even more frightening to admit for Ukrainian writers who, by some quirk of fate, saw themselves as the last hope of the enslaved nation.[6] And it is no coincidence that in his letter to Vasyl Stus about the latter's "A Phenomenon of Our Time," Stanislav Telnyuk wrote:

---

[5] Solomiia Pavlychko. Teoriia literatury. (Theory of Literature) — K.: Vydavnytstvo Solomii Pavlychko "Osnovy" ["Basics" Publishing House of Solomiia Pavlychko], 2002, 47-48.

[6] All participants in the populist discourse agreed with this opinion, from E. Malanyuk to O. Korniychuk. The same was demanded by ideological propaganda (both Soviet and anti-Soviet), which forced writers to educate the people. On the other hand, the "modern," now understood as the contemporary or the newest in every historical period, is *"the striving to update existing forms and c a n o n s, dynamism, the desire to match the level of the modern world's development, the achievements of the natural sciences, philosophy, psychology, technology, twentieth-century communications"* (Leksykon zahalnoho ta porivnialnoho literaturoznavstva / Bukovynskyi tsentr humanitarnykh doslidzhen. Kerivnyk proektu A.Volkov [Lexicon of General and Comparative Literary Studies / Bukovyna Center for Humanitarian Studies. Project Manager A. Volkov.] — Chernivtsi: Zoloti lytavry, 2001, 342). Adherence to tradition is declared reactionary by modern researchers, and this is quite true, as it opposes the ideas of a Eurocentric understanding of progress. However, when viewed from the point of view of anti-globalism, such a quixotic populist position, although felt to be unpromising, appears much more moral in relation to the mother — the biological mother, the motherland, the Earth mother, retaining, albeit in a constrained form, the possibility of otherness as another choice and another way of being human. The problem of Ukrainian literature is that our land, with its traditional

"Vasyl!
I may not have responded to your "A Phenomenon of Our Time" pamphlet. It is not addressed to me. I disagree with you and your pamphlet has not shaken me in anything. The facts provided are already known to me. The argument you use is familiar to me. I am even reluctant to confute it, just reluctant to expend phosphorus on it.
But the reason I set out to answer you is the following. There is a pamphlet passing from hand to hand in which mud is being thrown on the greatest Ukrainian poet of the last half-century [the underlining here and further in the text of the letters is done either by the investigator Loginov or the judge Dyshl to prove the anti-Soviet agitation and propaganda of Vasyl Stus — Dmytro Stus]. *And this is considered not only permissible, but worse — progressive, revolutionary, necessary, and so on and so forth. And NO ONE, I don't mean demagogues, but truly decent, truly thinking, truly independent people, NO ONE shouts: "Help!" NO ONE is indignant, NO ONE is shaking.*
... People are reading your "A Phenomenon of Our Time" calmly and smiling and do not think about the real PHENOMENON OF OUR TIME: 99 percent of the nation does not know and does truculently fails to perceive its most national poet! The nation refuses to accept him as if he were a foreign body in it. How much further could this nation go, a nation which catastrophically and categorically renounces all that is its own, which is categorically ashamed of all that is its own and rushes to be, as Franco said, a "tractive force for the fast trains" of other larger nations with more belief in their historical mission?

---

peasant way of life, is one of those points of great tension, where the archaic peasantry clings to life to the last, retaining a potential for a different development, i.e., the possibility of another choice for man and society. And preserving this "spirit of the earth" is the great tribute to populist discourse, in which the principle of hierarchy and succession—"*Kotlyarevsky was the spiritual father of Shevchenko, and Shevchenko was spiritual father of Franko*" (Sherekh Yu. Na ryshtuvanniakh istorii literatury / Sherekh Yu. Druha cherha (On the scaffolding of the history of literature: Second Turn) — [New York, 1978], 31) — outwardly "unpromising" in terms of progress, yet harmonizes with the "spirit of the earth" as an idea of a different, an alternative path of human development.

Let us renounce everything! Let us renounce language! Let us renounce Tychyna. He is not worthy to be one of ours, because no one has anyone like him, and we are ashamed not to be like everyone else!"[7]

Apparently, he was not ashamed, nor should Stanislav Telnyuk be ashamed of these literary oppositions, he who at the 1972 court hearing "hopelessly" tilted at the windmills of irresistible judicial logic. However, it was an uncommon expression of the extremely painful realization of the tragedy of his people's rejection of the work of one of the most original Ukrainian poets, the creator of one of those high-tension lines that determined the development of literature. If it did not shine brightly, it was extremely important for Ukrainian society, and then as now it was uncritically declared by the modernists to be "peasant," "outdated," "primitive," "backward," and so on.

Nevertheless, the writer works with material that presents him with real life, the world around him. And that reality was "archaic" compared to modern European literature. Therefore, it is not surprising that *"Ukrainian literature has always lacked educated people, both among its authors and in the broader literary environment."*[8] For the faithful performance of their task, such an education would most likely have been a hindrance. It would be like wearing European glasses that progressively distorted everything, and made it difficult to understand the process, artificially suspended in the 1920s, of dividing *"Ukrainian writers into two parties."*[9] This process could not develop naturally, when its participants were artificially driven into an "underground," which, on the one hand, contributed to transforming rural culture into an urban culture with rural roots, and, on the other, further distanced the intelligentsia from the people.

---

[7] The first letter of Stanislav Telnyuk to Vasyl Stus, no date (it can be approximately dated to 1971 or 1970) // Criminal case N 47 on accusations against Stus Vasyl Semenovych in committing a crime stipulated by the Art. 62. Part 1 of the Criminal Code of the USSR. Started: January 13, 1972; Completed: July 26, 1972 in 12 volumes. Volume 10, - 1, 9.

[8] Solomiia Pavlychko. *Teoriia literatury* (The Theory of Literature), 49.

[9] Ibid., 50.

In this situation, Stanislav Telnyuk expressed the point of view of progressive populists. Vasyl Stus was a defiant individualist who, according to the facts of his biography, combined in a chimerical way rural roots and tradition with — outside the family — a completely Russian-speaking urban environment (Donbas). The combination in one individual of two small and culturally diverse homelands often hinders the formation of an integral personality, but good language skills and an almost pathological capacity for work allowed a person from an uneducated family to acquire so much of European tradition that even a cosmopolitan like S. Gluzman, whom fate led to share a ward with Vasyl Stus in 1972, described him as a *"European-educated intellectual"* who helped him to discover the *"true Ukrainian culture, its depth."* Gluzman was especially impressed by the fact that Stus communicated this "knowledge" to the city-raised Gluzman, not in the language of tradition, but in the language of urban culture, allowing him to become acquainted with the greatness of a Ukrainian culture unknown to him since childhood. This is why, after hearing Gluzman swear, the peasant Stus could stop him and *"lecture for about five minutes, and I was terribly ashamed. I had never been ashamed in such situations, but at his side, I realized for the first time that I should be ashamed. Besides, it was not a Puritan who spoke, but an ordinary person and from the point of view of a completely different culture."*[10]

Actually, in hindsight, looking at Vasyl Stus' fate, the first thing you notice is his stoicism in defense of the native language and tradition on the one hand, and then an even somewhat excessive fascination with cosmopolitan world culture (literature, first of all), of which he was truly fond. And this second culture, a non-native one, became his spiritual bond and support during the hardest times of a difficult life journey. Rilke, Goethe, Pasternak, Italian emigrant poets of the middle of the last century, Tolstoy, Tsvetaeva, Pushkin, Kamya, Kipling — these are the can be called the poet's best friends in prison and exile. At the same time, we are not able

---

[10] Semen Hluzman. Dvadtsiat dniv u kameri z Vasylem Stusom [Twenty days in the ward with Vasyl Stus] // Znak neskinchennosti.[Infinity sign] — K.: Fakt [Fact], 2002. — P 10.

to mention any Ukrainian cultural figures, except for the small number of his friends, who, like him, strongly defended the right of Ukrainian culture to exist.[11]

Today we have enough material to advance a hypothesis: Vasyl Stus is not a truly organic figure among the sixtiers,[12] even though he belongs to this circle as a person who defended his parental rural culture. His complicated, European-focused poetry, his desire to synthesize "his own" with the "foreign," and a conscious desire to re-code national works in the international language of world culture, made his 1960s work too complicated in the context of poems more representative of patriarchal culture by B. Oliynyk, V. Symonenko, I. Drach, L. Kostenko, M. Holodny and many others Stus' generation. However, it should be noted that I. Kalinets, M. Vorobyov and V. Holoborodko worked in a similar direction. So it is not surprising that the works of these authors in the 1960s were the closest to Vasyl Stus.

However, the difference between him and these writers, who were close to him in spirit, was also quite significant. Kalinets, Holoborodko, and Vorobyov saw the reasons for the "dying out" of folk tradition primarily in the glaring contradiction between the national and Soviet (quasi-international) worldviews, whereas Stus took a somewhat broader view of the problem: archaic traditional national rural life has no place in the legalistic civilization of the Western world.[13] In fact, I can explain his long-standing fascination

---

[11] See.: Vasyl Stus. Tvory. U 4-kh tomakh (6 knyhakh). 5 i 6 (u 2-kh knyhakh) — dodatkovi. Tom 6. Lysty do ridnykh.[Works. In 4 volumes (6 books). Volumes 5 and 6 (in 2 books) — additional. Volume 6. Letters to relatives] — L.: VS "Prosvita" [Education Publishing Union], 1997.

[12] This is a common interpretation of the term, but is not the point of view of Ye. Sverstyuk, L. Svitlychna and other sixtier-dissidents, who tend to restrict the community of the sixtiers to the people who, at the very least, were in active moral opposition to the Soviet regime. Where the cultural aspect is concerned, however, such a restriction seems somewhat simplistic and excessively focused on personal qualities, rather than on his cultural orientations and preferences.

[13] This explains why Stus never actively sought to leave the USSR. When he publicly renounced his citizenship (in 1978 and in 1979) it was only because of the absence of basic human rights — the right to say goodbye to a terminally ill father, to preserve your own notes, keep poems, etc. As soon as the pain and resentment of the government's absolute arbitrariness and injustice subsided,

with existentialism ("always on the edge") and these well-known and hitherto misread lines only by the clear realization that the progress of the Western world inevitably brings death to national roots:

> I was not destined to hide from fate ...
> Thunderstruck — and immediately everything in life
> Has gone wrong. And here you are — all that dreamed about,
> As death-existence and life-death.
> So test, like gold, on trial
> Your beloved ones, relatives, friends and children:
> Would they go through a hundred of their deaths
> Following you? Would they
> understand your needs — at least at the end of life?
> Wouldn't they get terrified of chills in the heart
> From all misfortunes? Oh, I wish I knew ...[14]

The great symbol of almighty Destiny, of which You, man, can be worthy, runs through all of Stus' works. Only this explanation of the ontological symbol strikes me today as sufficiently motivated and convincing because it largely explains the life of Vasyl Stus himself.

Stus' extreme self-discipline, together with his desire to capture the vanishing world fully have so complicated and concentrated his poetry and thought that even the most profound researchers of his work — M. Kotsyubynska, M. Pavlyshyn, M.Heifets, M. Ryabchuk, Ye. Sverstyuk, V. Ivashko[15] — do not try to cover its

---

Stus immediately seemed to correct himself, saying "I don't really want to go abroad" or something similar. The same unwillingness to leave the country was evident during the "break" between prison terms, from August 1979 to May 1980, when, despite being invited to lecture at several universities, he made little effort to leave. On the contrary, according to his wife, and my own childhood memory, he was much more eager to get to "freedom" again, to the camp, where he could become "himself" again, without the constant humiliation, for him, of being unable to provide his family with material well-being, or shield it from the external pressure brought on by his uncompromising behavior.

[14] Vasyl Stus. Works: V.3: book 1, 83-84.
[15] See, in particular, their works: Mykhailyna Kotsiubynska. Poet // V.Stus. Tvory [Works]: Vol.1, book 1. - P. 7—38; Stus yak tekst [Stus as text] / Editor

entirety in their studies or articles, and either consciously or unconsciously limit themselves to certain aspects of Stus' life, work or myth.

Konstantin Moskalets, a hermit from Matiiv, came the closest to capturing the writer's perception of the world.[16] *"It seems that the only thing Stus wanted from his destiny,"* he writes carefully, *"was to be a tractive force, so that the life impulse and Dionysian power that knew no polarities, both in his individual existence and in the history of the Ukrainian nation, would not subside. Instead, he finds 'fragments of destinies,' the intervention of forces that are difficult to understand and denote with the concepts inherent in his language. Involvement in the life impulse, occupying the core of the current, a state "in which I do not write, but it is written by me" – these are for Stus ideal examples of human existence. At the same time, there is no shortage of texts in which he persistently set fate in opposition to unpredictability or which communicate his belief that fate, destiny, God form man beyond his conscious will, or that man is God's collaborator in the development of the individual soul ... This aspect of his thinking is worth the attention of Stus' future readers and researchers, because it may be that here, as in every archetypal figure, the principle of complementarity is at work, in which the extremes of a binary opposition are the condition for each other, and the connection between them and the function of the opposition itself are more important than the visible confrontation."*[17]

Moskalets very precisely determines the presence of clear opposition not only in the fate of Vasyl Stus, but also in his work. It is loyalty to Fate and the unpredictability of the individual, who is

---

and the author of the foreword M. Pavlyshyn. - Melbourne: Department of Slavic Studies, Monasha University; Mykhailo Kheifets. "V ukrainskii poezii teper bilshoho nema ..." [There is nothing more in Ukrainian poetry now ...] // Suchasnist [Modernity]. - 1981, Ch. 7-8; Mykola Riabchuk. "Nebizh Rilke" i "syn Tarasa" [Nephew of Rilke and Son of Taras] // Krytyka [Criticism]. - 1999, June; Yevhen Sverstiuk. Vasyl Stus – letiucha zirka ukrainskoi literatury [Vasyl Stus is a flying star of Ukrainian literature] // Yevhen Sverstiuk. Na sviati nadii.[At the feast of hopes]. - K.: Nasha vira, [Our faith], 1999; Vasyl Ivashko. Mif pro Vasylia Stusa, yak dzerkalo shistdesiatnykiv [The myth of Vasyl Stus as a mirror of the sixties] // Svitovyd.[Worldview]. - 1994, P. III (16), P.104–120.

16 Kostiantyn Moskalets. Strasti po Vitchyzni [Passions for Motherland] // Krytyka.[Criticism] – 1999, June.
17 Ibid., 12.

able not only to extend the tradition in time but also to change and modify it. More acutely and clearly than his contemporaries, the poet understood the need less to preserve, as sooner or later progress would win, as to recode tradition in the universal language of culture, so that it, like a viable species, would at least have some chance of materializing in new, unfavorable conditions.

Such awareness and honest conclusions—"I do not live, but it lives by me"—inevitably had to lead Stus to an understanding of the depth of the ontological crisis: he could not renounce either kin, because that is "undignified for a man," or culture (and Western culture first of all), although in letters and conversations he often speaks of the latter's "parasitizing" on human misery, blood, and suffering.

The search for a combination of Will and Unpredictability sooner or later had to lead either to collapse or to the creation of his own model of the universe (his "forming" according to Moskalets), greatly enriched by peasant anarchism, whose most characteristic feature is an ontological disrespect for imposed law, a law which contradicts the logic of life and the tradition of peasant life sanctified over the centuries.

And here we must pay attention to a problem, which, although present in Ukrainian literature since the end of the last century, still contains many unclear points and, unfortunately, undiscussed topics.

It is the question, in the newest studies, of the aggravation of the confrontation between the "modern" and the "folk," or, more precisely, the "populist" in Ukrainian culture and literature in general. The researchers of the new formation seem all, with the exception of V. Morenets, unconditionally to give priority to the (at first glance) more contemporaneous "modern," and devastatingly criticize the "populist," which in the pages of periodicals like *Krytyka* (Criticism), "Knyzhnyka-review" (Bibliophile-review) and even, in part, *Suchasnosty* (Modernities) has long been synonymous with the uneducated and even archaic in art in general and literature in particular.

Solomiia Pavlychko, an apologist for the modern, managed to do this most correctly, consistently and convincingly. In "The Discourse of Modernism in Ukrainian Literature," she seems to bridge the gap between the understanding of the modern as progress and of the populist as stagnation at the beginning and at the end of the past century: "Populism put forward the thesis of that the ground should be the "native," the authentic, as opposed to the foreign, the Western. To what extent was the authentic truly authentic? Both Franco and Efremov were influenced by Russian populism ... Fascinated by Russian socialism, which intellectually won out intellectually against the background of clerical populism, to say nothing of their Moscowphilia, Franco and the others failed to notice that along with this they transplanted into the Ukrainian field the hatred of the West distinctive of Russian populist socialists, their call to rely on their own native "ground," their mysticism (the people is the source of ultimate wisdom) and even a tendency to messianic exaltation."[18]

Assessing the situation during the late nineteenth and early twentieth centuries in Ukrainian literature, Pavlychko returned to the century-old opposition, a not particularly constructive one (in my opinion, rather militant), between the folk and the modern, the Russian-oriented and the Western, the "reactionary" and the "progressive."

Like every Ukrainian artist, Stus perceived that in their declining years, even the most enthusiastic modernists end up taking a populist position. Ukrainians in the relatively free western lands left those lands in search of better fortune much more often than residents of the despotic Russian Empire . In the country where he was destined to live the traditional populist discourse was preferred not only by most writers but also, more importantly, by the majority of their readers. And if before the early 1960s his fascination with fashionable existentialism prevailed, after the complete fiasco of his modern "Zymovi dereva" (Winter trees), even among a narrow circle of experts, Stus finally realized that he was conducting his search "not quite on the plane" promising recognition.

---

[18]   Solomiia Pavlychko, *Teoriia literatury* [The Theory of Literature], 71-72.

This realization was not easy. Yet, at the cost of several years of hopeless wandering, it struck him. And this was perhaps his greatest creative victory before his arrest in 1972. Accepting, if not with his mind then in his heart, that the people cannot be "blind," Stus realized that in being "uninteresting" for the reader, it was he rather than the reader who was guilty. This happened because Vasyl Stus had not found a music that would entice, beckon and lead the reader into his world.[19]

Eventually, he clearly recognized the popularity of the play "V stepakh Ukrainy" (In the Steppes of Ukraine) by O. Korniychuk, and the much greater interest taken in the poems of his contemporaries Vasyl Symonenko, Mykola Kholodny, Lina Kostenko.

After all, paving "the way" for the reader is the main task facing everyone. And the Ukrainian artist is not alone in striving to turn from a word-monger into a professional writer. Of course, most do not manage to accomplish this, but the very fact of the search indicates the seriousness of the writer's intentions and his certain professionalism.

Unfortunately, failures in this way are natural, and successes occur rarely and never or seldom show any regularity. "Modernists" pay the price of being misunderstood by the general public, "traditionalists" endure the superiority of critics and theorists of literature. The authors who pursue a synthesis often become strangers to both.

Who can forget the names of Pavlo Tychyna, Viktor Petrov-Domontovych, Mykhailo Yatskiv? To a greater or lesser extent, the works of these writers are still read rather superficially, or, in the case of Tychyna and Petrov-Domontovych, are condemned on pseudo-ideological grounds. The isolated voices of those who bring into correlation their own tragedy and dualism with the tragedy

---

[19] This situation regarding readers' perception/rejection of the "modern" Western art language was relevant for the country not only in the 1960s and 1970s, but also at the beginning of the last century. For instance, the modern theater of Les Kurbas in the 1920s never drew large audiences as the traditional and in many respects ethnographic theater in Kyiv or Kharkiv.

and dualism of the Ukrainian people in the twentieth century remain sporadic and have little impact on established modes of perception.

Something similar is happening with the works of Vasyl Stus. Some perceive him only as an aesthete and lyric poet, others as a fighter for the "independence of Ukraine" (in fact for the right of Ukrainian-speaking peasant culture to exist) with all the aforementioned quite naturally coexisting in him in a very complex, composite and not always a consistent way.

And, most importantly, Vasyl Stus could not betray any of these components. Because on the one side were mother, father, kin; and on the other the desire for the great, the pursuit of its realization, and the responsibility of a talent representative of God's spark as either a gift or a curse.

* * *

Vasily Stus' parents[20] got married in the autumn of 1920. Two or three years earlier, their marriage would have been difficult to even

---

[20] Regarding the male branch of the Stus family in the village of Rakhnivka, the archival work done by local historian Oksana Yatsyuk resulted in the article "Rodovid Vasylia Stusa" [Vasyl Stus' Ancestry], published in *Vinnytska Pravda*: *"On February 20, 1858, the cantonist Klymentiy Fedorovych Stus ... [Vasyl Stus'] great-grandfather, appeared in the census of the village of Rakhnivka of Haisyn district. Before 1858, the surname 'Stus' had not been seen in the village of Rakhnivka.*
Klimentiy Fedorovich Stus belonged to cantonists of a special status in existence in the Russian Empire since 1805. All the underage sons of junior Russian army officers were recorded as cantonists. They were the property of the military from birth and, due to their origins, were required to perform military service. The cantonist institution was closely connected to serfdom, for once a conscript was liberated from serfdom, he and all his offspring became the property of the military institution. And even the sons of those retired soldiers, the illegitimate sons of soldiers' wives and widows, abandoned boys adopted by lower-ranking officers' families, became cantonists.
Cantonists served in separate companies, where they were taught to read and write, mechanical and industrial arts, military sciences. Unfortunately, we know almost nothing about the life of the cantonist Clement Stus until 1858. Probably he was born in 1843-1844. His place of birth is unknown. It is possible that Vasyl Stus' great-grandfather served in the Kyiv-Podilskyi district of military settlements ...
In 1856, the cantonists were released from military service, and Klimentiy Stus was sent to Rakhnivka to become a "state property" peasant.
It is unknown why Vasyl Stus' great-grandfather was sent to Rakhnivka specifically, but he was destined to live most of his life in this village. In Rakhnivka he and his wife

imagine, because the difference in social status and wealth between Yilyna Sinkivska and Semen Stus was significant, and this is speaks against marriage. There was also Yilyna's despair, obviously connected to an unfulfilled love about which she remained tight-lipped.

They had no children for the first five years. "God did not provide," Yilyna Yakivna used to say. Semen Demianovich's two sisters, Marusia and Lusha, lived with the newlyweds in a small hut near the village pond. The revolutionary events that swept over Podillia at the turn of the twenties did not leave much of a mark on history, but the calm and level-headed Semen did his best to make the household prosperous and bring home the bacon. And they were indeed quite prosperous during this period.

Although the victory of Soviet power brought much that was incomprehensible to the people of the region, as long as the "New Economic Policy" (NEP) proclaimed by Lenin was in force, people did not particularly complain about their fate. *"My father gave us a cow,"* Yilyna Yakivna recalled, *"then the cow dropped a calf. He gave us a sow and she gave birth to twelve piglets in the spring before Easter. And so we lived. Then we bought a cart. Then we bought horses. We came through everything and served well and never argued with anyone. Somehow we lived well."*[21] By the mid-1920s life gradually settled, Semen's

---

Maria Hnativna raised three sons Demian, Semen and Fedor ... Semen and Fedor served in the army. Semen was killed in unknown circumstances. His wife Natalka and daughter Maria stayed in his native village. Demian, born in 1862, the eldest son of Klimentiy Fedorovich Stus ... lived in Rakhnivka. He had five children: two sons, Semen and Vasyl, and three daughters, Zinovia, Likera and Maria. He was married twice as his first wife Darka, Semen's mother and Vasyl Stus' grandmother, died young.
Semen Demianovich Stus ... like his uncles, served in the army.
In the 1930s, Semen Demianovich Stus worked as a zavhosp [supplies supervisor, second-in-command] at Rakhnivka kolhosp [a collective farm]. The head of the kolhosp was the brother of his wife Yilyna Yakivna. His name was Dmytro Sinkivsky."
A photocopy of this article is kept in the archive of Vasyl Stus, which, unfortunately, does not contain bibliographic references. Unfortunately, I was not able to contact O. Yatsyuk.

21 Ibid., 141. On the basis of the book, we can conclude that they were talking about 1934-1935; however, from additional consultations with and clarifications provided by Vasyl Stus' family members and relatives, it is clear that Vasyl Stus' maternal grandfather first helped the newlyweds get on their feet in the mid-1920s. and then after the famine of 1933.

younger sisters grew up and in 1926 their first child, Palazhka,[22] was born. Vasyl's older brother, Ivan, was born in the early 1930s.

The famine of 1933 was painful for Vasyl's parents, but not as terrible as for the vast majority of peasants: "My mother said that in 1933 they did not see the famine. Other people were starving, but ... they were not hungry ... There was a cow. It was bearable,"[23] Vasyl's sister Maria, who was a year older, recalled. And Ilyina Yakivna herself spoke about the winter-spring of 1933 without desperate strain: "Things happened! But it was different at home somehow."[24] However, the NEP was replaced by the policy of collectivization. The state increasingly needed funds for industrialization, and the pressure on the peasants, almost the only real "sponsors" of this policy, increased.

Everyone had to choose. Dmytro, Ilyina's brother, immediately took on a managerial role at the collective farm, but Semen decided not to hand over his hard-earned property to someone else. This worsened the already rather cool relationship between Dmytro's wife and Yilyna, and the pressure on Semen Stus grew more and more: "*He did not join the collective farm immediately. It was necessary to do it at once, but he did not.*"[25]

Evil tongues, envy and the harsh calculations of peasant life significantly worsened the situation of the people gradually enslaved in the village. The "new masters" were yesterday's poor people, who gladly took out their anger on the "old masters" or those who had managed, in the five or seven years of relative freedom, to get out of poverty. And at first, the collective farmers lived much poorly than those who, despite confiscatory taxes, remained outside of the collective farms. Such circumstances turned even close relatives into enemies. Thus, it is not surprising that Semen's stepsister Maria (Marusia) was thrown out of the house for a trifling tax underpayment, with the active participation of Dmytro Sinkivsky. When she and her four children later returned to their house, the

---

[22] Palazia, as rendered by Yilina Stus.
[23] Mariia Cherednychenko / Netsenzurnyi Stus. [Uncensored Stus], 161.
[24] Yilyna Yakivna Stus / Netsenzurnyi Stus, 141. She compares the famine of 1933 in Rahnivka with the severe famine of 1947, which Yilyna Stus barely survived.
[25] Yilyna Yakivna Stus / Netsenzurnyi Stus, 141.

"eviction" procedure was repeated even more brutally. The young woman tried to drown herself, neighbors only just managing to rescue her. The atmosphere of hatred and universal moral depression prevailing in Rakhnivka in the early 1930s was so terrible that Maria's husband, completely intimidated by the "kurkul [rich peasant] formation" process, decided to abandon the woman and her four children and flee. When he later returned to the village, the head of the village council *"forced him go to the ravine and killed, shot him."*[26]

The humiliation and the pain of existence, constantly accompanied by the threat of reprisals, forced many to look for any chance to escape their native village. The process of "kurkul formation" really left a man almost no other choice. If you joined the collective farm, you became a poor serf, deprived of your own land; if you run your own farm, you have to pay a tax, which is often higher than the harvest itself. *"They came to me. We were threshing grain. They took everything down to the last little grain ... And one neighbor came to us. And I am crying, crying. What are we going to do? Four children. Where can we go? That man says to me: 'Do you know that tomorrow you will have a court hearing?' I say: 'For what?' 'You were short.' They took the bread that we were threshing and added that I did not have enough for the allotment. There is nothing extra to pay for the allotment. 'It must be you and two other people.' Deal with it and go wherever you like. And then he, my grandfather [Semen Stus], hid somewhere in Kerch.*[27] *I then grabbed my bag and left. And I had never even been to the railway station. I came and told my grandfather. He says, 'You are getting confused. It could never happen that all the bread would be taken away and you judged. For what?'*

... I was the one to blame. All right. (My mother was still alive then.) I leave my children with her. I go from there back to my station. I am going home. It is already dark. I call on the neighbor who lives on the edge of the field. I say: 'Any word about me?' And she: 'One woman ran away and you ran away, and another was taken, and her husband was imprisoned

---

[26] Ibid.
[27] The reference is to the unsuccessful attempt by Vasyl Stus' father to find work in Crimea.

like kurkul' ... They gave her five years because she didn't have enough to pay extra ..."[28]

Fear grew greater, no one had any faith in the future. After a while, Semen Stus returned to the village and, under threat of being charged, was forced to write an application to join the collective farm. This meant the loss of all property, including the barn.

Semen Stus, a watchful and caring man, was appointed as *zavhosp*. This appointment was approved at the collective farm meeting, which he did not attend for some reason. It seemed to give him the chance to establish himself in the village, but as soon as the opportunity arose to escape, Semen seized it. In 1937, an official recruiting workers for industrial Donbas visited Rakhnivka. Donbas needed more and more workers, and these were actively recruited in the villages looted by the authorities. It was a chance not only for Yilyna and Semen but for their children, whom their parents wanted to educate, as well.

Yilyna Stus described the circumstances of their move as follows: *"He comes home and says: 'You know, there is a recruiter from Donbas. I will probably go.' He does not want anything anymore. He does not want to see those people. And I say to him: 'It is up to you.' He applied for a certificate to leave. The head of the collective farm and the head of the village council did not want to release him. They said: 'We will not let him go.' And they gave him nothing. No certificate. But the man, the recruiter from Donbas, says: 'You know what, I am taking you without any documents. I will take responsibility for you.' That is how we came here. He was so sick of those people who tortured him so much that we left ... Such misfortune drove him there. But now we say that it is good that it drove us out of those beets and that misfortune. And sometimes I dream that I am back home there and I am so sad and think: 'God, why did we come to this Donbas. Why did we do that?'"*[29]

And Semen left. Unlike his previous attempts, this trip was successful. He managed to find a job that allowed him not only to escape from the village but also to quickly move his wife and children to Donbas.

---

[28] Yilina Yakivna Stus/ Netsenzurnyi Stus,. 142.
[29] Ibid., 143.

However, no matter how difficult it was in the village, life there did not consist only of problems and trials. There were starry evenings and the quiet heartfelt intimacy of people forced to waste their youth for the incomprehensible ideals of a communist utopia.

The patriarchal heritage, and the unchanging concept of w h a t a f a m i l y s h o u l d b e even in times of trouble, did not allow Yilyna and Semen to limit themselves to two children: in 1937 and 1938 they had two more children, Maria (Marusia) and Vasyl.

The mother left the youngest, Vasylok, when still a baby, with his grandmother and took her two eldest children to distant Stalino[30] at the end of 1938 to try, like thousands of runaway peasants, to escape the humiliation of violence and poverty. In this emigration, on the industrial steppe, they had to start from zero. They became *hrachi*.[31]

A few words about the history of the city.

At a large rally, just after the Soviet victory in 1919, an inhabitant of industrial Yuzivka raised the question of changing the name of the settlement, which became a city a little later. The resolution was passed as follows: *"'It is a shame that the center of proletarian Donbas is named after the exploiter Hughes. To wipe out this shameful stain, it is necessary to rename the working city of Yuzivka as the city of steel — Stalino.' The name was adopted ... Only the railwaymen remained more conservative and called the station Yuzivka. Later they renamed it as well, probably in connection with Stalin."*[32]

And on the subject of *hrachi*, this is how Petro Hryhorenko, who spent his youth in Donbas, was repeatedly addressed, even though he held a relatively high Komsomol position. Once, at a store with his friend, he was treated with undisguised contempt, a hillbilly who was not from there, by a native Donbas resident, who lived there by right of birth and had long experience of survival in local conditions.

---

[30] The former name of Donetsk.
[31] "Hrach" — a rook (See the poem "Ty odyn mii, o hraivorone..." [You are the only one, oh my rook].
[32] Petro Hryhorenko. Spohady [Memoirs] /Translated by Dmytro Kyslytsia. — Detroit: Ukrainski visti [Ukrainian news], 1984, 82.

The insult hrach has many implications. In Donbas, this word "gleefully used by people who consider themselves to be a working-class aristocracy to addressed ordinary people, hillbillies."[33] And this division somehow laid the foundation for the hierarchy in the settlement. This division immediately indicates "the status quo: I am a local, a member of the community where you have just shown up, so try to survive, prove your right to be like me. Thus, even after learning from a saleswoman that he was dealing with a great Komsomol leader, the native was not at at all concerned, but told them both to their face: 'he is a secretary for you. But for me, he is a hrach, whatever his position is.'"[34]

It was right, I say. Surviving in freedom-loving Donbas, which operates according to its own unwritten laws, was always a difficult task. And not only because Ukrainians, Russians, Caucasians and other nationalities went there, in the midst of the Donbas inhabitants who were living there, but also because this region in all conditions preserved a love for freedom, practiced a cult of strength, valued strength of character and accepted all travelers, about whom, however, they were not specifically worried.[35] The land had been inhabited since ancient times, and offered a place for all those who were ready to meet force with force, openness with openness and sincerity with sincerity. They were always outspoken and if they were beaten, they admitted it openly, but without remorse. As in all times and places, most were unable to catch the bird of happiness, and, as a result, the loss of illusions and the overcrowded misery of the barracks were drowned in *horilka*, regularly arranging drunken "wall-to-wall fist fights." Strangers were disliked, but if anyone could stand up for himself, he was recognized as one of theirs.

It is believed that active settlement of the Donbas steppes started as early as the era of the Great Migration, and that the first

---

[33] Ibid., 83.
[34] Ibid., 83.
[35] Sava Bozhko in his novel "V stepakh" [On the Steppes] writes that under the rule of the Roman Empire, Roman law did not to apply to settlers in the Donbas, and any criminal, even one under a death sentence, who fled to the steppe could start life over with a clean sheet.

nomadic tribe was the Cimmerians, who came from the Don in the tenth century BC and roamed in the Kalmius basin and the Siversky Donets. After three centuries, the Cimmerians were displaced by the Scythians, seeking their fortune in that region, who during the next five centuries mixed with the Sarmatians,.[36]

Numerous traces in the form of stone *babas*,[37] left by these almost mythical ancestors, make their presence felt, though they are lower in comparison with other, truly Christian regional percentages.

The defining feature of Yuzivka-Stalino-Donetsk was also its border position: between cultures, between ethnic groups, between armies[38] and between states. What can I say, if even different judicial and executive powers in this region were not surprising? Greek immigrants, who moved to these lands by order of Catherine II at the end of the eighteenth century, elected a separate body to govern Pavlivsk,[39] combining administrative, judicial and police functions, the Mariupol Greek Court, the highest court in Mariupol County.[40]

The Japanese Hiroaki Kuromiya, who was also interested in Donbas, accurately described the nature of the region: *"'Class' and 'nation,' the two major concepts of political thought that arose in reaction to the Enlightenment, did not and do not apply comfortably to Donbas politics. The Marxists had a very difficult time in the Donbas even at the time of 'proletarian revolution' and civil war (or 'class war') in 1917-1920; so did nationalist parties at a time when they thrived elsewhere in the wake of the collapse of both imperial Russia and the Soviet Union.*

What has defined Donbas politics was (and still is) a fierce spirit of freedom and independence. Independence did not preclude the possibility

---

[36] Leonyd Rubynshtein. Knyha rekordov Donbassa [Book of Donbas Records]. (Donetsk: EAY-press, 2002), 7.
[37] *Baba* from "balbal," "babai" (from the Turkic, a strong, warrior hero inspiring respect).
[38] On April 30, 1746, the Russian Senate decided that the Kalmius river would mark the boundary between the Don Army and the Zaporozhian Cossack Army. Since then, the left bank of the river was attached to the Don, and the right to the Zaporozhian. For more details, see Leonyd Rubynshtein. Knyha rekordov Donbassa, 15.
[39] This was the name given to Mariupol.
[40] Leonyd Rubynshtein. Knyha rekordov Donbassa, 18. The Mariupol Greek court had jurisdiction only over the Greek population.

of a pragmatic alliance with foes and outsiders, behavior often appears to observers as unprincipled, mercenary, and lacking perspective. This spirit is a historical product. The Donbas belongs to an area that used to be called the 'wild field', a no-man's-land. No-man's-land attracted freedom seekers, and the wild field became a free, Cossack steppe land. Even after the free steppe was conquered, the frontiers closed, the Zaporozhian Cossackdom abolished, and the Don Cossacks incorporated into the Russian Empire, the metropolis's hold on the former frontier region remained weak, and the spirit of freedom endured. ...

Even in the Stalinist 1930s and beyond, the Donbas never lost its reputation as a safe haven for fugitives. Both before and after World War II, the Donbas attracted numerous people who sought to live new lives there. Such was the case with the numerous disenfranchised people such as the 'kulaks' and clergy as well as Jews ..."[41] Naturally, it was in Donbas that Ukrainian peasants, who had to flee physical extermination, sought refuge. After all, Donbas was not the Urals, or Siberia, or Kolyma, places to which people were not only sent away in trains with bars on the windows, but to which they went on their own (though not in large numbers). Only the most desperate dared to go into the completely unknown Far East, across the length of the continent, and often they went there seeking banal earnings. But Donbas ... this region still kept the illusion of a possible return ...

So, we can say that Vasyl Stus, was born in the village of Rakhnivka, Haisyn district, Vinnytsia region, on January 6,[42] 1938, but, during childbirth, his mother's thoughts were already far from their small home and only the birth of her child forced her to postpone moving to Stalino for a year.

We can say that the lot of his birth meant that Vasyl combined two components: peasant balance and wisdom, which ceased to be

---

[41] Hiroaki Kuromiya, *Freedom and Terror in the Donbas: A Ukrainian-Russian Borderland, 1870s–1990s* (Cambridge: Cambridge University Press, 2003), 335.

[42] There is a lot of confusion about the date of the poet's birth in the literature about Vasyl Stus. In different sources, the date of his birthday is indicated as January 6, 7 and 8. It is likely the birth certificate gives January 8 as the date. However, as Yilyna Stus admitted, she was simply afraid to register her son on January 6 and wrote down a different date. Vasyl Stus celebrated his birthday on January 6 and this was the date he used in all documents where not associated with registration records.

virtues in his lifetime, and Donbas freedom, rebelliousness and independence, without which it is almost impossible to strive for success. For some reason, he did not take the easy path of renouncing his roots and mother tongue, as most children of immigrants naturally do, to avoid the cruel mockery of his peers. That path is for the weak, and from his childhood Vasyl wanted to be strong. And, besides, his parents, as far as he could see, were not ashamed of their origins, preserving their religion in the family circle, as well as their traditional order and language. It is quite probable that his father or mother told him many painful details about their escape from Vinnytsia in the long dark evenings. They were able to tell the romantic young man about his native land in such a way as to instill in him an irresistible desire to defend the national dignity, a dignity that in Stalino you could read about only in historical legends about the Cossacks. Stus was not lacking in either character or perseverance for the task, and the difficult life of his parents only compelled him to set his teeth and jut out his chin proudly, as if to challenge: "Look who has come."

This life philosophy, which originated in Vasyl Stus' protest against parental abuse in his childhood and youth, was finally formed in the mid-1960s, but from today's perspective, we can say that it was largely to the result of the circumstances connected with his arrival in Donbas.

In the Donbas, "cursed" by his mother Rakhnivka, everything looked completely different in the ravines of Podillia, lost in the steppe, where rich land is found side by side with chronic poverty, where hands stained black from hard labor coexist with a powerful thirst for knowledge. This thirst could be suppressed only by the humiliations endured by half-starved peasants struggling to survive, by the hard necessity of the search for bread. Most cannot withstand this pressure and go into the ground to become the soil for future generations' growth. But sometimes there are happy exceptions to the rule and someone will stride with open pride to challenge man and God, to powerfully create his own Destiny, in violation of all precepts, but precisely because of this in time he becomes an example to follow. He becomes a world, and it does not matter what kind of world — real, poetic or just fictional — where those for whom Nietzsche predicted a lonely existence on the icy heights find the warmth of understanding. Or maybe everything is much simpler, and Podillia's rich land simply gave the world another man with a steel character, who from an early age was formed in free and independent Donbas, where not defending the right to one's own otherness meant either becoming an apostate or falling victim to the mockery of his peers.

Anyway, on an unsilent, non-festive Christmas Eve, a boy was born in a *hata* (house, home) on a steep, snow-sprinkled alley perfectly evoking the Moryntsi relief of the steppe.[43] This boy not only succeeded in achieving a defiant synthesis of modernism and a respected tradition, but also managed to live in such a way that his work developed and became life, and his life itself became creativity. The ground for this life-as-creativity was the eternal utterly shapeless body of the peasant Pantagruel, which needed to be transformed by a stylus into a new form of perfection, one which would not only *not* destroy the traditional national spirit but, on the contrary, emphasize it, make it recognizable and bring it close to the people of his land on a tangible sensual level. Being born in a village, the poet was well aware that due to the lack of education, his people could not comprehend either the meaning of his life and struggle or his creative achievements.

Around the late 1960s, Vasyl began to create not only his own poetic world, but also the myth of his own biography. Since 1972, the two have existed integrally and inseparably. Yet, at the same time, paradoxically, they remain completely separate from each other, as in his work Vasyl Stus did not really allow a place for publicizing declarations or the political statements that the Ukrainian poetic horde likes to make. Indeed, what does today's struggle against power mean in eternity? The struggle is required only to know yourself and to determine what you are capable of.

The poet put down the details of his childhood, in a somewhat mythologized biography, in a letter to his son dated April 25, 1979.[44] However, Stus' first attempts to create it date back to the late

---

[43] Moryntsi is a village where Taras Chevchenko was born.
[44] Vasyl Stus. Tvory... [Work] V.6: book 1, 345-350.

1960s,[45] when he was focused on looking for approaches to a new poetic language. After writing his work on Pavlo Tychyna, "Fenomen Doby, abo Skhodzhennia na Holhotu slavy" [The Phenomenon of Our Time or the Way to the Golgotha of Glory], the poet finally realized the duty of the writer, at least of the Ukrainian writer, to tightly intertwine destiny and work. At some moment during the writing of "Fenomen ..." Vasyl Stus finally understood: the higher the creative goal that you set for yourself, the more must you demand of yourself, because if you do not, you will not be trusted, and you will go down the well-travelled road of the jester.

In the late 1960s, Stus failed to draw up his childhood apocrypha. This happened ten years later, when, after an eight-year separation, he sincerely recounted his childhood in a letter to his son, trying at least in this way to prepare him for their meeting. He realized that they would have to get acquainted again. Only extreme sincerity could break the ice of mutual ignorance and misunderstanding. Describing the events of his childhood, which were deeply engraved on his memory, and, therefore, were the most important for him, he seemed to stake out at the fateful crossroads that formed him. For this reason, sometime quoting too long passages from this letter, I will allow myself to comment on or supplement them only in some respects.

Vasyl Stus' first conscious and, given his age, almost mystical childhood recollection dates to 1938, when he was not even a year old. That is why it is so difficult to distinguish the images of a child's memory from mystical imagination or the later, somewhat hagiographic schemes, in which the child's emotions are inseparable from his mother's memories and impressions from rather infrequent visits to Rakhnivka. "*I remember lying in a cradle (my mother was still working in the fields, on the collective farm, so I was less than a year old), and no one was there. The cradle hangs from a hook nailed to a beam ...*[46] *I am wet, I must have roared and I am bored. It is boring to lie down, so I am playing with my ears. I am crumpling them in my palms. I*

---

[45] The beginning of the story of his childhood is preserved in Vasyl Stus' family archive.
[46] In the late 1950s, Vasyl Stus' cousin, Mykola, built a house on this location. In 1959, the poet himself worked on its construction.

remember going to the nursery in Rakhnivka (my mother still lived in the village) and kissing all the snotty-nosed children there because I loved them all. I remember being frightened by someone else's dog and a shaman 'pouring out the fright,', circling a white egg around my head and repeating: dog-dog-dog, horse-horse-horse, sheep-sheep-sheep. It helped, although I spoke with a stammer a little bit as a child, even at school ...

> My mother was singing a lullaby over my crib ...
> My son, my son, do not curse your father,
> But remember kindly.
> I am the one who is cursed, I am your mother, –
> curse me.

When my mother later sang these sad words, I wept bitter tears. Why "don't curse your father"? Why is the mother cursed? I could not understand. And tears ran from my eyes and I hid them because I was ashamed of tears. And again:

> Oh, lyuli-lyuli, my baby,
> day and night,
> go, son, to Ukraine,
> cursing us.

And it is sad again: am I not in Ukraine? Where should I go then? Why ('cursing us' (my mother used to say 'cursing us' and I, being little, divided as follows: curs ingus and did not understand; then I realized that it was 'cursing us')."[47].

From an early age, my mother's emotional "pedagogy" posed several questions to Vasil and he searched for the answers to them all his life.

On the one hand, there was the "Ukrainian Ukraine," from which your parents were expelled by envy; on the other, the cruel multinational and eclectic conglomerate of Donbas, where although you were laughed at as a white crow, you were given the opportunity to live your own way. And my mother's tears. It is about the land of Podillia. It seems that Yilina Yakivna could not reconcile herself to its loss until the last years of her life. And it was

---

[47] Ibid., 345, 347-348.

so painful that even in her old age she could not forgive her *komnezamka*[48] relative the bag of flour that, on the basis of her report to authorities, had been taken from malnourished children whose parents were in applying to join the collective farm.

In 1940, when Semen Stus had somehow settled in Stalino,[49] and Palazhka was already in the eighth grade, Yilyna went to her husband with their son Ivan.[50] Little Vasyl, who stayed with his sister Marusia in Rakhnivka with their grandmother, often "repeated after her '*Our Father, who art in heaven*,'"[51] either unconsciously trying to calm his often weeping grandmother, or hoping to understand this mysterious adult world, which was unable to enjoy the sun, happily "*splash in the pond*" or smile on a new day.

In 1941, on the eve of the Easter holidays, Semen Stus went to Rakhnivka to pick up the children.[52] Yilyna Yakivna refused to do

---

[48] In the Ukrainian villages of the 1920s and 1930s, this was the name given to members of the committees of the poor peasants, who carried out most of the authorities' dirty work and took the bread from fellow villagers.

[49] Stalino at that time was significantly different from the Donetsk of today. Petro Hryhorenko described the city in the 1920s and 1930s as follows: "*Now, Donetsk is a big modern city. In my time, it was a collection of settlements whose natural center was a great metallurgical plant. The plant's shops were scattered over a large hollow, with settlements located above on the perimeter. In those days, there was a distinct, more or less populated area north of the plant referred to as a town. There were 16 tracks (streets). In the center of the town was a square ("maidan") 250-300 meters wide a huge marker (later a pestle). Around the square there was a church, located in its southern part, a cinema, a state bank and other buildings. The so-called tracks (streets) crossed and were numbered along First track (later Artema St.), with tracks 2, 3, 4, 5, 6 located on the one (eastern) side of the First track and 7, 8, 9 ... up to the 16th on the other (western) side.*". See: Hryhorenko Petro. Spohady [Memoirs], 82.

[50] Both Yilyna Stus and Vasyl Stus when referring to their son and brother called him Yivan.

[51] Vasyl Stus. Tvory... V.3: Book 1, 345.

[52] In the letter to his son dated April 25, 1979, Stus wrote about the year 1940, when his father took him and his sister Marusia to Donbas. A comparison of the memoirs of Maria Cherednichenko (Stus), Yilyna Stus and Vasyl Stus suggest that he was wrong, and Marusya and Vasyl's move to Stalino dated to the eve of the 1941 war. The only thing that casts doubt on this conclusion is that Yilyna Yakivna gives the same approximate age of the younger children by: "*Marusia was three years old and he was two*" (Yilyna Yakivna Stus / Netsenzurnyi Stus, 144). On Easter 1941, Vasyl was three years old and Marusia was four. However, the emotional memories of the same Maria and Yilyna Yakivna indicate that in the year of Palazhka's death (she died in the year that the younger

so: *"I do not want to go there anymore. We lived quite long there, it is enough."*[53]

However, it was not only the grudge against the villagers and especially her relatives that explained Yilyna's sharp refusal to go to Rakhnivka. On the eve of Easter, on Holy Thursday, her eldest daughter, Palazhka, fell ill with meningitis. In those days, few people managed to survive this disease. Life in the dirty and confined space of the barracks greatly contributed to the spread of infectious diseases. It should come as no surprise that, in the late 1930s, the Soviet Union was getting ready for a lightning offensive war. It had sufficient human resources, including slave labor in the prisons, peasants who could be used as serfs, and cheap labor in its industry. Therefore there was no need for the state to create even minimally sanitary conditions. The country's top management reasoned as follows: not all of them will die. And who were they supposed take care of? The former kurkuls and other runaways from the villages and cities who escaped their "fair" punishment in the camps only because Donbas needed workers? The people themselves did not perceive this terrible situation as a tragedy. In the first place, their psychological investment in the gigantic tasks of the state was of great importance, and Stalin's propaganda "infected" a large percentage of the workers. Secondly, the former peasants well understood that new life required sacrifices, and therefore were psychologically prepared for it. Sometimes you even get the impression that having paid this terrible price, a man seemed to feel some ease, forgetting the terrible events of 1933, the persecutions, insults and the loss of the traditional way of life. Having paid, a person seemed to gain the right to start life from scratch, renouncing the old culture and religion. The lure of a passport, which seemed to guarantee

---

children moved to Stalino) war broke out and her grave was crushed by military vehicles, strongly indicate that Maria and Vasyl moved to Donbas during the Easter holidays of 1941. This is also supported by the memoirs of Maria Cherednychenko: *"When we came here, my parents lived in ... a house in the settlement of Factory 107 ... We lived there for several months. Then the war began."* (Netsenzurnyi Stus, 165).

[53] Yilyna Yakivna Stus / Netsenzurnyi Stus, 144.

freedom of movement, and the opportunity to "teach" their children, played a very important role in this renunciation.

Such was life. And since no one in this multimillion depersonalized mass had the slightest chance to change it in any way, to survive they had to mix with the great crowd, one with power to attract a man into becoming a part of it. Thus drawn in, the crowd allowed to shed or at least ease the constant pressure of fear that prevailed in the country. And although the Stus family tried to preserve peasant customs in its own, such a social atmosphere could not but influence the children.

Later, contemplating his life in these two circles of family and society, Vasyl Stus saw quite clearly his place (and that of many like-minded men who became intellectuals in the first and second generation) in a world torn by another's will:

> *You are in the middle. Between two of my worlds*
> *my boat is sailing. As far as the eye can see -*
> *on the right hand – a steep ravine and a moat,*
> *on the left hand – it is dark and deep.*
> *Suffering has so wisely lifted us up*
> *above the sailing and over time.*
> *Put the broken oar into the water,*
> *and become, already memoryless, by yourself.*[54]

On the eve of the Easter holidays of 1941, Semen crossed half of Ukraine to pick up his children, children who had already forgotten what their father looked like. Yilyna, despite her daughter's fatal illness, *"went to work at night. I came back and went to the poor girl who was in the hospital. So I worked during the day and stayed with the child at night. I left, and the next day was Easter. I went to work, and I cambe back home and he is already at home with the children. He had arrived and brought them. And he said: 'I had a lot of trouble with them'. They did not recognize him. 'I just brought them here* [to the barracks where the Stus' lived in 1941 – Dmytro Stus] *and they are already trying to run away.'*

---

[54] Vasyl Stus. Tvory... V.3: Book 1, 171, 391.

I told him this and that, that a child, a daughter, was in the hospital unconscious. He left, sent her to the other hospital and she commended her soul to God there already on the second day of Easter ..."[55]

Vasyl Stus' memory, consciously or unconsciously, erases the facts not covered in the letter to his son. He could not, felt that he did not have the right to write that he had not recognized his father, because that would cast a shadow over his family ties! However, the poet has no real memories of this meeting with his father, a stranger to two-year-old Vasylko: *"I remember my Dad taking me together with Marusia to Donbas in 1941.*[56] *I still remember the smell in the car."*[57] That was all that he remembered — the smell.

Uncomfortable with such a lapse of childhood memory, however justified, Vasyl Stus adds: *"I remember my father returning from work in Rakhnivka – it was in 1939*[58] *and I was running from the mountain to the valley (a very steep mountain!) to meet him - to fall into his hands, and he lifted me above him."*[59]

This Easter was truly black for the Stus family. They had already lost their place in the peasant world and had just started the ordeal that would give them the right to exist in the industrial world. Vasyl's parents did not want to talk about this and the poet himself prefers to present the gap between the worlds by the memory of himself as a 2-year-old boy: *"I remember the women of the Donetsk barracks laughing that I was boasting about my long shirt walking in it: 'My grandmother sewed this shirt for me, with a pocket,' I said, and they were happy."*[60]

---

[55] Yilyna Yakivna Stus / Netsenzurnyi Stus, 144.
[56] 1940 in the text of the letter.
[57] Vasyl Stus. Works. V.3: book 1, 345.
[58] Most likely, this is either a layering of memory or a conscious mystification. This was almost a year after Semen Stus had been recruited to work in Donbas, and, therefore, could not have been in Rakhnivka. A meeting between father and son in 1939 or 1940 would only take place when Semen came to the village to pick up his wife. So, in order to please his mother, who was able to feed the children only thanks to her husband's parcels from Donbas, and who whispered in her son's ear: "Daddy has come, daddy has come!", a boy, between the ages of eighteen months and two and a half years, would really fall into the arms of a forgotten father.
[59] Vasyl Stus. Works... V.3: book 1, 346.
[60] Ibid., 345.

After moving to Stalino, Stus lived in the hostel of Factory 107, in a separate closet, where somehow the whole family fit. There was a common lavatory and kitchen for the tenants of the floor.

However, the peasant habit of having their own house and not living in a ward forced little Vasyl's parents to build their own house, despite the grief of losing their eldest daughter. Whatever the troubles in Donbas, they didn't even consider the possibility of returning to Vinnychyna, because, as Yilyna Stus said, "*we were driven to Stalino by such grief...*"[61]

In the painful disintegration of the peasant class in Ukraine, the Stus family was quite typical and differed little from others. One distinction, actually an all-important one, is that Semen did not drink and had extraordinary respect for education, which he himself had failed to obtain. That is why the cult of knowledge and curiosity reigned in the family. The children were much more willing to share the knowledge they acquired with their father rather than with their mother.

It is quite possible that this peasant stubbornness of his parents, who, despite the pressure of the environment, did not renounce their faith (although they rarely went to church), or language (spoken, not literary), or traditional Ukrainian values, allowed little Vasyl to feel his difference for the first time, some sort of separateness from others that accelerated his self-awareness as an individual. To some extent, the fact that Vasyl's parents were already elderly people also contributed, as they did had no great ambitions, which would inevitably force them to radically change their way of life. They simply wanted to survive and educate their children, and all they had to do was work. It fed them and fed them well. The painful loss of their eldest daughter even forced them to bear additional expense. To save their younger children (because who can guarantee that some other infection will not take one of them?) they rented a room in a house on Udarna Street. However, Stus did not have the time to build his own hut in the few months before war broke out.

---

[61] Yilyna Yakivna Stus / Netsenzurnyi Stus, 143.

Vasyl's early childhood coincided with the war years, which the poet mentions briefly and quite neutrally:
"*I remember the beginning of the war when our troops were retreating. A Tatar neighbor slaughtered a colt, beautiful and young. He cut its throat before my eyes. I cried as I felt sorry for him. And when he, the neighbor, wanted to feed me that meat (the whole corridor smelled of it!), I shed crocodile tears so that he would not force me to commit a sin – to eat a fine colt.*

I remember the rabbits we kept during the war. For some reason, they were blind and perished. The corpses laid in the swamp – oh, how sad I was! I did not want to live. Such a bitter time and I felt sorry for rabbits!"[62]

Two difficult years of occupation began when it was necessary to simply survive. No one thought to plan anything, because no one knew how the mayhem would end. Semen Stus was too old to serve, and being able to keep the breadwinner in the family was a great relief. It was not easy. But they did not have it worse than others. Judging by the recollections, the greatest misfortune during the war was the loss of sister Palazhka's grave. "*We were afraid of going to the cemetery,*" recalled Vasyl Stus' mother, "*as two boys returning from the cemetery had been killed by the Germans. You had no right to walk. And we did not go. So we still do not know where she is buried. They crushed it utterly.*"[63] When the war ended, with the destruction in the cemetery was such that no trace of the graves could be found.

During 1942-43, to survive, Vasyl's parents had to trade everything they had for food. "*Dad and Vanechka, the eldest son, used to go to trade.*"[64] At the end of the occupation, the family fell on evil times.

The liberation did not promise relief. In the Soviet Union, "persons who remained in the occupied territories" were treated

---

[62] Vasyl Stus. Works. Vol. 6: book. 1, 345. His sister Maria claims instead that "*during the war we lived in an apartment and kept nothing ... My father had rabbits when he was living in Rakhnivka ...*" (Maria Cherednychenko / Netsenzurnyi Stus, 166). It is possible Vasyl's childish fantasy is the figurative rendition of the loss of something significant for his parents, engraved in his memory, a loss which the little boy simply could not comprehend.
[63] Yilyna Yakivna Stus / Netsenzurnyi Stus, 167.
[64] Maria Cherednychenko / Netsenzurnyi Stus, 167.

rather harshly. And the need to prove loyalty to the authorities arose again.

In 1944, trouble came to Stus again: his brother Ivan died.

"*I remember in 1944,*" Vasyl Stus wrote, "*us planting cord in the field, digging wormwood out of the virgin land. I threw grains into the holes, and mother and Ivan, my brother, were digging…*

I remember Ivan's injury. I remember him lying with his left leg blasted off and his left cheek torn away by shrapnel. He looked like he was sleeping when my mother and I found him. 'The stars were falling from the sky on me,' he said when my mother, without shedding a tear (because her heart ached), woke him up and put his leg back, as if it could still grow together. He was unconscious till the end.

I returned home alone and saw Marusia there. Oh, how I did not want to tell her about the trouble! And when I climbed onto a window sill with her (maybe looking for our parents), I mustered up the courage to tell her what had happened to Ivan. We were both crying and a few hours later Ivan died. He was 15 years old … I remember being led to the body in the cemetery to kiss him for the last time. And I saw only a mole on his right cheek and did not want to either kiss or say goodbye to Ivan and his mole."[65]

In 1944 the Stus family was forced to return to the barracks of the chemical plant because they could not afford to rent the room in the settlement. In the fall, Vasyl's sister Maria went to school. Yet, whereas Semen and Yilyna were able to buy books and good

---

[65] Vasil Stus. Works. Vol. 6: book. 1, 346. Maria Cherednychenko recalls this episode as follows: "*Then, after the war, they took over the vegetable gardens. It was virgin land. They were digging. They took ten or fifteen hundred square meters. And they planted veggies on this virgin land. They planted corn, then potatoes, whatever they had. Then my mother went there with Vanechka … took the plot, and then other people went there. Mom says: 'Vanechka, you go back and tell them that we took the plot there.' Because they seemed to have … just … marked … And he came back. After the war there were … bomb craters … Such pits. And in that pit the boys were defusing a bomb … And when he came up … there was an explosion. Of one boy who of the boys, only pieces were found. And the second, they said, had his head blown off but his body was still running. And his [Ivan's] cheek was torn out, he got shrapnel in his heart and his leg was torn off. And the mother, as she saw … couldn't even imagine that it was her son. And he said, 'Mommy, don't cry. This is my destiny.' He said that, and she burst out crying. She had a heart attack that time. Then they called an ambulance. It took time as they were in the fields … And he was taken away. He lived for a few hours longer. Three, four or five*" (Maria Cherednychenko / Netsenzurnyi Stus, 169).

clothes for the older children, so that "everything is as it should be," Maria had to go in the clothes that she had. And the only thing that Semen told his daughter during her studies were the words: "*If you do not study, you will go to the railroad to work.*"[66]

Life went on. Little Vasyl, not wanting to stay at home alone — dad and mom were at work and kindergarten so soon after the war was too much of a luxury — followed his sister to school. He could read: during the war, there was nothing to do, no entertainment, so he was forced to learn the basics of how to read from his older brother Ivan, and his father and mother, to somehow entertain himself with the books he could find.

The teacher was easygoing about the situation, especially since the young Vasylko quickly became her best pupil. The teachers' good memories of his brother Ivan, who was one of the best pupils, also helped. It was only when the frosts came that the teacher began to worry and decided to talk to Yilina Yakivna: *"We did not even know ... that he was going to school ... I said: 'Vasechka, son, stay at home.' And we got land there, as we are Ukrainians, planted corn and other vegetable. And I would go for that corn and say: 'You, son, stay near the house, do not go anywhere.' And the next day Marusia came from the school and said: 'Mom, the teacher sent this note for you'... to see her. She, that teacher, lived nearby.*

I went early because I was going to the vegetable garden myself and I left the boy at home. He was not yet six years old. He would be six at Christmas ... I told her that I am Vasyl Stus' mother. 'Why is he going to school barefoot?' And I said, 'I don't know. He does not go to school, he is not six years old yet.' And he was already reading the newspaper. I said: 'I don't know why he goes to school. I am always on the go, in the vegetable garden, here and there, and I leave him to be the master at home. Why he went to school, I do not know. Why do you take him?'

And she said, 'And you know what I'm going to tell you: let him go to school. Let him go.'"[67]

---

[66] Maria Cherednychenko / Netsenzurnyi Stus, 164.
[67] Yilyna Yakivna Stus / Netsenzurnyi Stus, 144.

In spite of their poverty, his family made him a suit and Vasyl's attendance to Russian-language school №150 was made official.

Between 1944 and 1946, Semen and Yilyna managed to build a small one-room hut[68] on the land allotted to them. The four settled there. Semen had to take a loan of 10,000 old roubles for the construction. Material for the house foundation was gathered from the many ruins in Donetsk after an exhausting shift, as both the war and reconstruction were still going on. Semen Demianovich laid the foundation of the future family house, which would not be completed until the 1950s. All the money he earned at work was swallowed by loans and the construction. In the end, his health failed. In 1946, Semen had to go to the Monastyryshche for treatment. When Yilyna Stus saw her husband off, she wrote a letter to her mother: "*I sent Semen to the resort, but I don't know whether he will return or not. Maybe I sent him away forever.*"[69] But destiny or a sense of duty helped him to survive and return.

The winter of 1946-1947 was the most difficult in Vasyl's childhood: his father was gone, his mother earned little, and he had to accept alone[70] the savage injustice of the world:

"*When I was 9 years old, we were building a house.*[71] *My father was dying, bloated from hunger. And we were trundling a wheelbarrow, tempering clay, making adobe, putting up walls. I was hungry like a dog. I remember seed cakes made by my mother, and I got a headache from them.*[72] *That was when I was in the 3rd or 4th grade. Then, even with all that trouble, I studed well. I graduated from the 4th grade with honors and*

---

[68] There first house built by the Stus-Cherednychenko family still stands in Donbas. It is located in the Donetsk yard on 19 Chuvashskaya St. It is a small one-room kitchen.
[69] Maria Cherednychenko / Netsenzurnyi Stus, 166-167.
[70] Maria was taken to Rakhnivka by her aunt in March 1946, where she stayed for a year. For more details, see Maria Cherednichenko / Netsenzurnyi Stus, 166.
[71] Probably the house containing several rooms, which Vasyl's father started to build at the beginning of 1947, is meant.
[72] To treat the children's headaches, which frightened the parents after the death of their daughter Palazhka, they had to drink fish oil. Vasyl stubbornly refused, so his father Seen paid him 10 kopecks for each spoonful he took. From money raised in this way, after the war, Vasilko bought books that his parents did not own. For more details, see Yilyna Yakivna Stus / Netsenzurnyi Stus, 145.

till the end of school, I got certificates of progress and good conduct with the oval portraits of Lenin and Stalin on them.

I spent my whole childhood with a wheelbarrow. Once they took potatoes from the field, then I went to the vegetable garden with a sack to collect grass to feed a cow or a goat, then I carried coal, collecting it from a gob pile. It was hard work, the tendons almost breaking. But you have to trundle the wheelbarrow. I remember my mother crying because she had only one torn shirt, patched up many times, and Marusia and I wore rags.[73]

I remember grazing someone else's cow in 1946-1947 and I was fed for that. I knew that my mother was hungry and I could not eat alone. I asked to bring a bowl home to eat with my mother. Once I carried a bowl home, and my mother started scolding me severely, crying, telling me not to do it again. Because she really wanted to eat and it was hard for her to look at the food. And I could not eat at all after that.

I remember my mother sewing my first suit herself, sometime in the 4th grade. And I was very proud of it – made of black canvas."[74]

Abject poverty made it possible to identify oneself more clearly. When you do not want to lose your dignity, parental grief can neither be forgiven nor forgotten.

Despite all the problems, the trouble was confined to the house. The school was like another world that attracted and promised great prospects for the future. Ideologically-imbued Soviet education was delivered in such a way that, along with knowledge, the child gradually acquired the ability to see the world from the "right," Soviet, point of view. Therefore, it is not surprising that, in the late 1940s, Vasilko became a sincere pioneer who *"believed in books very much. He thought that everything discussed in books was true. He had great respect for Lenin and Stalin then. He raised his hand and declared: "For Lenin, for Stalin!" People who were present there* [at the

---

[73] This condition of the children's clothes was not at all typical of the pre-war period, when Semen and Yilyna were able to provide proper clothes for their children.
[74] Vasil Stus. Works. Vol. 6: book. 1, 346-347.

young pioneers meeting] *said:* "*Eto, naverno, sin kakogo-to raykomovtsa ili obkomovtsa*" [This is probably the son of some district or regional Party committee member].⁷⁵

Later, Stus would be too ashamed even to mention such happy moments of his childhood, but it was the belief in what he read that saved his from soul from erosion, kept him from hardening, and reading and discovering something new helped him to forget the constant feeling of hunger. Books became his only consolation, because only in them did good always defeat evil: "*I remember that the first books I saw were histories of the ancient world (with color maps, color drawings of the life of the Egyptians, Greeks, Romans). And the first book I read was* Maple Leaves *(this seems to be its title) by Vasyl Stefanyk. I took it from the library, the first book in my life!*⁷⁶

I remember reading Maxim Gorky's Mother *in the 4th grade and I was happy that Pavel Vlasov was so nice. I remember reading Nikolai Ostrovsky's* How the Steel Was Tempered *and* Born of the Storm *at the same time. The latter smelled very much of naphthalene. It was given to me by a girl, with whom I was assigned to the same desk (for a few days she was weeping).*

And around that time I decided that I myself would be like Pavel Korchagin, like Pavel Vlasov, working so that people would live better. And I also wanted to study hard, because living is hard. It was hard for mom. It was hard for Dad. So it must be hard for me, too, until it becomes easier for my father and mother, until it becomes easier to live for all the people in the world."⁷⁷

But, even captive to ideological delusions, little Vasyl did not lose his ability to see the world. And what he saw raised many questions that every child, out of self-preservation, seeks to avoid. But sooner or later they insist on being heard, and you, a person brought up on good books, forming a strong character, surmount your fear both spontaneously and as a result of extreme effort. And how could it be otherwise, when you constantly see the clash of "friends" and "foes": some are malnourished, others always have

---

[75] Maria Cherednychenko / Netsenzurnyi Stus, 171.
[76] Of course, it was not the first, but in the didactic purpose of the letter to his son, no exaggeration was too great.
[77] Vasil Stus. Works. Vol. 6: book. 1, 347.

enough to eat, although they have never grown anything in their lives; some are in rags, others choose fine clothes to wear; some have soot-blackened faces and calloused, worn hands and others sport a pampered look that is always pleasantly striking ...

This strange division intensified considerably in the summer, when Vasyl (sometimes with his mother, who, although she did not like Rakhnivka, still went there from time to time) went to his native village: *"I remember going to the village to see my grandmother in 1951. I was gathering ears of corn from the stubble. I was being chased by an overseer. I was running, but he had horses (a two-horse cart). He caught me, and started to pull out the contents of the bag, and I bit his ugly red hands. I was so angry (a 13-year-old boy!) that I snatched the bag. And the next day the stubble was ploughed."*[78]

This was the first (perhaps rather exaggerated and heroized for the sake of his son) protest of the 13-year-old boy.

Yet the time of this incident was quite significant. When the seventh-grader Vasyl Stus spent the summer of 1951 in Rakhnivka, he naturally knew nothing about an editorial article entitled "Against Ideological Distortions in Literature,"[79] which was published on July 2 in *Pravda*, in which Moscow Party ideologues "assaulted" Volodymyr Sosyura's poem "Love Ukraine." This article actually initiated the ideological war against manifestations of national features in Ukrainian literature, a war that extended into the pages of the central and national republican press.

Of course, that those ears of corn taken from the overseer coincided with another pogrom of national culture was purely accidental, but such "coincidences" in the fate of Vasyl Stus can be found frequently, and if the first semi-conscious protest, which coincided with the pogrom of Ukrainian literature, could be considered a coincidence, later coincidences provoke questions about their regularity. And although we can hardly make categorical statements about Stus' feeling regarding special crises in national life, I could not find any other satisfactory explanation for the fact

---

[78] The same.
[79] See: V. F.Verstiuk, O. M. Dziuba, V. F. Repryntsev. Ukraina vid naidavnishykh chasiv do sohodennia. Khronolohichnyi dovidnyk [Ukraine from ancient times to the present. Chronological guide], 510.

that Stus always defended the national dignity when no one else did and the atmosphere of fear intensified. Because: "if not me, then who?"

The habit of only momentarily resting from the overcoming of difficulties, acquired in childhood, toughened the character and habituated him to a life where you have to get everything yourself. The situation could be called hopeless, but, after all, Stus had prospects and they were substantial. And as a boy, Vasyl divined or felt that these prospects were inextricably connected to the practice of *"greater or lesser national betrayal."* The latter was associated with his parents, whose tradition he was organically unable to renounce. And since he could not see any way out of the situation, he nurtured the dream of geological exploration since childhood.

Much has already been said about the fact that the realities of life forced Vasyl Stus to perceive the clash between "friends" and "foes" quite early. That is why he was more and more attracted by culture, which increasingly seemed to him a zone of authenticity and unity for the world. It was in the realm of culture (but only there) that he was truly a man of the Universe. Stus wanted to work — and was willing to work hard — to gain a place in and a sense of belonging to world culture.

Obviously, it is in this search for belonging to the world, which has long left behind those who stood on the side of the road beaten by civilization, that we must search for the birth of the extreme alienation and cold felt in Stus' late poems.

Yet this is a rational explanation for the path taken. The young Stus trusted more in emotions and feelings, which seemed to direct his mind, determining the trajectory of the search for him.

At a quite early age, it became apparent that the poet was responsible for the formation of character: *"When I read Martin Eden by Jack London (around the 5th or 6th grade) the world was turned upside down. A man who suffered greatly was able to surpass those who overflowed with wealth! And this all was done by hard work (work, son, with special emphasis!) and through salty bloody sweat.*

I remember making my first radio set myself! There was not enough wire and I was listening through headphones in the cold, in a cold barn, putting on everything I could. And that detector set made my soul happy.

For some reason, I remembered for a long time B. Hmyria singing this song:
Throw off the shackles, give me freedom —
I will teach you to love freedom.
There were many other songs, but they vanished without a trace like straw or dust. But this one I remembered. In grades 4-6, I knew almost all of Kobzar by heart."[80]

Vasyl Stus provided his son with an orientation to the patterns of life that were important to him, which taught him to live, and not merely to drift, as he used to repeat, with the current. Even in adulthood, the poet was drawn to heroic-romantic literature, where strong personalities with integrity can throw down a challenge to time. Everything else is reaching after literary effect, literature for the weak, for those who are "like everyone else,", for those "without a heaven," who are "neither fish nor flesh." In this, Stus' worldview closely echoes the views of Ivan Franko, who at the beginning of the last century criticized the members of "Moloda Muza" [Young Muse, an informal modernist group of writers and artists in Western Ukraine, founded in 1906] for devoting themselves to details that had not achieved integrity, rather than for their aestheticism.

"And I was already in the 8th or 9th grade. And I was dreaming of geological exploration because I was mad about traveling. I loved traveling, solitude, watching the sunset, loved telling an old tale in the forest, the sun playing on the water, sitting on a "goat" (a sledge with a coarse iron rod) ride along the river at full speed against the wind, against the snow, against the darkness and the unknown world.

I raved about music. In the 7th grade, my dad bought me a guitar as a reward for my 'certificates of progress and good conduct.' I first learned to play 'I would take a bandura' [a Ukrainian, plucked string, folk instrument], then a few old romances, marches. But it was all wrong. And then I used to take the guitar and play my own tunes on one string. I played everything I heard, what I longed for, what I aspired to. I played everything. I was had no sense of time. I could spend 2-3 hours playing like that

---

[80] Vasil Stus. Works. Vol. 6: book. 1. - P. 347.

and I took no notice of the time spent. It happened later as well, already at the institute.[81]

I remember the first time I went to the Philharmonic Hall. I remember listening to a series of lectures on Beethoven, all 9 symphonies and many concerts. And how wonderful his sonatas were! And what kind of man he was! All his life he was in trouble, in misery, in torment. And he was alone against the whole world and won! That means that he remained steadfast against abusers and forces ranged against him: either the world will accept me as I am, as birthed by my mother or it will kill and destroy me. But I will not give up! And from every one of my moments, from every feeling and thought of my own, I will draw my portrait, i.e. a portrait of the whole world. And let the world know that it may have suffocated, bent me, but I survived, preserved myself and brought to others everything I wanted ...

And Beethoven turned my soul upside down ... How I regretted that because of my parents' poverty I could not ask them to buy me a violin or a piano. There was no talk about a piano, when my mother almost every month racked her brains over who to borrow a few roubles from to tide us over until my father's got his pay, which was not enough!

I did my best to help my parents. On my holidays I "rested" on the railway, where I changed rail sleepers, rails, spiked railroad ties, loaded rin (broken stone ballast). I worked hard and was almost ready to drop. However, 400-500 karbs. in old money added to dad's 600-700 meant something. It was help anyway."[82]

There is no deviation from the clearly chosen scheme in the whole text of the letter, i.e., romanticism plus poverty, the misery of his parents. That occurred only in our private conversation. When I began to broach topics that had long annoyed both in the school curriculum and in the general tone of Ukrainian life, Dad could not stand it. I would ask: "Why are these Ukrainian writers so lame, poor, tearful, tragic?" Dad replied: "Well, of course my

---

[81] Vasyl Stus's fascination with the guitar was forcibly ruptured by his military service, when he lost the phalange of his left finger. Yet, even after losing the ability to play this instrument "for a public," he sometimes played something for himself. Thus, in 1978, in the village named after Matrosov, in the Magadan region, Vasyl Stus played on one guitar string, and then wrote a melody for the poem "Ostannia pisnia" [The Last Song] in his wife's notebook.

[82] Vasil Stus. Works. Vol. 6: book. 1, 348, 349.

childhood was good. It was hard, with work and sweat, but it was also fun."

However, this truth is for private life, and there is only an elaborate concept of the "elevated" life, which rather resembles hagiography on paper. In the mature Stus' interpretation, even first love seems to lose its independent value and is transformed into an element in a much more important plot—its influence on the further choice of destiny: "*And so: there was the 9th grade and I liked one girl very much. At that time she seemed to be a living angel ... And I wanted to be worthy of this angel, that is, to lead the same angelic life. And I began to read more. And then I came across Franko, his 'Moses' poem. This is a wonderful poem. Like the whole story of Moses, it is beautiful. For a long time, Moses' people lived in captivity in Egypt. And he, the son of a wealthy man; the father, it seems, bathed in milk at the court of the Pharaoh. And there were his blood brothers — Jewish slaves living before his eyes. Life pampered Moses but did not kill his conscience and honor. And when he was 40 he roused his people to freedom. And he realized the ugliness of his past when he was taught to command his brothers, and he studied, believing that everything was as he was taught.*

... did you not study in Egypt's
Schools, so that better
You might know how to forge for our freedom
And honour strong fetters? And Moses brought his people out of captivity — through the desert, through famine, torment, drought and hunger ...

And having read this poem, I forgot all about geological exploration and became a writer."[83]

Emphasizing in the letter the main events that shaped him in this way, Vasyl Stus seems to be leading his readers to understanding him as a mature person: I have to be perceived in this context and not in some other context. And although since then we have managed to learn about other details regarding his schooling, they add almost nothing to what has been said. The only thing to which you should pay attention is what was said in conversation with his son: "*back in school, I started to confess every day to myself. What good*

---

[83] Ibid., 349-350.

and bad things have I done today?" And as such self-judgment is very cruel not only for a teenager but also for an adult, it is not difficult to understand the actions for which blushed with shame in front of himself. Stus learned quite early on not to do those. This ability to constantly perceive himself from the outside ensured that he would not veer off, deviate from his chosen code of dignity and honor, which was much more important to Stus than anything else. And when later the criminal code and the grief of his parents and wife came into collision with Stus' private code, the latter proved more important, and the poet followed it even unto death so as not to betray himself, a boy who managed to choose the path of his destiny from a thousand roads.

Later, in the preface to the collection of poems "Zymovi dereva" [Winter Trees] Vasyl Stus, summed up his schooling: *"Schooling was harmful. One is foreign and the other is stupid. The sooner you forget school, the better. In the 4th grade, I rhymed something about a dog. In Russian. It was humorous. It was soon gone but was born again in high school when love came."*[84]

We can say that his "good childhood," as the poet himself described it, raised a Ukrainian who felt that he belonged to the whole world. Although he still remained a patriot to his country in 1954, Vasyl's innate anarchist, positive spirit and sense of justice helped him to overcome the age-old "depressiveness" and fear of the world that had sunk deep roots in the souls of Ukrainian peasants after the famine of 1933, the repressions of the 1920-1930s, and tribulations of the war. The real consequence of this was that for decades all peasant children were forced to shed the label of being second-rate. The vast majority were happy to get to an institute or to work in the city — to such an extent that they felt the need to constantly give thanks, becoming debtor-creatures for a long time. Stus was ashamed of it. When he encountered an attitude of superiority, his soul filled with anger, and if nothing could be changed, he raised his pointed chin even higher, as if his pride could restore the self-esteem of millions of young people like him, young people for

---

[84] Vasyl Stus. Dvoie sliv chytachevi [A couple words to the reader] // Works. Vol. 1: book. 1. - P. 42.

whom it was often convenient to live just so. This pride became his soul bird, the ungovernable impulse that carried the young man, who graduated from school with a silver medal, into the wide world.

My people! Oh, serfs of the commune!
Nails foisted on the future!
Oak coffins are being carried for you all –
If only you would live up to the grave!
Tortured, needy serfs!
My passportless nation![85]

A year after Stalin's death, when the psychosis over the loss of the longstanding Soviet leader (for some the "father of nations," for others a bloody tyrant) passed, and society started to hope that some change would take place, Vasyl Stus graduated from secondary school. It cannot be said that he received a brilliant education, but thanks to his own work and perseverance, his knowledge was quite thorough. He chose the Ukrainian humanities, and the young man had only to try to make this dream come true. Because what life obstacles can get in the way of a person toughened in the environment of cruel Donbas freedom? Vasyl Stus was sure that the new social situation would open many doors that had been closed for him only the day before.

Bibliography

Burtseinyi P., Rubin M. Vinnytska oblast. [Vinnytsia Region] – K., 1967.

Entsyklopediia ukrainoznavstva. [Encyclopedia of Ukrainian Studies]. V.6. Republished in Ukraine. – L., 1996.

Vinnychchyna. Fotoalbom. [Vinnytsia region. Foto album] – K.: VF "Chorli", 1998.

Allen Van Atta Donald, Honcharuk Oleksandr, Perrotta Luiz. Ukrainske selo na zlami stolit. Sotsiolohichnyi ta antropolohichnyi zriz / Za red. Yu.I.Saienka.[Ukrainian village at the turn of the centuries. Sociological and anthropologic shapshot] – K.: In-t sotsiolohii NANU, [Institute of Sociology of National Academy of Sciences of Ukraine], 2001.

---

[85] Vasil Stus. Works. Vol. 1: book. 2. - P. 175.

Zenkin Sergey. Zhitiya velikih eretikov. Figuryi inogo v literaturnoy biografii // Inostrannaya literatura. [Life of grate heretics. Figures of difference in literary biography] // Ynostrannaia lyteratura.[Foreign Literature] — 2000, N 4, P. 123-139.

Pavlychko Solomiia. Teoriia literatury. [Theory of Literature] / Compilers Vira Aheieva, Bohdan Kravchenko. — K.: Vydavnytstvo Solomii Pavlychko "Osnovy" ["Basics" Publishing House of Solomiia Pavlychko, 2002.

Leksykon zahalnoho ta porivnialnoho literaturoznavstva / Bukovynskyi tsentr humanitarnykh doslidzhen. Kerivnyk proektu A.Volkov [Lexicon of General and Comparative Literary Studies / Bukovyna Centre for Humanitarian Studies. Project Manager A. Volkov.] — Chernivtsi: Zoloti lytavry, [Golden Timpani], 2001.

Sherekh Yu. Druha cherha.[Second turn] — New York, 1978.

Kryminalna sprava № 47 po obvynuvachenniu Stusa Vasylia Semenovycha u vchynenni zlochynu, peredbachenoho st. 62. ch. 1 KK URSR. Nachato: 13 sichnia 1972 r.; Okoncheno: 26 lypnia 1972 r. v 12 tomakh. [Criminal Case N 47 on accusations against Stus Vasyl Semenovych in committing a crime stipulated by the article N 62, part 1 of Criminal Code of Ukrainian SSR. Started on January 13, 1972; Finished on July 26, 1972, in 12 volumes]. Volume №10. — P. 1, 9. Zberihaietsia v arkhivi SBU, od. zber. 67524. [Deposited in the Archive of the Security Service of Ukraine, archival unit 67524].

Znak neskinchennosti.[Infinity sign] — K.: Fakt [Fact], 2002.

Stus Vasyl. Tvory. V 6 tt., 9 kn. [Works in 6 volumes, 6 books]. — L.: vyd. spilka "Prosvita" [Publishing Union "Education"], 1994-1999.

Stus yak tekst [Stus as text] / Red. ta avtor peredmovy M.Pavlyshyn. — Melburn: Viddil slavistyky un-tu im. Monasha [Editor and the author of the foreword M. Pavlyshyn. - Melbourne: Department of Slavic Studies, Monasha University], 1992, XII+93 p.

Kheifets M. "V ukrainskii poezii teper bilshoho nema ..." [There is nothing more in Ukrainian poetry now ...] // Suchasnist [Modernity]. - 1981, N 7-8; or in the book: Ne vidliubyv svoiu tryvohu ranniu ... [I did not stop loving my early fear] — P. 242 — 317.

Riabchuk Mykola. "Nebizh Rilke" i "syn Tarasa" [Nephew of Rilke and Son of Taras] // Krytyka [Criticism]. - 1999, June, P.14-19.

Yevhen Sverstiuk. Na sviati nadii. [At the feast of hopes]. Vybrane [Selected] - K.: Nasha vira, [Our faith], 1999.

Ivashko Vasyl. Mif pro Vasylia Stusa, yak dzerkalo shistdesiatnykiv [The myth of Vasyl Stus as a mirror of the sixtiers] // Svitovyd.[Worldview]. - 1994, Ch. III (16), P.104-120.

Moskalets Kostiantyn. Strasti po Vitchyzni [Passions for Motherland] // Krytyka.[Criticism] – 1999, June, P.4-14; See also in the book: *Moskalets Kostiantyn*. Liudyna na kryzhyni [A man on ice floe]. – K.: Krytyka. [Criticism] – 1999.

Netsenzurnyi Stus. Knyha u 2-kh chastynakh. Chastyna 1. Uporiadkuvannia Bohdana Pidhirnoho. – Ternopil: Pidruchnyky i posibnyky, [Uncensored Stus. Book in 2 chapters. Chapter 1. Compiled by Bogdan Pilhirny. – Ternopil: Textbooks and manuals], 2002, 336 pp.

Hryhorenko Petro. Spohady [Memoirs] /Translated by Dmytro Kyslytsia. – Detroit: Ukrainski visti [Ukrainian news], 1984, 758 pp.

Rubynshtein Leonyd. Knyha rekordov Donbassa [Book of records of Donbass]. – Donetsk: EAI-press, 2002, 304 pp.

Kuromiia Hiroaki. Svoboda i teror u Donbasi: Ukrainsko-rosiiske prykordonnia, 1870 – 1990-i roky [Freedom and terror in Donbas: Ukrainian-Russian border regions, 1870-1990 / Translated from English H.Korian, V.Aheiev; Foreword by H.Nemyria. – K.: Vyd-vo Solomii Pavlychko "Osnovy"[Basics Publishing House by Solomiya Pavlychko, 2002, 510 pp.

Verstiuk V.F., Dziuba O.M., Repryntsev V.F. Ukraina vid naidavnishykh chasiv do sohodennia. Khronolohichnyi dovidnyk. [Ukraine from ancient times to the present. Chronological guide] – K.: Naukova dumka [Scientific thought], 1995, 688 pp.

Yatsiuk Oksana. Rodovid Vasylia Stusa [Vasyl Stus' Ancestry] // Vinnytska Pravda. [Truth of Vinnytsia].

The Poet's Youth

> Poor raincoat!
> What does it think
> hanging on a peg?
> Vasyl Stus

The silver medal that Vasyl Stus got the year after Stalin's death offered opened all roads. Therefore, the 16-year-old man packed his belongings almost without hesitation and went to Kyiv, the capital of the real Ukraine he longed for and dreamed of. He left Stalino almost without hesitation, because the awareness of his own otherness and his unwillingness to be "remolded" into an inhabitant of Donbas, forced him to find a new place.

And this was Kyiv.

After the dirty train and the coal dust of the dilapidated Stalino station, the pile of the Kyiv railway station did not frighten the young man who came to pass exams and conquer the capital. His first impressions, which never resulted in poems, were shaped by the ocean of Kyiv greenery, which saved you from the burning hot asphalt of its unwashed streets. But Vasyl could not linger and headed for the admission commission of the Journalism Department of Kyiv University…

However, romantic dreams of Kyiv and the University collapsed at the very first stage:

"We accept only applicants born in 1937 or earlier …"

However, despair did not last long:

"I will be back as a victor," he threatened someone and hurried toward the railway station. "I will be back," he said, turning his head away for the last time on the red spot of the university, where his most cherished dreams had been thwarted.

* * *

From 1954 to 1959, I studied at the Donetsk Pedagogical Institute.

From Vasyl Stus' autobiography

Contrary to his expectations, frustration at the Kyiv exams was received by Vasyl's parents calmly and not without a certain satisfaction: after all, their son would remain at home.

Vasyl submitted an application to the Ukrainian Department of Stalino Pedagogical Institute.

The silver medal he had won at school exempted him from taking exams, so he worked all summer on the railroad, earning money for a suit and a "Ukraine" radio-gramophone[1] which remained in his parents' house until the early 1990s.

At the end of his first year of studies, in the spring of 1955, the students were informed that the institute's four-year course had been converted into a five-year university course, and in addition to a philology degree, the students would receive historicalical instruction. Fate allowed Vasyl to get some kind of university education. The study became more difficult not only because of the new university status but also because the faculty changed: the philological faculty was made into a historical-philological one. And since the tutors did not have much time to revise the program, they simply *"patched together the full-time four-year courses study of history and philology"*[2] and the students had to master the full courses of both philology and history in five years. However, if the majority had a hard time dealing with such a load, Vasyl was happy about the expansion of the institute's course.

The youngest student in the group, Vasyl quickly gained authority among his peers and soon realized that the teachers did not meet his needs. But you must take whatever is available. Every morning, Vasyl *"was the first to appear in classroom no. 38, sitting at*

---

[1] Mariia Stus. Slavnyi brat mii // Ne vidliubyv svoiu tryvohu ranniu. Vasyl Stus — poet i liudyna [My glorious brother // I did not not stop loving my early fear. Vasyl Stus — poet and a man] — K.: Ukr. pysmennyk [Ukrainian writer], 1993, 12.

[2] Anatolii Lazorenko. Shtrykhy do portreta Vasylia Stusa // Ne vidliubyv svoiu tryvohu ranniu... [Strokes to the portrait of Vasyl Stus // I did not stop loving my early fear...], 16.

the first desk and opening a textbook. He always had something to read in his bag: Kant, Nietzsche, Montaigne, and Feuerbach...

He learned Latin himself. He knew German well [...] read Heine in the original, without a dictionary. And in German classes, he translated a text without a dictionary and did sight-reading. He answered only in Ukrainian. The tutor Semernina requested Kira Boryskovska to translate Vasyl's translation into Russian...

He never trumpeted his knowledge, never embarrassed us, although we did not know as much as he did. And he was always very polite with teachers, respected them, even when he knew more. This was the case with the Old Slavonic language, linguistics, comparative grammar: 'I read about it somewhere, maybe I didn't understand it myself..."[3] He told his mostly indifferent tutors to follow the latest developments in their field, knowing perfectly well that they would be told about the main thing, the changes in the ideological winds, at Party meetings.

Vasyl spent a lot of time in the library, persistently studying literature. And although some curiosities, such as the ignorance of the Ukrainian language of one of the teachers, had a depressing effect, he learned to accept this as inevitable. Gradually, Stus grew in authority, and this worked in his favor. Seeing Vasyl's persistence and good performance, some tutors began to give him books from their own collections, including Kost Teslenko,[4] whom Vasyl knew since early school days, and Tymofii Dukhovny, a tutor of foreign literature. Thanks to these people, in 1954-1956, Stus was able acquainted himself with the early works of Pavlo Tychyna and Maksym Rylsky, the works of the then banned Mykhailo Semenko and Mykola Zerov, Volodymyr Svidzinsky and Arkady Lyubchenko, Todos Osmachka, and Mykhailo Drai-Khmara. The encounter with the prose of Mykola Khvylovy, Valerian Pidmohylny, Borys Antonenko-Davidovych and Volodymyr Vynnychenko, as well as with the dramas of Mykola Kulish,[5] was

---

[3] Zynaida Kononuchenko. Zghaduiu dobrom // Ne vidliubyv svoiu tryvohu ranniu... [I remember the good // I did not stop loving my early fear...], 13.
[4] Father of the writer Oleksandr Teslenko. The latter moved to Kyiv in the late 1960s and often visited the family of Vasyl Stus and Valentyna Popeliukh.
[5] It was arguably in Stalino that Vasyl Stus first became acquainted with some works (*Kulish's Novels* and *Alina and Kostomarov*) by Viktor Petrov-Domontovych.

extremely important for a true understanding of Ukrainian literature, in which Vasyl was already getting ready to work. The future poet would almost certainly have been deprived of all of this in Kyiv, where constant attacks on "Ukrainian nationalism" instilled in tutors a fear of students. But in Donetsk, there the opportunity, and Stus took advantage of it to the greatest possible extent.

In 1954, when Vasyl Stus had just entered the Pedagogical Institute, as mentioned by his institute and later Kyiv friend Oleh Orach, "*the spirit of Ivan Dziuba still was in the air*" (Dziuba had graduated from this university a little earlier). Contemporary with Stus, such well-known figures of Ukrainian literature as Oleh Orach, Volodymyr Mishchenko, Anatoliy Lazarenko, and Vasyl Zakharchenko studied at the Stalino Pedagogical University; and, a little later, Vasyl Holoborodko studied there for a year as well, but failed to get a degree.

The Institute's literary studio, which was headed by Tymofii Dukhovny,[6] abounded with national and literary life. Given the limited conditions of the Ukrainian language in Donbas, the level of literary studio members was quite high. And although not all of its members managed to reach literary heights, the national spirit, constantly provoking of intellectual growth, interesting discussions and healthy competition, all of which the leader of the group nurtured in his students, greatly contributed to their growth. And the very existence of this closed Ukrainian-language literary environment helped Stus to realize his own otherness more quickly and to react less painfully to the "lack of understanding" of Ukrainian by individual tutors.

Perhaps the greatest authority among the students was Tymofii Dukhovny, who, not only gave an interesting course of lectures, but also published works in national editions.

It is symptomatic that none of Stus' friends at that time stooped to denunciations, which were banal and rather conventional in that Ukrainian-Soviet humanitarian environment, neither

---

[6] Oleh Orach, "Vybir," in *Ne vidliubyv svoiu tryvohu ranniu*, 44.

out of fear of the omnipotence of the authorities nor for career reasons. Anatoly Lazorenko, one of the poet's close comrades of that period, stated in court in 1972 that he considered Vasyl Stus to be much more educated and "advanced" than himself, and therefore could not assess his actions or statements because he did not understand them. Afterwards, he greatly praised the poet's human qualities, with very sad consequences for Lazorenko himself. In 1972, it was a true action, because Anatoly well understood why he was summoned to court in Kyiv and what the consequences of such a statement. In the Soviet Ukraine of 1972, such a speech guaranteed the freezing of all prospects. However, the Donbas habit of despising even such a dismal prospect for the sake of "friends" appeared to be more important to Lazorenko, and outweighed all practical considerations and the pressure of the investigators and the court ...

By remaining loyal to his friend, Lazorenko appeared to pay tribute to the atmosphere of camaraderie and trust that prevailed in Tymofii Dukhovny's literary studio in the second half of the 1950s. The studio created not only strong preconditions for the maximum realization of the potential of all its members, and also provided the first tests of human decency, devotion to the ideas of goodness and friendship, and this was a great achievement in the Soviet system of higher education.[7]

---

[7] Of course, it was a two-edged sword. In 1971, Heinrikh Dvorko, who had reason to distrust one of Stus's friends, warned Vasyl that his comrade Leonid Seleznenko was cooperating with the KGB. Stus listened but calmly repied: "You see, it's quite possible that it is in fact as you say. But you have no facts... And what if he is not an informant? We can mortally offend a person with our distrust ..." Around the middle of 1971, many people stopped trusting Seleznenko, but Vasyl Stus continued to be sincere friends with him, often visiting his apartment. During the 1972 investigation, the seriously ill Seleznenko was broken by the psychological pressure exerted on him by the investigators, and he gave Stus several different—positive and negative—characteristics. However, the nature of these testimonies, which are preserved in Vasyl Stus' case file (Criminal case of Stus Vasyl Semenovych on charges of committing a crime under Article 62, Part 1, of the Criminal Code of the Ukrainian SSR, in 12 vols. Started on January 13, 1972, finished on July 26, 1972. Stored in the Archive of the Security Service of Ukraine under no. 67298-FP), allows us to conclude with a high of probability that in 1971 Seleznenko did not cooperate with the

Stus set great store by his first intellectual community, often inviting friends home and *"visiting... the dormitory almost every day after lectures and seminars."*[8] His need for such a literary and national community was so great that he even envied his friends, who, unlike him, lived in a dormitory and spoke together a lot.

However, at the end of the first year of his studies, the young man, enthusiastic about life, realized that it was not wise to talk openly with everyone. However, the realization is one thing and the ability to do so at the age of 16-18 is another. It was especially difficult to refrain from scathing comments, which have a great currency among students. One of these situations stuck in the memory of a member of his group, Anatoly Lazorenko:

"We... were studying[9] *the ingenious work of the leader,*[10] *where the 'all-knowing theorist' utterly defeated the vulgar and sociological views of Academician N[ikolai] Y[akovlevich] Marr.*

'What a man! Perhaps, he is gifted in all the spheres.'

'Sure!' Vasyl retorted. 'The materials of the All-Union discussion of linguists were used well ...' Suddenly he caught himself and cast a slow and confused look around all those present as if considering who would be the first to run to 'rat' it to the special agents."[11]

Given this impractical "inability" to remain silent when necessary, Vasyl had to be especially careful in choosing friends. Ivan Pryntsevsky and Mykola Raetsky were the ones closest to him during his student years. The fates of these people are typical of their whole generation.

---

authorities. In 1972, a judge and an investigator forced him to testify against some of his other friends under extreme pressure.

8   Ivan Sereda, "Tsokaie hodynnyk," in *Ne vidliubyv svoiu tryvohu ranniu*, p. 14. The room in the dormitory where Vasyl Stus' closest friends lived was often called *"the thirty-fifth canton." "It was the centerof soccer life, chess life and... the center, oddly enough, of card-playing."* Stus used to go there to play soccer and chess. See Oleh Orach's memoir in *Netsenzurnyi Stus*, ed. Bohdan Pidrhirny, Pt. 1 (Ternopil: Pidruchnyky i posibnyky, 2002), 226.

9   The year was 1955.

10 This refers to the article "Marxism and Problems of Linguistics" by Joseph Stalin.

11 Anatolii Lazorenkom "Shtrykhy do portreta Vasylia Stusa," in *Ne vidliubyv svoiu tryvohu ranniu*, 16.

Mykola Rayetsky was expelled from the institute in his fourth year on the charge of exercising a national-patriotic influence on students. Before that, he was summoned to the Donetsk regional committee of the Communist Party of the Soviet Union (CPSU) to talk to the KGB representatives. Obviously, there were suggestions that he give testimony against friends. He refused and did not try to feign remorse after a careless statement, and therefore was forced to leave the institute. He was lucky that, after Stalin's death, the Gulag was in the process of emptying rather than filling. It was for this reason that he managed to escape the camp. A few years later, he even graduated from Lutsk Pedagogical Institute and worked all his life in the Vinnytsia region, secretly doing translations. The translations were said to be good, but after his death in the late 1980s, there seemed to be no one to take care of Rayetsky's archives.[12]

The fate of the other of Vasyl's great friends of that time, Ivan Pryntsevsky, who was considered by tutors to be perhaps the most talented student of the Stalino Pedagogical Institute, was also tragic. Ivan was the son of a man repressed in the 1930s and therefore had to work hard to get excellent grades. As Oleh Orach recalls, Pryntsevsky and Stus *"wrote such conference papers that students from other groups attended. When Stus delivered a conference paper on Moses by [Ivan] Franko, people from the department of physics and mathematics came, because they knew that to listen to it would make them smarter."*[13]

Unlike their expelled friend, Stus and Pryntsevsky managed to graduate from the institute, but then...

"Eventually Ivan Pryntsevsky became a Candidate of Science [equivalent to a Ph.D.] *in Donetsk ... and a lecturer at the University, which was formed based on the Donetsk Pedagogical Institute. He was so well-mannered and delicate and evoked our [student] smiles... We called him a 'weak sister.' He had that kind of behavior. He was extremely gentle... It seemed to us that he was so weak and gentle that it did not suit a Cossack... So this weak... man, when he was bullied so much that could not stand it any longer, went home to his apartment, where he lived with*

---

12 See Oleh Orach's memoir in Netsenzurnyi Stus, Pt. 1, 230-231.
13 Ibid., 226. Later Vasyl Stus' essay "Roses and Grapes" won the first prize in the Republican competition of student works.

his wife and little daughter, got on his knees by the bed, fitted a slipknot to the side of the bed and strangulated himself... They say that he left a note to his daughter saying: 'Daughter, I am guilty only before you.'"[14]

But this was the fate of their whole generation, before whose eyes the dismantlement of the seemingly unshakable Stalin system took place.

For students at the Stalino Pedagogical Institute, awareness of the changes in 1956, when the struggle for power in Moscow launched a campaign to debunk the personality cult of Joseph Stalin. Most of those in the vanguard of the process were the same people who contributed the most to the creation of the cult.

The same thing happened at Stalino Pedagogical Institute. *"Very excited with something, the lecturers announced that some important meeting would take place. Mad after eight hours of listening to lectures, hungry and angry, cursing the meeting."*[15] Students slowly gathered in the assembly hall. However, *"after the announcement of the agenda by the secretary of the Party bureau, [the same students] forgot about everything else in the world ... The [CPSU] Central Committee resolution 'On overcoming the personality cult of Stalin' was read out."*[16]

What happened?

How did this happen?

After all, most of them well remembered the *"days of March 1953.*[17] *At mourning rallies, people sincerely, openly wept, asking each*

---

[14] Ibid., 226.
[15] Anatolii Lazorenko. Shtrykhy do portreta Vasylia Stusa // Ne vidliubyv svoiu tryvohu ranniu... [Strokes to the portrait of Vasyl Stus // I did not stop loving my early fear...], 16.
[16] Ibidem.
[17] Thousands of people died in mourning rallies the Stalin's funeral procession to. They were trampled by grief-stricken streams of people that filled the maidans and squares in an incomprehensible quest to pay their last respects to the leader who had sacrificed millions of lives to the moloch of the industrialization of the Soviet state. However, from the point of view of the state, those sacrifices were not in vain. Even though all of Stalin's successors used only the mechanisms of power he formed by him, the state structure built by his hands lasted for more than thirty years.

other: What will happen now? We have no leader of the peoples anymore!"[18]

And although many people experienced in those days the apocalyptic horror of the death of their idol and helmsman, in three years the system created by this idol cruelly gobbled up its creator, who rashly went to a better world. And this system's servants, the cogs in the machines, whose functional and mechanistic roles in the state machinery was the essence of their lives, these same functionaries in a few years' time were more or less psychologically ready to debunk the former deity, so as not to lose their place in the state mechanism created by Stalin's iron will.

At that meeting of 1956, Stus was frustrated above all by this lack of loyalty and devotion by servants who quickly denounced the former god.

To Stalin's Critics
Yes, Stalin was a tyrant. But I regret –
Why did he not destroy you, his choir?
Those who sang hallelujah
To a leader in a bloody crown.
Why didn't you go to the coffin then,
You who once licked his feet,
you would be saved a little from disgrace,
Because there is honesty in slaves' fidelity as well...
Every day I hear your late cry,
and I am crying myself, losing my head with rage:
"Come back, Stalin, come and visit,
and pull out their black tongues.[19]

Such a poem, written by a young man who seemed to be concerned about whether the tyrant was "good" or "evil," was an eloquent

---

[18] Anatolii Lazorenko. Shtrykhy do portreta Vasylia Stusa // Ne vidliubyv svoiu tryvohu ranniu... [Strokes to the portrait of Vasyl Stus // I did not stop loving my early fear...], 16.

[19] Draft autograph in a general notebook. Deposited in the Manuscripts Department of the Institute of Literature of the National Academy of Sciences of Ukraine, record group 170, storage unit 746, sheet 27. First published in Dmytro Stus, *Zhyttia i tvorchist' Vasylia Stusa* (Kyiv: Fotovideoservis, 1992), 36–37.

fact. The poet comprehends the subject on the ethical level, which was already one of the most important for Vasyl Stus.

The poet wrote a lot at that time, but later viewed most of the poems of that period as unimportant for his work, and did not even include them in his early collections *Circle* and *Winter Trees*.

The members of the literary studio also testified to this in their recollections. They mentioned that Vasyl Stus rarely read his poems to them, and at Tymofii Dukhovny's poetry studio he behaved more like a critic.

An exception was "Impulse" (1958), included in both *Circle* and *Winter Trees*, and a kind of declaration of the young poet's aspirations.

Impulse
Do not stop loving your early fear, –
that land where the horizon shimmers in cloudiness,
where the evening winds are weaving
the silky dove-color without hesitation.
Let's go. We have a space to go — vast roads,
still bluish in the cool mist.
We have a space to go — on the waves, over the ground –
Ways — like horizons — are far and transparent.
Make noise, spring and days! Shine, evenings!
Mornings, send us sly smiles!
Go ahead, helmsman! Let youth burn out –
We are devoted to life and will be rewarded with glory.[20]

In his last year at the institute, Vasyl Stus prepared his first real collection of poems and, probably through Tymofii Dukhovny, sent it to the *Literaturnaya gazeta*[21] editorial office. Its foreword was written by the almost legendary Andriy Malyshko: "*It seems that the work of a 21-year-old teacher from the Vinnytsia region, Vasyl Stus, contains good poetic seeds ... in particular, originality of approach to the phenomena of life and an ability to generalize lyrical reflections (rather than to speak*

---

[20] Vasyl Stus, *Tvory*, Vol. 1, Book 1, 152.
[21] Now called *Literaturna Ukraina* [*Literary Ukraine*].

about them in general terms). Thought and artistic image often live in his works organically, merged together. The verse is clear and expressive. Good language skills determine the general culture of this young talented writer."[22]

A selection of three poems was already published in the leading literary newspaper of Soviet Ukraine when Stus was serving his compulsory military service. But it was this publication that was the main result, a report, at least for himself, on the work of his apprenticeship period and a "breakthrough" for the young poet.

But the world is not only literature and not only poetry.

It is important to note that his active intellectual life during his university years allowed the young Vasyl to free himself from the psychology of the "cog," the man who is a function of the state mechanism, which was instilled in young people by the Soviet ideological machine. The poet paid special attention to primary sources — ancient and classical philosophy, the poetry of Johann Wolfgang von Goethe (in the original in his last years of study), which was spiritually close to him, Rudyard Kipling, Boris Pasternak, and works in various areas of knowledge, from the philosophy of nature to mathematics and physics.

Many of Vasyl Stus' lecture notes from his studies at the Stalin Pedagogical Institute have been preserved. It is precisely them which allow us to draw certain conclusions regarding the mastery and comprehension of material by the young writer.

The white notebook of 1957, which included mostly extensive and short extracts from inaccessible books, attracts attention as it reveals Stus' desire to structure and systematize the knowledge he acquired.

Thirty-one pages of the notebook are covered by Stus' notes on cognitive theory in its historical development, with extensive quotations from the works of Kant, Descartes, Avenarius, Leibniz, Aristotle, and others. In addition to these notes, where even a few of his chess games were included, there are all sorts of ideological assessments, knowledge of which was especially required for the

---

[22] Andriy Malyshko, "Dobroi puti: Poezii Vasylia Stusa," *Literaturna hazeta*, December 22, 1959.

exams on historical materialism and dialectical materialism — the surrogates for the study of philosophy and history in Soviet times.

This was followed by six pages of quotations from Nietzsche's *Thus Spoke Zarathustra*, borrowed from someone, with Stus' comments, placed in between the thoughts he found most interesting thoughts:

"I love those who do not know how to live, except by going under, for they are those who cross over [from monkey to superman].

"Virtue is the will to down-going, and an arrow of longing." "I love him who reserves no share of spirit for himself, but wants to be wholly the spirit of his virtue"

Nietzsche hates the angst of modernity, in which persons are more levelled (more differentiated, but scattered and torn by contradictions ...).

Nietzsche thinks that this leveling (when there will be no shepherd and flock!!??) will stop progress.

Forget "I have to," learn "I want"...

This world is imperfect.

My self has learned: not to hide my head in the heaven-sand anymore, but to hold it high, an earth head creating the meaning of the earth.

It is "the sick and dying who despised the body and the earth and invented the things of heaven."

"The body is a big sagacity, a plurality with one sense, a war and a peace, a flock and a shepherd."[23]

In his third year at the Pedagogical Institute, Vasyl Stus developed his own method of taking notes. What he reads becomes part of his own world reflections, while other people's insights and reasoning are an Ariadne's thread, which prevents you from getting lost in the labyrinth and saves time in overcoming difficulties, letting you cover distance with a fast car, rather than being an object of admiration for the collector of knowledge.

One more essential feature draws the attention of those accustomed to working carefully with primary sources. As though conducting an examination of someone else's wisdom, Vasyl records

---

[23] Vasyl Stus' notebook with a torn white cover and marked "z. 17", sheets 18–19. Kept in the archives of Vasyl Stus' family.

THE POET'S YOUTH   125

his emotional impression in the margin. Next to a quote from Nietzsche's *Thus Spoke Zarathustra* – *"I love those who do not know how to live for today, oh supermen!"* —Stus noted: *"You're lying!"*[24]

As we can see, a high degree of rigor,[25] which Ivan Dziuba called one of the characteristic features of Stus' personality, was already active in him at the age of 19–20. And this is not surprising, because youthful maximalism is commonly found in the vast majority of idealistic romantics. However, by being based on the treasures of world culture, the peculiarity of Stus' emphatic moral criteria is that they had a foundation strong enough that he did not renounce his youthful maximalist demands in later years. In this inner readiness to face life's trials lies one of the greatest mysteries of his personality, the unsolved mystery of the "forging"[26] of Stus' character, a character which until the last years of his life saved him from despair and hatred of a world that was too harsh for him.

Turning further the pages of Vasyl Stus' notes on philosophy, in the midst of his studies of Hegel (sheets 22–36), we suddenly come across occasional records of the poetry of Hölderlin, which allows us to speak of the Stus' early acquaintance with this author, who was half-banned in the USSR. Several pages are devoted to the philosophy of Bentham and Spencer.

In parallel with his philosophical studies, Vasyl pays a lot of attention to expanding his knowledge of the history of Ukraine and the history of Ukrainian literature.[27] Aware that many pages of the histories of both were ideologically edited, the young man gleans and rereads virtually everything he can from books published in the 1920s. In particular, in his notebook of that period many pages

---

[24] Ibid., sheet 21.
[25] Ivan Dziuba, "Svicha u kamyanii pit'mi," in Vasyl Stus, *Palimpsest: Vybrane* (Kyiv: Fakt, 2003), 7–32.
[26] See Kostiantyn Moskalets, "Strasti po Vitchyzni," in his *Liudyna na kryzhyni* (Kyiv: Krytyka, 1999), 209–254.
[27] This undertaking, according to Ivan Dziuba, was greatly supported by Andriy Vasyliovych Klochchya, whom Vasyl Stus mentioned with great reverence and respect until 1972. After 1972, when this former member of the Molodniak literary group, twisted by Stalinism, was forced by the KGB to provide necessary characteristics regarding the poet, in his letters Stus allowed himself to mention him disrespectfully. See Dziuba, "Svicha u kamyanii pit'mi," 10.

were devoted to summarizing *Valerian Polishchuk* by Ivan Kapustyansky and *Creativity of V. Sosiura* by Mykhailo Dolenho, and included little-known information about Ivan Hulak-Artemovsky and Mykola Kostomarov.[28]

This combination of two cultural components, equally important for Stus, the native and the world, allowed him better to see the flaws and a certain underdevelopment in the national literature, largely provoked by Ukrainian history, which, despite many heroic pages, was struck by the virus of defeat, the lack of a will to win and structure, as well as by nihilism.

With the eagerness of a desperate young man, Stus dreamed of providing a "damning" treatment of his father's culture and looked for ways to modernize it. At this time, he was actively testing himself as a critic and even a culturologist in his student environment and in the literary studio of Tymofii Dukhovny. His words were listened to: "*He analyzed meticulously, in detail, convincingly, demandingly, even as he remained, so to say, within the limits of delicate goodwill.*"[29] The critic's role not only allowed him to see the flaws in the works of others, but also to extrapolate these impressions to his own work. This helped him to bear the thought that the poems of this period represented only a stage of his apprenticeship and were the preparation for something more significant.

In his senior years, Vasyl became more and more attracted to the history and theory of culture, and to the history of the development of civilizations. Although this knowledge, like the history of non-Marxist philosophy, had to be gained from the waste paper of vulgar sociological Soviet criticism, the search itself widened his horizons and allowed him to see Ukrainian culture in the context of

---

28   From the general notebook with the torn white cover. In Vasyl Stus' lecture notes we also come across the names of Koryak, Vynnychenko, Leites, Khvlovy, and other Ukrainian authors of the 1920s and 1930s, whose very mention in the 1950s was sedition. In conversation with me, in late 1979 or early 1980, dad mentioned that at the institute he re-read a lot of works by writers of the Ukrainian Executed Renaissance.

29   Oleh Orach. Vybir / Ne vidliubyv svoiu tryvohu ranniu… [Choice // [I did not stop loving my early fear…], 44.

historical world progress rather than as a phantom or epiphenomenon.

And at some point during that stage, he made the final choice in favor of philology. The metaphor for this choice was Ivan Franko's poem *Moses*, and the very life of Moses, briefly mentioned by Stus in a letter to his son dated April 25, 1979. He presents the key to understanding his essence, saying,

> *Suffering has so wisely lifted us up*
> *over the sail and over time.*
> *Put the broken oar into the water,*
> *and become, already memoryless, by yourself,*[30]

as if revealing the recipe for his self-creation in *Palimpsests*, given to him by fate as its most permanent adept. However, like everything from Destiny, Vasyl was able to accept this gift only through hard work. At the institute, however, he believed only in the youthful dream of modernizing the culture of the fathers, which sooner or later must stop devouring or ejectin its own children. His believed in the possibility was strengthened as such attempts, quite successful ones (!), were made before– Stefanyk, the dramas of Lesya Ukrainka, Tychyna, Rylsky, Yanovsky, Dovzhenko, and Petrov-Domontovych faced with the neo-classicists. He knew all of this, he admired it, and the fact that the bar was high, made him seek to surmount it even more.

At the end of his studies, Vasyl Stus wrote a paper based on the material of Maksym Rylsky's collection *Roses and Grapes*. It was a success. The paper won the national competition of students' works and even gained some notoriety. However, this did not really convince Vasyl of its value and he sent it to Maksym Tadeyovych personally.

Rylsky probably paid attention to this work even though his works were studied not only in schools but also by serious scientific researchers. After all, not only distinction of the paper itself, but the

---

[30] Ibid., Volume 3: book 1, 171.

region from which it was sent, Russified Stalino, would have attracted attention. Although no written evidence of Maksym Tadeyovych's assessment of this paper was found, he considered it necessary to answer Stus, who showed the letter at the institute.[31]

Army service lay ahead. That Vasyl could not avoid. Thus, when postgraduate work assignment meant that someone had to go to a remote village in the Kirovograd region, after a few days of thought, Stus decided to release Zinaida Kononuchenko from a forced minimum of 3 years' "exile."

"Don't go to the commission yet, I will go first," he told her. "I will join the army soon, so I will take the Kirovohrad region."[32]

It is difficult to say what dictated this choice more—his desire to help a member of the group, or the "longing for the real Ukraine, not Donetsk,"[33] Before joining the army, Stus decided to breathe the fumes of Ukrainian power on the border between the Kirovograd and Vinnytsia regions. And it happened that the distance from his place of destination to his native Rakhnivka was not more than a hundred kilometers. However, whatever the poet's motives, departing for the sake of someone else, in a symbolic sense, became a kind of prelude to his whole future life, a life in which self-actualization was not a selfish goal but must influence the world. Only thus was he able to write before death, without great effort, the following: "I feel good that I did nothing evil in my 40 years. I helped people in need, and when sometimes I got into trouble, I neither sniveled nor complained. Because this is life, Destiny..."[34]

---

[31] Zinaida Kononuchenko. Zghaduiu dobrom // Ne vidliubyv svoiu tryvohu ranniu... [I remember kindly // I did not stop loving my early fear...], 13.
[32] Ibid., 14.
[33] Vasyl Stus. Dvoie sliv chytachevi [Two words to the reader]. // Works. V.1: book 1, 42.
[34] Vasyl Stus. Lyst do syna vid 25.04.1979 [A letter to son of 25.04.1979] // Tvory [Works]. V.6, book 1, 350.

Bibliography

Ne vidliubyv svoiu tryvohu ranniu... Vasyl Stus — poet i liudyna.[I did not stop loving my early fear. Vasyl Stus — poet and man] — K.: Ukrainskyi pysmennyk [Ukrainian writer], 1993, 400 p.

The criminal case, part 47 of Stus Vasyl Semenovych on charges of committing a crime foreseen by Article 62 Part 1 of the Criminal Code of the Ukrainian SSR in 12 volumes / Started: January 13, 1972 — Finished: July 26, 1972 — Deposited in the Archive of the Security Service of Ukraine №.67298 fp.

Netsenzurnyi Stus. [Uncensored Stus]. Knyha u 2-kh chastynakh. Uporiadkuvannia Bohdana Pidhirnoho. [Book in 2 parts. Compiled by Bohdan Pidrhirnyi.] — Ternopil: Pidruchnyky i posibnyky [Textbooks and manuals].

Chastyna 1. [Part 1]. — 2002, 336 pp.

Chastyna 2. [Part 2]. -2003, 320 pp.

Zahalnyi zoshyt iz avtohrafamy Vasylia Stusa. — Zberihaietsia u viddili rukopysnykh fondiv i tekstolohii Instytutu literatury im. T.H.Shevchenka NAN Ukrainy. [General notebook with Vasyl Stus' autographs. — Deposited in the department of manuscript collections and textology of the T.H.Shevchenko Institute for Literature of the National Academy of Sciences of Ukraine.] F.170, F.170, №746.

Stus Dmytro. Zhyttia i tvorchist Vasylia Stusa.[Life and work of Vasyl Stus] — K.: MP "Fotovideoservis", 1992, 88 pp.

Stus Vasyl. Tvory u chotyrokh tomakh (shesty knyhakh). Z dodatkovymy 5 i 6 (u dvokh knyhakh) tomamy. [Works in 4 volumes (6 books). With additional the 5th and the 6th (in two books) volumes]. — VS "Prosvita" ["Education" All-Ukrainian Union], 1994-1999.

Lesyn V.M., Pulynets O.S. Slovnyk literaturoznavchykh terminiv. [Vocabulary of literary terms]. — K.: Rad. shkola [Soviet school], 1965, 432 pp.

Zoshyt iz konspektamy istorychnykh i filosofskykh prats Vasylia Stusa z notatkamy i nacherkamy rannikh virshiv Vasylia Stusa y napolovynu vidirvanoiu obkladynkoiu biloho koloru z poznachkoiu "z. 17". [Notebook with notes of historical and philosophic works of Vasyl Stus with comments and writings of early poems of Vasyl Stus and half torn white cover with mark "z.17".] Could be dated by the second half of the 1950s — early 1960s — Stored in the archive Vasyl Stus' family.

Stus Vasyl. Palimpsest. Vybrane. [Selected] — K.: Fakt [Fact], 2003, 432 pp.

Moskalets Kostiantyn. Liudyna na kryzhyni [A man on ice floe].—K.: Krytyka. [Criticism]—1999, 256 pp.

Kapustianskyi Ivan. Valerian Polishchuk.—Kh., 1925.

Dolenho Mykhailo. Tvorchist V.Sosiury. [Works of V.Sosura].—Kh.: DAOU, 1931.

Zahalnyi zoshyt z avtohrafamy poetychnykh tekstiv Vasylia Stusa kintsia 1950-kh—pochatku 1960-kh rokiv.—[General notebook with Vasyl Stus' poetic texts autographs of late 1950—early 1960.]—Deposited in the Department of Manuscript Collections and Textology of the Taras Shevchenko Institute of Literature of the National Academy of Sciences of Ukraine, record group 170, No. 746, sheet 741.

Malyshko Andrii. Dobroi puti. Poezii Vasylia Stusa. [Save travels. Vasyl Stus's poetry] / Literaturna hazeta. [Literary newspaper]—December 22, 1959.

Meetings and Leave-Takings (1961–1963)

> "The world is fascinated by the poetry of mistakes, rather than a not guilty verdict of history …"
> (Alexander Verbychenko)

And he still missed Donbas. He missed it deeply, feeling a pain in his soul, the unbearable, hard-to-contain despair of wanting a lungful of that special smell over the city's gob piles, even though Donetsk's squares of the 1960s were completely covered in flowers. As if on wings, Vasyl flew over the railway tracks to get lost in the crooked streets of his native settlement, which was located just behind the station, shyly hiding piles of garbage and slag, as integral attributes of the landscape as gardens and orchards, in an endless line behind the houses. Vasyl walked over the paved sections of the sidewalks, sparing him from getting stuck in the late autumn mud of his native streets. On this occasion, the thick, almost greasy yellow-pink smoke belching from the neighboring plant smokestacks did not irritate him at all, but served as a kind of confirmation signal: Well, I am home.

Despite all his declarations of longing for the real—non-Donetsk—Ukraine, Vasyl's feelings of "home" were still connected to Donetsk, where his parents lived, where his house was, and where he had close friends left.

At home, at first glance, there had been no change. Sister Maria taught at the school, her salary allowed the family to somehow teeter on the edge of poverty. It could hardly be otherwise, when the mother, who almost never worked in industry, received such a miserly pension that it was only enough for bread. His father's industrial work record (work for the collective farm was not taken into account) was barely enough to get him a minimal pension. Maria was having an affair then, and Vasyl did not guess the reason for the dark circles under his mother's eyes. But the joy of "liberation" and long-awaited meetings with friends outweighed household routines that could be postponed.

Pretty soon, however, it became clear that there was no way to rest. He needed to set about work. Without even a month off and looking for the opportunity "to crash out" of the monotony of household routines, Vasyl agreed to move to neighboring Horlivka, where starting in December 1961 he began teaching Ukrainian language and literature in secondary school N 23.[1]

To teach the Ukrainian language in Horlivka, you needed an outstanding character. The children hardly ever heard or even knew the living language and their parents, settlers from other regions of Ukraine, were ashamed of it, switching to the "common language" as soon as they could, because there was no benefit to be gained from an unregarded language. That is why they did not want their children to learn Ukrainian, multiplying their requests/demands that their children be released from the study of "Ukrainian language and literature." In these conditions what should a teacher, who has not lost his self-respect and become indifferent to everything that not connected to his career and benefits, do? The young teacher Vasyl Stus, ignoring the program, read his own poems to pupils and recounted interesting episodes from Ukrainian history to keep the pupils interested in the subject. Checking notebooks was a very boring task but one that had to be done, willingly or not.

At first, the routine was not too annoying. Having fallen greedily on books, as the fresh wind of change blew, along with the seemingly irreversible democratic transformations in the country, Vasyl hid in the back room of his own world, luxuriating with the works of those who truly interested him.

Summarizing this period, the poet would say: *"The post-army period was already a time of poetry. It was the era of Pasternak and my indiscreetly great love for him."*[2]

Seeking solitude, Vasyl Stus immediately rented a room in Horlivka, that quickly brought a varied bundle of adventures and

---

[1] "On December 7, 1961, he was employed as a teacher of Ukrainian language and literature in secondary school N 23 of the town of Gorlovka [Russian form of Horlivka]. Grounds: Order of the City Department of Education N 2012 of 07.12.1961" — Work record book of Vasyl Stus. Kept in the poet's family.
[2] Vasyl Stus. Tvory. Volume 1: book 1, 42.

entertainments into his bachelor life. Frequent meetings with Mykola Kolisnyk, Volodymyr Mishchenko, Volodymyr Buts (Verbychenko) and Borys Doroshenko gave the impression of a fully creative and intellectual life. It was in Horlivka that true love first came to Vasyl.

They got acquainted on January 6, 1962.

In the chemistry department student dormitory, where Vasyl's friends — Ukrainian language teachers Polina Denisova and Borys Doroshenko who were soon to be married — lived, there was a party on the occasion of Vasyl's 24th birthday. There was a crowd in the room, and the volume of alcohol-fueled noise did not allow them to hear each other. As a result, none of those present, except Vasyl, responded to the cautious, uncertain knock on the door. Shura Frolova had come to consult with her sister's friend Polina.

Getting to his feet to greet the late guest sarcastically, Vasyl gave the door a yank and saw a small, plump young woman. He looked her over with an ironic glint in his eye and said through his gritted teeth.

"*So small?*"

"*Hello!*" *she replied, not at all confused.*

"*Hello,*" *he said indulgently, not meaning to drive off an unexpected guest.*

"*What is going on here?*" *She spoke in such a friendly way, and with such interest, that the boy's proud demeanor relaxed, and, abandoning his sarcasm, indicatede his non-proprietary colleagues.*

"*We are all school teachers, and we are celebrating a birthday.*"

"*Whose birthday is it?*" *The girl was not calming down.*

"*Well, now I will undress you, hang a fur coat on a peg - I will find a place somewhere...*"

"*My name is Vasyl. Welcome, company. And how shall I call you?*"

"*My name is not nice, I do not like it myself... Alexandra... in honor of Makedonsky.*"

Vasyl listened politely and responded to statements in Russian in pure Ukrainian. And Shura[3] *understood him because she had worked in Donbas.*

---

[3] Alexandra Frolova, a woman loved by Vasyl Stus in his youth and mentioned in conversations with Ivan Kalynychenko in 1979, was born in the village of

The party was over. They started to leave ... They went out together with Shura. There was a lot of snow, the snowstorm was blowing white ice. He put his hands on the girl's shoulders, hugged her, and tilted his lips to hers. Shura suddenly squatted. The boy was so fast. She pulled away from him.

"What is this?"

"Look at her."

... He looked at her in dismay ... The realization of defeat brought him sharply back to his senses and the alcohol evaporated instantly. He put his hand to his flaming cheek, which felt a hitherto unknown caress, and disappeared into the darkness...

On the third day, Polina, who had left the party earlier, called her at work.

"Shura! Where did you put Vasya?"

"What do you mean where?... Gone home!"

"But he did not go home," the teacher sighed and Shura felt acute anguish in her voice.

"I slapped him. Told him to keep his hands to himself. I may be rather small, but will stand two meters high somehow!"

"He was taken to the police that evening," Polina Petrovna said tightly and Shura understood that the teacher disapproved of her words.

"But how is that? He is the Deputy Head of the school!" Shura retorted.

"There you are!" Polina sighed"[4]

That was how the first meeting between Vasyl and Alexandra ended.

The next time Vasyl went to Shura was on March 8. She was already living in a dormitory.

Voronezh, where her mother, a Ukrainian from the Khmelnytsky region surnamed Bogdanovich, moved in the 1930s when "the displacement" from Podillia started. There she married a Russian, Fedor Frolov. There were six children in the family, two, including Shura, were identified in their passports as Ukrainians, the rest as Russians. For more details, see Volodymyr Verbychenko. Vistria plasta [The Layer's blades]. — K. DP "Redaktsiia zhurnalu "Okhorona pratsi" [State enterprise "Editorial office of "Labor Protection" magazine], 2004, 93-94.

[4] Volodymyr Verbychenko. Vistria plasta, 94-96.

"*Shurochka! A guy is asking for you, the big one, who keeps a low profile,*"⁵ *the duty woman knocked on her door. "These contrasting features amused her so much that Shura, without thinking about who it was, started down the stairs. There was Vasyl in the corridor, holding a bouquet of snowdrops in his hand/*"⁶

Since then, they went out together on an almost daily basis. In the evenings, holding hands, they used to promenade in the city streets and talked, and talked, and talked ...

On several occasions they parted "forever," being on opposite ends in their understanding and perceiving their different priorities in life. But a whole year of Vasyl's life, from the spring of 1962 till the summer of 1963, passed under the sign of contact, which each of them saw and interpreted differently. It is quite possible that a diary Stus kept for occasional notes, which he started to keep in April 1962, also served to get a better understanding of both himself and the nature of his attitude towards Shura.

"*12.04.1962. Having gathered his wits, he decided to start a daily record. There were so few stimulating outside factors, at least memories in the light of new facts would give some input. I sent a letter to V*⁷. *I read for the third time 'Smert Shevchenka,' [Death of Shevchenko] poem by Ivan [Drach]. Compared to 'Nozhem v sertse' [Knife in the Heart], this work is much weaker. I have the impression that there is a lot of unenduring and undue things in the noise of thoughts and 'effusions.' The direction is good, but the execution is weak, the 'second delusion' (Ukrainian Sparrows) is a kind of bad reaction, a 'stick with two ends,' an unconvincing satire. 'Dalekyi divochyi holos' [Distant Girl's Voice] is good:*

*I have been waiting for you for years and years
Letting go the rainbow out of my sleeve
To your intended troubles (?)
To your threatening words.*

---

⁵ Ibid., 97.
⁶ Volodymyr Verbychenko. Vistria plasta, 97.
⁷ Probably to Vikror Didkivsky, an engineer-metallurgist and Vasyl's friend from his student days with whom the poet kept an active correspondence in 1961-1962.

He remembers from the time of Shevchenko's exile 'dark-skinned and thin Zabarzhadi.' And all this poet's glory with the masquerade appearances of Beethoven, Pushkin and Goya is not glory, but only the desire for it. Ethically, all is still not well here.'[8]

To find something in common, Vasyl and Shura went to Donetsk, where they often went to theaters and concerts. After the performances, they went to the Arctic, a cafe located near the Donetsk Opera House. They ate ice cream and drank good Tokai wine. At such moments, Vasyl forgot that he was on a date and he had to talk about something else. He perceived Shura as a muse and an audience for his critical exercises, rather than a sensual woman with her own wishes. He needed a muse, and Shura[9] was embarrassed by the idea.

"Why are we not like others?"

Vasyl was annoyed by this reaction, but he preferred not to pay attention to it, at least for a while, because he had the main thing, the creative impetus of a sensual woman who was open to him.

"09.07.1962. I sent two poems to A. Klochchya.[10] There is no reply yet. Five of my poems are included in the almanac. Bozhenko from 'Literary Ukraine' responded positively, but there is no news. It is on impulse.

I have no appetite for dances, although I am trying very actively to find one. This is due to some ancient chimeras of my psyche (or not only that). This is from the relationship with Valya.[11] Bitterness remained as she was very weak in her defeat (= in her feelings), and then, without

---

[8] "Diary" of Vasyl Stus. Deposited: Institute for Literature of the National Academy of Sciences of Ukraine. The department of manuscript collections and textology, F. 170, dep. item 1200. Cited for the first time.

[9] Vasyl's attempts to include Shura into the world of art, strange to her, were in vain. Natural and practical, she considered it a male eccentricity, maybe a pleasant one, but superfluous to real life. And how could it be otherwise, when she, a person without higher medical education, performed the most difficult baby deliveries better than any graduates, relying mainly on the instinct of her hands and her own senses? At the end of her career, Alexandra Frolova became the Head of the obstetrics department of one of the Donetsk maternity hospitals.

[10] Andriy Klochchya is a critic and prose writer. At the time he was the editor-in-chief of *Donbas* magazine.

[11] One of Stus' friends at the time.

getting an answer, she proudly fell silent. My first exam with her made me very sad. It was a surprise for her friends and only of consequence for herself.

Ustenko[12] said that she sent greetings to me jokingly and bitterly. How can she understand me? How can I understand myself? And everything that was done in our best times and later, was like an influx, subconscious, but premature and not planned. There is a crowded crossroads but the road is lonely and lost somewhere at sunset.

I was reading Ehrenburg. The impression is good, but it is shameful to read. It is a shame on them, the elders, and on myself, our generation, which is not, unfortunately, the one Malyshko is thinking about so brightly (I did not like his poem. He is wrong, he just closes his eyes or leads by the hand in the wrong direction). 'Silence' by Bondarev is something bitterly bold and desperate. It is somewhere close to the heart. It is strongly perceived, although not artistically impressive. It is being read with indifference for some reason.

A quarrel with Sasha would be useless, childish and unnecessary. There will be no need for a visit but it already lies ahead, like a date. He will be.

24.07.1962 Sasha asks me, again, why we are not like others, why we do not have a common rhythm, as we would like to. It is impossible. The insult to my words, that we have little in common, has grounds. But is it possible to eliminate its foundation? The visit was a trance. The lost Proust came to me by memories with his psychoanalysis..."[13]

Disappointment with Alexandra grew. Vasil became more and more aware that her nature meant that she would not be his companion on the road he was following. This was annoying because the poet needed the warmth of women, and all his other friends actually lost out to Shura. Internal dissatisfaction was strengthened by uncertainty regarding publications:

"I knock on the door of the editorial office, but so far without success. Every dog wants to reach its behind with its nose. It is not very pleasant to haunt the doors!"[14]

---

[12] Valentyn Ustenko, a historian, was a friend of Vasyl. He was considered the hope of Ukrainian archeology. He died tragically.
[13] "Diary" of Vasily Stus. Institute for Literature of the National Academy of Sciences of Ukraine. F. 170, dep. item 1200, sheet 5.
[14] Vasyl Stus. Tvory. V.6: book 2, 25.

The distance between the reality of Donbas and Stus' internal development was growing. Vasyl began to avoid parties, preferring books and his thoughts. This is proved by the diary entries of this period: "*08.08.1962. From the latest deep impressions, I would like to note the Enchanted Desna and the sea by Dovzhenko.*[15] *These works are ingenious, though patchily written (especially the second work). The author's voice sounds in such high registers that you wonder how we can have it.*

He foretells without being ashamed of the prophetic toga, and it is all warmed by such love that one hears the voice of a son, dreamy and intelligent, addressing his mother.

Sparrows and linnets will condemn the eagle for flying badly in bushes and hemp plants.There is a battle going on. White pigeons fly over the battle, as in a typhoon, and blasts of air buffet them from side to side, to the ground, to the fire.

Here is a mother, broken by separation from her daughter. Throwing her hands in the air she is shrinking to a point, and no one notices her, a saint.

He [Dovzhenko] *raises a man as much as he can with his good hands and at the same time warns that the land is taking revenge for betrayal.*

When it comes to a modern teacher for Ukraine, you will not find another one. It is a source of eternal inspiration, a man who has broken away from his time and, among other things, even reflects this time in his impulse.

On August 2, two poems were published in 'Radianska Donechchyna' [Soviet Donetsk Region]. Acquaintance with Tonya[16] *(after Dovzhenko it sounds different). Boris was a friend in a dream. We were not even joking. I have not mentioned him lately...*

More broadly I versify freely, exempt from rhyme, and sometimes rhythm. There is very little success. Success lies ahead."[17]

---

15 The reference is to two films, *The Enchanted Desna*" (1957) and *Poem of the Sea* (1959) by Alexander Dovzhenko.
16 Tonya was one of Vasyl Stus' passions in 1962.
17 "Diary" of Vasily Stus. Institute for Literature of the National Academy of Sciences of Ukraine. F. 170, dep. item 1200, sheets 5-7.

In the early 1960s, the *Obriy*[18] [Horizon] club of young writers was established at the Donetsk regional organization of the Communist Party of Ukraine (CPU). Many young and talented beginners from all over the region gathered there. The "dizziness" with the freedom that, after the revolutionary decisions of the XXII Congress of the Communist Party of the Soviet Union (CPSU), reached even Donetsk, inflamed and provoked discussions. Vasyl Stus was at its center: "*The speeches of the teacher from Horlivka, Vasyl Stus, were always passionate and socially acute. He promoted the works of Ukrainian 'sixtiers': I. Drach, M. Vingranovsky, Lina Kostenko, the critics I. Dzyuba, I. Svitlychny, Ye. Sverstyuk. These names and the passionate interpretation of the speaker filled our hearts with hope for the future of Ukraine,*" Vasyl Zakharchenko recalls. "*In addition, Stus read his strange, hard to hear poems. He read them in a blistering, torrential voice, read like a spell. Older writers brought up on empty agitprop poems did not accept such poetry at all and were sharply critical. The young ones liked it, and Vasyl immediately became the center of attention for the club members.*"[19]

Sharp criticism partially closed the young poet, but self-belief provoked an even more uncompromising position. Another conflict happened that evening. Most of the beginners made their first attempts in Russian, and one of the participants even provoked a discussion "*about this wild, primitive Little Russian dialect.*"[20]

Vasyl, of course, did not remain silent. A quarrel arose. Stus was supported by Ivan Pryntsevsky, Volodymyr Mishchenko, Ivan Bily and Mykola Kolisnyk, who forced "*passionate Ukrainophobes*" into silence by quotations from Lenin's works on national policy. One of the opponents was an official of the Donetsk regional committee of the CPSU, who, although forced to "close" the seemingly unfounded discussion, "took note" of the ardent "Ukrainians."[21]

---

[18] Vasyl Zakharchenko. Vin peremih // Ne odliubyv svoiu tryvohu ranniu. [He won // I did not stop loving my early fear], 26.
[19] Ibid., 27.
[20] Ibid.
[21] Ibid.

The incident did not lead to the closure of the literary studio, although Vasyl Stus found the atmosphere suffocating for young writers.

It was around that time that Stus received the offer to join the CPSU, being enticed with the promise of a position as school principal. However, dreams of postgraduate studies and a literary career did had not left Vasyl, and he refused almost without hesitation. The decision to focus on literary work matured. A push was needed, i.e., the opportunity to escape from an environment that no longer satisfied either his intellectual or emotional needs.

In literature – as in the cemetery:
Some lie and others' graves are still being dug,
Do not cry, slushy, wipe away tears,
Did you see how the living are buried?

In literature – as in the cemetery
On a stupid night. Break in the dark.
Whenever you see phosphoric letters.
Step on them. Step. Hope.[22]

The feeling of otherness struck the young teacher so suddenly that Vasyl needed time to transform himself into a chrysalis and grow wings for future flight. But there was too little time for such maturation. And the creation of his own of other-dimensional world had already begun ...

The pain of losing Podillia gradually changed into the fear of losing Ukraine. Is it possible in such a situation, to pay attention to minor life matters, as everyone around does?

Gradually, he felt more and more intensely his own dissimilarity from the official, almost classical, Ukrainian Soviet literature, from its poor content and the too exaggerated courage of the authors themselves. The younger generation, later called the 'sixtiers,' had not yet achieved anything special, but were

---

[22] Vasyl Stus. Tvory. Volume 1: book 2, 38.

spiritually close to Vasyl. So, there was the "era of Pasternak," who was an aesthete and whose every line "vibrated with meaning."

It was from this poet that Vasyl learned the balanced elegance of the poetic line, the ability to concentrate the content, to fill the poem with musical sound. He was also attracted by a hereditary aristocracy of the spirit, which does not erect an idol, but, and this is perhaps even more important, is not in a rush to tear down the existing one, because "the holy place is never empty." For Pasternak,[23] this was obvious, but Stus had to grasp this simple truth on the verge of emotional collapse ...

It was difficult for Vasyl to learn to say "no" softly but firmly, something that, according to D. Dontsov, was hard for the vast majority of Ukrainian intellectuals because of their inherent softness.

He was preparing "to get through" to a postgraduate study program, although he understood that he was not expected at the chair of the Donetsk Institute. The school was becoming more and more an obstacle to his preparation, and he intended to leave it at the beginning of the new year so as to give his mind completely to science in 1963.

Circumstances also contributed to this. In the first days of December 1962, a group of Lviv University graduates arrived in Horlivka. These young romantics hoped to "awaken the national spirit" of Russian-speaking Donbas. Among them was a teacher of Ukrainian language and literature, Vasyl Shymanskyi, who was assigned to the same Russian-language school where Vasyl Stus worked.

---

[23] Undoubtedly, the "harassment" of Boris Pasternak, organized in 1959 by the Soviet system, which did not excuse his willingness to publicly renounce the Nobel Prize, was important for Vasyl Stus' becoming more oppositional. The psychological demeanor of a romantic man brought up in the USSR had already been formed and it promoted a positive perception of everything that was persecuted. So it was not surprising that Pasternak's book of poems was a constant companion of Stus' in Horlivka. To some extent, this fascination with high poetry released national pains in the mind, and provoked taking the path of the artistic "bead game." Later, this would be perceived by Stus as a "great sin." In letters from the camps, the poet would talk about the "sinful nature of art," which flourishes only in service to the rich and powerful.

The acquaintance turned out to be a pleasant one, and, after a while, the young teachers started having lunch together and talking in the evenings.

On December 8, after completing their lessons, the two Vasyls went to the local workers' canteen. On that day, an advance payment was handed out at the mine located next to school N 231. And every advance payment in the mining town meant a good amount of drunkenness, which, in the end, was typical of all working-class suburbs.

Talking with each other, the Vasyls stood in line, the flow of gravity leading them to the small window where they would order food. Vasyl Shymanskyi, who was first, said:

"*Please give me borscht for the first course, schnitzel with mashed potatoes for the second, and compote.*"

His literary Ukrainian, made worse by a Western accent, irritated an drink-fueled miner. Being in a large group emanating wine vapor gave him courage.

"*Can't you, you bastard, speak our words? What the hell is: 'give me for the first,' 'give me for the second' ... Can't you, bitch, speak like a normal person?*" He was growing enraged, feeling the silent support of his comrades.

The woman serving the dishes tried to defuse the situation with a *surzhik* [a range of mixed (macaronic) sociolects of Ukrainian and Russian used in a certain region of Ukraine and adjacent lands] familiar to the miner's ear:

"*Shame on you. These are the teachers at our school!*"

But his rising temper was too far gone, and the additional strength provided by his friends provoked even greater boldness:

"*I don't give a damn that they are teachers. We did not kill these Banderivtsi [Ukrainian nationalists, the term derived from Stepan Bandera] in 1945, so we should finish them off now.*"

Vasyl Shymanskyi recalled the development of the situation as follows:

"*Vasyl Stus turned around (I didn't have time to put down the tray), grabbed that scoundrel and lifted him (I have already that Stus has never shouted, and he did not then), telling him angrily:*

'*Shut up, you scoundrel, or else we will throw you out of the canteen!*'

More reasonable miners ran out of the queue, and calmed the situations, and we went to eat our lunch."[24]

This was the ordinary situation that Ukrainian-speaking men in Donetsk, Kharkiv, Horlivka, and many other cities in eastern Ukraine had to face if they did not resort to jaded *surzhik* or Russian. And it was irritating, because "the Ukrainian language," correct and even somewhat simplified (because the truly fine one would not be understood) was a sign of difference, contrasting with the mass, whose main rule was to "blend into the crowd."

This time Vasyl was truly "fed up" with it. Full of rage, irritation and helplessness to change anything, he walked up and down in his small room, hopelessly trying to find peace:

> What did you say? Pest, — what did he say?
> Like bullets were clicking as wolves' yellow fangs.
> You promised — had wrapped it up forever
> The pain-high day and the light is no longer visible?
> What did you say? That you are going to strangle
> Me, my children, my wife,
> All nationalists from Ukraine with a garrote,
> Red fascist, you will take the land
> And put us on the platform — to the Siberian swamps,
> Will you use human bones to make fertilizer?
> I am your enemy — I am building a wall for your
> Empire. I am trying hard, at a furious pace
> Twisted like a snail with rheumatism,
> I am digging in the sand, searching feverishly,
> Gold for you. For your not communism.[25]

This rough draft shows an outright rejection of reality at the emotional level, but freed from the contextual specifics of the situation, the poet did not return to this text, until, in 1972, it was

---

[24] From the memoirs of Vasyl Shymanskyi // Stored in the archives of Vasyl Stus.
[25] Vasyl Stus. Tvory. V.1: book 2. — P.110.

exhumed by KGB. However, Vasyl did not find peace. Too many major and minor conflicts had already raged and all that hurt. It had been too affecting to see that his friends of yesterday put up with all that, forced to adapt to the dictates of an aggressive lumpen who increasingly felt empowered, especially as regarded the Ukrainian language and culture.

This time Vasyl, as it were, made it go. And he did not calm down until he had sent a letter to Andriy Malyshko:

"Dear Andriy Samoylovych!

I am writing to you for advice. And I would appreciate it if you could offer anything. Sometimes, focusing on the monotonous impressions of the environment, anticipating the end result of a very rapid process of denationalization of a large part of Ukrainians, I feel that this is madness. This is a tragedy that sometimes you do not feel due to our indifference (a national trait) and, maybe, a little to our religious belief that things are getting better. And then you recall one poet, it seems, Rasul Gamzatov, who, within the orthodox framework, confided his secret: if his language were to disappear tomorrow, he would rather die today ...

Donetsk is a purely Russian city (or almost purely Russian). I took a job assignment in deep Ukraine – in the Kirovohrad region, although I felt that it was out of my helplessness and an escape. But escape is not the way out. It's shameful ...

Now I teach my native language in Horlivka, in a Russian (of course) school. There were a few (2-3) Ukrainian schools in Horlivka that did not survive long. There do not seem to be any in Donetsk. So, the picture is very sad.

We have no future. The roots of the nation are only in the village, and we will not live long as a 'peasant' people, if we remember the influence of the city, the army, and all the other channels for Russification.

In Donbas (and not only there!) to teach the Ukrainian language in a Russian school is folly. You need to endure some moral traumas to do that.

Only one spoken statement from the parents is required to keep their children from learning the language of the people who raised these parents. Is this not a hopak [a Ukrainian folk dance] theater with horilka [a Ukrainian alcoholic beverage] and sharovary [a kind of men's pants, part of the national costume of Ukrainian Cossacks – wide at hips, often gathered at the waist, narrowing at the bottom around the ankles]? We consider it mandatory to study the German, French, English languages but not the native one.

When there is such a law, there is a right, and then what shall we expect? Why is this law not for everybody? Why is there no maximum implementation of this law, why do we play unfairly – against ourselves?

*It is shameful! I would like this law to come into full force, then many people would be see even more clearly how our culture has **flourished**, socialist in content, national in form.*

*Sometimes it seems that our cultural figures are doing useless work. They sing when the tree on whose branch they are siting is rhythmically shaken by the axe ... How can their calm be understood? How can one understand the weak sighs, the feeble care for the fate of the village of Dream, the weak complaints, when there must be **rage** and **rage** and **rage**!?*

*If the wave of Russification is an objective process and necessary for the future (historically fair), then why should not our cultural figures serve **progress**? Why not 'retrain' then, so as not to put a spoke in the wheel of the cart rolling over the corpses of such don quixotes, like the Cossack chroniclers, and Kapnist, and the brothers, and Taras, and hromadiany [citizens]*[26], *and Drahomanov, and Franko and etc. and so on.*

How can we wait longer? How can you put up with all this? It is not at all difficult to see the facts of the rudest chauvinism, the most shameless national humiliation ... Why are we so indifferent, where do we get so much obedience to fate as to doom?

I believe that the fate of Donbas is the future fate of Ukraine when there will be only nightingales singing ..."[27]

The December incident convinced him even more of the correctness of his decision to leave the school, because "to cultivate reason, kindness and eternal values" is to succumb to the vain

---

[26] Hromadiany refers to *hromadas* [communities], centers of the Ukrainian intelligentsia, which in the second half of the nineteenth century, taking advantage of the liberality of the government of the Russian Empire, were engaged in national and cultural work. The first *Hromada* was founded in St. Petersburg in the late 1850s. Its members included M. Kostomarov, P. Kulish, T. Shevchenko and others. With the financial support of Ukrainophile landowners, the *Osnova* magazine was founded, which, in 1861-1862, published works by Ukrainian writers.

[27] Vasyl Stus. Tvory. V.4, 370-373.

illusion of populists who did "what they could" to appease their consciences, rather than really try to change the situation. "No, in the current situation in Ukraine, only science and high literature can, if not help, at least form a monument that would prove that there were people here, too," Vasyl reasoned. And to teach the Ukrainian language in the Donbas environment, you need to endure "some moral traumas."

His general dissatisfaction with the environment grew, and seeped into his relationship with Shura, whose Russian-speaking began to be really annoying:

My native language
You forgave me like a weirdness...
You probably loved me,
Because you just frowned,
When I talked about love,
Which my ancestors called kohannia [love]
...once said:
- Even your language,
I think I could have loved it...[28]

Meanwhile, dissatisfaction with life's circumstances had reached its limit. The rejection of his works by older writers, intensified by the numerous creative defeats brought about by experiments with form, forced Stus to close himself off from the world in his own shell. At this time, he assembled a large notebook of poems, united by the eloquent title: "CASE №13" — the publishing house was *Sampishsamchit*[29] [I write read myself].

This notebook can be considered the first self-published collection by Vasyl Stus, made, however, not so much for distribution among friends, but as a record of the achievements of a certain period, 1962.[30]

---

[28] Vasyl Stus. Tvory. V.1: book 2, 31.
[29] Deposited: Institute for Literature of the National Academy of Sciences of Ukraine. F. 170, dep. item 744.
[30] Later, the poems of 1963 were included in "CASE N 13". Unfortunately, the complete notebook was not preserved. When the poet was preparing the manuscript of the collection *Kruhovert* [Turnover], he cut out the sheets with

Among his reading of that time were Berdiaev, Shestov, Heidegger, Camus, studies of German classical philosophy (Hegel, Kant, Schelling, Fichte), as well as Descartes, Spinoza, Hume, Skovoroda, the Cossack chronicles, and materials on the history of the "Ukrainian Revolution" of 1917-1921.

We can say that it was in Horlivka that the foundations of Stus' worldview were largely formed. Such a process of active formation inevitably entails falling under influences, and contains traces of a transitional, more or less long-lasting, fascination with philosophical doctrines or poetic worlds, being in the force fields of bright discoveries ...

Vasyl Stus had all this also. Perhaps it was this intense intellectual growth in "foreign" force fields that was the cause of the relative creative failures of Stus as a poet.

Once the period of intense searching gave way to cold-eyed analysis, Vasyl Stus assessed the situation more realistically. After some time, he even forced himself to apologize for that letter of December 1962 to Andriy Malyshko. *"Two months ago, I sent you a letter in which, pouring out my pain over the many cruel 'whys' and requesting some help. Your silence appeared to be a stark answer to me. Excuse me. I have also kicked myself for that letter, which I probably had no right to send."*[31]

He really blamed himself for that letter, being well aware of the complexity of the existence of the "great personalities." And what right do you, just entering life, have to evaluate them? Who are you and who are they? And given that their love for the homeland is not less than yours, how strong was the pressure placed on Tychyna, Rylsky, Malyshko for them almost "voluntarily" to put on the toga of the Soviet patented classic? And so what if, after a while, reborn, they even began to like it?

In January 1963, Vasyl Stus quit his job at school and returned to his parents in Donetsk. And since money still was still a pressing problem, he started working in the mine in March.[32]

---

what he regarded as the most complete works, attaching them to the manuscript of the book sent in 1963 to the publishing house Molod [Youth].
[31] Vasyl Stus. Tvory. V.6: book 2, 29.
[32] Ne vidliubyv svoiu tryvohu ranniu..., 395.

Vasyl tried not to miss a single meeting of the *Obriy* [Horizon] Literary Club of Young Writers. On January 26, 1963, he wrote in his diary: "*Several meetings of the young writers' club have already taken place. We have pleasant discussions there. We have antipodes there. Interesting things happen. L. Beryinsky, Nadiezhdin,*[33] *and some others present. Situations are acute, sometimes ugly, with unfriendly conversations. On January 19, I was involved in a fight. I was criticized for both protecting Jews and 'nationalism,' not explicitly mentioned but alluded to.*

...Yesterday – about my "Poryv" [Impulse] – was said "in a couple of years he will be a great poet."[34] *I am rarely wrong on these matters ...*

10.03.1963 ...They say that when Twardowski had a meeting with Khrushchev to give him Solzhenitsyn's short novel, he said, referring to Pasternak: if I am anything, in front of B[oris] L[eonidovich] I am a pygmy. This is first of all heroic. For this alone, you forgive him his rather gray writing and see that an honest person always has an excuse for himself without looking for it. One abstractionist, asked by Khrushchev where he got the paint (probably he meant to say that the people gave it to you, and you waste it on 'nonsense'), replied: 'I steal it like everyone else!'

This 'hooliganism' is characteristic of youth. It can be seen that spring sap begins to ferment under the old peel, and will pierce this peel by the end of the century and let new sprouts (maybe a new peel?) grow.

They predict that in the future there will be world despotism, that the emergence of the robot is evidence of human degeneration, evidence of the need to find some excuse for their misery.

Kipling:
We're foot – slog – slog-slog-sloggin' over Africa!
Foot – foot – foot – foot-sloggin' over Africa–
(Boots–boots–boots–boots–movin' up and down again!)
There's no discharge in the war!"[35].

In early March 1963, the party organization of the Donetsk region decided to start publishing a Ukrainian-language version of *Sotsialisticheskiy Donbass* [Socialist Donbas] newspaper. They

---

[33] Russian-speaking poets and translators.
[34] Said by A. Klochchi.
[35] "Diary" of Vasyl Stus. Institute for Literature of the National Academy of Sciences of Ukraine. F. 170, dep. item 1200, sheets 11-13.

needed young people with a good command of Ukrainian. Thus, Volodymyr Buts (Verbychenko), Valentyna Drozdova, Alla Surovtseva, Svitlana Kolodina, and the literary critic Konstantin Spasenko appeared in the newspaper. Vasyl Stus[36] was one of the last to go to the editorial office.

Most of the employees involved in publishing Ukrainian the version of the newspaper had been well known to Vasyl since his days at the Stalino Pedagogical Institute.

They worked mainly in the afternoons editing the "roughly" translated materials. Most of the translators were ignorant of the living Ukrainian language, but agreement on a recommendation for admission still outweighed the irritation of the tedious editing.

As a relief from the editorial routine, Vasyl often went down to the basement of the neighboring canteen of the Ministry of the Coal Industry on Artema Street, where he finished each order with a regular: *"and a bottle of beer."*[37] During these "relaxing" bouts, he quickly became friends with the ironic Butz, who was stood out for his good knowledge of the language. Sometimes the friends hotly debated literary and political topics, mentioning the names of Hrushevsky, Vynnychenko, Petliura, and Bandera *"in the context of information unofficially spread against Soviet apologetics."*[38] In commemoration of Butz, there was even "Na rannih poezdah" [On the early trains] (1945), a book by Boris Pasternak left for Vasyl exchanged for a collection of poems by Voznesensky.

Both were aware that the "thaw" was coming to an end, which was difficult to accept. And it was not in Stus' character to be silent or talk about something in a low voice. In his memoirs, Butz writes that at that time Vasyl Stus was interested in the imagery of A. Voznesensky and the political "bite" of Ye. Yevtushenko. This is confirmed in the diary:

"15.04.1963. The latest events. About a week ago in Komsomolskaya Gazeta [Komsomol Newspaper]*, an article*

---

[36] 'March 26, 1963 — Employed as a literary editor in the editorial office of the *Socialist Donbas* newspaper. - Order №27 of March 28, 1963." From the "Work record book" of V. Stus.
[37] Volodymyr Verbychenko. Vistria plasta [The Layer's Blades], 100.
[38] Ibid., 101.

"Khlestakovshchina" [bragging] *by three authors about Yevtushenko's "Autobiography" was published. He had to write it for the United States, where they started publishing his works and now he sells them in France. 09-10.04. The ideological meeting took place in Kyiv. They scolded Drach, Letyuk, Vingranovsky, Lina Kostenko. They were united in this. Vingranovsky did not confess his sins, but defended himself irresolutely. And his poem 'I am a sword. I am not a servant. I am a son,' they say, finished him off. Victor Nekrasov said that if he repents to please his friends-advisers he will not respect himself as a person."*[39]

The mention of Mykola Vingranovsky's name in the diary is not incidental. The poems of the young Vingranovsky, whose typewritten manuscripts were given to Stus by A. Klochchya, made such a big impression on Vasyl that he even copied them on a typewriter to distribute among friends ...[40]

In May, the poet went to Odesa for a monthly seminar of young literati. He was invited by Volodymyr Pianov, who was in charge of working with youth in the Union of Writers. There, in Odesa, several meetings took place, which gave Stus the hope that the illusory dream of the Kyiv postgraduate program would become a reality. Victor Ivanysenko, who headed the young poets' section, suggested to Vasyl Stus that he enter the postgraduate program at the Taras Shevchenko Institute of Literature of the Academy of Sciences of the USSR, and promised to support him.

The entrance exams for the postgraduate study program were passed almost "without nerves": a brilliant knowledge of theory and research methodology, awareness of "what" was worth talking about, and about "what" it was better to remain silent, helped avoid pitfalls and surface checks. Additionally, the "Donetsk" roots of the boy with good Ukrainian persuaded the members of the admission committee to allocate one place "meant for Stus."

---

[39] "Diary" of Vasyl Stus. - Institute for Literature of the National Academy of Sciences of Ukraine. F. 170, dep. item 1200, sheets 11-13.

[40] Volodymyr Verbychenko. Vistria plasta [The Layer's blades].—P.102. The poems were "Ia siv ne v toi litak", "Spalenyi, spechalenyi pechalliu ...", "Trynadtsiat ruzh pid viknamy tsvilo ...", "Tak, ye narod ..." ["I got on the wrong plane." "Burned, grieved with sorrow ...," "Thirteen roses were blossoming under the windows ..." "Yes, there is the nation ..."]

He returned to Donetsk in jubilation.
He wanted to joke, laugh, share his success with the whole world.
Verbychenko was in the editorial office.
To celebrate his success they went down to the usual subministerial café. While having a shot they got the idea appeared to play with the botched Russian calques, scattered around Donetsk, in the pages of a newspaper.
They return. Volodia calls the Head of the city department of culture, and Vasyl listens to the conversation on another line. However, they do not converse in Ukrainian.
"Look, a person who lives in Ukraine and does not know the Ukrainian language is involved in culture!" Vasyl was exuding bile.[41]
An hour later, a letter was written to Literaturna Ukraina [Literary Ukraine], which was published on October 18, 1963, in the section "Around the Word":

"LET'S BE POLITE TO EACH OTHER"
Not so long ago, a reader of Literaturna Ukraina, *being in a good mood, expressed a fantastic idea:*
"I wish a linguist would come up with a dictionary of the distortions and perversions occurring in newspapers, magazines, books, signs, etc."
We are for such an idea! And we offer linguists the following words:
"perva" means "first";
"kolia" (emphasis on the "a") – "kolia" (emphasis on the "o");
"Donesky" – that is, "Donetsky";
"Ekonomichny" with an "э" – "ekonomichny";
"Donetskzhilbud" – "Donetskzhitlobud";
"MZ of the USSR" – "Ministry of Health Protection of the USSR";
"Donetsky oblzdravviddil" – we can't translate it either.
"Tekstilshveitorg" – "Tekstylshveitorg."
We could exemplify a dozen more words, but we think that is enough!
V. Buts, V. Stus, employees of the Sotsialisticheskiy Donbass newspaper.

---

[41] Ibid., 103.

P.S. We certainly respect railroad workers, municipal employees, trade and medical workers. But they should also respect grammar. As they say in a trade let's be polite to each other."[42]

But he was already as if on the other side of life: on November 1, 1963, Vasyl Stus became a postgraduate at the Institute of Literature of the USSR Academy of Sciences, which promised a successful career and seemingly bright life prospects.

But Horlivka and Donbas remained in the work of Vasyl Stus as the theme and image of one of his program poems, which the poet worked on over ten years:

A night fire is burning out on Lysa Hora *[Bald Mountain]*
and the autumn leaves on Lysa Hora *are fading,*
and I have forgotten already where the Lysa Hora *is, and I do not know*
whether the Lysa Hora *would recognize me.*
It is mid-October, it is time for your evenings,
For your distrust and disbelief and the autumn wind.
And half of life is forgotten. Sin
Is already forgotten. Grief and joy are simple.
Mid-October of your thin-necked separations,
and I don't know anymore, I don't know, I don't know, I don't know
whether I am dead, or I live or I am dying being alive,
for everything has stopped ringing, blossoming and faded and stopped playing around.
But your sad palms still smell,
and the lips are too bitter right up to being salty and still smell,
and the Lysa Hora *is flown over by a flush bird,*
and deafly, in swollen aortas, pigeons are buzzing heavily.[43]

In general, the Horlivka-Donetsk period was extremely fruitful for Vasyl Stus in terms of creativity. It was there that the foundation of the *Kruhovert* [Turnover] collection was laid, a collection which he was no longer ashamed to submit for publication. And although

---

[42] Quote from: Volodymyr Verbychenko. Vistria plasta, 103-104.
[43] Vasyl Stus. Tvory. V.1: book 2, 159.

most of the poems were later amended to reach a certain level, it was Donbas, not Kyiv, that formed both Vasyl Stus' creative personality and his attitude to the world.

In Kyiv only a rigorous selection of works brought by him from Donetsk was carried out, and the first collections were finally formed, supplemented by a small number of more artistically perfect poems, in which the writer began searching for a new form and a new poetic language, finally achieved in 1972 in the temporary detention facility of the Kyiv KGB.

Similarly, it was in Donbas, not in Kyiv, that the civic formation of Vasyl Stus took place. It was there that his opposition to or, more precisely, his rejection of, many aspects of official Soviet society was established. However, his position can hardly be interpreted as anti-Soviet. Rather, we should talk about Stus as a patriot to his native land and culture, which he defended and maintained every way possible.

Bibliography

Stus Vasyl. Tvory u chotyrokh tomakh (shesty knyhakh). Z dodatkovymy 5 i 6 (u dvokh knyhakh) tomamy. [Works in 4 volumes (6 books). With additional the 5th and the 6th (in two books) volumes]. - VS "Prosvita" ["Education" All-Ukrainian Union], 1994-1999.

"Diary" of Vasyl Stus of 1962-1963. — Deposited at: Institute for Literature of the National Academy of Sciences of Ukraine, Department of manuscript collections and textology. F. 170, dep. item 1200.

Volodymyr Verbychenko. Vistria plasta [The Layer's blades]. — K. DP "Redaktsiia zhurnalu "Okhorona pratsi" [State enterprise "Editorial office of "Labour Protection" magazine], 2004, 150 p.

Ne vidliubyv svoiu tryvohu ranniu. Vasyl Stus — poet i liudyna. Spohady, statti, lysty, poezii. [I did not fall off my early anxiety. Vasyl Stus — poet and a person. Memoires, articles, letters, poems]. — K.: Ukrainskyi pysmennyk [Ukrainian writer], 1993, 400 p.

Stus Dmytro. Zhyttia i tvorchist Vasylia Stusa. [Life and work of Vasyl Stus] — K.: "Fotovideoservis", 1992, 88 p.

Dovidnyk z istorii Ukrainy (A — Ya). [Reference book on the history of Ukraine (A-Z)] — K.: Heneza, 2002, 1136 p.

Kasyanov Heorhii. Nezghodni: ukrainska intelihentsiia v rusi oporu 1960—80-kh rokiv. [Dissenters: Ukrainian intelligentsia in the resistance movement of 1960-1980.] — K.: Lybid, 1995, 224 p.

Zahalnyi zoshyt Vasylia Stusa u fioletovii obkladyntsi. — Zberihaietsia v IL NANU. [General notebook of Vasyl Stus in purple cover. — Deposited in the Institute for Literature of the National Academy of Sciences of Ukraine.], F.170, dep un. № 743.

The Bastion of Your Own Self (1963-1965)

November 1, 1963,[1] was the day of Stus' victory. He finally forced Kyiv to accept him.

Most of all, Vasyl sought new contacts with people he had heard so much about from acquaintances. The names of Svitlychny, Dziuba, Symonenko and Drach intrigued him, and he was subconsciously convinced that at least some, if not all, would become his good friends.

But he wondered whether he would be disappointed in them and they in him.

Vasyl banished these unwelcome thoughts from his mind as the train approached the Kyiv railway station, and trying think instead about literature and his future postgraduate studies. He had dreamed of this work for so many years. He now found himself in a completely new situation and his dreams were coming true.

The dormitory office was lost inside a one-story private building. Three five-story buildings and the postgraduate dormitory at 59 Kapitanivska Street[2] were congruent with it.

He was lodged on the fifth floor. He shared a room with Vladimir Osetrov, a postgraduate student at the Institute of Botany.[3] A bed had become vacant because Mykola Dubyk, who had previously shared the modest postgraduate space with Osetrov, moved to another block.

The circumstances of this "voluntary-forced" removal need to be related separately.

---

[1] On November 1, 1963 Vasyl Stus was enrolled in the postgraduate program, specializing in "Theory of Literature," at the T. G. Shevchenko Institute of Literature of the Academy of Sciences of the USSR. "Work record book" of Vasyl Stus. Stored in the poet's family archive.
[2] It is now 61 Vernadsckogo Blvd.
[3] Leonid Seleznenko // Netsenzurnyi Stus. Chastyna 1.—Ternopil: Pidruchnyky i posibnyky, [Uncensored Stus. Part 1.—Ternopil: Textbooks and manuals], 2002, 242-243.

The Russian-speaking postgraduates' group, which happened to be studying in Kyiv during the thaw, lived poorly but happily. Young people were interested in everything in the world, in particular socio-political, scientific and artistic news. But Ukrainian literature was of little interest to Vasyl's future neighbors, who outside the area of their scientific preferences—they were chemists, physicists, botanists—found time only for resonant artistic phenomena. Ukrainian studies did not fall into this category, so most of the erstwhile villagers deliberately switched to Russian, even in daily life, frightening others with their ugly accent.

Usually, they gathered in the room of Osetrov-Dubyk. They listened to the Voice of America, arguing about social issues, drinking, bringing women, or simply bragging about their successes on with them, telling "salty" or sharp political jokes, sharing successes, and sharing a drink after temporary setbacks. In a word, everything was as it was everywhere and at all times. Thanks to their gifts, the most talented people from the poorer strata of society broke into the local capital and were preparing for future achievements. They had already tasted the pleasure of local victory, because the status of a postgraduate, and in the future a researcher, in the USSR was almost a guarantee of a prosperous, full life in science, where you could do more than elsewhere, had more opportunities, prospects, and ... And in addition, there was the period of the "thaw," which coincided with their years of. The fear was gone and it was possible to openly argue about various topics.

However, it seems that Dubyk was a snitch. He signed a document stating that *"there is ... an anti-Soviet organization that even has a password."* According to Ivan Kalynychenko: *"The situation was complicated by the fact that the 'patriot' was beaten by someone when he was caught listening ... Therefore, [the postgraduates] became a matter of concern for the police and a special commission was set up at the Academy of Sciences."*[4]

---

[4] Ivan Kalynychenko. Zustrichi zi Stusom / Kamerton,[Meetings with Stus / Camertone], 20.

But it all worked out. The seditious scientists were "taken note of," but received nothing beyond reprimands. The academic commission decided that no anti-Soviet organization existed, and that no password existed, but *"the overheard words 'Crud, open up!' were misinterpreted."*[5]

This investigation had a practical purpose as well: to stop the postgraduates listening to "hostile voices," as Western radio programs were then called, a commission of the Academy of Sciences decided to install radio in the dormitory.

Anyway, the block residents were quite scared. It was at just that time that Vasyl Stus took up his lodging there.

Of course, the newcomer was not trusted. A snitch, who else would be put in a block with unreliable persons?

Vasyl's roommate was not enthusiastic about him either. A few days later he complained to Leonid Seleznenko:

"There was a very strange person put in my room. He says that he is a poet. He walks back and forth, reciting poems, muttering something ... In short, some weirdo, completely nuts."[6]

However, the ice of the postgraduates' reception was broken very quickly. Leonid Seleznenko, who became one of Vasyl's closest friends for several years, contributed to this greatly.

Sometime in mid-November 1963, he brought a lot of Polish magazines to Osetrov, which he got in gratitude for translating for a group of Polish historians and scholars at the request of Yaroslav Isayevich.

They started talking. After a while, Osetrov fell asleep, and Leonid and Vasyl *"talked late into night. I must say,"* Seleznenko recalled, *"that [Vasyl] was very friendly ... I think I made a good impression on him, or he felt a person feeling. We discussed different subjects with him. He took a suitcase out from under the bed and showed me, for example, photos, reprints from some old newspapers and books. There was*

---

[5] Ibid. See also Vladyslav Dmytrovych ta Viktoriia Kazymyrivna Tabielievy // Netsenzurnyi Stus. Chastyna 2 — Ternopil: Pidruchnyky i posibnyky, [Uncensored Stus. Part 2 — Ternopil: Textbooks and manuals], 2003, 184-185.
[6] Leonid Seleznenko // Netsenzurnyi Stus. Chastyna 1.[Uncensored Stus. Part 1.], 242.

Petliura or Konovalets. I looked at them with fear, not for myself, but for him. You know, on the very first time! It was already about 2 a.m."[7]

This is how Vasyl's first Kyiv friendship was formed. It is difficult to say what attracted the always balanced and collected Vasyl to the sincere but soft, almost amorphous Leonid, but the friendship arose almost immediately. In addition, Seleznenko's role in introducing Vasyl to Kyiv intellectual society can hardly be exaggerated.

The postgraduate chemist, who was interested in poetry and literature, had good connections in both the technical and cultural spheres and was able to open the door to the almost closed Kyiv societies for the alien. The Club of Creative Youth had already received considerable pressure from the authorities. In the second half of 1963, most of the sixtier writers were almost stopped from publishing in the official press and were forced to publish their most important and polemical articles by *samvydav* ["self-publishing"],[8] presaging the need for closed circles.

At the Institute, the process of joining the team was a long one. The seniors — I. Svitlychny and M. Kotsyubynska — already held a certain position, so the postgraduate could not try to make friends with them. Postgraduates had long been acquainted with each other, and departmental life was quite monotonous. In addition, the opportunity to use the well-stocked library of the Institute of Literature left almost no time to establish closer contacts with colleagues.

A dormitory is something else. Despite some suspicions, which were perfectly understandable, Vasyl quickly made the acquaintance of his comrades. It was the opportunity to overcome alienation that moved him to show off his clippings to Seleznenko: we may be from Donetsk, but we still know something. And Lenya answered in kind. Being in need of man-to-man friendship and intellectual conversation, he found an educated and good friend in

---

[7] Ibid., 244.
[8] See Borys Zakharov. Narys istorii dysydentskoho rukhu v Ukraini (1956 – 1987). [Sketch on the history of dissidents' movement in Ukraine (1956-1987)] — Kh.: Folio, 2003, 81 – 85.

Vasyl, helped him make new acquaintances and reported on interesting events in Kyiv life. And the most important thing—he was the complete opposite to those Vasyl met at the Institute.

Gradually, Stus got involved in the initially interesting but finally rather monotonous life of the postgraduate institution: boring academic boards, Komsomol meetings, somewhat more interesting and lively department meetings, escalating debates about the role of "ideological front fighters" who should be enrolled or employed at the Institute of Literature. However, it would be untrue to say that it was too annoying. After all, it was always possible to escape to the library, to lectures on philosophy or the German language. Moreover, the circle of friends gradually formed by fellow postgraduates was growing.

Stus scrupulously attended almost all literary evenings, trying at least in this way to jump, however hopelessly, on the bandwagon of "thaw," which was quickly disappearing over the horizon of the present, becoming no more than a pleasant memory of the past.

Sometime in late November, Vasyl got to know better Ivan Svitlychny, who was Executive Secretary of *Soviet Literary Studies*[9] magazine. Conversations with him only confirmed the generally gloomy Kyiv impressions, the feeling that you are hopelessly late for the holiday.

On December 4, 1963, Stus made notes about his impressions of the Kyiv atmosphere: "*After a summer evening devoted to Lesya Ukrainka (July 30) they still cannot clarify what and how.*[10] Such things

---

[9] See Dobrookyi. Spohady pro Ivana Svitlychnoho.[Memories about Ivan Svitlychny].—K.: Chas, 1998, S. 6.

[10] On July 30, 1963, young Ukrainian writers decided to informally honor the memory of the writer. Officials immediately treated the sixtiers as an "anti-Soviet group" and labelled them "bourgeois nationalists." When the participants gathered in the Kyiv central park of culture and recreation, it suddenly became clear that the summer stage had not been "prepared" for the event, and holding it was "undesirable." Despite their not having microphones, it was decided to carry on with the evening, but one of the park "landlords" ordered pop music to be player over the loudspeaker. The participants went to Dynamo Park Stadium and spent the evening there. "*I. Dziuba, I. Drach, M. Vingranovsky, I. Zhylenko, St.Telniuk and an actress, T. Tsymbal, performed by the light of torches.*" See Kasianov Heorhii. Hezhodni: Ukrainska intellihentsiia v

have never happened before. And here they accuse Borys Dmytrovych [Antonenko-Davydovych] and Mykhailyna [Kotsyubynska] of organizing all this. That resulted in the decision of the regional committee, where the facts were distorted (L. Kostenko etc.). Symonenko has fatal cancer. They say it is incurable. Izvestia newspaper commemorated Kotlyarevsky's anniversary in a rather original way. M. Rylski spoke about it in the evening at the teacher's house, answering questions.

I reminisced about Symonenko during a meeting with Ivan [Svitlychny]. A man with a mustache who jokes rudely but the hosts like it. About my poem ('To black prophets'), he said that he was sorry that I did not use bullets. He seemed to me mushy, with his vanity, with — perhaps — envy (and yet, perhaps, it was Ukrainian disbelief — a reference to Poplar by Vingranovsky and Dovzhenko). But he was self-confident, proud of his position and I didn't like it, because his collection did not impress for me.

On the 2nd [of December 1963] the four of us were discussed in the Union.^{11} Everything was about Kholodny. The members of his working group were stupid adherents. He had a colorful sweater, uncombed hair, a manifesto and weird poems. He was 5% a poet and 95% was devilry. Behind him, there were 5 or 6 of his followers — workers and students. Kholodny said about Shevchenko: 'a beatup hopak, Taras.' This is an eternally threatening hohlatstvo [a pseudonational presentation of Ukrainian life]. Ivan Svitlychny wrote an article about language. This, of course, is not a small matter considering our terms and our opposition.

Poetry should be given thought. It needs to be taken deeper and wider. You need to pull yourself away from the classicist gilding of gladhanding and vivacity. There is grief, but it is the grief of dawn. And this should always be kept in mind.

24.12.1963 On Sunday, December 15, Symonenko was buried. Kyivites and Lviv residents (among them Dziuba) came. Speeches at the cem-

---

rusi oporu 1960-80-h rokiv. [Dissenters: Ukrainian intelligentsia in resistance movement of 1960-1980]. K.: Lybid, 1995, P.27; Ivan Dziuba. Poiasniuvalna zapyska // Suchasnist. [Explanatory note 1968, ch. 8.—S. 87—94. // Modernity]. 1968, part 8, 87-94.

11   The reference is to a discussion of poems by Nadiya Kirian, Mykola Vorobyov, Vasyl Stus and Mykola Kholodny in the SPU [Union of Writers of Ukraine].

etery. The best, they say, was Dziuba's. He, Vasyl, died on Friday, bequeathing his rights to his family (about his mother, after 27 years of work in the collective farm, and now 'the first day after my death will be the first day of her hand-to-mouth existence'). He, Symonenko, writes that for literature it is a small loss – his death.

On Saturday (in Odesa, on Sunday, here on Monday or Tuesday) an evening will be given to his memory in Lviv.

An evening was held almost incognito in the medin[12] hall in Kyiv. Svitlichny made a report, before the record "keep off, Americans and Russians" was presented. Then there were telegrams from Drach, Shevchuk, Drozd. His poems ('Obelisks') were read. Spies. Mykhailyna Kotsyubynska recited 'Blue Distance,' Yurko[13] read 'Burned ...,' Kholodny read his dedication. Sverstyuk spoke very well. I recited Shevchenko's 'Isaiah, chapter 14.'"[14]

Vasyl Stus' meeting and subsequent rapid friendship with Ivan Svitlychny, which began in December 1963, may be said to be his de facto introduction to the circle of the sixtiers and the Club of Creative Youth. Having not even had the time to get properly acquainted with the oppositional, albeit Russian-speaking, dormitory environment, Vasyl entered into a completely different circle, the circle of the creative Ukrainian intelligentsia, which lived with the same pains and hopes as he did. Stus' one meeting with the terminally ill Symonenko, rather distanced him, but at the same time was somewhat significant. Despite ethical warnings, the young man with the Roman profile could not help but feel *"in the atmosphere of Kyiv Symonenko's cherished word."*[15] This was exactly what Vasyl lacked so much in Donetsk and why he went to Kyiv. According to Yevhen Sverstyuk, from *"the very beginning ... he found himself in the*

---

[12] Medin is the academic Boujmjltw Medical institute
[13] Yurii Badzo, postgraduate of the Institute of Literature.
[14] Diary notes of Vasyl Stus on some sheets of 1963-1964. Deposited in the Institute of Literature of the National Academy of Sciences of Ukraine, fund 170, dep. un. 1201, sheet 1.
[15] Yevhen Sverstyuk. Bazyleos //Ne vidliubyv svjiu gtryvohu ranniu... Vasy Stus – poet i liudyna. Spohady, statti, lysty, poezii. [I did not stop loving my early fear. Vasyl Stus – poet and a person. Memoires, articles, letters, poems]. – K.: Ukrainskyi pysmennyk [Ukrainian writer], 1993, 193.

same literary environment in which Symonenko matured, and read the same samvydav ... *Vasyl Stus embarked on the path of opposition just when the air smelled of gunpowder and caution dictate wearing the mask of loyalty.*"[16]

However, Vasyl Stus was interested in more than the figure of Ivan Svitlychny. A large library was collected in Svitlychny's tiny apartment. Vasyl Stus had had the opportunity to read "officially" and unofficially banned or confiscated literature in Donetsk, but it was nothing compared to Svitlychny's library. Here was philosophy, Ukrainian periodicals of the 1920s and 1930s, *samvydav*, and *tamvidav* [published abroad] that came to Ukraine, sometimes through Svitlychny himself.

However, the figure of Ivan Svitlychny was important not just because of this. Since 1964, especially after the disbanding of the Club of Creative Youth, he devoted most of his time to working with young Ukrainian writers, critics and artists, seeking to somehow promote a new generation of creative intellectuals who, due to the country's socio-political life, had to urgently decide on which side of the barricades they stood. Of course, he did not provoke or push anyone to move outside of the official narrative, but to those who found themselves there, he extended a helping hand, uniting and gathering them around him, helped them not to waste their talent and succumb to despair.

Naturally, the people who chose a career fell away, but those for whom youthful ideals were not empty words, but the meaning of life, started uniting more and more closely around Svitlychny. That's how Vasyl Stus got into this company.[17]

It is safe to assume that making the acquaintance with Ivan Svitlychny was the most important connection Vasyl Stus made in Kyiv. Ivan was almost the only person who did not treat Stus' poetic experiments with skepticism; on the contrary, he supported

---

[16] Ibid.
[17] Later, he would proudly write to his student friend Oleg Orachev: "Please believe that I have not changed since my student years. And if I have changed, it is as the result of conditions that have been too much for me." See: Netsenzurnyi Stus. [Uncensored Stus]. Part 1, 228.

them, encouraged faith and inspired further "non-publication" (the admiration of his Donetsk friends and comrades in the poetry studio paled into insignificance because Vasyl was well aware of the difference in level).

A few words should be said about the circle that formed around Svitlychny from 1964 through 1965. Lyudmyla Semykina and Vasyl Stus, Ivan Dziuba and Halyna Sevruk, Vyacheslav Chornovil and Alla Horska, Mykola Kholodny and Les Tanyuk, Lina Kostenko and Roman Korogodsky, Mykhailyna Kotsyubynska and Borys Dmytrovych Antonenko-Davydovych, Gorin's brothers and Panas Zalivakha used to come. And for everyone, Ivan had time a word of encouragement. Svitlychny related with each so precisely that everyone was convinced that it was himself whom Ivan Oleksiyovych paid the most attention. And if Svitlychny was busy with you, then your work has got to count for something. After such conversations, people seemed to grow wings and new creative ideas and plans appeared.

In a few months' time, Vasyl Stus was inside of this environment, and it turned out to be the life-giving humus in which Stus' talent matured and started actualizing.

In the middle of 1964, the poet submitted to the Molod [Youth] publishing house the *Kruhovert* [Turnover] collection of 137 typewritten pages.

The collection consisted of three sections—"Rozheve pivkolo" [Pink Semicircle], "Bil—Bilyi den" [Pain—White Day] and "Kruhovert" [Turnover].[18] In 1964, the book seemed to Stus a certain achievement. Unfortunately, it is impossible to completely reconstruct its text, because after arrangement was scattered in 1965, the poet did not preserve the manuscript. When preparing the collection *Winter Trees* for publication, he simply removed the typewritten pages of several dozen poems and added them to the new book.

The poems of each section were written at different times: the "Rozheve pivkolo" poems were written before Stus' army service,

---

[18] See Vasyl Stus. Tvory [Works]. V.1: book 1.

those in "Bil—Bily Den" in the army, and the "Kruhovert" - poems were written after 1961. Schematically, the plan of each section was as follows: "1. War—soldiers. 2. Work. 3. Feelings. 4. Territory. 5. Landscapes."[19] However, civic-sounding poems could be found neither in the reconstructed collection nor in the poet's archive. It can be assumed that these poems either had to be added eventually to the sections established in such a rational way, but were never written, or else were cruelly thrown out by the author not only from the book but also from his archive immediately getting the manuscript back from the publishing house.

The last section of *Krohovert* formed the basis of *Zymovi Dereva* [Winter Trees], so it is impossible to say anything about the composition of this section.

A prelude specific to each section, serves as introductory verse, i.e. the emotional and rational understanding of the place of man in space and the world:

When you believe in the good forever,
Then believe in the land. Believe in death and anxious screams
of women in labor. Since the earliest times there has been no
Easy faith and easy delights.
[...]
Learn to take faith. How they take
Sheaves on the shoulders. How the shovels are taken
By gardeners to dig the Ground
And to fertilize...
Take fatigue and sadness from work,
Deepen in joy, deepen in suffering,
Consult them as a touchstone,
Hardening the heart like steel.
Learn at work as a people.
To believe in the good to the last gasp.[20]

---

[19] Ibid.
[20] See: Vasyl Stus. Tvory. V.1: book 1, 207.

It is, so to say, a "mandatory" program poem in which the poet, wanting his book to be published, had to show the positive transformations and achievements of the Soviet country. He had to introduce optimism into the poem outline and testify his adherence to communist ideals.

As we can see, the poet did not succeed in this (we can even say that the attempt leads to obvious poetic defeats). Instead of chanting achievements, the poet speaks of human self-development, an example of which can be the hard labor of working people.

It is not surprising that when the time came "to kill" the collection of poems, already in the process of printing, it was not very difficult for an "experienced" internal reviewer to justify it.

"*On the basis of certain poems, stanzas and even lines, the young poet Vasyl Stus is a talented man,*" Nahnybida says at the beginning of his review. "*I can ... cite a lot of good poems, precise stanzas from the poetry of Vasyl Stus. But they do not, unfortunately, determine the form, content and spirit of the whole book ...*

On re-reading ... I am surprised that the young man, a contemporary of our turbulent, heroic, and sometimes dramatic events, managed to dissociate himself from them, to hide from them in the world of rueful feelings and vague aspirations ...

The world is full of events of historical significance, the work of millions of people of the socialist camp, who by their efforts transform the world, man, amaze mankind with their discoveries, feats ... Life is full of miraculous manifestations of human heroism in the pursuit of a great goal.

But all this (in most of the manuscript poems) lies outside the attention of V. Stus. He is interested in trifles that are far from life. His lyrical self is fascinated by rueful feelings, a conditional philosophicity which has nothing to do with true philosophy invading life, people's feelings, their destinies. That's why we have few plot poems in the book, and the lyrics are dominated by indifferent "blue sky thinking," in which the poet abstracts his mind from actual life, its characters.

Let Vasyl Stus not be offended by this truth, because this is precisely where the main flaw of the manuscript lies."[21]

---

[21] Internal review of M. Nagnybida of the *Kruhovert* collection by V. Stus. The copy is stored in the poet's family archive.

Yet not all of Nahnybida's accusations were baseless. In particular, when the reviewer claimed that the poet sought to *"deliberately complicate the poem, to twist the word inhumanly,"*[22] many of Vasyl's friends could have subscribed to this opinion if it did not mean "killing" the book.

They did not want such poetry. Kholodny's publicism corresponded to the spirit and mood of the time, but Vorobyov's metaphoricity or Stus' complicated philosophicity seemed to come from another planet. This is confirmed by the discussion at the Union of Writers, which Vasyl remembered discontentedly for a long time. But this is probably always the case. The publicist poem is clear, easier to digest and better regarded by the public. At the same time, the accumulation of images and metaphors still makes demands if it is to be perceived and understood. And when you don't understand something, it seems dangerous.

The internal reviewer did not hide his irritation with the book: *"when you carefully scan the deliberately complicated poems of V. Stus, you notice that the idea behind them is sketchy and their thoughts are worthless."*[23] Because how else can you explain this unsubstantiated statement by a man belonging to the "system"? Formal imperfections, still felt in Stus' poems of this time, allow M. Nahnybida to call the author's internal organicicism a boundless arbitrariness, which disrupts and destroys the established order of things.

Researcher Mykhailyna Kotsyubynska offers another view of the early collection:

"The lyrical persona of Stus' poetry, that of a man inwardly free, is always a priori free, despite the circumstances, contrary to them ... [The poet] from a young age consciously built such a bastion out of his own 'I.' This allowed him to remain a Man and a Poet. This is connected with the

---

[22] Ibid.
[23] Ibid.

constant emphasis, in different life situations, on adherence to one's destiny, the unwillingness to 'hide from destiny,' proclaiming the primacy of Destiny over the Mind."[24]

This was typical of the early, pre-army, work of Stus, in which future achievements could only be guessed ("Mynuli mrii vydiatsia maibutnim") [Past dreams will be seen by the future].

Later, the poet complicates the composition, experiments a lot with form, trying to achieve the maximum concentration of the poetic text:

Sky. Cliffs. Abyss. Water.
Sun. Seagulls. High waves
Are absorbed by the thickened remoteness.
We are fishermen who have taken rest.[25]

In the context of Stus' work at the turn of the 1960s, these lines allow us to speak of a conscious search for a synthesis of traditional, modernist and postmodernist principles,[26] something that was especially difficult for the poet. And what did such a creative method mean if not a betrayal of the ideals of realism and socialist realism? And the reviewer M. Nahnybida was right, claiming that a book with such a philosophical basis trespasses against the "sacred cow," i.e., socialist realism as the creative method of Soviet artists.

And, perhaps, a blind eye could have still been turned on this "sin," but the young author's outright reluctance to pander to or comply with the mandatory requirements made this impossible. This was not simply a matter of pride, which particularly affected

---

[24] Mykhailyna Kotsiubynska. Vasyl Stus u konteksti sohodnishnoi kulturnoi sytuatsii // Slovo i Chas.[Vasyl Stus in the context of today's cultural situation // Word and Time]. 1998, 6, 18.

[25] Vasyl Stus. Tvory. V.1: book 1., 135, 390. One early poem later included in *Zymovi dereva* In the *Krohovert* collection it was called Z dytynnoho viku" [From the age of childhood].

[26] M. Naienko. Vystup na pershykh Stusivskykh chytanniakh // Slovo i Chas. [Speech on the first Stus' readings // Word and Time]. – 1998, 6, 26 – 28.

the older generation of Ukrainian writers, often forced to compromise their conscience for the sake of saving lives. And the less talent the author had, the more devoted was his service.

Thus, the sin of subjectivism, the sin of perceiving the world not as an objective reality, but as an object for the metaphysical development of the speaker, caused the angry and exceedingly intolerant remarks of M. Nahnibida.

However, the Stus-poet's individualism is too strong, and his aching 'I' is so expressive and powerful that even in love and landscape poetry, the publicist stream is distinctly felt through which the pains and wounds of the world become a part of the narrator's inner world, urging him to take responsibility for the external world, which has already become a part of the author's nature. *"A distant, strange dream ... As if a dream were grass ... // Stop, tired, with an unknown desire. // The steppe has already turned yellow. In a blue whisper // You didn't catch his hidden words ... "; 'Life Symphony, Symphony of Spring'// and satanic – with screams – Manevych ... // Jew – up to his neck. And up to his neck – disbelief, // up to his neck – delusional and wise snow."*[27]

The configuration of the section "Bil – bily den" [Pain – White Day] is a bit more complicated than the declared scheme suggests. Here the sprouts of pre-experience acquire historical roots, and the whole world, from the sphere of intimacy to that of public life, is marked by these patterns of history.

The section opens with the poem "1875" (in *Zymovi dereva* [Winter Trees] the title was removed; the first line is "*One hundred years passed since the Sich's [Zaporozhian] death...*"). The dominant tendency is the personal responsibility for creating the present-day history, and even ancient history, because the tragedy of the people and their kin becomes part of the inner world of the lyrical persona, who seems to take responsibility for everything that has happened. At such maximal rates, there can be no question of any caution or action concerning censorship. Because the unrepentant inconsistency of the ancestors with the high requirements of history leads

---

[27] Vasyl Stus. Tvory. V.1: book 1, 206, 205.

not only to the tragedy of the people—"*Howl like an animal, drink horilka ...*"; "*In the collective farm*" —but also brings the corrosion of cynicism into the sphere of feelings and love, probably the highest sphere in Stus' hierarchy of this period:

* * *

A late hawthorn sprinkled our way,
The autumn land groans underfoot,
  and the fiery sun
is leaving a purple trail on the branches.
Let the October evening be yellow and green,
and evening remoteness shows crimson.
  Someone's sadness
was carried on the wing in trains
  by the last cranes.
And you and I are making a fire,
Having gathered brushwood. And with this fire
The mournful night, torn to pieces,
is tracing out ink silhouettes...
... It got cold. Your dream is over,
the blackened night wraps us together.
"I so want to ..."
You always want, — she answered, —
and still you do not know what.[28]

Vasyl Stus' poetic growth during this period was so intensely fast that when, after making a speech at the Ukraina cinema in 1965 in defense of his arrested friends, the printer's type for his book (his first collection of poems) was "scattered" a month before its publication date, the author took it quite calmly. The vast majority of poems from the first parts were never included anywhere.

The conscious decision to "grow up" augmented Stus' already extremely high working capacity. There was the thesis subject ap-

---

[28] Vasyl Stus. Tvory. V.1: book 1, 216-217.

proved by the Academician Shamota, his thesis supervisor, and, obviously, discussed with Ivan Svitlychny: "Sources of the emotionality of an artwork (based on modern prose)."

At the same time, Vasyl Stus wrote several review articles on new Ukrainian poetry, in which he formulated his own understanding of poetry:[29] "*Unfortunately, many of our poets lack deep intellectual significance. When you get acquainted with the poetic products of the last two years, you feel that we have a limited number of real successes. Moreover, some generally good collections, poems, thoughts, are almost lost in the slag of ordinary poetic thinking, superficial cleverness, the attributiveness characteristic of poetry.*"[30] And summing up: "*Our poetry, especially the new one, needs to do a lot to endow itself with the huge artistic achievements made by the poets of the 19th and 20th centuries.*"[31]

At the same time, Vasyl was surrounded by friends, almost all of whom were members of the newly disbanded Club of Creative Youth. The closest friends of that time were Alla Horska and Les Taniuk, Ivan Svitlychny and Ivan Dziuba, Mykola Vingranovsky and Yevhen Sverstyuk, Mykhailyna Kotsyubynska and many others, who, despite numerous reprimands, maintained the spirit of disobedience and continued to hold forbidden and semi-forbidden evenings wherever it was possible to promote the national culture.

This semi-legal "second wave"[32] of the sixtier movement captured Vasyl. Even the realization that joining with these "newfound" friends would endanger his scientific prospects did not stop him. Indeed, a man cannot betray like-minded people when they are threatened.

The summer of 1964 cooled passions. Some went on vacation, and Vasyl went to his parents. The tension of an escalating adversarial relationship between the young participants' cultural activities and the authorities seemed to have eased. Surrounding himself

---

[29] Vasyl Stus. Na poetychnomu turniri [At the poetry tournament] // Dnipro.—1964, 10, 150—153; Nai budem shchyri [Let us be sincere] // Dnipro.—1965, 2, 142–150. See also Vasyl Stus. Tvory. V. 4, 165–189.
[30] Vasyl Stus. Tvory. V.4, 173.
[31] Ibid., 172.
[32] Popeliukh // Netsenzurnyi Stus. [Uncensored Stus], Part 2, 28-29.

with books, Vasyl luxuriated in the comfort of his parents' house, enjoying the solitude. During this summer, he reread almost everything written by Khvylovy, Pluzhnyk and Vynnychenko that he managed to get. Rilke[33] and Hölderlin somehow broke Pasternak's hegemony. Among the philosophers on Stus' table there increasingly appeared Kierkegaard, whose existentialism largely determined the philosophical basis of *Zymovi dereva* and Ortega y Gasset, whose New York edition of *The Revolt of the Masses*, in Ukrainian translation, was passed from hand to hand. Somewhat later, after critical reviews from Soviet philosophers, Vasyl Stus became acquainted with the philosophical doctrines of Heidegger and Jaspers, as well as the work *Sex and Character* by Otto Weininger.[34]

His parents' house in Donetsk became a hiding place, where he privately made some important decisions, the main one being to avoid, if possible, open confrontations of a clearly political nature, and to pay more attention to literary and perhaps scientific work. Although the poet considered the latter, according to a letter to Igor Nyzhnyk dated March 22, to be a forced compromise: "*Stus would like to be a scientist, you don't believe him. He is "d'On'tbelieve.*"[35] At that time, it seemed that, despite the "winding up" of the policy of relative democratization in the country, "not looking for trouble" seemed enough to provide the opportunity for active creative work. But the world and Fate offered him such rough conditions that none of the things envisioned was accomplished.

---

[33] Vasyl asks Yury Badz in a letter dated July 29, 1964: "Yur! - Yesterday I was in a foreign bookstore. Rilke was not there. I beg you, if there is any opportunity, get it. It may not be worth ordering from Chernivtsi. Maybe Roman Korogodsky would help in Kyiv, heh?
It would be very good if you did not send me a fee, but would buy Rilke. For God's sake, Yurko! I will pray for you forever ...
I am reading more prose now, including Tolstoy, Hemingway, Böll, Moem, etc. My Pasternak books are in Kyiv at Hritsko's. And it is easier without him. I am reading more, and most importantly — chasing new emotions. I want to wear myself out with chasing, not wanting to do it any more in Kyiv ...
Rylsky's death, I knew it, shocked me. I loved him not "**once upon a time**. I loved him. It all is terrifying ... "- See Vasil Stus. Tvory. Vol. 6: book. 2, 34.
[34] Ivan Dziuba // Netsenzurnyi Stus. [Uncensored Stus]. Part 2, 238-239.
[35] Vasil Stus. Tvory. Vol. 6: book 2, 33.

On his return to Kyiv, Vasyl felt as though he had not been absent there for a month and a half. Friends were coming back from various practices, expeditions and vacations and again started gathering in the evenings. Meetings with Ivan Svitlychny also became more frequent. The troubles, especially in his relationship with the "slightly weird" supervisor, Academician Shamota, were not very pleasant, but they did not seem to be a great price to pay for the positive things that Vasyl Stus gained from postgraduate study. So he had to be patient.

One September evening, he returned to the dormitory more annoyed than usual. Recent events and news: Panas Zalyvakha was excluded from the Union of Artists, there were attacks on Lvivians, there was increasing ideological pressure at the Institute of Literature—these, and Ivan Svitlychny's troubles, somehow made him especially nervous and did not allow him to concentrate.

To dispel the unwelcome discontent, Vasily decided to walk alone to the University metro station. Having walked up from Khreshchatyk along Lenin Street, he came to Volodymyr Cathedral. But this time he did not pass by, as usual, but decided to stand before the silence of the icons. He lit a candle. Making no request, just for destiny ...

Peace did not come even in the church. Crossing the street, Vasyl wanted to dive into the metro, but at the last moment changed his mind and went for a walk in the University Park. He did not notice how he came to the Khreschatyk metro station.

On the escalator, his hand habitually reached into his pocket for a book, but his eyes fixed on the profile of a beautiful young woman going a little below him on the escalator.

Forgetting about the book, Vasyl slowly went down the steps of the escalator. Having stopped one step above her, he watched intently the graceful movements of the stranger. They had a calming effect on him.

Feeling someone's piercing gaze on her back, the woman turned. "Well, it was me, actually," Vasyl thought, but did not avert his eyes. "What an insolent fellow! You cannot look at a woman you do not know like that," her eyes reproached him.

Still feeling discomfort and not wanting to sink into the slough of the situation, Vasyl instinctively, rather than intentionally, rushed down the steps, touching her "with his wing," as Valia later remembered.[36]

"*What are you doing? Approaching a woman on the street has never been your forte. God knows what she will think. Get on the train, lazybones, and go to Bolshevik.*"[37]

However, having run down the escalator, he did not hurry to dive into the train, but stopped in the distance, watching the strange lady approaching.

"*I wonder where did this naturalness came from here in Kyiv?.. What is her name?*"

The woman blushed and walked down the steps, not looking at the forward young man, who seemed to be devouring her with his deep eyes.

"*Did you really like this brat?*" she asked herself, realizing that she would respond with pleasure to any expression of attention.

He followed her with his eyes.

"*We are going the same way,*" he pronounced as she turned in the direction of Bolshevik.

The black of the tunnel was cut by the headlights of a train approaching the station. The car doors did not open for some time, and Valia noted out of the corner of her eye that the young man was watching her from under his brows as if reflecting whether "to go for it or not."

"*What a brat! Who is this big appraiser?*" A part of her was indignant. However, another objected: "*He may be a brat, but you felt warm when he touched your shoulder on the escalator.*"

The door closed, and caught up in her own thoughts, the woman did not even notice that at the last moment Vasyl jumped into the next car and was watching her through the window.

---

[36] Valentyna Popeliukh // Netsenzurnyi Stus. [Uncensored Stus]. Part 2. — P. 28-29.

[37] "Bolshevik" metro station is now called Shulizvskz. For a long time it marked the end of the Sviatoshin line.

Well before the Polytechnic Institute, she was saddened to find that the young man was no longer in the car. The chance meeting threatened to turn menacingly into a brief vignette, which suddenly appeared and disappeared just as suddenly, becoming a pleasant and strange memory.

Taking the escalator to the exit, she again felt the same look that bored into her abruptly and warmly at the Khreshchatyk station.

Vasyl at first could not decide for a long time whether to get in the same car with this strange woman, whose figure suddenly caught his eyes on the escalator, immediately distinguishing her from the mass of identical ladies, Kyivans and non-residents, or stay on another one to watch her unnoticed. He leapt into the next car as the door almost closed in front of his nose.

"*I made it in time*," he thought, making his way to the end door window and trying not to lose the facial features that were fast becoming familiar. He enjoyed the bewilderment of the woman, being afraid to admit that he was very pleased to watch her. He was pleased to see her shrinking into herself, ignoring the lustful gazes of the young men, who, like him, did not take their eyes off her, traveling alone in the almost empty car of the evening metro.

At the Polytechnical Institute station, he went over to her car and was even upset that, being self-absorbed, she did not pay the slightest attention to him. The woman did not raise her head even when he almost touched her as he passed her by.

Almost offended by such inattention, Vasyl overtook the crowd of evening idlers and climbed the steps of the escalator. Having stepped on it, he for some reason immediately regretted that he did not dare to speak to her in the car:

"*And what if somebody is waiting for her upstairs? It could be a man she's dating or a friend. It would be so uncomfortable to watch the two of them. But how shall I meet her? I will approach her on the street. I will definitely do it,*" Vasyl decided.

After walking through the glass door marked EXIT, he hid among the trees, watching the crowd slowly following him, and trying not to miss the woman, who attracted him more and more.

The flow of people was thinning but she did not appear.

"*Did she go back, accidentally passing the right stop?*" He did not have time to be frightened, as his eye caught the now familiar figure in the crowd. The woman was almost walking towards him, but, as if avoiding an invisible obstacle, she suddenly turned away and headed for the fifth streetcar, which Vasyl used to take to the dormitory.

The streetcar was empty. The young woman who, for some reason, Vasyl was sure had noticed him among the trees, as if on purpose, took a double seat, provoking him to take sit next to her.

However, he did not dare do so at once, and only the new passengers, who started getting on the streetcar at the Harmatna stop, threatening to take it, Stus' seat, pushed him to approach the strange lady:

"*May I?*" he asked, embarrassed and feeling the unnaturalness of speaking in Russian, which, however, diminished the inconvenience of such an acquaintance.

"*Sure,*" she replied.

Worryingly, conversation did not begin. However, it turned out that even sitting silently next to her was pleasant.

Near the Chervony [red] excavator the swollen clouds broke into a drizzle, which allowed Vasyl to raise the window, through which raindrops were falling directly on his clothes, i.e., to renew his attentions.

"*It appears we are neighbors,*" Vasyl said suddenly, waiting for her to react to his Ukrainian.

She answered in Ukrainian!

On the fourth cutting, where the streetcar track ended almost at the forest glade, the two of them got off the streetcar. Not yet knowing each other's names, but what do names matter, when after 15-20 minutes they both had the feeling that they had known each other for a very long time ...

Their meeting lasted until late into the night. Even without kisses. Vasyl was afraid to destroy the ethereal and fragile contact he had with this woman by a careless word or action.

"Fate knows how to endow," he thought, walking to the dormitory long after midnight.

This is how Vasyl Stus met Valentyna Popeliukh. The poet hardly ever dedicated poems to her, but all the female images of his poems and translations bear the imperceptible stamp of Valia's personality. It was she to whom, like Eurydice, he confided a secret, as if thanking her for believing in the "truth" and love of the yet unknown expression of eyes that September evening, giving herself away without any reservations or demands and always showing a readiness to share the consequences of any of Vasyl's decisions.

Valia was the royal prize for the worn-out poet, as he had never met a woman like her. For some reason, he did not like the intellectual women from the institute who swarmed around him, just as before he did not like the Kylina-women, who in the search for life benefits were often at a loss in the simplest collisions of life, turning into women-for-one-night. And Shura, Shura, who still hurt and, he felt, would hurt for a long time. Shura belonged to the past life, in the pre-Svetlychny era.

After this meeting, he was haunted by the feeling that Valia, Valentina Popeliukh, his Cinderella, would provide him with what he needed most: loyalty and faith, even without understanding the motives of his actions.

When Vasyl returned to the dormitory, nobody in his block was asleep. Someone was having fun with a new acquaintance, someone, already well drunk, pressed on with pseudo-intellectual conversations, so as to preserve the sanctity of the meeting. So he dived into the night and wandered until the dawn when he got to the fence of her Svyatoshinsky house.

That autumn, he appeared much less often than usual at literary evenings, contenting himself with brief meetings with Svitlychny at the Institute of Literature. However, the love stamp was so obvious that Svitlychny did not even try to restore his younger friend in love to society, allowing him to devote himself to the charms of love.

Sometime later, Vasily tried to read her his poems. Valya listened as if inattentively, reluctantly, and at first Vasyl even thought that they were indifferent to her. But when one day he, as if stumbling, broke off one in the middle and experimentally tried to read a piece of another one, she immediately noticed it and was even offended. Based on barely noticeable head movements or small reactions Vasyl learned to distinguish whether she liked a poem or not. Soon enough, Valia became the first listener of Stus' poems, because he seemed to believe in her unconditionally — perhaps not in her taste, but her feeling.

Autumn was passing.

Life was gradually assuming a slow pace. Vasyl even began to gradually introduce Valia to his cohort, inviting her to an exhibition or a literary evening. At first, he was a little annoyed by her awkwardness among the intellectuals or her unwillingness to be constantly in the spotlight. For Valia, it seemed enough to be in his shadow. And although Vasyl kept repeating that she should be bolder in defending her own views, thoughts and feelings, realizing her reluctance to expose her inner world to the public and seeing how she locked herself in the shell of her own experiences and impressions, not wanting to change her chosen behavior at any cost, he decided not to take her with him to the evenings, but invited her to the theater, cinema or some art exhibition, where there would be an opportunity to hide from prying eyes.

And so they lived. From time to time, Valia visited the dormitory, where the technical and natural science society of that year gained a philological newcomer, Yurko Pokalchuk.[38]

The first meeting impressed Stus. A graduate of the Leningrad Institute of Oriental Languages, he generously shared his knowledge of the East with his senior fellow postgraduate. Although it soon became clear to Vasil that it was not as deep as he had come to acquire.

However, when Lenya Seleznenko blurted that he was flitting, *"a little there, a little there, nowhere solid, everything is easy for him ...*

---

[38] Later, invoking Yuri Pokalchuk's good knowledge of Spanish, Vasyl Stus suggested that they make joint translations of Lorca, of whom they were both then fond.

like a ballerina with a suitcase,"[39] Vasyl immediately took up his cause: you cannot come to a final conclusion based on a few impressions. And when Yurko was hospitalized at the end of the year, Vasyl was almost the only person who visited the patient regularly. The reason was, perhaps, not so much their friendly relations, which had not yet formed, but the utter loneliness of Yurko. As Ivan Dziuba recalled, Vasyl's strong will was always "aimed at asserting moral height and purity. This will was so strong that he did not allow himself the slightest indulgence in anything ... We need to go to a friend who is ill. Late hour, fatigue. Someone else would say — I will leave it for tomorrow, when I'm not so tired, when I have more time ... He did it *immediately* ... *When there was a need for a moral reaction to things, he did it right away, immediately, taking into account neither his condition, nor his fatigue, nor any other part of his situation."*[40]

Vasyl often secretly "escaped" from the premises of the Institute of Literature and went to the Museum of Ukrainian Art, where Dmitry Gorbachev worked. Thanks to him, Vasyl had the opportunity to look at not only the exhibition but also the paintings kept in storage. Gorbachev said that Stus already had developed an artistic taste: "*he distinguished first-class artists from secondary ones. He liked Petrytsky, for example, very much. The Boychukists ... Pieces by the cubists-futurists also attracted him ... He spoke little about it. I just saw a lively reaction to these things. And he spoke little because in general, even art experts find it difficult to speak about this art."*[41]

The amazing richness of Ukrainian painting thus opened to Vasyl, attracted him to the museum, as you could only dream about such a collection in Donetsk.

On October 23, 1964, Vasyl Stus again *"went ... to the Museum where Dima Gorbachev worked. I saw the family (from the triptych by F. Krychevsky), Kateryna. I saw also Palmov (war theme, hatas [Ukrainian houses], heavy green background, flag, planes, etc.). The second canvas, a mother with a child, simplified body types with a chimerically heavy and densely solid colored background. There is a wonderful 'Invalids' by A.*

---

[39] Leonid Seleznenko // Netsenzurnyi Stus. [Uncensored Stus]. Part 2, 248.
[40] Ivan Dziuba // Netsenzurnyi Stus. [Uncensored Stus]. Part 1.—P. 19
[41] Dmytro Horbachev // Netsenzurnyi Stus. [Uncensored Stus]. Part 1.—P. 19

Petrytsky, awarded the first prize some time around 1930 having beautiful, ribbed chord, fierce and hard.

There are wonderful pieces by Palmova, 'Rybalka' [Fisherman] in particular. There are other compositions with unfinished backgrounds. There is a breaking of hues. Bogomazov is a god! His 'Pylshchyky' [Tuning Saws] is an outstanding thing, as well as a portrait of his wife. Cubism is reflected here. There are beautiful Caucasian motifs and the cat. There is a nice prison with a gloomy and angry blue-gray sky. The white spot is an owl. I saw a cut canvas (portrait of Pastushenko?) of one of the Boychukists [a group of Ukrainian artists who studied and worked with Michailo Boychuk, monumentalist and graphic artist] – Tsedlar."[42]

After such visits, Stus was particularly taken by the patriotic peasantry and tried to avoid meetings with those who, with pseudo-patriotic rhetoric, vulgarized and profaned both the achievements of Ukrainian culture and its tragedy. Ivan Dziuba said: "*Vasyl was sick of all forms of* malorosiystvo *[Little Russian identity was a cultural, political and ethnic self-identification of the Ukrainian who identified themselves as one of the constituent parts of the triune Russian nationality] ... He rejected some, so to say, medieval forms of patriotism connected with a kind of hatred and resentment of people of other nations. There are also such forms of patriotism. Vasyl did not accept that at all ... I think it was in him 'originally.' In this case, he did not even need to bring it up himself ... It was in his nature.*"[43]

And given that there are always fewer people with such tolerant views because it is much easier to blame strangers for all their troubles, the sixtier movement at this time already fractured: "culturalists" seemed to break with "politicians." When Leonid Brezhnev became the new General Secretary of the CPSU Central Committee in October 1964, it became clear to many that the "thaw" was over.

---

[42] Diary notes of Vasyl Stus on some sheets of 1963-1964. Deposited in the Institute of Literature of the National Academy of Sciences of Ukraine, fund 170, dep.un.1201, sheet 2.
[43] Ivan Dziuba // Netsenzurnyi Stus. [Uncensored Stus]. Part 2, 234.

However, the younger generation, brought up in the atmosphere of liberalization, was not ready to accept the policy of cutting down the national movement.

The *Prolisok*[44] [snowdrop] Creative Youth Club, established in Lviv that year, had already assumed a completely different position than Kyiv's culturalists. While the "public" demands of Kyivites, so intimidating to the authorities, were limited to demanding the truth about the Bykivna tragedy and defending, as Ivan Gel put it, "*the cultural rights of the nation,*" the goal of the Lvivians was the "*fight for Ukrainian independence.*" And the most radical among them, Ivan Gel, did not conceal that he was a supporter "*not only of the word 'struggle' but of the armed kind as well. And he believed that the struggle confined to the word is a kind of an intellectual invention.*"[45]

Only the balanced approach of Ivan Svitlychny, who, according to Mykhailyna Kotsyubynska, was a "living bridge"[46] between Kyiv and Lviv, persuaded the *Prolisok* members to refrain from armed struggle, limiting themselves to legal forms of confrontation—"*to be outspoken about what we think of the existing state of affairs.*"[47]

Not surprisingly, as early as 1964, Ivan Drach warned the Lvivians about possible arrests.[48] They did not happen then. But once the new power was in place in the Kremlin, a wave of arrests,

---

[44] *Prolisok* was headed by Mykhailo Kosiv, a literary scholar and postgraduate at Lviv University. The group included psychologist Mykhailo Horyn, art expert Bohdan Horyn, historical department student Ivan Gel, the university tutor Mykhailo Osadchy, poets Ihor Kalynets, Iryna Stasiv-Kalynets, Hryhoriy Chubai and artist Stefania Shabatura.

[45] Audio interview with I. Gel conducted by B. Zakharov in 1997 // Archive of the Kharkiv Human Rights Group (hereinafter - KhHRG), 4-5; cited in Boris Zakharov. Narys istorii dysydentskoho rukhu v Ukraini (1956—1987). [Essay on the History of the Dissident Movement in Ukraine (1956-1987)], 84-85.

[46] Mykhailyna Kotsyubynska. "Good-eyed" // Good-eyed, 108.

[47] Audio interview with M.Horyn taken by B.Zakharov in 1997 // Archive of the KhHRG, 5; cited in Boris Zakharov. Narys istorii dysydentskoho rukhu v Ukraini (1956-1987). [Essay on the History of the Dissident Movement in Ukraine (1956-1987)], 84-85.

[48] Ibid., 86.

most likely under the instructions of the Kremlin ideologue Mykhailo Suslov, swept across Ukraine.

The direct proxy of the Suslov stance in Ukraine was the Secretary of the Lviv regional committee, V. Malanchuk. So it is not surprising that most of those arrested were in Western Ukraine. In Lviv, in particular, they arrested the Horyn brothers, I. Gel, M. Osadchy, M. Kosiv, S. Baturin, G. Sadovska, M. Zvarychevska, M. Masyutka, and Ja. Menkush; in Ternopil, I. Gereta and M. Chubaty; in Lutsk, V. Moroz and D. Ivashchenko; in Ivano-Frankivsk, M. Ozerny, V. Ivanyshyn and P. Zalyvakha. In the central regions, arrests had a lower profile, and the most famous sixtiers were spared except for I. Svitlychny[49] in Kyiv and S. Karavansky in Odesa. It is quite possible that the First Secretary of the Central Committee of the Communist Party, Petro Shelest, was against the arrests because he believed that this would increase Malanchuk's influence in Ukraine. However, he could not oppose the arrests of those whose contact with the Western "radicals" seemed obvious to investigators.

There was a clear inconsistency in the actions of the authorities, and even a certain disorientation. An article by M. Masyutko was published in *Literaturna Ukraina* [Literary Ukraine] after his arrest, and discussion continued about the previously published review by M. Kosiv, a reproduction of a painting by Panas Zalyvakha, also arrested, was published in the October issue of *Mystetstvo* [Art] magazine. And at the workshop for media specialists held in the spring of 1966, the linguists from the Academy of Sciences of the USSR mentioned articles by M. Ozerny and S. Karavansky.

When news of the arrests reached Kyiv, not everyone believed them. But no doubt remained after they called Lviv.

Those staying in Kyiv thought of ways to inform the public about the arrests.

The solution proposed by Ivan Dziuba seemed the best. On September 4, a few days after the arrests, a public preview of the film *Shadows of Forgotten Ancestors* by S. Parajanov was to take place

---

[49] Ivan Svitlychny was arrested on his way from Lviv to Kyiv.

at the Ukraina cinema. Ivan and Marta[50] were close friends with Sergei Parajanov, so Dziuba suggested that Chornovil, taking advantage of the gathering of a large number of people, announce the arrests of Ukrainian intellectuals before screening the film.

"*I hope Serhiy won't object,*" he said.

Parajanov did not object and even seemed happy that thanks to this action, his film, having received several prestigious Western awards, but without being screened in Ukraine, would gain resonance.

Fearing that the KGB agents would get to know about their plan, the "conspirators" decided not to involve anyone except Parajanov.

When Vasyl Stus was on his way to the cinema to see the film, he did not yet know about the arrest of Ivan Svitlychny. Only a strange fright in the dormitory raised the alarm, but Vasyl took little account of it. Svitlychny's phone did not answer; as it turned out, from August 31 to September 2, thorough searches[51] took place at Leonida Svitlychna's apartment.

It was only once he got near the Ukraina cinema that Vasyl learned that Ivan had been arrested. And although he did not know any details, it seemed that Svitlychny was eating "government" food.

Vasyl was not in the mood to see *Shadows of Forgotten Ancestors*, but the Svitlychnis' phone still did not answer and Vasyl decided to attend the preview.

Having found his seat, he collapsed into the chair, trying with all his strength to order his thoughts: What to do? How to help Ivan? Is it worth protesting? And will his protests help Ivan? But is it possible to keep silent when a newly found comrade, who imperceptibly became Vasyl's closest friend, is, without any doubt, unfairly thrown into prison?

What will happen now to the circle that gathered around Ivan, where it was so nice to meet a writer who had not been seen for a

---

[50] Ivan Dziuba's wife.
[51] Leonida Svitlychna. Poruch z Ivanom // [Nest to Ivan] Dobrookyi, 27-29.

long time? How to help Liolia? How will he live without the Svitlychny's house, where you were always warmly received by friendly hosts?

Stus recalled how, embarrassed, he once went up to the fifth floor on Umanska Street, where the couple lived. He recalled as he crossed the threshold, not knowing where to put his hat, which for some reason turned out to feel almost ridiculous in his hands. He almost smashed a ceramic toy in a tiny corridor and was so upset that he intended to leave immediately, but when he looked up he saw such human kindness in the "mustachioed master" and the hostess Liolia that, after a few minutes, he did not even remember the many hesitations he suffered before the door of the Svitlichny apartment opened to him.

This memory echoed in Vasyl's soul with such pain, he felt such despair, a despair made more acute by this unfairness that Vasyl began to think of action. Involuntarily, he rose from his seat and hurried to sit only when he saw that Serhiy Paradzhanov and Yurko Yakutovych[52] were giving the floor to Ivan Dziuba on the stage.

Vasyl was suffering: *"My God, how can we talk about art, when a wave of arrests swept across the country yesterday?"*

Dziuba began to thank the costume designer Baikova, who for some reason was overlooked by the organizers. He handed her a bouquet of flowers. After that, he broached the subject that, while the cultural community of Ukraine welcomes the worldwide recognition of the film *Shadows of Forgotten Ancestors*, arrests were being conducted behind the walls of the hall. Ivan Svitlychny, Bohdan and Mykhailo Horyn[53] were arrested ...

Dziuba was not allowed to continue. The director of the cinema was the first to attack him, shouting and pushing him off the stage. A siren wailed.

Ivan Dziuba recalled still standing on the stage: *"And at that time, Vasyl got up. I am absolutely one hundred percent sure that his*

---

[52] Yury Yakutovych was the art director on *Shadows of Forgotten Ancestors*.
[53] Ivan Dziuba // Netsenzurnyi Stus. [Uncensored Stus]. Part 2, 243.

movement was purely spontaneous. It was not planned, nobody spoke about it ... nobody then even thought that Vasil would do it, and nobody addressed him ... There simply was such an atmosphere, the mixture of tragedy, bitterness and this brutality when they silenced you with sirens and put hands on you. And Vasyl got up,[54] *something spoke in him. And he shouted for all those who protested against the arrests to stand up or to please stand up. A few people rose immediately, then more, then more, then more. But not all. About half of those present rose, and half sat."*[55]

From the hall it appeared differently:

"There were, according to Roman Korogodsky, three or four dozen at most. I don't think there were even four ... but I want to tell you about Stus, what was he like. He was terrible. He was so shaken, pale and as if he was having convulsions. I remember him shouting that our indifference would lead to what had already happened – 1937."[56]

During the film, Vasyl was on pins and needles: they, these people, did not get up, his people were afraid, his country was afraid, his state was afraid. They were one complete-complete-complete fear, intensified by thousands of frightened eyes, covering the whole country in shadow. It was disgusting, disgusting.

And later it hurt that Pavlo Tychyna, whose early poems he valued so highly, debased himself by saying that he was indignant that a group of young men violated the quiet atmosphere of a film screening.[57]

But most insidious was another paradox of the totalitarian era: the planned speech meant to inform the public about the arrests in Ukraine took place, but the public preferred to forget everything

---

[54] Different people remember this moment differently. Some, like Ivan Dziuba, remember that it was Stus who called on those present to stand up in protest. Mykhailyna Kotsyubynska writes in her memoirs that the call to protest against tyranny belonged to Vyacheslav Chornovil, and Vasyl Stus only took up the topic.

[55] Ivan Dziuba // Netsenzurnyi Stus. [Uncensored Stus]. Part 2, 243-244.

[56] Roman Korohodskyi // Netsenzurnyi Stus. [Uncensored Stus] Part 2. Chastyna 2, 83

[57] Ivan Dziuba // Netsenzurnyi Stus. [Uncensored Stus]. Part 2, 243.

they heard that evening: *"there was such a paralyzing fear that even public forms of protest and information were powerless."*[58]

When the lights were turned on, everyone thought only about whether he would be arrested or not. But although by the end of the film the entire cinema was surrounded by KGB special forces and young men dressed in civilian clothes, there were no arrests.

On Tuesday, September 7, Vasyl Stus did not hurry, as usual, to get to the Institute by 10 a.m. and allowed himself to drink coffee, but the presentiment of something bad did not leave him.

"You are summoned to the directorate!" Vasyl shuddered at these words, which seemed to pierce the heavy, almost rubbery silence that hung in the corridor of the Institute.

"I am coming," he said carelessly and exchanged a few words with Yurko Badz, with whom he had become friends.

"Now you will be asked to write an explanation. Everyone who was there has already written one, including me, Svitlana,[59] *Mykhailyna Kotsyubynska ..."*

Stus said: *"And what shall I explain to them? That it is 1937 starting again? That the executive secretary of the Institute's journal is arrested, and everybody keeps mum and pretends that nothing happened?"*

Stretched taut. Vasyl did not enter but burst into the office of the Deputy Director of the Institute of Literature, Serhiy Zubkov.

The red-splotched face of the leader, who had already got a good scolding about the Party line, promised nothing good. Shaking with anger and irritation, Zubkov said: *"Well, sweetheart, you have got yourself into trouble. — You have not only created problems for yourself but also exposed us to danger! Well, you will flunk out of the Institute, but you still have the chance not to wind up behind bars like your friend Svitlychny."*

What exactly was said behind closed doors is unknown, but they say that the conversation ended in shouts. Vasyl Stus left the office trembling with nervous tension. When Zubkov's face, flushed

---

[58] Ibid., 245.
[59] Svitlana Kyrychenko, the wife of Jury Badz.

and distorted with hatred, appeared at the door, it became clear that Stus could no longer study at the Institute.

In a few hours Stus sent his explanation to the directorate:

EXPLANATORY NOTE

On Saturday, September 4, there was a speech by the director of the film Shadows of Forgotten Ancestors *and its participants and then, afterwards, a speech by I. Dziuba, who was not allowed to talk about the number of arrests made (he was pushed off the stage by people shouting that no one was arrested). I acted in the same way. I was outraged by the brutal treatment of I. Dziuba, the fact of the arrests, and the atmosphere of concealment of this fact, which was most clearly revealed in the meeting with the director and crew of the film. There were frantic shouts: "This is a provocation," "this is a lie," "this is not the place," etc. And I could not stand it.*

I spoke with indignation that the suspiciously covert arrests revealed a kind of depressing atmosphere in Kyiv, especially for young artists. These suspicious arrests paved the way for terrible analogies. The shadow of the bloody year of 1937 is too close not to evoke such symptoms. I could stand it neither psychologically nor civilly. Under such circumstances, **silence is a crime***. A crime against those high ideals of communism on which I was brought up.*

The fact of the ugly drowning of a speaker outraged me as well! If the arrested are guilty, then why hide it? How can we say that there are no arrests? How can we reconcile ourselves with the situation when some symptoms in the environment contradict the truth of Leninism, the truth of high civic duty, and the rights of Soviet man?

I could not stand it. I could not remain silent. After the film, I wanted to say that we, the Soviet people, could not forget that Stalin undertook some anti-socialist measures, using the name of Lenin. Khrushchev did the same, conducting a number of his experiments, theories, etc. I wanted to say that using the sacred name of Lenin to cover up our not-always-Leninist activities forced us **to fight for the real Lenin***. Not the one seen by Stalin or Khrushchev but the one he is: the ideal of all the most progressive things that mankind has produced, communist social progress over the centuries. I had to say that Stalin's executions of many innocent people were done against Leninism. And I believe that every honest person, every* *honest communist (whether he belongs to the Party directly or not) must do everything to ensure that the pure name of our leader of the Revolution is not used in their interests (perhaps simply because of their specific individual understanding). I spoke because I felt that the atmosphere that arose in the cinema indicated the fact that there were forces in the country that could continue to perform dishonest, actually anti-Leninist work. I believe that every honest person, every honest communist, **must** defend the revolutionary gains, our socialist system, our Soviet democracy. Every honest person must fight for Lenin.*

*We are committed to doing it by the memory of the millions of people who fought for a true **socialist, the most truly democratic** social system, the memory of the people who sacrificed their lives for the high fire of the Revolution, for the happy future of their descendants.*

*But the siren wailed out, drowning out my voice. This is terrible. I was trying to speak about **the duty of every Soviet person** to fight and defend democracy, socialism, the real revolutionary Leninist doctrine. And the siren was wailing. It stopped me from speaking, sealed my mouth.*

V. Stus
07.09.1965[60]

The appeal to Lenin in the Explanatory Note is not accidental. We see the same in Ivan Dziuba's text, "Internationalism or Russification." In a "closed" society, such as the Soviet Union, Lenin's name made it possible to "legally" introduce the most acute problems into official public discourse, defending the gesture with quotations from Lenin's works and opposing the "perverted" practice of socialist construction. There was no other way to have a dialogue with the state.

Therefore, Stus' appeal, taking the offensive, and not aiming to defend himself, was, first of all, a well-thought-out strategy, a desire to seize from the attackers their own weapons.

However, it did not have any effect on the experienced ideologue Zubkov. The young man whom he invited into the cabinet not only refused to "admit his fault and repent," by saying that it was a mistake of youth, something that happened to everyone, he

---

[60] Vasyl Stus. Tvory. V.4, 374-375.

accused Zubkov of inaction, and spoke about the shortcomings in the policies of socialist construction of Stalin and Khrushchev.

However, even this could have been excuse, but for the "cheek" of the young man, who not only did not try to hide his outright hostility but harshly demanded respect.

On September 20, an order was signed to expel the postgraduate Stus *"for the systematic violation of the rules of conduct of postgraduates and staff of the scientific institution."*[61]

The worst thing was that expulsion from the postgraduate program meant the loss of his place in the dormitory, from which Stus was immediately dishoused.

Of course, it was possible to stay with friends for a while, but the question immediately arose: What would he do next?

Vasyl immediately felt a void around him. Viktor Zaretsky, Alla Horska and Nadezhda Svitlychna were on a long creative trip in the Donetsk region, Ivan was behind bars. And he had to go to the dormitory in secret. All his plans for scientific and literary work crumbled at their very beginning. It was also necessary to help at least a little bit his sister Maria, who was bringing up a child by herself. Only Valya and Leonid Seleznenko ...

Vasyl started looking for a job. Lonia decided to help him. But they had no positive result. In the first place, there was the lack of registration. Secondly, potential employers were frightened off by the "political" entry in the work record book; and, thirdly, his higher education. In the USSR there was a rule: do not employ persons with higher education for regular working job positions.

Finally, Leonid learned that it was possible to work in a brickyard on Korchuvate, where they would take someone even without Kyiv registration.

They went there. Vasyl, who had already received several rejections, was nervous. The ulcer that had bothered Vasyl for a long time worsened. The acidity increased sharply. Halfway there, they jumped out of the bus near a park because Vasyl was nauseous.

---

[61] Work record book of Vasyl Stus. Stored in the poet's family archive.

They got to the personnel department. Leonid was the first to enter. Being usually timid and awkward, he was sometimes prepared to act when it came to others. That was the situation then, because Vasyl, who was extremely nervous and ready to lose his temper at any moment, could ruin everything with one harsh word.

After a while, Leonid left the personnel department and said that the case seemed to be settled.

"*Come in and bring only the necessary documents.*"

However, when Vasyl entered the office of the Head of the personnel department, he was met with a rebuff:

"*Vy ponimaietie, v danyi momient u nas miesta niet, no vy zvonitie, vy ponimaietie ...* | [62] [You understand, at the moment we have no opening, but please call us, you understand ...]

Silently they went outside. In desperation, Vasyl turned yellow. Leonid, in whose apartment Stus was staying, was even afraid of him. Just half an hour later, Vasyl took a book out of his pocket and began to read ...

A few days later friends advised Vasyl to seek help from the 47-year-old poet Mykola Samiylenko, who worked at the Institute of Gardening as a master of the construction brigade, and who, before, they said, had spent several years in Stalin's camps.

They met and got acquainted. It was only possible to get a job in the construction brigade, but Samiylenko promised that he would find a job for Vasyl where he would be able to work separately, although as part of the brigade.

As Mykola Samylenko recollected: "*there was a pit dug for about a hundred tons of lime. It was necessary to slake it. I set him to do it. He took a good stirrer and put [lime] into the pit, filled it with water, and stirred it. He worked like that, apparently, for more than a month and a half. It got cold. He started in late September. And when it got cold, he went to the boiler house. It was heated by coal.*"[63]

Vasyl, together with a partner, had to service two boilers. The shift lasted eight hours. There was no ventilation. So, in solid coal

---

[62] Leonid Seleznenko // Netsenzurnyi Stus. [Uncensored Stus] Part 1, 251-252.
[63] Mykola Samiilenko // Netsenzurnyi Stus. [Uncensored Stus], 327-328.

dust, the boilers were first loaded, then, in two or three hours, furnace slag was scooped out, and then the task was repeated. He worked like this for one or two shifts because sometimes he had to replace a partner. There were some advantages. In the interim between loading and unloading, he could read without suffering from either excessive supervision or the prying of other people's eyes.

When he got to work, Vasyl felt his feet again and finally dared to talk to Valia, whom he had avoided for a long time, wondering if he could afford the luxury of marriage with all his troubles.

After a brief separation,[64] Vasyl finally informed her about the arrests, as well as the change in his social status. Marrying a postgraduate of the Institute of Literature was one thing, marrying an unskilled worker who slaked lime was another.

Valia's reaction shocked him:

"And what, you will become different because of that?"

"Not different. It is just when you are up in the air, it is hard to plan, especially to take responsibility for someone ..."

"Then we will not plan. I am fine with you, and everything else is nonsense." She closed the conversation.

That same day they decided to get married. They decided to register their marriage for November 25,[65] but when they went to the registry office to apply, it turned out that it was possible only on December 10.

"Let it be the tenth," they decided. *"Is there any hurry about it?"*

This simple decision of the beloved, who accepted everything as it was, without thinking of possible life sorrows, but, on the contrary, trying at all costs to support the beloved in **his** decisions, was very important for Vasyl: he found the one he had been looking for for many years. That day, for the first time since Svitlychny's arrest,

---

[64] At the end of August, Vasyl went to visit his parents, and Valia had a rest in a rest home, the permit for which she got accidentally at the Kyiv Mechanical Plant, where she worked as a design engineer. See Valentina Popelyukh // Netsenzurnyi Stus. [Uncensored Stus], 29-31.

[65] Vasyl Stus' letter to Viktor Didkivsky dated October 23, 1965. See. Vasyl Stus. Tvory. Volume 6: part 2, 37.

he realized that his "pathological" inability to remain silent when he saw injustice was not so absurd. It turned out that many people around him felt as he did, and were not only ready to verbally empathize with someone else's trouble but also to help to overcome it.

That same feeling was felt a few days later during a meeting with Roman Korogodsky, who said that the Central State Historical Archive of the USSR, where he often worked, had openings, one of which Vasyl could apply for. He had already asked some people about this, and they, in turn, had spoken with the management, which had only one requirement: Vasyl should get at least a temporary registration for the Kyiv region.

Impressed by such support from people he barely knew, Vasyl promised to think about doing something in this regard. On the one hand, work at the Institute of Gardening suited him, because there was a lot of time for creativity. However, Vasyl was very sorry for the hours that could be better devoted to literary and scientific work. He was already in a hurry to live, worrying that he might not "*rise to the top of world culture*"[66] and to do this he needed at least the minimal conditions that would allow him to work in some area of the humanities. And he was increasingly suffering from whooping cough caused by the constant coal dust, forcing him to think about his health and the rest that would allow the ulcer that was really bothering him to heal.

Talk with Roman was more and more turning into a heart-to-heart conversation between two old comrades, and Vasyl, who was reluctant to share his personal affairs with others, blurted out:

"*You know, the main thing for me in all this ... is to know that you have reliable backing. I do not have to think about her as I do about myself. Because I do not think about myself.*"[67]

It was the time of the swiftly approaching group of "sacred cows" and their sixties movement, who until September 4 looked

---

[66] Dmytro Horbachov // Netsenzurnyi Stus. [Uncensored Stus].—Part 1, 205.
[67] Roman Korohodskyi // Netsenzurnyi Stus. [Uncensored Stus].—Part 2, 86.

at Stus only as a novice poet who wrote chimeric poems, but after his action accepted him as an equal.[68]

On December 6, Vasyl, together with Yevhen Sverstyuk and Lina Kostenko, went to Leonida Svitlychna.

They sat late past midnight. They asked about Ivan, talked about cases, about the possibility of further developments and the danger of *samvydav*, which had become almost the only opportunity to publish.

When Yevhan and Lina started to leave, Liolia, who had learned that Vasyl was staying with friends at that time, told him that he could stay with her.

That night, the first version of one of Stus' program poems appeared in the apartment on Umanska Street:

I can't do without Ivan's smile
to survive this slushy winter.
In the abysses of the night when Kyiv is asleep,
and my friend is being slandered diligently somewhere,
I can't close my eyes for a moment,
like a star he beams in from the gloom,
but he says nothing, nothing, nothing, nothing ...

All brave men sit in the cracks,
all truth-seekers, damn you.
Or human kindness is only kindness,
while being without strength, courage, rights
to help, remedy, stand up for,
shelter the afflicted
and dare to fight to live,
and dare to die to live?

When you, beloved, are punished —
where shall I flee from shame and disgrace?

---

[68] See, in particular, Mykhailyna Kotsiubynska. U svichadi pamiati // Ne vidliubyv svoiu tryvohu ranniu [In the mirror of memory // I did not stop loving my early fear], 130.

Then forgive, farewell, cursed land,
the homeland of cowards and murderers.
06.12.1965[69]

All this was watched by an attentive and evil stranger's eyes. As it turned out later Lina Kostenko, Yevhen Sverstyuk and Vasyl Stus went to visit Liolia with a "tail." And when about 1 a.m. the first "tail" discovered that Svitlychny's wife was visited by two men and one woman, and only one man and one woman came out, Ivan immediately learned about it.

The next day, the investigator, as if by the way, asked sarcastically:

"Ivan Alekseevych, are you not interested in who your wife spends her nights with?"[70]

Svitlychny stopped the conversation, although who knows what efforts of will he required to overcome the inevitable doubts and suspicions that occurred to every person arrested, cut off from any information from the outside.

In those same days, Valia's father, Vasyl Karpovych Popeliukh, was summoned to talk to the secretary of the Party organization.

An unknown man in civvies was in the office. The conversation lasted almost three hours, during which Vasyl Karpovych was persuaded to influence his daughter, who was going to marry an unemployed man (Stus had just taken the work record book from the Institute of Gardening in the hopes of being employed by the Historical Archive as a junior research associate after the wedding).

"What can you do if she loves him?" Vasyl Popelyukh replied, ignoring the "iron" arguments of the KGB. *"We talked to her. But this is destiny."*

This is how *diedia* [grandfather] described this difficult conversation when, shortly before his death, I asked him to explain to me

---

[69] Vasyl Stus. Tvory. Volume 1: book 1.—P.93-94.
[70] Leonida Svitlychna. "Ne mozhu ya bez posmishky Ivana ..." // Ne vidliubyv svoiu tryvohu ranniu. ["I can't do without Ivan's smile ..." // I did not stop loving my early fear.], 88.

how he, a communist since the 1930s, had agreed to let his daughter marry a man who openly opposed the state. "*Fate*," he said. "*And Valia was shining with happiness then.*"

And nothing more. For him, "fate" and "love" were much more important than all practical considerations. And it all mattered so much to him that he took his daughter's side, even though his wife Olga, to put it mildly, did not approve of the marriage.

Anyway, having been convinced that they would not be able to change Valia's decision, the parents insisted on celebrating the wedding, saying that they would be ashamed before people otherwise, although the young couple thought only of a simple ceremony at the registry office.

Leonid Seleznenko was to be best man at the wedding. However, when the time came to complete the documents, it turned out that he had left his passport at home. So Yurko Pokalchuk became the best man.

Vasyl was half an hour late to see his bride as he and R. Korogodsky were choosing flowers in Besarabka for a long time, and telephoned Stus' neighbors in Donetsk to find out if his parents were coming ... Valia was in despair: it was time to get married, but there was no groom ... When everyone was finally together, it turned out that there was still a lot of time left before the ceremony.

After the official greetings by the official at the civil registry office, everybody went outside. Vasyl's first words were:

"'*I have to smoke, and now no one say anything.*'

'*He was smoking,*' Roman Korogodsky recalls, '*and was worrying a lot ... he was very upset, agitated ...*'

'*Well! I have done smoking. Now we guys will go and have a good drink.*'"[71]

They celebrated in Sviatoshyne, in a one-story eight-apartment house where his wife's parents had their apartment. During the war, the Germans kept horses there, and after Kyiv's liberation, the premises were provided for veterans' families.

---

[71] Roman Korohodskyi // Netsenzurnyi Stus. [Uncensored Stus]. — Part 2, 89.

After the wedding, the newlyweds went to Vasyl's parents' in Donetsk for a few days. Vasyl's mother Yilyna Yakivna for some reason kept repeating: poor, poor Valia.

She immediately accepted her daughter-in-law, anticipating, however, the young woman's difficult fate. Mykhailyna Kotsyubynska had the same feeling: *"I was present at the wedding. For the first time, I saw Valia in such a tense situation and immediately understood and felt that it would not be a festive marriage."*[72]

However, their minds were not on troubles. There was a return to Kyiv ahead, where Vasyl was promised a place in the State Archives. He dreamed about a better life, hoping that all would go well for him in the new place.

Bibliography

Netsenzurnyi Stus. [Uncensored Stus]. Knyha u 2-kh chastynakh. Uporiadkuvannia Bohdana Pidhirnoho. [Book in 2 parts. Compiled by Bohdan Pidrhirnyi.] - Ternopil: Pidruchnyky i posibnyky [Textbooks and manuals], 2002, 2003, 336+320 p.

Kalynychenko Ivan. Zustrichi zi Stusom / Kamerton, [Meetings with Stus / Camertone]. — P.20-23.

Zakharov Boris. Narys istorii dysydentskoho rukhu v Ukraini (1956 — 1987) / Kharkivska pravozakhysna hrupa. [Essay on the History of the Dissident Movement in Ukraine (1956-1987) / Kharkiv Human Rights Group]. — Kh.: Folio, 2003. 144 p.

Kasianov Heorhii. Nezghodni: ukrainska intelihentsiia v rusi oporu 1960 — 80-kh rokiv. [Dissenters: Ukrainian intelligentsia in the resistance movement of 1960-1980.] — K.: Lybid, 1995, 224 p.

Dziuba Ivan. Poiasniuvalna zapyska // Suchasnist. [Explanatory note // Modernity]. 1968, Part 8. - P. 87 — 94.

Ne vidliubyv svoiu tryvohu ranniu... Vasyl Stus — poet i liudyna. Spohady, statti, lysty, poezii. / Uporiadnyk Orach (Komar) O.Iu. [I did not stop loving my early fear. Vasyl Stus — poet and a person. Memoires, articles, letters, poems / Compiler Orach (Komar) O.Ju.]. — K.: Ukrainskyi pysmennyk [Ukrainian writer], 1993, P.193.

---

[72] Mykhailyna Kotsiubynska. // Netsenzurnyi Stus. [Uncensored Stus]. — Part 2. — P. 60.

Stus Vasyl. Tvory u chotyrokh tomakh (shesty knyhakh). Z dodatkovymy 5 i 6 (u dvokh knyhakh) tomamy. [Works in 4 volumes (6 books). With additional the 5th and the 6th (in two books) volumes]. - VS "Prosvita" ["Education" All-Ukrainian Union], 1994-1999.

Stus Vasyl. "Zoreplavtsiu" ["Star explorer"] // Donbas. — 1963, p.1, P.72.

Stus Vasyl. "Nich skulptora" / Prapor [The Sculptor's Night / Flag]. — 1963, p.1, P.35.

Stus Vasyl. Virshi [Poems] //Dnipro. — 1963, p.10, P.92-93.

Nahnybida Mykola. Vnutrishnia retsenziia na zbirku V.Stusa "Kruhovert". [Internal review for "Turnover" collection of poems by V.Stus]. — Copy is stored in the poet's family archive.

Kotsiubynska Mykhailyna. Vasyl Stus u konteksti sohodnishnoi kulturnoi sytuatsii // Slovo i Chas. [Vasyl Stus in the context of today's cultural situation // Word and Time]. — 1998, p.6, P.3-23.

Naienko Mykhailo. Vystup na pershykh Stusivskykh chytanniakh // Slovo i Chas. [Speech on the first Stus' readings // Word and Time]. — 1998, p. 6, P. 26 — 28.

Malaniuk Evhen. Knyha sposterezhen. — Toronto. Nakladom Vydavnytstva "Homin Ukrainy" [Book of observations. — Toronto. By the edition of "Sounds of Ukraine" publishing house], 1962.

Prosalova Vira. Kontseptsiia myttsia u tvorchosti Ye.Malaniuka i V.Stusa // Aktualni problemy ukrainskoi literatury i folkloru. Vypusk 2. Naukovyi zbirnyk. — Donetsk: Kassiopeia [Concept of the creator in works of Ye.Malanniuk and V.Stus // Actual problems of Ukrainian literature and folklore. Ed. 2. Scientific collection. — Donetsk: Cassiopeia], 1998, P.88-92.

Stus Vasyl. Na poetychnomu turniri [On the poetic tournament] // Dnipro. — 1964, p.10, P.150-153.

Stus Vasyl. Nai budem shchyri [Let us be sincere] // Dnipro. — 1965, p. 2, P. 142-150.

Dobrookyi. Spohady pro Ivana Svitlychnoho / Uporiadnyky: Leonida i Nadiia Svitlychni. [Memoires about Ivan Svitlychny / Compilers: Leonida and Nadiya Svitlychny]. — K.: Chas [Time]1998, 572 p.

"And All That Is Like the Gifts of the Lord" (1966–1972)

> "Every executioner
> loves red wine,
> heated to 36°"
> (Vasyl Stus)

How little a person needs for happiness.

He needs his favorite job, basic conditions, peace for family and friends.

If this simple set of life's benefits is not endangered, a person may even think that his life is rather insipid.

But once the balance is broken everything goes wrong. "Misfortune never comes alone," people say. Once this balance is lost, most of us are willing to pay any price to get it back.

However, one of the paradoxes of our lives is that forward movement is usually possible only when there is no sustainable balance. When a person is open to thousands of winds he has no other guarantee than his own willingness to offer sweat and blood on the altar of self-esteem every day. And the greater the losses, the greater the opportunities. Although who can boast that he has taken full advantage of these opportunities?

The vast majority prefer to flee as soon as they realize that they have to follow their chosen life journey on their own. And there are no signposts, no ready-made solutions. Try not to fail, or miss the necessary turn in life, when so many troubles from all sides fall on the lonely head of a reckless wayfarer. And the only salvation is the constant readiness to accept losses and the unforeseeable and the refreshed will.

That is how the faithful endure as long as they can follow their Fate, which, as if mocking desperate men, offers them increasingly more complicated tasks. Can you do it? Will you withstand it? Can you bear it?

Once a person finally copes, a new trick awaits him—fatigue. No one can escape its tight claws. It is followed by irritation, intolerance ... When the poor man, having overcome all obstacles, finally reaches the goal, it turns out that ideals are no longer very important, and the result seems to lose its value ...

So, against our wishes, we have to look back at the road traveled, the price of whose overcoming is life itself, spent only in avoiding the trails of life strategies followed by those who have gone before. We must learn to accept defeats gracefully and carry on, preserve our human dignity under any circumstances ...

This last is the most difficult. It is a litmus test, "checking" your every step, provoking you to react to various situations unrelated to the sphere of *"practical politics and practical political action or behavior"* directly affecting a person's destiny. Ivan Dziuba believed that the immediate reactions and ill-considered speeches of Vasyl Stus had the greatest impact on the poet's fate. But could he have done otherwise when, as Dziuba said, it was in the sphere of Vasyl's *"moral existence in this world, where everything is largely determined by external pressure. It is determined in the sense that, if it were a question of ordinary human existence in a normal human society, there would be no need for it and it would not be expressed ... in such a form. And when a person is placed under terrible artificial conditions and there is great inhuman pressure, it provokes answering forms resistance.*

In Vasyl's case, it seems to me, it originated in human dignity. Things could have been different, he would have been himself, he would have been as he was, but his life would have been different if he had not been artificially driven to this ... He is just a victim in this respect ... The opinion, which for many reasons is unpleasant to me, is often expressed: They say if ... he had not had this tragic fate, we would not have such a poet as Vasyl Stus. First of all, I don't think it is the right way of putting the question. It borders perhaps on the consolation that others suffer the fire around and pull chestnuts out of the fire. It is not good. It comes from our desire to have victims, but for someone else to be a victim, and for you to be proud of the Ukrainian people for being capable of sacrificing themselves ..."[1]

---

[1] Ivan Dziuba // Netsenzurnyi Stus. Chastyna 2. — Ternopil: Pidruchnyky i posibnyky [Uncensored Stus. Part 2. — Ternopil: Manuals and textbooks], 2003, 255.

In Ukrainian society, this incomprehensible need to have an iconostasis of martyrs sometimes takes ugly forms. At first, society seems to shrink, the self-defense or career goals of each of its members creating the most uncomfortable situation for a person, and then either finds fault with the person who could not bear the status of victim or else glorifies his ability to sacrifice, devaluing other — seemingly less important — virtues.

But every victim needs an executioner who will use the victim for their own purposes.

At the end of 1965, in the Western Ukrainian region, V. Malanchuk the then Secretary of the Lviv regional committee of the Communist Party of Ukraine, became an executioner. The arrest warrants for the Western supporters of cultural activities that he sent to the Head of the local KGB became a jumping-off point for his future career. Having assessed the possible benefits of such Party "vigilance" against a principled stand, he felt able not to agree on the matter with the First Secretary of the Central Committee of CPU, Peter Shelest.

At the same time, in Kyiv, where the executioner was not, only Ivan Svitlychny was arrested and prosecuted on the grounds of having close personal ties with the Western Ukrainian dissidents.

And we must admit that, after the Lviv arrests, Kyiv was frightened. Most turned their heads away, quietly hoping that this "cup" was not for them. This is where the individual characteristics of each person began to be revealed. In 1965, Viacheslav Chornovil and Ivan Dziuba could not remain silent, speaking not so much out of solidarity with the prisoners (because how would such solidarity be helpful?) but out of an inner need to be in the vortex of events. The chain reaction caused by their speech affected Vasyl Stus and several other people, who also could not remain bystanders. And only chance and the lack of interest of official Kyiv in extending repressions in the capital saved the three from arrest.

Incidentally, Viacheslav Chornovil had his own interpretation of the events in the Ukraina cinema: *"The appeal to people to protest by getting up has been mistakenly attributed to Vasyl Stus. He spontaneously joined the action. Everything was prepared by me and Ivan Dziuba ... Dziuba was telling about the arrests and they switched on some kind of a whistle from the projection booth, but he managed to say the main thing. And after him, I called on all those who were against the return of Stalinism to stand up. Most of the audience stood up, despite a lot being present at the invitation of the Central Committee.*

...We went outside — d for some reason they didn't take us. We also agreed to go to Parajanov in the morning and apologize for spoiling the premiere of the film. At the time, we did not think that that had been the best advertisement for Parajanov."[2]

Chornovil's harshly individual motivation — "for some reason they didn't take us" — provoked the arrests of many people, who then and later situationally supported his actions, in which he had thought "for himself." The oratory and courage of V. Chornovil worked, and this motivated people who were not ready to undertake a desperate act, at least for a moment. The temptation to do so has always been too high, so there was always support. However, when the time came to answer the emotional impetus, which was interpreted by the punitive authorities as "anti-Soviet agitation and propaganda," a person who had no such intentions in his mind started to hesitate. On the one hand, it is somewhat shameful to justify and "repent," but, on the other, a three- or five- or even seven-year term for an emotional outburst is too much. That is how people "broke," and often provided testimony about themselves and their friends out of an elementary bewilderment at the openly cynical pressure of the punitive authorities. And why, in fact, should such a person not have "broken"? And more generally, is it correct that human weakness and an unwillingness to "serve time" be called "breaking"? After all, if someone went to see a movie or read "forbidden" literature or took part in an action, he did so out of curiosity or a natural sense of justice but without any political motivation.

But after the 1965 arrests, the wheel of repression had already started to turn, so communist ideologues who had linked their career interests to the struggle against "Ukrainian bourgeois nationalism" had to find more and more victims. Thus, they had to fan

---

[2] Interview of V. Chornovil to the *Moloda Gvardiya* [Young Guard} newspaper dated June 24, 1990 // Petro Shelest: 'Spravzhnii sud istorii shche poperedu ..." ["The real court of history is still ahead ..."], 702.

the fire of persecution of the Ukrainian intelligentsia, using the individual character features of individual Ukrainian charismatics. Failures also joined the movement. They found it easier to link their own defeats to Moscow's anti-Ukrainian policies than to their own inability. All this created the illusion of an organized opposition in Ukraine.

And since civility had never been a hallmark of the government, a situation occurred when it was necessary to choose "one's side" of the barricades: either a chance for official recognition and infamy, or "holding your head high" and a proud posture, but ... no chance of prosperity or career advancement.

The majority, as always, sought a compromise and achieved little, because the further this confrontation progressed, the more severe obedience the state demanded. There was also a fear of judicial and extrajudicial repression, threatening not only an individual person but also his family. By 1965, this fear had paralyzed the will of many people: the "forgetting" of the events at the Ukraina cinema by the great majority of those present for more than twenty years only confirmed this.

For Vasyl Stus, such behavior was unacceptable, because the loss of dignity was for him to the same as the loss of talent, the loss of the ability to create, and, therefore, death and capitulation.

For Vasyl, the preservation of dignity meant overcoming circumstances and being himself. And this desperate desire to remain human in an almost inhuman set of circumstances, the ability to overcome the feeling of being a cornered wolf, when he was hunted like a wolf, gave such a powerful impetus to his creative and personal realization that since 1966 Stus started to create. He created in conditions seemingly completely hostile to creation, the autographs of poems and collections multiplied and multiplied. Some of were lost, but most of the written works survived in at least one or two versions.

Life forced Stus to decide on a situation caused by three rather random factors: the arrest of Ivan Svitlychny, the decision of Dziuba-Chornovil to inform the public about the arrests, and the siren, which was switched on by the director of the cinema for fear of losing his position. Reacting emotionally to the injustice and not backing down from it under Zubkov's pressure, Vasyl Stus doomed himself to the "way of the cross," along which the loss of a place in a postgraduate program was the least of all possible disasters.

However, Stus' choice had obvious advantages.

After the events in the Ukraina cinema, the young poet, whose "fame" was limited to his friends, was recognized not only by the sixtiers' circle but also by people on the other side of the "barbed wire,"[3] people who were a paragon of resilience and moral virtue for Vasyl. Returning in January with his young wife from his parents', Stus for the first time realized that, accidentally sensing the zeitgeist, he managed not only to withstand it but was also able to respond. And on the path that chose him (or maybe her?), the glory of the man would make the glory of the poet—the most important for him. Therefore, even under inhuman conditions, he must create himself, because only in this way could the people of his nation, whose recognition counted for Stus above all, pay attention to his quest in the realm of the spirit and perhaps even understand his life and poems.

This realization, which at first seemed completely fantastic, was ruthlessly pushed out of his consciousness. However, it had already become a conscious way of fighting for attention for his own work. And, setting foot on that frosty January morning on the platform of the Kyiv railway station, Vasyl already knew that he would not betray this path.

Thus began Stus' "formation." A new round had begun, which imperceptibly changed into a vertical growth, in which the creator distributed his efforts so that they became the life history of an uncompromising and honest man. This man, notwithstanding any mitigating circumstances, did not pander to evil, and the poet—the second "self" of this man—fixed borderline cases, which had to confront the individual in the struggle to preserve himself in this hostile, cruel, but at the same time good and just world.

---

[3] Mykhailo Horyn // Netsenzurnyi Stus. [Uncensored Stus]. Part 2, 264.

Vasyl's well-being of this period grew so clear that he was not even surprised that he obtained a position as a junior researcher at the State Historical Archive of the Ukrainian SSR without any ado.

It was a victory over circumstances, failures, and finally over his constant financial troubles. His new status somewhat smoothed out some of the misunderstandings with the wife's mother, who, like every mother, responded painfully to her son-in-law's problems with the authorities, which could result in numerous difficulties for the young family. And how can we forget the *voronoks* [a specific black car used by the NKVD for arrests] that, in Stalin's time, which suddenly seemed quite recent, in the middle of a stupid night, dres up to the houses, where in every apartment there was a tense wait, wondering if it was for us or the neighbors? Or for both? And only when the noise of the engines subsided, was it possible to breathe calmly and try to guess, before going to sleep, who in the morning would be declared an enemy of the people.

Vasy's housing situation also bothered him. The small two-room apartment in which Valia's parents allocated the newlyweds a separate but walked-though room, staying in the other with their youngest daughter Alexandra (Shura), forced him even at night to work mindful of the peace of his relatives.

But Vasyl luxuriated in work.

After a few days, he met Vasyl Kuk, a former head of the OUN [Organization of Ukrainian Nationalists] Security Service who worked in the same archive. And although Vasyl wondered how lucky he was to survive, the poet did not dare to question the living legend. Kuk kept himself apart from most of his staff, but Stus immediately tried to make friends with him, at least to get first-hand information about the history of armed resistance to the Soviet occupation in Western Ukraine.

We cannot say that there was trust between them but it is well known that Kuk repeatedly persuaded Stus to refrain from sharp polemical speeches and to focus on scientific and creative work.

There was no need to convince Vasyl of the latter. Having gained access to almost unknown archival sources, he devoted all his free time to studying historical chronicles and documents on the modern history of Ukraine.

During the five and a half months that Stus worked at the Archive, he re-read and made notes on everything related to the Ukrainian revolution of 1917-1919. Vasyl was so absorbed in the material that he accepted, more calmly than he expected, the letter from the *Molod* [Youth] publishing house informing him that the *Krugovert* [Turnover] collection, the typesetting for which had been ready for a long time, was rejected by them. At any other time, it would have taken him long to recover from the news, but in January 1966 he was only interested in the archive.

The young scientist's vigilance and diligence were noticed by the management, and on May 3 Stus was promoted to the position of "senior researcher."[4]

The Deputy Director of the Institute of Literature, S. Zubkov, soon got to know about the meteoric career of the recently expelled postgraduate student and used all his Party and administrative-scientific influence to get the former student, who spoke so rudely to him in September 1965, removed from a Soviet scientific institution.

In his autobiography, in an entry dated July 23, 1966, Vasyl Stus described the situation as follows: *"I worked at the CSHA* [the Central State Historical Archive] *as a researcher, then as a senior researcher, but was resigned 'voluntarily' at the seemingly unscrupulous insistence of comrade Zubkov from the Institute of Literature (I learned about this from comrade Mityukov in the Central Committee of the CPU)."*[5]

However, even a few months of scientific work allowed Vasyl to accumulate material that formed the basis of an article, unpublished in his lifetime, "Deshcho z dumok nashykh poperednykiv ..."[6] [Some thoughts of our predecessors] and gave him invaluable material for his most thorough literary article — "Fenomen Doby (Skhodzhennia na Holhofu slavy)"[7] [A Phenomenon of Our

---

4   Work record book of Vasyl Stus.
5   Autobiography of Vasyl Stus. The manuscript is deposited at the archive of Humanist Center of Vasyl Stus.
6   Vasyl Stus. Tvory u chotyrokh tomakh (shesty knyhakh). Z dodatkovymy 5 i 6 (u dvokh knyhakh) tomamy. Tom 4 [Works in 4 volumes (6 books). With additionally the 5th and the 6th (in two books) volumes. Volume 4]. - VS "Prosvita" ["Education" All-Ukrainian Union], 1994, 381-397.
7   Ibid., 259-346.

Time (A way to the Golgotha of Glory)] devoted to the creative rise and fall of Pavlo Tychyna, who was "*destined to be a genius.*"[8] It was completed only in the middle of 1971, but never became a notable *samvydav* phenomenon, because the exceedingly meticulous author spent a long time consulting with friends and researchers of Tychyna's work on one or another of his assessments, and, after his 1972 arrest, two typewritten copies kept by people were burned.

"Fenomen doby" will be discussed in the next chapter. Below there are a few quotes from the article "Deshcho z dumok nashykh poperednykiv ..." [Some thoughts of our predecessors], regarding Vasyl Stus' ideas about the role and place of the writer in the life of a people:

*"The people and the whole world need the artist when he is **modern**, when his work goes touches the very nerve of life, when it merges with the cry of his nation.*

Where is modernity to be found for today's Ukrainian artist, for today's Ukrainian intellectual? It lies between the blade of a great power's sword and the throat of the Ukrainian nation. There and only there did our predecessors, local writers-great martyrs, most of whom became victims of Russian tsarism and the newest despotism look for and find modernity...

*Let us not be afraid of them, let us not be frightened, let us remove the labels glued to them by the enemies of Ukraine. As the long-forgotten legendary Ukrainian traveler of the first half of the 18th century, Vasyl Grigorovich-Barsky, wrote: "**do not be afraid of what I have written here, because I wrote all this in the passion of my heart ... and besides, I am writing this book for those who are too lazy to be a witness. So let these people get to know everything, at least by reading ...**"*[9]

The passion of the heart, which Grigorovich-Barsky emphasized, became dominant for the poet in his work and in life itself. "Literary work must be needed by the people, otherwise it loses its essence. Because when a writer has no hope that someone will need his words even after his death, such a writer fills the already dense ranks of graphomaniacs and barren fig trees, produced in great

---

[8] Ibid., 260.
[9] Ibid., 382.

numbers on our earth." That is what my father told me on another occasion, in 1980, shortly before his second arrest.

Whose thoughts seemed to Stus so concordant that he "melted" them down into an article? They included Stepan Rudansky, Serhiy Yefremov, Oleksandr Dovzhenko, Oles Honchar and Ivan Pulyuy.

The stunning picture of the decline of national life (not only the language but also the traditional life of the Ukrainian peasant, schooling, book printing, etc.) ended with figures taken from official Soviet statistics, based on which Vasyl Stus concluded with remarks the increasingly threatening Russification of the cities and the oppressed state of the titular nation in Ukraine:

"Just as before the revolution, the indigenous Ukrainian population of the republic, compared to the Russians and the Jews (living in the cities), is kept in the background and the normal cultural development of the Ukrainian nation is being slowed down and impeded in every possible way. The rural Ukrainian population ... does not in fact have access to the city, cannot join the urban population and take the Ukrainian language out of the village. Collective farmers are doomed to permanent, non-exit residence exclusively in the villages. Without passports, they are in fact **enslaved** *in specific collective farms."*[10]

Analyzing the tragedy of the "new Greece", as Ukraine was called by the German philosopher Herder in his note to Catherine II, referring to the transformation of the civilized land into a wordless and uneducated people, Stus formulates the task as follows. *"To save this modern "Greece", with its singing language, people who carried through the ages its humanity, hospitality, kindness to all peoples of the world, to any smallest brother nation, - what could be more joyful,* **natural** *for the Ukrainian intellectual than this purpose, which our predecessors sacrificed all their might and even their lives to!"*[11]

"Addressing history," as the poet later called the period of his archival life, was crucial for his further self-determination and positioning in the world. His seeming populism and championing of the people of the land, did not presuppose, like the actual populists,

---

[10] Ibid., 394.
[11] Ibid., 397.

"going" to that people and was, it could be said, even an escape from that people to archives, scientific institutions, modern world literature and culture.

Realizing that he was a representative of a nation with a "toppling tree crown," one that against its will found itself in a situation of cultural stagnation, he tried to rescue the names of officially permitted writers from the pseudo-patriotic mud and sought to introduce forgotten authors into contemporary literature. Therefore, the task of the article was to show how representatives of different branches of knowledge at different times nurtured cultural continuity, preventing it from rupturing in the most difficult historical periods. And the newest intellectuals of the sixties, it is as if Stus emphasized, must do everything possible not to be the last in this line. It was no longer enough to go to the people, to take up armed struggle or just write or paint. It was necessary to fight with all possible resources to create the conditions that would ensure the constant flow of the national element, which has nourished the national culture since ancient times, into cultural centers. That was why the struggle for the liberation of the peasants, Ukrainian schools, Ukrainian universities, high and even elite Ukrainian culture and science was becoming so important. And this path presupposed, first of all, legal forms of struggle, compromises, search for ways out of the crisis that had grown threatening.

Not everyone thought like Stus. Therefore, his circle of nonradical like-minded people was much narrower than the circle of the sixtiers. Supporters of cultural activities, who avoided confrontation with the authorities, but were willing to do their best to achieve this goal, in the mid-sixties formed an even smaller circle. After the return of Viktor Zaretsky and Alla Horska from a creative trip to Donbas and the release of I. Svitlychny on April 30, 1966 as "*socially undangerous*,"[12] the apartments of these people became a place of informal, albeit semi-forbidden, meetings and dissenters' discussions. This circle included Ivan Dziuba and Lina Kostenko,

---

[12] See.: Leonida Svitlychna. Poruch z Ivanom [Next to Ivav] // Dobrookyi. Spohady pro Ivana Svitlychnoho [Memoirs of Ivan Svitlychny].—K.; Chas [Time], 1998, 31.

Halyna Sevruk and Yevhen Sverstiuk, Roman Korogodsky and Nadiya Svitlychna, Lyudmyla Semykina and Viktor Ivanysenko, and Vasyl Stus, as well as a wide range of the technical intelligentsia who kept in touch with cultural activists especially through Leonid Seleznenko, at that time a very important figure for this cultural movement.

Svitlychny's release from jail under growing ideological pressure was a real victory for all these people and, perhaps, the only real consequence of the events at the Ukraina cinema. The victory was a really hard-fought one, and not gained by the "good will" of the authorities. Lina Kostenko had collected signatures of "masters" for a statement demanding the release of Svitlychny, not only from M. Stelmakh and A. Malyshko but also the academician M.A mosov and the aircraft designer O. Antonov. The English writer Paul Tabori, who headed the Amnesty International Commission in charge of imprisoned artists, helped the *Slovo* [Word] Association of Ukrainian Writers bring Ivan Svitlychny's case to a general session, resulting in a congressional resolution condemning "*violence against Ukrainian writers in the USSR.*"[13] The support of the technical intelligentsia, strongly defending the well-known Ukrainian writer and demanding that the authorities release the "unjustly detained" author was of particular importance. The senior KGB executives did not dare to disregard these views.

However, the euphoria was short-lived. The joy of Ivan's release was overshadowed by the pressure on M. Kotsyubynska at the Institute of Literature, trials in Lviv and Ivano-Frankivsk against the Horyn brothers and P. Zalyvakha, the dismissal of Vasyl Stus, the obstacles to publication for B. Antonenko-Davydovych, G. Kochur Ye. Sverstyuk and many other writers, whose works, even when included in periodicals, appeared under pseudonyms or even other people's names.

At the same time, the first splits occurred among the sixtiers. The relationship between I. Svitlychny and V. Chornovil, who understood differently the tasks of Ukrainian intellectuals under the conditions of total state pressure, gradually worsened. Perceiving

---

[13] The same.—P.30.

the small number of the new Ukrainian cultural elite and trying to save it from elimination in the camps, Ivan Svitlychny considered it expedient to limit himself to cultural and informational work. This made it possible to transmit information about arbitrary power in Ukraine to Moscow and from thence abroad, publishing the most interesting literary texts in Czech and Polish Ukrainian-language periodicals that did not face such harsh censorship. Viacheslav Chornovil insisted on more radical methods. He believed that a positive result could be achieved only by a tough confrontation with the authorities: mass illegal and unjustifiable arrests, in his opinion, would draw attention to the catastrophic cultural situation in Ukraine.[14]

The conflict reached its apogee in 1967, after the publication of "Lykho z rozumu" (Portrety dvadtsiaty "zlochyntsiv") ["Woe from Wit" (the portraits of twenty "criminals")], in which Chornovil collected documentary accounts about the sixtiers repressed in 1965. The publication had a significant resonance in the West and was even awarded the International Journalism Prize in Great Britain.[15] Yet they managed to avoid a final split within the community of the opposition-minded intelligentsia. The KGB "helped."

Viacheslav Chornovil was arrested on August 3, 1967.[16]

And if the greater or lesser disagreements between the conventional culture supporters and the conventional "politicians" among the sixtiers had seemed fundamental before, the court verdict (three years in prison) handed down by the Lviv Regional Court helped them all to realize that they still had much in common, and it was necessary to rise above trivial contradictions. Tactical and strategic considerations "won" over "ethical" ones: really, you cannot leave it to the whims of fate.

---

[14] Vasyl Stus' position on this was rather inconsistent. Accepting the correctness of I. Svitlychny's position and generally supporting it, the poet became a true radical when he witnessed any instance of injustice against a particular person.

[15] Ukrainska hromadska hrupa spryiannia vykonanniu Helsinskykh uhod: V 4 tomakh. T.1: Osobystosti / Uporiadnyk Ye.Zakharov [Ukrainian Public Group to Promote the Implementation of Helsinki Accords: In 4 volumes. V.1. Personalities / Compiler Ye.Zakharov]. — Kharkiv: Folio, 2001, 172.

[16] Ibid., 172-173.

The summer of 1966 turned out to be difficult for Vasyl Stus. Just after being removed from the State Historical Archives, the words of his wife came as a real shock:

"*Vasyl, I'm ... expecting a baby.*", - He heard the words one evening when, after another failed attempt to find a job, he was telling himself that he, a man, a breadwinner, could not support his family.

"*How can you be pregnant?*" He said, realizing that he had made a fool of himself. "*Valia, I am out of work. Arrests are possible, how can we bring a child into this world in which you and I have no certainty about tomorrow?*"

"*When God gives a child, He also gives the clothes,*" Valia revealed her thoughts with the proverb. "*One way or another we will manage. I will give birth to a baby.*"

In a few days, Vasyl managed to find part-time work constructing the metro and, on September 17, he was employed as a senior engineer at the Technical Information Department of the drafting bureau of the Ministry of Construction Materials Industry of the USSR.[17]

The work, of course, was far from perfect but provided the minimum income required for survival. Editing technical texts was uninteresting and not in the least creative but left some free time.

Late in the evening, when his wife's parents and her sister Alexandra fell asleep, Vasyl sat over poems until the dawn. In the difficult winter of 1965-1966, walking with Valia around the Svyatoshinsky forest, his attention was suddenly caught by the beauty of frost-covered leafless winter trees. No excess, no external ornaments —nothing covered over the essence of the majestic or twisted trunks and the skeletons of branches, which in majestic peace contemplated the bustle of human life.

"*Poetry should be like that,*" Vasyl reflected, "*free of the husk and layers of daily life, the mud of coincidences, only the quintessence of being, the human experience of every moment that a man has lived in the world. Zymovi dereva [Winter Trees] is a brilliant title for a new book of poems. Has no one used this image yet?*"- The poet was straining his memory,

---

[17] Work record book of Vasyl Stus.

trying to extract from it any hints or associations. *"No, I do not seem to have encountered such a title. That will be the book's title!"*

At night, resisting the temptation to lie comfortably in a warm bed with his wife, he forced himself to sit at a desk cluttered with unfolded manuscripts and focused on revising his poems or systematizing the information he had accumulated over several months of archival work. That was the first time that anyone had thought of Tychyna as a singer of the Ukrainian revolution. He was broken, however, like the revolution itself. Even geniuses get smaller in the tragedy of defeat. That is what should be written about in work on Tychyna, who became the singer of the greatest rising of the Ukrainian spirit in the twentieth century, and, uplifted by a burst of national greatness, reached heaven. When the force of the impulse vanished, he fell into the hopelessness of despair.

On the same desk, or in the kitchen, where he often went to smoke, Stus also wrote his letters—both to friends on the outside and those behind barbed wire fences: "*Panas!*" He addressed the imprisoned artist Zalyvakha, trying to support his spirit at least by letter. "*I wanted to tell you something. The Head of the Council of Ministers Kosygin has been to Donetsk recently. He also went to the mine where I worked for a short time as a slab after Horlivka. This is the* Oktiabrskaya *mine in Donetsk. My friend talked to him and the conversation somehow turned to you, the prisoners. The friend said that you were being treated roughly and reported some facts, including how they were treating Daniel and Karavansky. Kosygin said that he did not know that, and would come down hard on those bastard-governors so that they would remember it forever. He is a determined man, and I think that you will have new camp commanders if your "educators" do not show more brains. So, the friend told me and I decided to tell it to you in a letter so that you (and others) would not be in the dumps. But you wouldn't, would you? I know your area. I did military service in the northern Sverdlovsk region 5 years ago and traveled through your blessed lands. I just did not know that all that would one day have the glory of an intellectual mecca, where the best minds would gather under a corporal's observation.*

... I have a feeling that I am already sorry – Why the hell didn't the local bastard cast me there with You. Being there for a few years wouldn't hurt anyone ...[18]

Recently Mykola Kholodny[19] *came to me (today I have enriched myself with a son!) with some ugly Vasyl Hlynchak from Lviv. Mykola is completely afraid of everything. We calmed him down a bit. Because it is no picnic to be evicted from Kyiv. I am reading all sorts of ministerial reports and Dürrenmatt's novel Once a Greek. Prose attracts me, but I regret that I had no zek [an inmate of a forced-labor camp] practice other than stroybat [construction battalion]. Do you know whether I could take an internship as a junior zek?.*

I also have the following news: in about a month Pluzhnyk will go out. I have already seen the third set of proofs.[20] *Novichenko has written a huge preface, which is long and tedious. There will be two poems by Yevhen Pavlovych included. We had an evening in memory of Zerov recently. G. P. Kochur told an interesting story about concealment. He was reciting some prison letters. It was interesting. Yevhen*[21] *also is good at it but always with a dose of romance, which he likes. I saw one of Pluzhnik's autographs. He has clear, confident, not at all playful handwriting. 'Stone has one preserve – to be silent.' Do you know Pluzhnik?*

For sure he is a genius...

Good luck to you, Panas!

Good luck to my fellow friends, it has been more than a year now. And then your term will come to an end and you will have free time.

With wishes for a good mood, Vasyl. "[22]

---

[18] Karl Bryullov called the landowner Engelhardt "a pig in Torzhkov's shoes" when he went to see him to redeem Shevchenko from serfdom.

[19] Mykola Kholodny often visited Kyiv and often stayed at Stus' apartmenton 62 Lvivska St. In 1967, Valia's parents and sister Alexandra moved to the Voskresensky massif, where V. K. Popeliukh, the poet's father-in-law, got a two-room apartment. Afterwards, friends often stayed in the small two-room apartment with Vasyl and Valia. But Kholodny "got to" Valia a lot, as his dirty socks were often scattered all over the apartment.

[20] Yevhen Pluzhnyk. Vybrani poezii.[Selected poems] – K.: Radianskyi pysmennyk [Soviet writer], 1966.

[21] The reference is to Yevhen Svertiuk.

[22] Vasyl Stus' letter to Panas Zalyvakha of 15.11.1966. // Vasyl Stus. Tvory: Volume 6: book 2, 39-41.

Despite the warnings of the "cautious," Vasyl was quite active in his correspondence with prisoners, concerned about the fate of Vasyl Holoborodko, who *"escaped from the power of the small baits and charms of our world, and in the bare emptiness freedom, torn by teeth, felt such fatigue, such challenging grief for himself and for the world turned upside down."*[23]

Stus even was afraid that Holoborodko would do something "irrevocable," but a lot of people were in that state then. A man, however, gets used to everything. Gradually, a new life in opposition to the government became commonplace.

After his wife's parents moved to their new apartment, Vasyl's life normalized, but little Dmytryk, as the poet named his son, only ceased to remind him of his existence when he slept.[24] However, the living space expanded considerably and the poet even allowed himself the "luxury" of a typewriter which, after 1967, he used for typing his poems.

In general, 1967 happened to be quite calm. Svitlychny persuaded Vasyl to start work on "Fenomen Doby" and a new collection of poems, which consumed almost all of his free time.

When he had to be alone, Vasyl went to Leonid Seleznenko, who had a one-room apartment in Akademmistechko. But the poet's moral state was deteriorating. In a letter to Bogdan Horyn, he wrote: *"Bogdan-friend! I apologize a lot for ... the previous dirty letter. I have heard that your eyesight is worsening. It is very difficult to feel all your unhappiness, to see what is being done here, and to feel my own helplessness. There are some threads of hope, fragments of lines but there is no thickening. Everything consists of episodes that are perceived as a whole only when you look (look back) far back. Then it gets a little easier ...*

Recently, a friend of mine,[25] *who likes to cry like a woman next to me, said that we are a lost generation. In fact, we, the people who reach (or have crossed) the line of the age of 30, have less than half of what is possible and given to us. In that time, we endured only the rage of discontent — our*

---

[23] Vasyl Stus' letter to Bohdan Horyn of December 1966 – January 1967 // Vasyl Stus. Tvory: Volume 6: book 2, 42.
[24] Ivan Kalinichenko recalled that when he went to visit Vasyl Stus in the late 1960s, the little baby cried and wept all through his stay.
[25] The reference is probably to either Leonid Seleznenko or Mykola Kholodny.

locomotives 'on the other side of passion.' This rage of ours will one day again (or more than once) bring us back to youth. And perhaps it will be a sad reason to extend our bitter youth to death. The longing of the unfinished, rage before the unattainable (as if unattainable), night pollution instead of actions – this is ours. I remember poor Joyce, who carried his Ireland in his heart, who made out of it a spiritually disembodied intellectual reality and lived as any (even Ukrainian) intellectual lives: without hands, without balls, without deeds. One more thing: imagine an object in motion. The object is lost, say, it has burned up. All that was left was movement as a memory of the object and the longing of the object, the dog's pectoral alert for the moon. Do you recognize us in this?

I recall many of our martyrs who stood before and beyond a barrier. And 'over barriers.' Everyone had her, full-blooded, like a whore, like a drunkard, like a prostitute, like a so-and-so. And then he was anxious for her, loving, already crazy with rage. As in Galileo:[26] *virtues on ugly soil, a flower that grew out of yesterday's latrines. And this pederasty, this virtue, on the contrary, this gangrene of pain is claimed as patriotism.*

Excuse me. This rage was added to me by **Myna Mazailo** *and Malakhy,*[27] *whom I read yesterday. This joy of memory, the Walpurgis night of comprehension, this orgasm of once again experienced destiny is ours. Everything ugly is ours, everything dumb is ours, everything blind is ours, everything good is ours. Ignorance is ours. The blinding of spiritual buds is ours.*

In him, being wise in a special way I feel the barbed wire o justice and the smile of the 'active young man' and the orgy of the savage.

I do not know. I have already dug the tunnel to my last strength of faith. I am standing over the edge and I am happy with skepticism. What is here? I apologize for my rage.

The news is as follows. All magazine products are pushed to the ideal level of 1946-1947. They cut the short novel by E. Gutzal, many other

---

[26] In 1967, Vasyl Stus worked on the translation of the poetic parts of Bertolt Brecht's play *The Life of Galileo*, which was translated into Ukrainian by Zinaida Joffe. Later he edited the entire translation and wrote the foreword, "On Bertolt Brecht's Play *The Life of Galileo*" (See: Vasyl Stus. Tvory [Works]. Volume 5, 241-335). However, precisely because Stus translated the poems, Zinaida Joffe's translation was removed from the edition of Brecht's works. Vasyl was greatly depressed by this and even apologized in writing to the translator in a letter dated April 25, 1968 (See: Vasyl Stus. Tvory [Works]. Volume 6: Book 2, 46-47).

[27] *Myna Mazailo* and *The People's Malakhy* are plays by Mykola Kulish.

prose pieces, they say, good ones (Gutzal too). They made a clean sweep of columns as if there were a sabbath of beautiful Amazons from the Bald Mountain!
I settle down to prose ..."[28]

In that transitional year, Vasyl Stus experimented a lot and, as we can see from the letter, even settled down to write prose works: the autobiographical short novel *Podorozh do Shchastivska* [Journey to Shchastivska] and the short stories "Dzvinok" [Call], "Bevz", "Shchodennyk Petra Shkody" [Diary of Petro Skoda], "Tak buvalo uzhe ne raz" [It happened not once], "Khuga" [Snowstorm].[29]

Prose, however, detained Stus for only a short time. The possibility of a much broader, panoramic, revelation of time and man's inner state, which so impressed Vasyl in the recently read *Ulysses*, was quickly replaced by the sober realization: despite everything, he was closer to the nature of the poetic word. And he was closer to the compact stylistics of an essence detached from philological waters, where one can hide behind the image of a lyrical hero, disengaging oneself from personal experiences and troubles.

Vasyl remembered Valia's tears. He could not forgive himself for them. When he got off the plane with his baby son in his arms, the child had a fever. How could he know when he sent his son to his parents in Donetsk that the baby's health was so poor? The wife did not say a word, just looked so sad that it gave him goosebumps.

"We need to get rid of this haunting remembrance somehow," he said and forced himself to concentrate on something else.

He looked at his watch. *"Damn, I am almost late!"* Today he was going with Lenya to a gathering hosted by the Ukrainian-speaking chemist Henrikh Dvorko. Lenya told Stus that, for a long time, Dvorko organized gatherings of Ukrainian poets and artists who find a grateful audience: young Ukrainian-speaking scientists in both the natural and technical disciplines. Lenya said that a large group of people had already formed around him, and even took

---

[28] Vasyl Stus' letter to Bohdan Horyn of 1967 // Vasyl Stus. Tvory. Volume 6: book 2, 43-44.
[29] See Vasyl Stus/ Tvory. Volume 4, 3-159.

their rest together. It was necessary to go. It seemed to be nearby, in Academmistechko.

As he walked up to the entrance to Dvorko's apartment house, Seleznenko was certainly nervous.

"*I'm starting to worry about it*," he muttered, looking at his watch. "*You are not late, as a rule*," Leonid finished by stammering. He grabbed the poet by the sleeve and pulled him to the next house. "*They are already waiting for us.*"

"*Wait a minute. Let me catch my breath.*"

"*You will get it there. It is improper to be late.*"

It was really improper to be late. At the entrance, they met a young historian, Yaroslav Dzyra, who was also going to the Dvorko's.

Entering the room, Vasyl noticed the familiar faces of Borys Mozolevsky and Viktor Ivanysenko, who were in a lively discussion about something with strangers. Ivan Kalinichenko was perched in the corner, ready to join the discussion at any moment. "*Well, it looks like my people are here*," Vasyl decided and sat on a chair in the corner of the room, listening with interest to the conversation about political "frosts." "*It seems that, unlike my colleagues in the humanities, they are not afraid that their conversations may be overheard*," Vasyl noted with pleasure.

In a minute, the room was filled with the thick smell of the coffee offered by the hostess with the unusual name of Gelia. Later, Vasyl learned that Gelia was an abbreviated version of Engelsina, the name her parents gave her.

He liked the company more and more, and when the owner, a powerful and strong man, asked him to recite something from his poems, Vasyl agreed after a brief hesitation.

It was easy to recite and Vasyl basked in the attention of the audience, an attention he had never felt before. In order not to overwhelm his listeners with the too complex figurative constructions and existentialist motifs of poems from the *Zymovi dereva* [Winter Trees] collection, he decided to end with a publicist poem:

A hundred years since Sich perished.
Siberia. And Solovetsky cells,

deep night all around
a hellish land and a hellish scream.

A hundred years of tortured hopes,
expectations, faith, and blood
of sons, who are branded for their love,
a hundred hearts like a hundred blazes.

They grow up out of bast shoes,
sharovary, from a smoky hut
slaves grow up to be sons
of their mother – Ukraine.

You will no longer perish, you a hardy
land robbed for centuries,
and suppressors will not execute you
by sibireas and solovkis.

You are still aching with pain,
You are still torn to pieces,
but you are already cool and rebellious,
you straightened up for freedom,

you grew with anger. Now
you will have no peace from it,
it will grow and grow until
the prison doors will collapse.

With joyful stormy thunder
lightnings are falling from the sky,
Taras' prophetic birds –
words are hovering over the Dnipro.[30]

Vasyl made a good impression on the hosts: "On the one hand, he treats people with great respect, and, on the other, he is an independent, proud, noble man ... very attentive to everything that is

---

[30] Vasyl Stus. Tvory. Volume 1: book 1, 90-91,

happening ... a completely independent man. This is not the kind of person you can influence in any way."[31]

Whenever he had the chance, Vasyl liked to join this group. And although it did not happen very often, once every two or three months he visited these poetic-singing-cultural evenings, which were attended by "*Mozolevsky, Kordun, Kholodny, Vorobiov, Ilya ..., Goloborodko.., Orach.*" The hosts were not too puritanical and professed "*the principle of one bottle ... As a rule, they made coffee, sandwiches. And one bottle. They drank the bottle ... In fact, it was a confrontation. Everyone knew perfectly well,*" as Henrikh Dvorko recalled, "*that we gathered here, that they came to us ... the scientific intelligentsia met the humanist one. They did not like it very much.*"[32]

And how could they like it when it was there that the foundation of a strong friendship was laid, which withstood not only the test of time but also the arrests of the early 1970s. When I. Svitlychny was arrested, the Dvorkos family financially supported his wife, the Dovhans couple helped the Vasyl Stus family; others helped the children of those repressed to enter a technical higher educational institution (humanist ones were closed to them).

Sometimes Vasyl brought young poets to these gatherings. And although a car with special eavesdropping equipment started making an appearance under the windows of the apartment in 1968, it did not affect the atmosphere of friendliness that prevailed in the community.

Neither can one ignore the meeting at the Zaretskys' apartment, where the temperamental and fearless Alla Horska, "*the soul of the of the sixtiers' community,*"[33] presided and set the mood and atmosphere.

A tender, very warm relationship was established between Vasyl and Alla almost immediately. There were even rumors that they were a little romantic with each other. However, Roman

---

[31] Henrikh Dvorko // Netsenzurnyi Stus.[Uncensored Stus]. Part 2, 196.
[32] Ibid.
[33] Mykhailyna Kotsiubynska. Vocabulary of names, used in letters // Vasyl Stus. Tvory. Tom 6: book 2, 192.

Korogodsky, who was in close communication with them both, denied this: "*I knew Alla very well. She would kiss with the guys when we were dating. I once told her:*

'You have such beautiful horse's lips. They are soft and warm and big.'

'You are paying me such compliments,' Alla said. 'I don't even know if I should slap you.'

'I just love you a little.'

'I love you too,' she replied, 'not a little, but a lot.'

'Thanks.'

'But, you know, I am eager for Vasyl Stus to tell me that.'

'How on earth? The vulgarity that I said? But he is not capable of that. What are you talking about?'

'That's my point. I can't kiss him anyhow ..."[34]

Vasyl Stus and Alla Horska were *"people of the same structure, but with different psychotemperaments,"* Mr. Roman proceeded. *"They loved each other very tenderly. They loved each other as much as people on the same plane can, they shared the same, spiritual, height.*

Vasyl was a man doomed to go to his Golgotha out of love ... He was a man who did not want anything for himself, he did not need anything. He had everything necessary: shoes, a suit, pants, sweater... He did not need anything except those cigarettes ... Later it seemed to be tea."[35]

It is difficult to say anything else about the nature of the relationship between these two extraordinary personalities, who, although they met only rarely always carried on their conversation as if it had not been interrupted, shared many common preferences, and, in a quite natural way, immediately created around them an extremely attractive aura of absolute trust and openness.

These private culturological (largely closed to outsiders) companies, which met in the apartments of Svitlychny, Zaretsky, and the Dvorkos, starting in 1967 began to play an important role in the consolidation of the "new," as it were, sixties movement. It created an environment for those who were ready not to compromise with the authorities and were ready to defend the national culture and

---

[34] Roman Korohodskyi // Netsenzurnyi Stus [Uncensored Stus]. Part 2, 93.
[35] Ibid., 93.

not renounce arrested comrades, even in conditions of political "frosts."

And intellectually they were more interesting than those officially held in the palaces of culture or the Writers' Union. Here you could talk about Rilke and Hölderlin, argue about the latest trends in painting or literature, discuss current political events, "moan" about creative crises and always have at least a few, surprisingly grateful listeners.

Almost imperceptibly, Vasyl Stus became one of the leaders at these gatherings. His opinion was sought after. As Ivan Dziuba recalls, the leaders of the new sixties movement were "*Ivan Svitlychny, Yevhen Sverstyuk, Vasyl, Mykhailyna Kotsyubynska, Alla Horska ...*" And when some disputes occasionally arose, they occurred mainly outside the circle of these people.[36]

It is very probable that the most resonant text of the sixties, *Internatsionalizm chy rusyfikatsiia* [Internationalism or Russification] by Ivan Dziuba, which for decades was decisive for many thinking people and even changed the worldview of some, was first tested in this circle. Perhaps the author consulted more with Ivan Svitlychny.

"*Internatsionalizm* was an intellectual response to the arrests of 1965, perhaps even a new program, sent to the leadership of the Central Committee of the Communist Party of the USSR and the Soviet Union at the end of 1965.[37] Already in 1966 the book, which the leadership of the republic even printed for ideological party workers with the label "For official use," became a *samvydav* hit and was actively distributed throughout the republic.

The seventh chapter of the book. "The Phantom of 'Ukrainian Bourgeois Nationalism' and the Reality of Russian Great-Power Chauvinism as the Principal Obstacle to National Construction in the USSR," was especially relevant. In this chapter, I. Dziuba not only defended "Ukrainian bourgeois nationalism," a formula made

---

[36] Ivan Dziuba // Netsenzurnyi Stus [Uncensored Stus]. Part 2, 237.
[37] Ukrainska suspilno-politychna dumka v 20 stolitti. Dokumenty i materialy. Tom III [Ukranian socio-political thought in the 20th centure. Volume 3] / Compiled by Taras Hunchak i Roman Solchanyk. — Suchasnist [Modernity], 1983, 200.

"GIFTS OF THE LORD" 221

nasty by the official Soviet ideological machine, but also demonstrated the danger to the unity of the USSR posed by Russian chauvinism, brought to the level of state policy.

Ivan Dziuba believed that the main task of *Internatsionalizm chy rusyfikatsiia* was to explain to the Russian-speaking people of the republic that in the USSR "*conditions are created that force people to refuse to switch to Russian instead of Ukrainian ... that all this fits into a great strategy and political history.*"[38] As both Russian-speaking and Donbas-born, Dziuba, as few others, was alive to all the dangers of official, almost coercive Russification. That is why he made the arrests of Ukrainian patriots a trigger for a serious theoretical discussion.

The second task that Ivan Dziuba set for himself was to show "*the leadership that they are doing destructive work in general, destructive for themselves and for the ideas of communism and socialism.*"[39]

The author also addressed the Ukrainian patriotic community. Warning against the practice of confrontational and illegal forms of protest, caused by speeches of opposition-minded youth, especially in Western Ukraine, Dziuba formulated a theoretical action program for Ukrainian patriots under the existing conditions and convincingly argued that the priority of the Ukrainian intelligentsia was to revive Ukrainian culture and Ukraine as a whole.

He considered it a mistake to confront the authorities openly, proposing instead to achieve "*legally all that is promised to us by all constitutions, programs and declarations.*"[40]

The evident moderation of the text greatly contributed to the growth of nationally-minded youth, and it was only after this development, in mid-1972, that *Internatsionalizm* was labeled an "anti-Soviet" work and simple ownership of a copy could lead to repression (seven years after its writing!).

Influenced by the book, the traditional annual commemoration of Taras Shevchenko, which informally took place every May

---

[38] Ivan Dziuba // Netsenzurnyi Stus [Uncensored Stus], 251.
[39] The same.
[40] The same. — P.252.

22, became in 1967 a true demonstration of protest against the policy of "Russification."

At 10 p.m., a police *voronok* drew near the monument and an officer with a megaphone demanded that the gathering break up. People who had been peacefully singing songs with Shevchenko's lyrics not only ignored this demand but shouted "Shame! Shame!" in reply and blocked traffic on Vladimirska Street. Police *voronoks* immediately disappeared from the site, taking with them the five people who were closest to the cars. The rally, which had been about to end, swelled with a bang. More and more people joined the protesters, and when a young doctor, Mykola Plakhotniuk, offered to go to the CPU Central Committee building and demand that the detainees be released, about three hundred people went to defend justice. They were not deterred even by the fact that trucks had been used to block the road. There were attempts to instigate a clash and disperse people with water cannons.

At 2 a.m. the Minister of Public Order Protection Golovchenko went out to the people and promised to *"release the detainees by morning."* At dawn the next day, they were indeed released from the police station without explanation.[41]

This unfortunate defeat in the struggle against the increasingly organized cultural national movement forced the authorities to increase vigilance and gave new life to the supporters of the "tough" policy of suppressing the disobedient. Young cultural activists, who quickly joined the national movement, became more and more active. They were not deterred even by the danger of losing their job or being expelled from an institution of higher education.

The natural result of this confrontation was a letter from 139 public figures representing the fields of science, literature and art, addressed to the General Secretary of the CPSU Central Committee,

---

[41] See: Boris Zakharov. Narys istorii dysydentskoho rukhu v Ukraini (1956—1987) / Kharkivska pravozakhysna hrupa. [Essay on the History of the Dissident Movement in Ukraine (1956-1987) / Kharkiv Human Rights Group].—Kh.: Folio, 2003, P.92-93; Kasianov Heorhii. Nezghodni: ukrainska intelihentsiia v rusi oporu 1960—80-kh rokiv. [Dissenters: Ukrainian intelligentsia in resistance movement of 1960-1980.]—K.: Lybid, 1995, 71-72.

"GIFTS OF THE LORD" 223

L. I. Brezhnev, the Chairman of the USSR Council of Ministers, O. M. Kosygin, and the Chairman of the Presidium of the Supreme Soviet of the USSR, M. V. Pidgorny.[42] Representatives of the humanist and creative intelligentsia sounded the alarm about political repression, expressing concern that *"the political processes of recent years have become a way of suppressing dissidents, civic activity and the social criticism necessary for the society's health. They testify to the growing restoration of Stalinism, against which I. Gabay, Y. Kim and P. Yakir warn so strongly and courageously in their appeal to the public figures of science, culture and art of the USSR. In Ukraine, where violations of democracy are complemented and exacerbated by distortions of the national question, the symptoms of Stalinism are even stronger."*[43]

Sergei Parajanov was the first to sign this letter. Vasyl Stus also added his voice to the protest.

The letter caused found some resonance in the wider world. Viacheslav Chornovil was released in February 1969 "under amnesty."[44]

In April 1968, the collection of 150 signatures for the letter started, and included Stus'. It condemned the practice of "closed" trials against members of the creative intelligentsia of Kyiv, Ivano-Frankivsk and Lviv.[45]

The authorities' retaliation was not long in coming: the Ukrainian writer Oles Honchar was harassed for his novel, *Sobor* [Cathedral]. The campaign was headed by the Chairman of the KGB under the Council of Ministers of the USSR Yu. Andropov. In his letter to the CPSU's Central Committee, he described the novel

---

[42] See the complete text of the letter in Ukrainska suspilno-politychna dumka v 20 stolitti. Dokumenty i materialy. [Ukrainian socio-political thought in the 20th century. Documents and materials]. Volume III. – Suchasnist [Modernity', 1983, 238-241.
[43] Ibid., 239-240. The letter was sent in March 1968 and was published on October 11, 1968 was in the *Svoboda* [Freedom] newspaper.
[44] Ukrainska hromadska hrupa spryiannia vykonanniu Helsinskykh uhod. Tom 1: Osobystosti. [Ukrainian Public Group to Promote the Implementation of Helsinki Accords. Volume 1: Personalities]. – Kharkiv: Folio, 173.
[45] V.F.Verstiuk, O.M Dziuba, V.F Repryntsev. Ukraina vid naidavnishykh chasiv do sohodennia. Khronolohichnyi dovidnyk.[Ukraine from ancient times to the present. Chronological guide] – K.: Naukova dumka [Scientific thought], 1995, 568.

as "*a politically harmful work that promotes elements of nationalism and depicts Soviet reality in a distorting light.*"[46]

It was at this time that Vasyl Stus finished compiling the *Zymovi dereva* [Winter Trees] collection and on May 12, 1968, submitted it to the *Molod* [Youth][47] publishing house.

For some reason, this book by an unofficially banned difficult young littérateur was immediately included in the publishing plan and preparations for its publication began.

Unfortunately, the original version of the collection has not survived. Ivan Drach wrote a generally positive internal review and "*strongly recommended*"[48] the book for publication. However, after Vasyl Stus' letter to the Board of the Writers' Union of Ukraine regarding O. Poltoratsky's article, "Kym opikuiutsia deiaki humanisty" [Who is Protecting the Humanists], published in *Literaturna Ukraina* [Literary Ukraine], became public, the collection was removed from production and the manuscript was returned to the author.

Not wanting that his letter would be published in the newspaper of Ukrainian writers, V. Stus sent copies to the Secretary of the CPU's Central Committee, F. D. Ovcharenko, and to the editorial board of *Vsesvit* [Universe] magazine. This reckless, but emotionally understandable, step was provoked by the poet's indignation at Poltoratsky's pasquil, in which his comrades were maligned and the content of "List 139-ty" [The letter of 139] was perverted. Vasyl just could not help but react to this:

---

[46] Ibid.
[47] Vasyl Stus. Tvory. Volume 1: book1, 355.
[48] The typewritten copy of the internal "Review of the book manuscript of *Zymovi dereva* - poems by Vasyl Stus" written by Ivan Drach. Stored in the archives of the poet's family. In his diploma paper, "Ranni roky zhyttia Vasylia Stusa" [Early years of Vasyl Stus' life], which was later published in a book entitled *Zhyttia i tvorchist Vasylia Stusa* [Life and Work of Vasyl Stus] (1992), the author of this book, not then having the complete version of I. Drach's review, allowed himself to call it positive and superficial. Now that the full text of the review has been found in the archives of Vasyl Stus, I would like to apologize to the esteemed Ivan Drach for my disrespect due to the incomplete material. This internal review is an important source of information about the *Zymovi dereva* version of 1968.

"As is well-known, the 'black hundred' cult supporters have resumed their pogroms since the middle of 1965. Over the next year, dozens of people were convicted, including artists, scientists, engineers, teachers, students... [M]any scientists and qualified editors were dismissed; many students were expelled from institutions of higher education; many talent-filled books by M. Osadchy, M. Dalko, M. Kholodny, V. Kordun, M. Vorobiov, L. Kostenko could not be published; thousands of souls were injured. Many of these pogroms were mentioned in V. M. Chornovil's letter to the government ... Repressions continue even now. Most recently M. Kh. Kotsyubynska, the paleontologist H. Bachynsky, the physicist I. Zaslavska ... have been dismissed from their jobs, the artists A. Horska, L. Semykina, G. Sevruk ... have been expelled from the Artists' Union, one of the most gifted contemporary Ukrainian poets V. Holoborodko has been harassed and sent to do military service.

O. Poltoratsky, refuting the 'hostile slanders,' mentions only S. Karavansky and V. Chornovil.

My question is: Why did not Poltoratsky and Co. write their pamphlets when mass arrests were being conducted? Why did Poltoratsky arm himself with his talented pen only when the St. Bartholomew's nights of the past years were talked about in the West?

...It is well known, that in their letter, almost one hundred and fifty Kyiv residents stood for the constitutional rights and democratic freedoms of the Soviet people. Poltoratsky consciously bypasses this main component of the letter since it does not aid him in his 'destructive criticism.' The author of the article dwells only upon a few select facts, but even in this, the meticulous literary filibuster lies very incompetently.

The whole article is based on excursions into the distant past of Karavansky (and Poltoratsky is not embarrassed that this name is not even mentioned in the letter)...

Poltoratsky is also a talented liar when he 'exposes' V. M. Chornovil ...

...It is very painful to feel that Poltoratsky always has the right both to murder and to rehabilitate yesterday's victims. And there are a lot of people like him...

In the damned old times, people like Poltoratsky were challenged to a duel. Today there is no such threat to Poltoratsky... Besides, deliberate slanderers have always avoided an honest fight: cowardice is just another *name for baseness."*⁴⁹ Vasyl Stus concluded the letter expressing his greatest pains.

The poet began to implement the program principle of Ivan Dziuba, formulated in *Internatsionalizm chy rusyfikatsiia*, of constitutional forms of protest against injustice. The individual form of protest seemed safest as, in the Criminal Codes of the Ukrainian SSR and the USSR, articles assigned criminal liability only to the instigators of group letters. " *"Before his arrest, Viacheslav Chornovil reacted to every injustice with letters. Now, apparently, my time has come,"* Vasyl reasoned. *"At least someone has to defend justice."*

The *Zymovi dereva* collection removed from the press was mercilessly reframed by Vasyl. The book was remade to such an extent that its original version is unlikely ever to be restored. What did Ivan Drach like in that version of the book?

"When you re-read these poems for the second and third time, only then do they reveal their full force," writes the reviewer of the young poet's poems. *"They breathe with the condensed sharpness of time, which might sometimes be clumsily expressed, obscured somewhere between the lines, but this sharpness, precisely the inflexibility of Vasyl Stus' muse is a very important and symptomatic sign of his interesting talent. His poems are not easy to read. But mostly it is real poetry."*⁵⁰

The reviewer notes the "richness" of the Vasyl Stus' poetic world: *"rich in color, rich in moods, multi-level, unforced complexity,"* which *"finds its words and is expressed by those words. Here you cannot fix exact or inaccurate metaphors, here you catch the accuracy of feeling, the weight and significance of the word, its unlimited capabilities of worldview, its anthropological function."*⁵¹.

The formation of the new version of the *Zymovi dereva* manuscript was completed by the poet in December 1969. In late December or early January 1970, Vasyl Stus made several typewritten copies of the collection, one of which he submitted to the *Radianskyi*

---

49 Vasyl Stus. Tvory. Volume 4, 375-381.
50 Ivan Drach. Review of the book manuscript of *Zymovi dereva* - poems by Vasyl Stus."
51 Ibid.

pysmennyk [Soviet Writer] publishing house, and six others were sewed and bound by him.[52]

Unlike previous collections and even the *Zymovi dereva* manuscript submitted to", this version opened with an author's preface, "A Couple of Words to the Reader," which say more about the author and his collection than any reviewer could.

A COUPLE OF WORDS TO THE READER

My first poetry lessons were given to me by my mother. She knew many songs and could sing them very intimately. There were as many songs as old Zuiha, our compatriot, had. And they were the same. The greatest mark on my soul was left by my mother's lullaby "Oh, lyuli-lyuli, my baby." Shevchenko over the cradle – this is not forgotten and it is sung sadly: "You go, son, to Ukraine, cursing us" – still worries. It is something like a sad tombstone lament from "My Testament": "Oh bury me, then rise ye up and break your heavy chains and water with the tyrants' blood the freedom you have gained." These are the first signs of our spiritual anomaly, sorrow as a baby's first feeling in the world. There were also impressions from childhood, a good childhood.

Schooling was a failure. One is foreign and another is stupid. The sooner you forget school, the better. In the fourth grade, I rhymed something about a dog. It was in Russian. It was humorous. That effort vanished quickly and was reborn in high school when love came.

The institute years were difficult. The first poetic publicism was connected with history. I admired Rylsky and Verhaeren. The disembodied spirit wanted something else. And again it was love. Longing for the real (not Donetsk) Ukraine, I went to work as a teacher in the Kirovograd region, near Gaivoron. There I warmed my soul, freed myself from student asceticism. The army accelerated this process. I felt like a man. I almost did not write poems as I had shoulder straps. But I encountered Bazhan there. At the same period, in 1959, his first poems were published.

The post-army period was already a time of poetry. This was the era of Pasternak and an unquestioningly intense love for him. I got rid of it

---

[52] Vasyl Stus. *Zymovi dereva*. Authorized typewritten copy of the manuscript collection in *samvydav* format with a dedicatory inscription to G. P. Kochur. Stored in the Institute of Literature of the National Academy of Sciences of Ukraine, repository 170, archival unit 926.

only somewhere around 1965-1966. These days I love Goethe, Svidzinsky, Rilke the most. The Italians are wonderful (those whom I know). Particularly Ungaretti, and Quasimodo.

I also love the "thick" prose of Tolstoy, Hemingway, Stefanyk, Proust, Camus. Also, I am very much attracted by Faulkner.

Among the younger contemporaries, I appreciate V. Holoborodko the most. Then comes M. Vingranovsky. And, of course, L. Kyselyov. I hate the word "poetry." I do not consider myself a poet. I consider myself a person who writes poems.

And my idea is as follows: a poet must be a human being first and foremost, that is, full of love, overcoming the natural tendency towards hatred, he frees himself from it as from filth. A poet is a human being, above all. And a human being, above all, is charitable. If I lived better, I would not write poems but would work on the land.

I also despise politicians. And also I appreciate the ability to die honestly. This is more valuable than versification exercises!

One of my best friends is Skovoroda."[53]

The last name in the foreword is, so to speak, conceptual. It testifies to the author's conscious choice of tradition, in which the national is closely intertwined with the cosmopolitan, and aesthetics dominates over social significance and actuality. And although Skovoroda's tradition is less influential in Ukraine than Shevchenko's, it is recognized all over the world.[54]

The *Zymovi dereva* version of 1970 differed significantly from the original one: instead of six cycles, the new version of the book consisted of three sections, only the third of which had a title: "Early Poetry and Experiments." The collection included poems written during 1968-1969: "Otak zhyvu, yak mavpa sered mavp ..." [Here's how I live: like an ape among apes...], "Dazhd nam, Bozhe, dnes ..."

---

[53] Vasyl Stus. Tvory. Volume 1: book 1, 42. Despite the fact that some quotations from "Dvoie sliv ..." [A couple ...] were included, I consider it necessary to quote this text in full, so as not to destroy the kind of self-portrait presented by the writer, who tried to get the reader to imagine the author of *Zymovi dereva*.

[54] This thesis is, of course, contradictory and perhaps even provocative. However, it is in tune with Stus' task: to recreate the national cosmos in the international language of world culture.

[Give us, O Lord, this day our daily bread], "Vchysia chekaty, druzhe ..." [Learn to wait, my friend], "Prysmerkovi sutinky opaly ..." [Dusky twilight has fallen], and others.

The book made its way to the West in a rather specific way.

Vasyl Stus' sending the manuscript to the *Radianskyi pysmennyk* [Soviet Writer] publishing house did not mean that he was counting on its publication. Out of desperation to see the book published, the poet made six self-published copies. He presented one of them to Leonid Seleznenko.

At that time, Lionia was looking after a student from Czechoslovakia, Hanna Kotsurova, who was one of the first to go to the USSR after the suppression of the Prague Spring of 1968. He introduced the young woman to Ukrainian culture, which was already clearly in opposition to the regime, and Hanna told him about the events in Czechoslovakia after the Soviet troops' military intervention.

Among the books Seleznenko gave her to read, including self-published ones, was *Zymovi dereva*.

"Lenya, this is a wonderful author, I will keep the collection for a few days," Hanna said.

Seleznenko did not object.

A few days later, Kotsurova went to Czechoslovakia for a week and took Stus' poems with her. In Prague, she showed the work of the unknown Ukrainian poet to Bohdan Chapryna and Bohdan Levytsky.

"Listen, Hanna, there is an opportunity to publish this collection. Do you think the author would mind?"

"Why would he mind?" The woman was surprised by the question.

A few months later *Zymovi dereva* was published in the UK.[55]

On her return to Kyiv, Anna told Seleznenko that she had left the book in Prague. Lenia was not thrilled, although he agreed that

---

[55] The statements by Ye. Sverstyuk support Britain as the place of publication. The Brussels-based *Literatura i mystetstvo* [Literature and Art] publishing house, mentioned in the original data, seems to be nothing more than a conspiracy to associate the author's name with well-known Western OUN publishing houses.

Kotsurova's decision was logical: the collection would not be published in the country.

The book, published abroad, came into the author's hands only in the autumn of 1970. It was his first printed collection. It came as a pleasant surprise. If in 1969 he still had some hesitations about sending the book abroad, in 1970 there was no doubt that his poems would not be published in Ukraine.

Finally, he got his book!

Vasyl was pleasantly surprised by the foreword by Ariadna Shum, whom he did not know, which noted the main features of poetic creativity, gently helping the reader to perceive the complex poetic constructions.

The critic remarked the extremely wide range of Stus' lyric, which *"goes from attempts at the Italian sonnet, through folk-song stanza-built constructions to the most daring free verse."* However, according to Shum, *"the most interesting aspect of Stus' work is not its instrumentation, rhythm or rhyme but the figurativeness of his phrasing, which, connected to a very peculiar worldview, gives us the style of an original imagist poet with some marks of surreal composition."*[56]

Realizing the crisis of the traditional poetic word, which for too long had been overloaded with social, populist, moral, class and other functions, the Stus the *Zymovi dereva* period waded into the deep stream of imaginative searches for a "new motivation" or a "new reality" of the word.

Zymovi dereva was an undeniable success for the young author. This was understood even in *Radianskyi pysmennyk*, where the instruction to "kill" the book had already been given. The publishing house's management decided to do so at the hands of internal reviewer Yevhen Adelheim, who was rumored in Ukrainian-speaking circles to "stifle" anything national. In the late summer of 1970, he submitted the following review to the publishing house:

"We are too late in releasing young poets into the world. This leads to their 'getting past their prime,' to forced self-isolation, to a loss of the 'running start' needed to gain the desired flight speed.

---

[56] Ariadna Shum, Vstupna stattia [Opening chapter] // Vasyl Stus. *Zymovi dereva*, 1.

*Something similar happened to Stus, a man gifted with a worldview that was **too** independent to remain painlessly within the framework of the established norms. Is there a need to talk about the fear of this **too**? The fear of a too powerful expression of personality, a too great dissimilarity from others, a too strong desire to **remain true to oneself** under any circumstances?*

I must admit that it is these features that attract me the most in Stus' work because they ultimately make up the 'quality of being specific,' which is a true feature of poetry.

Stus is a poet of dramatic feelings, he lives in a world of complex or – more precisely – incredibly complicated feelings and, in addressing them, does not want to 'smooth out' anything, as less sincere or less gifted writers do.

*Personally, not accepting many of the poet's conceptions, I just want to say that his **absolute openness of self-expression** can form a reliable ground for the same open polemic and a probable condition for overcoming gloomy moods, which are already beginning to corrode the personality ...*

There is a cross-cutting theme coming through the Zymovi dereva collection – that of the Human being and of Man and Humanity, along with its narrower aspect – – 'I' and the people around me. The poet is often lost in the complexity of the question and, struggling with its contradictions, seeks a way out where it cannot be found – in proud 'Byronic' loneliness ... Obviously, Stus himself feels the subjectivity of his mood and tries to overcome it to some extent ...

*Whatever Stus writes about, he returns to the core of his thoughts – the human being. The poet's 'I,' this or that intimate experience is ultimately reduced in the collection to broader reflections on the Human being **in general**, on the essence of his existence before the Universe, Death, Eternity or on the moral categories, taken in their greatest dimension, **as Absolutes**.*

Without objecting in principle to these dimensions, at the same time I must say that the poet is the least prepared for them. On such an infinitely large scale, the specificity of lyrical characteristics in the collection is too often lost and, most importantly, so is the very opportunity to view a person within the time of history, the stages of social progress...

It seems to me that both the poet's pessimism ('In thirty years you were born only to understand: you are dead in a dead world') as well as his despair and painful sense of defenselessness and loneliness arise from a very abstract concept of the Human being torn from time and examined within the framework of the immovable Absolute, to which the young poet so aspires with his undisciplined imagination, romantic excess and inability to think dialectically.

When Stus writes:
A man is a weather vane. Yes. A man – weather vane,
Dependent on the wind, not on himself ...
then I see in this statement ... a tragic inability to find a synthesis of the historical determination of human behavior and freedom of choice and self-chosen solution...

The questions that the poet always raises are not meaningless: 'Who are you? And what are you? And where are you?' They are caused by the desire to understand – what does a human being **begin with** *and where is the limit beyond which he* **loses** *his personality, independence and the very opportunity to make a choice."*[57]

Yevhen Adelheim, who was one of the most attentive readers of *Zymovi dereva*, points out that Stus' metaphor often grows out of the ugly and horrible aesthetics of the present time. And since the author of the book is *'undoubtedly gifted with the skill of unexpectedly drawing together distant associations, a very original metaphor is born."*[58]

The parallels that the reviewer finds between the works of Vasyl Stus and Mykola Bazhan's *Hetto v Umani, Trylohiia prystrasti, Sliptsi*[59] [Ghetto in Uman, Trilogy of Passion, Blind People] are also interesting. These echoes are especially noticeable when it comes to the "vertical" of time – the connection of the present time with the ancient Slavic ground, its language, its type of thinking, its philosophy.

"Pagan Kyiv," – which, due to historical progress, was filled with hotels, suburban trains, streetcars, Paton Bridge and "clumsy Khreschatyk houses of" ("To Millennium Kyiv") – asthmatically suffocates in the industrial decor of the new time. This decor se-

---

[57] Yevhen Adelheim. Review for the "Zymovi dereva" collection of poems by Vasyl Stus. Authorized type print. Stored in the archives of the poet's family, 1-4.
[58] Ibid., 5.
[59] Ibid.

curely hides pagan customs, the natural and living spoken language, ancient traditions; and no matter how much you want to swear "*may God damn you,*"[60] you must be silent, because a flock of pioneers running down the street, cleansed of your ancient currents, is directing its steps to your future, Kyiv.

So, Kyiv was silent, thinking that almost everything was lost and nothing could be returned. At least in the metaphysical sense. As Ye. Adelheim noted it did not work out with the dialectics that Stus employed.

The reviewer finishes his review by concluding that it is not only "**possible**" but "**necessary**" to publish the collection.[61]

Nobody expected that. Vasyl Stus, impressed by the attention paid to him by Adelheim, wrote a letter to him on August 25, 1970:

"Dear Yevhen Georgievich!

First of all, I would like to thank you very much. Not so much for a positive review, as it is called, but for that and, perhaps, only because your review is a very human response to the work of an author whose many opinions you do not share. In the author of the Zymovi dereva review, I recognized a nice man. Thank you for this: humanity is the greatest and hence rarest merit of a modern artist.

I even wanted to make a self-review for you.

In my opinion, pessimism does not differ much from optimism. Like all antinomies, Siamese twins include: good and evil, night and day, etc.

My pessimism comes from understanding the futility of human life and its impossibility at the same time. The only meaning is contained in the proverb: people should be mourned at their birth, not at their death.

But there are wise ideas: it is preordained, it was destined; given by God and so on. This reasoning seems to me the fairest. It means no complaints about life, they are even absurd.

My optimism-pessimism: It is not me who lives, it is lived by me. Nature is living through me, so I have to live – I have to, at the level of the ability of my existence.

---

[60] Vasyl Stus. Tvory. Volume 1: book 1, 105.
[61] Yevhen Adelheim. Review of the *Zymovi dereva* collection of poems by Vasyl Stus., 8.

A person respects life even when it is difficult or unbearably difficult for him. But the candle of individual human existence, lit by nature, the earth, God, etc., should burn as long it is given.

When it seems to you that it is difficult for me, it is because it is difficult for the living being – in the dead world of poisonous social integrations. It is difficult because survival is taken for a full existence, and the attempt at flourishing is perceived as antisocial.

And one more thing: my appeals are global, not some narrow-term, regime ones, etc....

Yours sincerely

Vasil STUS"[62]

Although the trials around *Zymovi dereva* were the most painful for Vasyl Stus at the turn of the 1970s, they were not the only ones that indicated a clearly directed movement towards the "state" doors, which were about to open for the "young" intellectuals forced out of official literary life.

Vasyl asked his wife rhetorically: *"Why don't they summon me? Almost all my acquaintances have already had interviews with representatives of the KGB, but I am not touched ..."*

Valia answered: *"Bite your tongue. Thank God that they do not touch you."* -. Somehow she immediately perceived that a confrontation between her husband and the state apparatus of coercion was to be expected.

Vasyl was growing more and more nervous. He wrote letters to various institutions, protesting against the authorities' arbitrary actions, which resolutely pushed the opposition either to Moscow, in the case of Les Tanyuk, or to the margins, with Gorska, Svitlychna, Goloborodko, Antonenko-Davydovych and Vasyl Stus himself. It threw the most disobedient, without any hesitation, behind bars. Some were able to "serve their sentence."

At the end of the turbulent summer of 1970, having served five years in the Mordovian camp №385,[63] the artist Panas Zalivakha

---

[62] Vasyl Stus. Tvory. Volume 6: book 2, 66.
[63] Shevchenkivski laureaty. 1962 – 2001. Entsyklopedychnyi dovidnyk / Vstupne slovo I.M.Dziuby. Avtor-upor. M.H.Labinskyi. [Laureates of Shevchenko prize. 1962-2001. Encyclopedic reference book./ Opening remarks by I.V.Dziuba. Author-compiler M.G.Labynsky]. – K.: Krynytsia [Well], 2001, 178-179.

returned to Ukraine. The only crime of this talented person born in Slobozhansky region was his love of painting and Ukraine. Besides these qualities, he had a deep sense of human worth, which would not allow him to sink to repentance, remorse or the denunciation of friends.

He served five years for that.

When Zalivakha's *zek* hairstyle appeared on the platform of Kyiv railway station, its owner was quite surprised. An unforgettable evening worthy of a true hero was organized for him by Ivan Svitlychny and Alla Horska. After all, Panas was a hero who withstood the pressure of unjust imprisonment without whining or crying.

He returned to Ukraine via Moscow, where he was given a warm reception by the Tanyuks, who *"gave him good coffee, put on good shoes on his feet and sent him to Kyiv! And in Kyiv, he was given a gala dinner at Natalka[64] surrounded by high-quality company."*[65]

The company was really remarkable. On one side of the hall was the circle of Svitlychny-Stus-Horska, on the other was their *toptuny*[66] and KGB agents in civilian clothes.

But the latter got little attention. The party were drinking wine and *horilka*. They were talking. They were singing and dancing almost until dawn, because the most important — moral — victory was won by one of them: he was not broken.

And although Panas returned to Ukraine with almost no hope of gaining even a foothold in a provincial town, communication with friends restored his faith: he would find a place in Ukraine.

In the KGB, they went crazy:

"It goes beyond all boundaries. They meet zeks like heroes."

---

[64] Natalka restaurant is located on the Kyiv-Boryspil highway. Its walls were decorated with frescoes by Alla Horska.
[65] Opanas Zalyvakha. Nikhto ne proide za tebe tvoho shliakhu // Dobrookyi. Spohady pro Ivana Svitlychnoho. [No one will walk your path for you // Dobrooky. Memoires about Ivan Svitlychny], 203.
[66] *Toptuny* [field surveillance] or *shpyky* [company spotters] belonged to the pre-revolutionary period, used of KGB officers who spied on the leaders of the sixtiers for a long time, looking for some compromising material.

After that night, the pressure increased. Vasyl, who finally really got to know Panas, asked him about the *zek*'s daily life. Panas said that he dreamed of only one thing: to paint.

"Don't seek to get there, Vasyl, there is no possibility for actualization there. It only puts pressure on you."

Stus looked at Zalivakha with genuine admiration: how much suffering had he experienced, a person cut off from his métier, but still he did not give up, did not break.

Panas Zalivakha's life gradually improved. He even managed to settle down in Ivano-Frankivsk.

Around this time, Alla Horska died near Kyiv under mysterious circumstances. Late in the evening of November 28 of the frightening year 1970, her mutilated body was found in the cellar of her father-in-law's house in Fastiv by Nadiya Svitlychna, who went there as if expecting something evil. Before her arrival Horska's father-in-law died as well. He had been pushed in front of a suburban train. The second death "helped" investigators to "close" the case, indecently hinting that the father-in-law may have been responsible.

Fearing that Alla Horska's funeral would turn into a protest rally, the KGB had conversations with most of the deceased's friends: do not go to the cemetery if you do not want to lose your job or face new problems.

They did not talk to Stus. Until then, the role of this emotional young man in the cultural movement of the sixtiers, which the authorities believed to be controlled by someone, remained a complete mystery to them. He was perhaps the keenest, but spoke only on his own behalf, not taking sheltering behind the authorities or the support of friends. He was probably either Don Quixote or a madman **who**, besides, reads completely incomprehensible things: "1. Berdyaev, *Filosofiya svobodyi.[Freedom Philosophy]* 2. *Voprosyi literaturyi [Literary Issues]* – Sartr, N 11.69. 3. *"Iskusstvo i elita". [Art and* *the Elite]* 4. Bogomolov. 5. Shvarts *"Ekzistentsializm v evropeyskoy literature"* [Existentialism in European Literature][67].

In a dark mood, like a strained nerve, Vasyl went to the cemetery. He knew about the preventive "conversations," the "mysterious" deaths, the "ugly" hints ...

Vasyl carried a portrait of Alla Horska on his way to the grave. It was so bitter, so unfair, so unbearable to feel the loss of a loved one.

He hardly listened to the speakers, and when he had the opportunity to say a word, he began:

Today – you. And tomorrow – I,
and God will let us get to the pit of hell,
where for our eternal pain – ran away,
the earth frightened to death.
For we are very few. We are a pinch
for prayers and hopes,
we were all destined to early death,
for we are geared to a late goal.[68]

In the dead silence over the grave, Vasyl choked as he said that it was a murder, a deliberate murder and the best of them was viciously struck from their ranks ...

After this loss, Stus was not able to *"return to himself"*[69] for a long time.

The last entries in Stus' diary date from the 1970s to the beginning of 1971.

"30.11.1970. It would be worthwhile to write a book about today's poetry. So poets are timeless or poets are without modernity. Show the complexity of loss – the earth, life, human form. Void dreams. Blind seers. Loss of the vertical and horizontal existential line. Getting from here – into madness, anarchy, misanthropy, etc.

---

[67] Yevhen Sverstyuk's "Borhova zapyska" [Debt Note] referring the books he took from Vasyl Stus together with "Zymovi dereva". See: Yevhen Sverstiuk. Bazyleos // Ne vidliubyv svoiu tryvohu ranniu ... [I did not stop loving my early fear], 194.
[68] Vasyl Stus. Tvory. Volume 1: book 1, 320-321.
[69] Vasyl Stus. Tvory. Volume 6: book 2, 70.

02.12.1970 I read Anna Akhmatova[70] yesterday. I was surprised by her high, lofty suffering, calmness. She perceives suffering as the Lord's punishment and rises above it, remaining an aristocrat, a person devoted to beauty. Any of our writers would burst into screams of "save us," cursing and, in the worst cases, would be saved through their own ethical death and go into "service."

He thought that M. Rylsky, one of our greatest aristocrats after 1930 was lying about the outdoors and then he paid for his well-being with his conscience and self-respect. Others, like I. Drach, started with a fee for being released. These are our indulgences, the pre-human period of Ukraine.

Infantilism, the existence of pre-experience is a normal human existence, it is a world without the rust of social integration. Yes, I need to buy something, I take off one shoe (it costs 4 krbs) and pay. It is like a child's position in a world of gangsters: something is moving with a complete loss of causality.

08.12.1970. There is a great need to return the communicability of artists, being single diligently in today's world. How can an artist, a painter, for example, not be able to bring his works to the people? Painters do not see their canvases with wider eyes, musicians do not hear their works, writers do not read theirs. This is lifelong loneliness...

29.12.1970. It is possible to upgrade a variant of the Veselyi Tsvyntar [The Merry Cemetery] by enriching it with surreal situations. It is like an old retired collective farmer grazing a black chicken tied to his leg in an empty yard. These are elements of a refined existence – say, rags hanging on a pole – chickens, cars, quarrelling neighbors, etc. That is the first. Secondly, the theme of Ukraine is a subject for great comprehension, which, in the case of a serious undertaking, can take a lifetime to reach the goal. It will take many years. As a title for the collection, Neolith [The Neolithic] could be used. (He carved a mammoth's outline on a rock and then went to the grocery store to buy oranges.)

21.01.[19]71. Yesterday I was told by p.O.[71] : On July 19, 1941, I.St.'s[72] mother Lyudmyla Mykhailivna Starytska-Cherniakhivska, the

---

[70] The reference is to her "Rekviiem," which was kept by the poet as a self-published collection.
[71] O.: I could not determine who was meant.
[72] I.St. – I. Starytska-Cherniakhivska, the daughter of the writer L. M. Starytska-Cherniakhivska.

Academician Krymsky and the gynecologist Vylegzhanyn were taken to the East in a truck laden with barrels. Mother died on the way, the Academician Krymsky died in prison in Aktubinsk or Akmolinsk[73] on January 22 (?), 1942. On his birthday on January 22, 1941, when he was awarded the Order of the Red Banner of Labor, the Academician Krymsky greeted Jews, Turks and other representatives in their languages. On the evening of January 19, 1971, A. O. Ishchuk spoke about his acquaintance with Krymsky, when he so brilliantly opposed Masalsky's doctoral dissertation 'The Language and Style of Shevchenko.' He named himself Ahatanhel Yukhymovych.

25.03.1971. I recently read an interesting article by the former rector of the University of Edinburgh, Malcolm Muggeridge, "The Great Liberal Death Wish." This exactly accords with my frequent thoughts. And if the mood takes me a lot of ambiguities became clear: education gives nothing to many people. It gives, but only to a few people, it is a feature of education, which is unable to influence world development. So, there is one more narrow unresolved question: what does education give to these singletons? Maybe nothing? Maybe they create a carousel for other singletons? Is a carousel independent of the world? One more important thing: the planet can no longer withstand excessive mental evolution. Is a mind the latest plague, pestilence, the most successful way to bring about the self-destruction of humanity, its immanent antipode and enemy?

*19.03.1971. Myth-making psychology is brought about by the growing distance between a human being and the world because a human being loses the very tangible sense of the world and therefore any given life situation is unexplained in many of the most important relationships. That is why it is time not to know, but to feel what is known, to determine its relation to existence, the sensory content of man. And maybe fill with fear. It will all depend on the extent of our fear – either it will stimulate a return to "square one," or it will propel us to where there is at least the certainty of the **usual unknown** achievements of civilization.*

In myth-making psychology, there is something close to primitive parallelism, the nature of allegory, symbolism. Myth is a search, fear and feverish self-awareness in a critical situation.

---

[73] The academician Krymsky died (more precisely, he perished) on January 25, 1942 in a hospital for prisoners in the Kazakh city of Kustanay. H was buried in a mass grave with other prisoners. See M. Kutynskyi. Nekropol Ukrainy [Necropolis of Ukraine] // Dnipro. - 1996. Part 10, 142–143.

On a business trip, visited Yevhen Kontsevich.[74] He frightened me with his smile and his rootless optimism; pure fleshless spirituality, pure spirit of the eyes. What is his life? Memories, reading, a window, a prison that is not felt as such and it is good that it is not felt, because otherwise — you would climb the wall. One of his greatest pleasures is talking about pigeons, which are methodically stolen from him. He knows how to talk about them — and feels the sky, space, freedom from them.

31.03.1971. I remembered Malory's book and again the same opinion about the book. The spirit of Ukraine is a kind of article about folklore — our songs, perhaps narrower — Cossack or just lyrical, where the "eternal theme" is better expressed, like looking into the sky and Skovoroda and Shevchenko and Stefanyk, and Lesia or Saints Cyril and Methodius or Drahomanov and Tychyna, and Svidzinsky. It would be to my liking, and, moreover, it would be possible to reveal the essence of the thing with the objectless essence.

01.07.1971. Sometime recently I was at B.A.'s.[75] He asked about the orgnabir [organizational recruitment] in 1929.[76] I answered that the only important thing was that S. O. Efremov wrote a personal diary, which was ... hidden by his nephew Pavlushkov. Pavlushkov had an insidious beloved, who got to know about the secret and during a search revealed its whereabouts. It was as if S. O. Efremov was given a choice: either we draw blood, or just like that — you will pass from the picture because of the forgery,

---

[74] Yevhen Kontsevych was a Ukrainian prose writer and translator, author of the collections of short stories, *Dvi krynytsi* [Two Wells] and *Iduchy vulytseiu* [Walking Down the Street]. Starting in 1952 he was bedridden with a serious illness. He was close to the circle of the sixtiers, who often visited him at his parents' house in Zhytomyr.

[75] B.A.: Boris Dmytrovych Antonenko-Davydovych.

[76] The *orgnabir* of 1929: the political arrests of 1929-1930, as a result of which 45 representatives of the older generation of the Ukrainian intelligentsia were put on trial, including two academicians, S. Efremov and M. Slabchenko. Their trial, called "the trial of the case of The Union for the Liberation of Ukraine" (ULU) lasted from March 9 to April 19, 1930 in Kharkiv. The younger generation of the Ukrainian humanist elite did not publicly support the elders. But the phrase "music by GPU, opera [agents] ULU" became popular. From 1937 to 1939, 13 of the 45 convicts, on the judgment of various local troikas [three officials who issued sentences] were shot at their places of detention. See, in particular, *Dovidnyk z istorii Ukrainy* [Reference Book on Ukrainian history]. - K .: Heneza, 2002, 813-814.

with the guarantee of a more merciful end. And he seemed to agree. He, S. O. Efremov, was a courageous man and agreed..."⁷⁷

The intelligentsia again became too inconvenient for the authorities, and Alla Horska's death only confirmed this belief.

But was there an urgent need to go camping? Maybe Les Tanyuk was really right. He decided to spend these "winters" in Moscow, where it was a little easier to breathe, and the superhuman state's pressure on a living human soul was not so strong.

Vasyl, who had been thinking for a long time about the possibility of entering the Moscow High Courses for Scriptwriters, submitted the *Ozhidanie*⁷⁸ [Expectation] script to the creative competition.

After a while, an invitation to the competition came from Moscow, and a few days later, a refusal ... Later, mostly from whispers, he learned that his candidature was opposed by the Central Committee of the Communist Party of Ukraine.

The absurdity was at its very worst.

The absurdity of existence, when someone's evil pushes you out of the sphere of culture into the political arena, forcing you into open confrontation — because how else can you preserve dignity? This wass transformed into the sarcastic lines of poems that marked a new stage in Vasily Stus' work.

A few months after A. Horska's death, the poet finished compiling the experimental collection *Veselyi Tsvyntar* [The Merry Cemetery]. This book is easier to understand when you know that the impetus for its creation was the death of Horska, and that it was written during the show trial of Valentin Moroz, the author of *Reportazhu z zapovidnyka imeni Berii* [Report from the Beria Reserve], and during the production of the "Ukrainskyi visnyk" [Ukrainian Herald] *samvydav*, headed by the just-released Viacheslav Chornovil.

---

[77] Diary notes of Vasyl Stus. Deposited in the Institute of Literature of the National Academy of Sciences of Ukraine, fund 170, dep.un.2102, sheet 2, 4-7.
[78] Vasyl Stus. Tvory. Volume 4, 126-139.

Vasyl Stus laid out his political views in letters to the government and the Communist Party leaders, hoping not so much to influence the irreversible process of the new Stalinization, but out of an inability to remain silent. In "To the Central Committee of the Communist Party; to the KGB at the Council of Ministers of the USSR," he wrote:

"Now it is clear to everyone that we are living on the eve of some significant changes. This is discussed in samvydav *texts, speeches at plenums of the Central Committee, in the conversations of passengers and at private family meetings.*

The last decade has been a period of almost systematic deterioration of material and spiritual living conditions. The general devaluation of values is proceeding — starting from the ruble to many economic, political, ethical and aesthetic concepts.

I am sure that today there are many aesthetic problems that to be solved and that this is almost equally felt by A. Solzhenitsyn and Yu. Andropov, V. Nikitchenko and V. Moroz, V. Kozachenko and I. Dziuba, I. Svitlychny and M. Shamota.

The problem of being able to have a healthy dialogue is growing. A referendum is needed on many issues. Unfortunately, healthy discussion ... is forbidden. Certainly, discussion is taking place, but under abnormal conditions — either at closed Party meetings or in samvydav literature. And the abnormality of conditions prevents finding the truth, leads to the fact that even the truth that is found remains abnormal: existing only for individuals, being "secret," it meets a natural resistance from the public ...

The lack of the dialogue necessary creates excellent ground for exaggerating disagreements and differences. Each of the participants in the silent discussion is perceived as if through a magnifying glass. A person who has a different position is perceived by his partner as ... an enemy!

It is terribly painful and embarrassing to think about the fate of Valentin Moroz, who was arrested two months ago for writing several publicistic articles. This is exactly an example of a person being refused existence. Because what else does it mean to forbid a person to think and express his thoughts?

...I beseech you to do everything possible so that the possible trial of Valentin Moroz does not become a new shame for all of us."[79]

Certainly, Vasyl Stus was not "naive" and was well aware that even this balanced letter could be interpreted as "anti-Soviet agitation and propaganda," but he could not remain silent and watch the world falling into the abyss.

The surrealism in *Veselyi Tsvyntar* creates a kind of dominant background, here and there revealing itself as surreal transformations, in which the world's madness reaches its apogee. The everyday dull reality of pathologies, the dementia of the daily existence of people-functions that long ago came to terms with the world of false mirrors, mirrors that have finally deformed not only human souls but life itself—this is the humus out of which Stus' new book grows. The world of this book is completely sky-free, sun-free, human-free ...

I followed the coffin of a friend and thought:
Some have all the luck:
Lifted his legs and had no problems;
For the last time shone with the white thighs of the deceased,
and let the world turn upside down.
But when we came to the cemetery,
saw so many cars, vans, catafalques —
far from approaching,
we could not even poke head.
There was a huge queue for pits.
Everyone tried to seize a plot of land
(you can get in hand 1.5 x 2 meters).
Our turn was eight hundred and sixty-three.
How could we wait for it,
when so many villains appeared d —
that is one disabled in the first group,
that has a right, that holds a baby in her arms.
And that simply — drank to the point of having his eyeballs float from the very morning
and wends his way to get in anywhere,

---

[79] Ibid., 404. Also published in the *samvydav* "Ukrainskyi visnyk," 1970, 3.

it doesn't matter whether to get cabbage or death.
We had to return home with nothing ...
And this is where she is approaching us
An old woman with two baskets
(sells vegetables in the cemetery)
Do you need a pit? She asks
I can let you have my own
For one hundred and fifty krb.
It can be found cheaper,
but it is only called a pit,
and mine is as soft as a feather-bed...[80]

Not having the slightest hope for the publication of *Vesely Tsvyntar*, the poet freely experiments with form, shifts and mixes styles, accumulates images and explodes with lyric surrealism (*"Liudyna fliuher ...," "Vertannia"*) [Man is a weather vane ..., Returning).

Twelve copies of the collection,[81] which, according to Stus' own confession, made to Vasyl Zakharchenko, the poet was not very pleased with — *"it is not what it was supposed to be,"*[82] — as it were fixed malnourished modernity's free soaring above the horizon where the deformed lines of destinies become illustrations of the undiscovered realizations of the very meaning of human life.

The book was also a free experiment with verse form: the traditional stanza of *"Na Lysii hori ..."* [On Bald Mountain ...] is adjacent to the unrhymed poetic kind of a play *"Tsia piesa pochalasia vzhe davno ..."* [This play started a long time ago ...] and the completely avant-garde *"Vperiodrozghornutohobudivny ..."* [In the period of launching a constr ...].

---

[80] Vasyl Stus. Tvory. Volume 1: book 1, 162-163.
[81] The only copy of *Veselyi Tsvyntar* not confiscated by the KGB, or burned by frightened owners during the 1972 arrests, was kept by Heinrich Dvorko. The first publication was based on this version: Vasyl Stus, *Vesely Tsvyntar* [The Merry Cemetery]: Poezii [Poetry]. - Warsaw: Publishing agency of Union of Ukrainians in Poland, 1990, 109.
[82] The lesset to Vasyl Zakharchenko of 16.01.1971 // The same. Volume 6: book 2, 69.

However, formal searches were secondary. The paramount task was to recreate the spirit of the time. This implies that the narratives of individual poems, weighed down by the accumulation of surreal situations, reveale to the maximum the loneliness, helplessness and existential absurdity of a person long deprived of "intimate" space, his own thoughts, and at least a little hope for the best ("*Vertep,*" "*Os vam sontse ...,*" "*Ia yshov za trunoiu tovarysha ...,*" and others [Nativity Scene, Here's the sun ..., I followed the coffin of a friend ...]. Tragedy becomes absurdity.

And that absurdity disappears only in the poems dedicated to bright figures who laid down their lives for the right to be themselves—"*Yarii dushe, yarii, a ne rydai ...*" and "*Kolesa hlukho stukotiat ...*" [Burn bright, my soul, burn bright and do not weep ... and The Wheels are thumping ...], to the memory of A. Hurska and M. Zerova:

> The wheels are thumping,
> like a wave against a ferry,
> meet, comrade Charon,
> with evil, and with good.
> The wheels are beating, the wheels are beating
> Beating a path somewhere,
> Already. They cannot be back home
> Cannot be back home.
> The wheels are thumping, the wheels are thumping
> they are beating a path, wheels pounding
> in Christ, in the leader, in all the gods
> and in the mother and the name of the devil.
> Moscow, Bear Mountain, Kem
> and Popov Island—the way
> behind bars, behind guards,
> swollen on the tears.
> And again Vyatka, Kotlas, Ust-
> Wim. Then to Chibyu,
> of Soviet-socialist-concentration-camps union,
> forgotten by God,
> And by the devil too.

> Now another god rules here:
> Marxist, racist and cannibal —
> one in three.
> Moscow — Chibyu, Moscow — Chibyu,
> Pechora concentruck [concentration camp]
> Creates a new time
> on blood and bones.[83]

Thus, memory in the context of *Vesely Tsvyntar* poses a real challenge to the authorities: only the past retains its purity, and it is a tradition in which the poet seeks authenticity. From here sprout the philosophical lyrics of *"Palimpsesty,"* which could occasionally be glimpsed in *Zymovi dereva*.

However, the time of *Vesely Tsvyntar* is not the best for thinking about the future:

> *I am looking into tomorrow — there is darkness and black*
> *darkness. And black darkness. And black darkness.*
> *Only black water. And the black dense forest.*
> *But there is not your Svyatoshin here.*
> *No sister, no mother, no father.*
> *No wife. Son, let me hear from you.*
> *Numb friends. Black causeway*
> *in the dark. The dark — a dime a dozen.*
> *Only trembling, like faith in disbelief,*
> *Is penny candle on the table*
> *and around the apartment,*
> *there are your griefs rushing up and down.*
> *Rustling and whispers and pains –*
> *Are you recollections days*
> *splashed by the oars of the trireme,*
> *burning in St. Anthony's fire.*
> *All life is like looking back*
> *in the last century. Over the shoulder.*
> *No fear, no pain, no hesitation*
> *before death. And God says:*

---

[83] Vasyl Stus. Tvory. Volume 1: book 1, 166-167.

*find the ancient masonry by touch,
go and rest in it,
in a forgotten century. A warm memory
will be of use on the Day of Judgment.
June 2, 1970*[84]

This is already close to the resilient style of the apocrypha-like "Palimpsests," in which there is an awareness of the distorted forms of a new Ukrainian patriotism, formed under conditions of total anti-Ukrainian terror, as well as of a man of the Universe, who is restrained from cosmopolitanism only by the deep recognition of the fact that *"it is impossible... for the Ukrainian to be a man without being a patriot."*[85]

"Coercible patriotism" — this newest cross of the Ukrainian, Irish or any other patriot belonging to an enslaved people provokes Vasyl Stus to realize the loss of the national not as something specifically his own, but as an irreversible result of the crown of the universal tree. Because when it lacks the twig of your kin, it is forever. And as a man belonging to humanity, as Vasyl understood himself, he had to stand guard over the national element and the national word, and live as if he were the last defender of the native language. In this — and perhaps only in this — there is a great similarity between Taras Shevchenko and Vasyl Stus.

Psychologically, Vasyl already felt that the prison gate had opened before him, but Destiny gave him a few more holidays.

In July 1971, Vasyl, Valia and their son went to the headwaters of the Pripyat River for a few days, where a large group of like-minded people gathered.

The leader was Heinrich Dvorko.

Mykhailyna Kotsyubynska dedicated a series of songs to his wife, Engelsyna Ponomariova: "Enhelsyno, vidchyny-no ..." [Engelsina, open up ...], which was a recasting of the shameful "Catherine ...".

---

[84] The same. 196, 410.
[85] Ivan Dziuba. Svicha u kamianii pitmi // Vasyl Stus. Palimpsest: Vybrane. [The Candle in the Stone Darkness // Vasyl Stus. Palimpsest. Selected works]. — K." Fact, 2003, 19.

There was a host of children—young devotees of the Pripyat element, who performed a "big blorp" with a smiling Svitlychny and studied a map of the starry sky with Viktor Ivanysenko.

The adults used to go to the banks of the flooded Pripyat at least for a while to relieve the incredible psychological pressure of Kyiv.

The Stus couple arrived there on the eve of the biggest holiday—the birthday of the Leader's Wife.[86] They thought they would go there for a long time, but it turned out to be only for a few days. An untreated tooth tortured him so much that even the pain-resistant Vasyl was forced to return to Kyiv after a few days.

However, he left the company the finished "Fenomen doby" [A Phenomenon of Our Time] and the memory of himself as Neptune: when the sun had just started setting, an orchestra comprised of jugs, metal bowls, all sorts of spoons and homemade musical instruments struck up, and a homemade flag made of swimming trunks, shorts and even socks was hoisted up. And then a boat came over from the island in front of the Pripyat campers. "*On the front of the boat there was ... a tall, thin, but ... heavily-built man, covered with ... water lilies ... There was a wreath of something green on his head and two mermaids accompanied him ... Halyna Sevruk and Lesia Zaboy.*"[87]

The performance was so unexpected that even Belarusians who were fishing nearby with nets swam closer to see it. Vasyl was inspired in his role. Though in general not a big fan of jokes and improvisations, he spouted jokes, started singing songs, prompted children and adults to play games and pranks ... It was one of the funniest days of the Stus' life ...

---

[86] "*On July 17, we are going to Prypiat. This is near Turov, the stop is called Hvoyensk. If you dare (or as a group), it would be nice. There is a large kish [temporary post] of people—writers, scientists, artists—about twenty souls with families. It is desirable (i.e., necessary!) to have a tent (when you are with the family) and a sleeping bag. For food we have fresh fish and wild berries. From Hvoyensk, the kish is 1.5 km downstream, where you can walk, asking where there are tourists with a bearded man, the tribal leader. This is Heinrich Dvorko, a doctor-chemist, the tribal leader*". From a letter of Vasyl Stus to Vasyl Zakharchenko. See Vasil Stus. Tvory. Volume 6: book. 2, 73.
[87] Mykhailyna Kotsiubynska // Netsenzurnyi Stus. [Uncensored Stus]. Part 2, 57.

The next day, when he had to take a rocket to Kyiv, he was completely pale from the toothache that could not be tamed even by the omnipotent Nadia Odarych, who was a "citizen" of the noisy and merry Pripyat Republic.

It was swelling on the Kyiv Sea, suppressing the anxiety that had somehow settled over Vasyl's soul. For some reason, Vasyl remembered the previous summer, when he tormented himself for a few days with the little capricious Dmytryk in Prokhorivka, where his wife took a trade union permit but could stay only for half the term. He had to spend the second half with his son and stop working. As if in reality, Vasyl saw a sandy road going down the mountain of Maksimovich, along which he "walked away" from his son, who felt guilty and ran after him crying:

"*Daddy, come back, come back ...*"

And although his heart was torn with pain, Vasyl continued walking, because the naughty little boy, who did not seem to stop fussing for even a moment, still had to be taught.

When his son's cries subsided, Vasyl heard:

"*And 'vot' [what] 'sall' [shall] I, poor boy, 'to' [do] ...*"

It was beyond his power to go on. Even without finishing the lesson, he held the child, reproaching himself for involuntary cruelty ...

Memories grew into a line of an as yet unwritten verse: "*and the son runs like blood runs down the throat ...*"[88] Vasyl thought: "*I should use it in one of the poems... - Why is it so sad, so unbearable at its heart?*"

Kyiv ensnared Stus with nervous and rather unpleasant meetings and impressions. With each passing day, the space of his uncertain freedom diminished and the feeling of danger and uncertainty in the future grew. Even Sunday escapes to the forest did not save him, because the presence of "foreign" eyes was felt there as well.

---

[88] A line from the poem "*Nasnylosia, z rozluky naverzlosia ...*" [Being separated I was dreaming and it was striking me as...]. See Vasyl Stus. Tvory. Volume 3: book 1, 77.

It was also annoying that despite his outspoken position and active communication with "yesterday's" zeks and people in opposition to the government, he was still stubbornly not summoned to the KGB, although "unofficial" surveillance of meetings, travel and correspondence grew increasingly cynical.

On November 15, 1971, on Dmytryk's fifth birthday, a large group of people gathered in the apartment of Valia and Vasyl in Sviatoshyne.

Viacheslav Chornovil arrived in Kyiv and, as Ivan Dziuba recalled, wanted to gather *"in a narrower circle to talk about ... things, where and what was being done. In that period the movement was already passing into another state because in its legal forms it was basically suppressed. We had to choose: either adopt to some extent illegal forms or reject everything and look for forms of purely cultural work. The crisis was sorely felt by everyone. We gathered to talk about all this ... We were... arguing for a long time.*

At that time, "Ukrainskyi visnyk," *being a purely underground edition had already started to appear in Lviv. And there was a different attitude to it — whether it was worth publishing or not. Whether it was justified, or could only provoke repression ... There were various disputes, but conducted peacefully and in a friendly way. It was clear that this was being monitored and under surveillance. And I have the impression that after that, precisely because the conversation took place in Vasyl's apartment, they [the KGB] decided that he held some key position in the movement, and after that, they put him on the line."*[89]

The debates lasted almost till the dawn. Dmytryk had long ago fallen asleep. Valia went to bed. But Svitlychny, Chornovil, Dziuba, Sverstyuk, Stus, and many others could not decide: what had to be done next?

The investigators did pay special attention to that meeting, questioning whether any anti-Soviet organization had been set up there. Ivan Dziuba seems to be right when he says that the simple fact that the most famous sixtiers gathered at Stus' apartment finally convinced the authorities that Stus should be imprisoned!

---

[89] Ivan Dziuba // Netsenzurnyi Stus.[Uncensored Stus] Part 2, 239.

They had to find a reason. In fact, a reason for the arrests had long been sought, although the situation had remained uncertain also because there was no unanimity in the upper echelons of the Ukrainian Party leadership: should the sixtiers be arrested and tried or not? And, if yes, then which ones exactly?

The pause stretched out. Vasyl received a permit to one of Morshyn's sanatoriums and went there to *"patch up ... his stomach"*[90] because the ulcer that had been tormenting the poet since his military service flared up again.

On the way to Morshyn, Stus stayed in Lviv for a few days and by chance agreed to go there for the New Year and Christmas holidays.

Vasyl took with him several volumes of Rilke and a book by Jaspers, all in German.[91] During the three weeks that he stayed at the *Svitanok* [The Dawn] sanatorium in Morshyn, he translated all of Rilke's elegies.[92]

Before the New Year holidays, Vasyl used to escape the sanatorium almost every day and wander the outskirts of the Western Ukrainian town, enjoying the hours of solitude, which were so few in his life. In the frosty evening forest, he searched for the best way to "deliver" the text of Rilke's elegies in Ukrainian and thought about the incomprehensible situation in which he would be forbidden to do what he most desired all his life: to write. Stus did not know how to get out of this mess, but convinced himself that *"there are no situations which one can't get out of."*

The sanatorium society did not cheer him up: P. M. Matskevich, V. V. Kyslynsky and V. I. Sydorov, who were there with him, seemed as though they wanted to provoke Stus into sharp political discussions, and he, not wanting to do so, started

---

[90] Vasyl Stus' letter to Zinaida Yoffe // Vasyl Stus. Tvory. Volume 6, book 2, 74.
[91] Kryminalna sprava № 47 po obvynuvachenniu Stusa Vasylia Semenovycha u vchynenni zlochynu, peredbachenoho st. 62. ch. 1 KK URSR. V 12 tomakh. Tom N 1. - Zberihaietsia v arkhivi SBU, N 67298 fp. Ark.141-142. [Criminal Case N 47 of Stus Vasyl Semenovych on on charges of committing a crime stipulated by article N 62, part 1 of Criminal Code of Ukrainian SSR. In 12 volumes: Volume N 1. Deposited in the Archive of Security Service of Ukraine. N 67298 arch.un., sheets 141-142].
[92] Ibid., Sheet 142.

arguing with them. Although what is the use of such disputes with "compatriots," who are interested only in women and money?

The new year of 1972 found Vasyl Stus in Lviv, in the apartment of Iryna and Ihor Kalyntsiv,[93] where a circle of like-minded Lviv people gathered, whom he regarded with interest.

At Christmas, in a large group, they took a walk around Lviv, caroling to the friendly hosts, who hospitably opened the door to the carolers. Yet the mood was depressing. Anxiety gnawed at him and Vasyl sighed with relief only when he boarded the train to Kyiv.

Already when, after diving into the woods,
you drank greedily Subcarpathian mourning,
for the last time partaking of the sacrament of its
age-old alienation ...
[...]
... then when the evening
cherished your magical loneliness
between the figures of enchanting rogues ...
[...]
a troubled premonition entered your footsteps
and a scent of trouble ran in advance.
Spoiled by the mugs of drunkards,
debauchers, prostitutes, vagrants, sucking
and crazy countrymen,
it is a wicked sinless dump place
was trembling, swaying like a swamp,
surrounded by whispering indifferent jokers,
wishing to please one and all –
such cold blew on me
in this alienated homeland, here,
where the land seemed to be the heart of the heart,
and a moan of blood – the horizon signified!
   ...Then already,
when the last yuletide was being celebrated
(There was a holy night and carol and noise

---

[93] Ibid.

*Of a child's voiced carol),
you heard about it. When about unknown Lviv
I was walking at random, drawing close my time
(Right here, right here, right here you are, farewell occasion,
that overtook the meeting), even then,
when hoping for happy wishes,
the crowds of patients from the clinic were watching us,
and solemn memorable singing
was a dam for noisy streetcars
and late bypassers, I realized:
this all – one excessive farewell –
to the Motherland, the world, life.*[94]

With such sentiments, Vasyl Stus returned to Kyiv, where his arrival was met by a search warrant issued in connection with a Belgian tourist, and, at the same time, a kind of Ukrainian patriot, Yaroslav Dobosh.

The latter was "locked up" at the border with *samvydav* literature and some materials that he allegedly received from Svitlychny and other sixtiers. A terrified Ukrainian patriot with a Belgian passport, to whom the KGB interrogators brightly described his "merry" prospects in a Soviet camp, gave testimony on the basis of which, on February 12, arrests were made across Ukraine. Later, during the trials of Ivan Svitlychny and Yevhen Sverstyuk, Viacheslav Chornovil and Vasyl Stus, Iryna Kalynets, and Stefania Shabatura Dobosh were not mentioned. It was from this "agent of enemy intelligence" that mass repressions against the particularly active sixtiers, who had long irritated the party leadership by their independent behavior, were justified. "Certain" leaders showed political acumen and came to the logical conclusion that the trial of foreign intelligence "allies" and nationalist elements promised an accelerated career.

The arrests began.

Vasyl had hardly changed from his traveling clothes before they rang the bell of his apartment. The search lasted all day. In the

---

[94] Vasyl Stus. Tvory. Volume 3: book 1, 59-61.

evening, when Valia returned home with their son, manuscripts, books, and loose typewritten pages lay in a large heap in the middle of the room and a whole group of KGB agents stared in confusion at the still full bookcase, each book of which could potentially contain additional evidence of Vasyl Stus' "subversive anti-Soviet activities."

Frightened, Dmytryk hid from the dreaded guys behind a large armchair, trying to shoot them with an arrow from a toy bow. When he succeeded, someone yelled angrily:

"*Any sledite za rebonkom* [Now then, watch your child]."

"What do you mean watch, it is time for him to sleep!"

"*My rabotaem* [We are working]..."

Towards five o'clock in the morning, Vasyl kissed the weeping Valia and went out the door. The process of making an uncompromising ideological enemy of the Soviet system out Vasyl Stus by state officials and the KGB was entering its final stage.

Bibliography

Netsenzurnyi Stus. [Uncensored Stus]. Knyha u 2-kh chastynakh. Uporiadkuvannia Bohdana Pidhirnoho. [Book in 2 parts. Compiled by Bohdan Pidrhirnyi.] - Ternopil: Pidruchnyky i posibnyky [Textbooks and manuals], 2002, 2003, 336+320 p.

Petro SHELEST: "Spravzhnii sud istorii shche poperedu ...": Spohady. Shchodennyky. Dokumenty. Materialy / Za redaktsiieiu Yuriia Shapovala. [The real bar of history is still ahead ...: Memories. Diaries. Documents. Materials / Edited by Yuri Shapoval]. — K.: Heneza, 808 p.

Work record book of Vasyl Stus. Kept in Vasyl Stus' family.

Stus Vasyl. Tvory u chotyrokh tomakh (shesty knyhakh). Z dodatkovymy 5 i 6 (u dvokh knyhakh) tomamy. [Works in 4 volumes (6 books). With additional the 5th and the 6th (in two books) volumes]. - VS "Prosvita" ["Education" All-Ukrainian Union], 1994-1999.

Dobrookyi. Spohady pro Ivana Svitlychnoho / Uporiadnyky: Leonida i Nadiia Svitlychni. [Memoires about Ivan Svitlychny / Compilers: Leonida and Nadiya Svitlychny]. — K.: Chas [Time]1998, 572 p.

Ukrainska hromadska hrupa spryiannia vykonanniu Helsinskykh uhod: V 4 tomakh. / Uporiadnyk Ye.Zakharov [Ukrainian Public Group to

Promote the Implementation of Helsinki Accords: In 4 volumes. / Compiler Ye.Zakharlv]. — Kharkiv: Folio, 2001.

Pluzhnyk Yevhen. Vybrani poezii. — K.: Radianskyi pysmennyk [Selected poems]. — K.: Soviet writer], 1966.

Ukrainska suspilno-politychna dumka v 20 stolitti. Dokumenty i materialy. Tom III / Uporiadkuvaly Taras Hunchak i Roman Solchanyk. [Ukrainian socio-political thought in the 20th century. Documents and materials. Volume III / Compilers Taras Hunchak and Roman Solchanyk]. — Suchasnist [Modernity], 1983, 381 p.

Zakharov Boris. Narys istorii dysydentskoho rukhu v Ukraini (1956 — 1987) / Kharkivska pravozakhysna hrupa. [Essay on the History of the Dissident Movement in Ukraine (1956-1987) / Kharkiv Human Rights Group]. — Kh.: Folio, 2003, 144 p.

Kasianov Heorhii. Nezghodni: ukrainska intelihentsiia v rusi oporu 1960 — 80-kh rokiv. [Dissenters: Ukrainian intelligentsia in the resistance movement of 1960-1980.] — K.: Lybid, 1995, 224 p.

Verstiuk V.F., Dziuba O.M., Repryntsev V.F. Ukraina vid naidavnishykh chasiv do sohodennia. Khronolohichnyi dovidnyk. [Ukraine from the ancient to modern times. Chronological reference book] — K.: Naukova dumka [Scientific thought], 1995, 688 p.

Drach Ivan. Retsenziia na rukopys knyzhky "Zymovi dereva" — virshi Vasylia Stusa / Mashynopysna kopiia vnutrishnoi retsenzii dlia vydavnytstva "Molod". - Zberihaietsia v arkhivi rodyny Vasylia Stusa. [Review of the book manuscript of "Zymovi dereva" - poems by Vasyl Stus / The typewritten copy of the internal review for the "Youth" publishing house. - Stored in the archives of the poet's family].

Stus Dmytro. Zhyttia i tvorchist Vasylia Stusa. [Life and work of Vasyl Stus] — K.: MP "Fotovideoservis", 1992, 88 pp. (Seriia "Biblioteka ukraintsia") [The Library of Ukrainian].

Stus Vasyl. Zymovi dereva. [Winter trees]. Authorized typewritten copy of the collection manuscript in "samvydav" format with the dedicatory inscription to G.P.Kochur. — Stored in the Institute of Literature of the National Academy of Sciences of Ukraine, repository 170, archival unit 926.

Stus Vasyl. Zymovi dereva: Persha zbirka poezii. [The first collection of poems]. — Brussels: Literatura i mystetstvo [Literature and Art], 1970.

Leksykon zahalnoho ta porivnialnoho literaturoznavstva / Bukovynskyi tsentr humanitarnykh doslidzhen. [Lexicon of General and Comparative Literary Studies / Bukovyna Center for Humanist Studies] — Chernivtsi: Zoloti lytavry, [Golden Timpani], 636 p.

Adelheim Yevhen. Retsenziia na zbirku poezii Vasylia Stusa "Zymovi dereva". Avtoryzovanyi mashynopys. [Review for the "Zymovi dereva" collection of poems by Vasyl Stus. Authorised typewritten copy]. — Stored in the archives of the Vasyl Stus' family, 9 p.

Shevchenkivski laureaty. 1962—2001. Entsyklopedychnyi dovidnyk / Vstupne slovo I.M.Dziuby. Avtor-upor. M.H.Labinskyi. [Laureates of Shevchenko prize. 1962-2001. Encyclopedic reference book./ Opening remarks by I.V.Dziuba. Author-compiler M.G.Labynsky]. — K.: Krynytsia [Well], 2001, 696 p.

M.Kutynskyi. Nekropol Ukrainy [Necropolis of Ukraine] // Dnipro. - 1994. 1999.

Dovidnyk z istorii Ukrainy (A—Ya) / Pid zah. redaktsiieiu I.Z.Pidkovy, R.M.Shusta. [Reference book on the history of Ukraine (A-Z) / under general editorship of I.Z.Pidkova, R.M.Shust] — K.: Heneza, 2002, 1136 p.

Stus Vasyl. Shchodennykovi zapysy. Avtohraf. — Zberihaietsia: IL NANU [Diary Notes. Autograph. Deposited at: Institute for Literature of the National Academy of Sciences of Ukraine]. F. 170, dep. item 2102, sheets 2, 4-7.

Vasyl Stus. Vesely Tsvyntar [The Merry Cemetery]: Poezii [Poetry]. - Warsaw: Vyd. agenstvo Obiednannia ukraintsiv u Polshchi [Publishing agency of Union of Ukrainians in Poland], 1990, 109 p.

Stus Vasyl. Palimpsest: Vybrane. [Selected works]. — K.: Fact, 2003, 432 p.

Kryminalna sprava №47 po obvynuvachenniu Stusa Vasylia Semenovycha u vchynenni zlochynu, peredbachenoho st. 62 ch. 1 Karnoho kodeksu URSR. V 12 tomakh: Tom №1. — Zberihaietsia v arkhivi SBU: № 67298 fp. [Criminal case N 47 of Stus Vasyl Semenovych on charges of committing a crime stipulated by Article 62 Part 1 of the Criminal Code of the Ukrainian SSR in 12 volumes: TVolume N 1. — Deposited in the Archive of the Security Service of Ukraine: №.67298 fp].

"Creativity Time / Dichterzeit"

> The Great is connected by a functional dependence with the Whole. The Great Personality, apart from his individual value (genius, talent, will), radiating his own moral energy, must feel a constant influx of the environment's energy. Because even the greatest Personality can only be a motor; he cannot be the fabled Perpetuum mobile, which does not exist in nature.
>
> Yevhen Malanyuk

On January 13, 1972, the investigator of the Kyiv Oblast office of the KGB under the Council of Ministers (CM) of the Ukrainian SSR, Senior Lieutenant V. I. Loginov, *"having studied the materials of the search of the apartment of STUS V. S. conducted on January 12, 1972, by instruction of the Lviv Oblast office of the KGB under the CM of the Ukrainian SSR and taking into account that during the search at STUS V. S.', the items and documents confiscated indicated that he was systematically engaged in the production and distribution of documents slandering the Soviet state and social order, guided by items 5, 98, 113 of Art. 94 of the Criminal Procedure Code of the USSR.*

HAS RESOLVED AS FOLLOWS:
To initiate a criminal case against STUS Vasyl Semenovych on the grounds of the crime stipulated by Art. 187 of the Criminal Code of the USSR.
To accept the case and start its investigation.
To send a copy of this resolution to the prosecutor of the Ukrainian SSR and the 10th Department of the KGB under the CM of the Ukrainian SSR."[1]

The chief of the Investigation Department of the KGB under the CM of the Ukrainian SSR, Colonel Pivovarets, agreed with this subordinate's conclusion. It is difficult to say how it was in reality, but it seems obvious that the KGB agents had prepared the warrant for

---

[1] Kryminalna sprava № 47 po obvynuvachenniu Stusa Vasylia Semenovycha u vchynenni zlochynu, peredbachenoho st. 62. ch. 1 Karnoho kodeksu URSR. V 12 tomakh. Tom 1.—Zberihaietsia v arkhivi SBU: N67298, ark. 1 (hereinafter Criminal Case N 47) [Criminal Case N 47 regarding accusations against Stus Vasyl Semenovych of committing a crime stipulated by article N 62, part 1 of Criminal Code of Ukrainian SSR. In 12 volumes, Volume 1. Deposited in the Archive of the Security Service of Ukraine].

the temporary custody of Vasyl Stus even before starting their search.

On January 15, 1972, Vasyl Stus' "detention" was also authorized by the Prosecutor of the Ukrainian SSR, 1st Class State Counselor of Justice F. Hlukh, who testified that Loginov had "collected sufficient evidence regarding the case showing that STUS during 1968–1971 produced and distributed documents and poems that slandered the Soviet state and social order."[2]

Yaroslav Dobosh, whose case appeared to be the pretext for the arrests of almost all the sixties, was not even mentioned.

In fact, the Ukrainian patriot from Belgium was mentioned in only one—the first- interrogation on January 13, 1972.

Vasyl Stus arrived at the KGB internal prison at 3 a.m.[3] He was received by a sergeant on duty, Mazur, who noted as one of the "specific traits" of the new arrival: "*talkative*."[4]

This was followed by the tedious and humiliating procedure of mandatory rituals: "Ruki za holavy, razdvin yagaditsi, agali galovku" [Hands on the back of your neck, spread your buttocks, expose head]. This immediately struck and paralyzed the will with the routine of repetition. Finally there was the cell, or rather, a dungeon with a tiny window just below the ceiling.

When the door opened, Vasyl was most impressed by the incredible thickness of the wall: you could not break it with your head ... His gaze fell on the parquet floor, which looked very surreal below the bare stone walls. There was a five-liter pot on the floor, bunks, a bedside table and that was all. Nothing more.[5]

"Apravka dva raza v dien. Utram i viechieram" ["Toilet is allowed twice a day—in the morning and the evening" (Russian)], the guard said to Stus' back.

As soon as the door closed, a terrible silence fell, which seemed to engulf everything.

---

[2] Criminal Case N 47. Volume 1, Sheet 12.
[3] Ibid.., Sheet 4.
[4] Ibid., Sheet 5.
[5] Semen Hluzman // Netsenzurnyi Stus. [Uncensored Stus]. Knyha u 2-kh chastynakh. Chastyna 1 [Book in 2 parts. Part 1.]—Ternopil: Pidruchnyky i posibnyky [Text books and manuals], 2002, 216.

Vasyl paced the small space of the inner prison cell, not stopping, as if treading a diagonal path—from corner to corner—that vibrated with his energies.

"What comes next?"

"So they summoned you ..."

"Poor mother ..."

When the window in the door opened and lunch was brought, Vasil did not even pick up the spoon.

The food was taken away after a few minutes.

He did not pay any attention.

The door opened at about 4.00 p.m.:

"Stus, get out!"

He went out.

"Hands behind your back." —For some reason, he obeyed the command.

There was a loud sound of fingers snapping. From afar somewhere further down the corridor the same sound was heard.

"Litsom k stienie! Bystro! [Face the wall! Quickly!]" They flattened him against the wall, behind the nearest offshoot of the corridor.

Everything was like in a fog.

"I need to harness my willpower to sleep," Vasyl decided, but the harshness and categorical nature of the seemingly lenient requirements were strangely depressing. He could not focus his strength after the night search, Valia's tears and a quarrel with the warrant officer who "accepted" him at the internal prison.

Finally, they climbed the stairs and entered an office with high ceilings.

At the table, there was the narcissistic and sealed-off face of the investigator, Loginov, whom Vasyl disliked during the search on Lvivska Street.

The clock showed 4:03 p.m.[6]

"STUS: Regarding the questions asked I can state that I do not know the mentioned Belgian citizen Dobosh Yaroslav. I do not know anything about his arrival in Ukraine and I have not met him. I can also add that I

---

[6] Criminal Case N 47. Volume 1, Sheet 5.

have not met any Belgian citizens. I cannot explain in what way Dobosh got the photo. I did not give my photos to any of the residents of Kyiv or Lviv. This statement does not apply to employees of the personnel departments of the institutions where I worked.

LOGINOV: Did you write the article "A Place in a Massacre or a Battle" and a letter in defense of Ivan Suk?

Answer: I did not write the article "A Place in a Massacre or a Battle."[7] *I wrote the letter in defense of Ivan Suk, and this letter I sent to the Central Committee of the Communist Party of Ukraine, the Presidium of the Verkhovna Rada of the Ukrainian SSR, or to another government institution, which one, exactly, I do not remember right now. I do not remember whether I gave anyone the text of this letter and I cannot respond precisely to this question.*

LOGINOV: Did you write the article "The Phenomenon of Our Time" and to whom did you show the text of this article?

STUS: The article "The Phenomenon of Our Time" was written by me. I worked on it for a long time, about half a year. I turned to experts for advice on this article.[8]

Then Loginov asked about *Zymovi dereva* and the story of its publication abroad:

STUS: The collection was published abroad without my agreement, because I intended to publish it in the **Radianskyi Pysmennyk** *[Soviet Writer] Publishing House and this collection received positive reviews from Nahnybida*[9] *in 1965, Drach in 1968, and Adelheim in 1970–1971. I believe that recently the publication of Ukrainian authors abroad has become widespread and, in my opinion, this is not the fault of the authors, but of the existing general practice of publication of manuscripts in Ukraine. I set out my views on this issue in detail in letters to the Central Committee of the Communist Party of Ukraine and the Presidium of the Writers' Union, which I sent around November 1971."*[10]

At 5:50 p.m., Stus left the investigator's office.

---

[7] Stus' article was entitled "Mistse v boiu chy v rozpravi" ("A Place in a Battle or a Massacre").

[8] Criminal Case N 47. Volume 1, Sheets 113-114.

[9] The author has not been able to find any information about M. Nahnybida's review of this collection. Above, Nahnybida's devastating review of *Krugovert* was noted.

[10] Criminal case N 47. Volume 1, Sheet 115.

No agreement was reached. Stus behaved provocatively and demanded the return of his German-language volume of Goethe, saying that otherwise he would refuse to cooperate with the investigation, and, within a week or two, the investigators met the prisoner's demand.[11]

The first day at the KGB passed randomly and uncertainly. Nervous tension would not allow him to relax or gain balance. He had another sleepless night. Again he thought about his wife, son, parents.

Investigator Loginov, on the contrary, slept. It was time to think about how the drafts and manuscripts confiscated from Stus would be "smelted" into a criminal case. And he had almost no doubt that if it would be enough for Prosecutor F. Hlukh to authorize the detention of Stus as a particularly dangerous criminal, it would be enough to secure a prison term. For him, it would mean at least one more star on his shoulder straps: by any measure, a success in this case.

What did they confiscated from Stus' apartment?

Besides numerous draft letters and statements, as well as poems and the typewritten collections *Winter Trees* and *The Merry Cemetery*, the police search seized the following items. The notebook "A. Solzhenitsyn. Miniatyuryi. Ozero Segden" [A. Solshenitsyn. Miniatures. The lake of Segden], *samvydav* poetry collections by Hryhoriy Chubay ("Postat golosu" [Figure of the Voice]), Mykola Kholodny ("Kryk z mohyly" [A Cry from the Grave]), a sheet with the text of V. Symonenko's poem "De zaraz vy, katy moho narodu..." [Where Are You Now, the Executioners of My People...], Lina Kostenko's collection *"Poezii" (Smoloskyp)* [Poetry (Torch)], *Vybranyi Kazimir Edshmidt* (München, 1960) [Selected Kaszmir Edschmidt (Munich, 1960)], the typewritten text «Krutoi marshrut. Khronyka vremen kulta lychnosty» [Steep Route: Chronicle of the Times of the Cult of Personality], a typewritten copy by M. Yu. Braichevsky "Pryiednannia chy voziednannia? (Krytychni zamitky z pryvodu odniiei kontseptsii)" [Consolidation or reunifi-

---

[11] Semen Hluzman // Netsenzurnyi Stus. [Uncensored Stus]. Part 1, 213.

cation? (Critical notes on one concept)], a photocopy of Ivan Dziuba's book *Internatsionalizm chy rusyfikatsiia* [Internationalism or Russification], a typewritten copy of Lina Kostenko's collection *Zorianyi intehral* [Star Integral], Emma Andievska's book *Bazar* [The Market] (Munich, 1967), two letters by Stanislav Telnyuk regarding "Fenomen doby," a self-published collection by Iryna Kalynets *Pidsumovuiuchy movchannia* [Summing up the Silence] (Lviv, 1970), a book by Vira Vovk *Kappa Khresta* (Suchasnist, 1969) [*Kappa of the Cross* (Modernity, 1969)], a film about C. G. Jung's work and an Erika typewriter №4525453 model 30, made in the German Democratic Republic, which the poet used to type his own works. Instead of signing the list of materials confiscated during the search, Vasyl Stus added the following statement: *"Given that these items confiscated from me during the search cannot, in my opinion, be related to the person against whom a criminal case was initiated* [the reference is to Yaroslav Dobosh concerning whose case the search was conducted — Dmytro Stus], *I consider the removal of the items specified in the search report to be groundless."*[12]

On January 14 and 15, they did not summon Stus for interrogation, hoping that complete isolation and uncertainty would depress him and make him more yielding.

On the 16th, at 2:50 p.m., Vasyl was again brought to Loginov for interrogation and the investigator, as if playing a trump card, placed on the table the article "Mistse v boiu chy v rozpravi" (A Place in a Battle or a Massacre).

---

[12] Criminal case №47. Volume 1, Sheets 15-22. During the repeated official searches (there was also an unofficial search, which was secretly conducted when no one was in the apartment), which took place on February 4, 1972, the following books were confiscated and attached to the case: P. Rohachev. M. Sverdlin, *Natsyy – narod – chelovechestvo* [Nations-people-humankind] (Moskva, 1967); V. Malanchuk, *Torzhestvo leninskoi natsalnoi polityky* [The Triumph of the Leninist National Policy] (L., 1963); *Ukrainskyi istorychnyi zhurnal* [Ukrainian Historical Magazine] 1966. – N. 11; V. Ievdokymenko, *Krytyka ideinykh osnov ukrainskoho burzhuaznoho natsionalizmu* [The Critique of the Ideological Foundations of Ukrainian Bourgeois Nationalism] (K., 1967), and draft autographs of poems by V. Stus. Instead of the signature of V. Stus' wife, there was a remark made by Loginov: *"Popeliukh refused to sign the minutes and stated that she would like 'her husband to be present during the search for him to see what was confiscated.'"* Criminal case N 47. Volume 1, Sheets 24, 27.

"STUS: During the last interrogation, I testified that I did not write the article 'Mistse v rozpravi chy v boiu.' Reviewing the above-mentioned document presented to me today, I would like to make an amendment to the effect that I do not remember whether I gave such a title to the letter addressed to L. Dmyterko or not.

*Question: Were you familiar with samvydav document called "Ukrainskyi visnyk" [Ukrainian Herald]. If so, from whom did you receive and to whom did you return it? Do you know that your letter addressed to L. Dmyterko was included in "*Ukrainskyi visnyk*"?*

Answer: I was not familiar with the samvydav document called "Ukrainskyi visnyk" and I do not know that my letter to L. Dmyterko was included in this document.

Question: In the letter to L. Dmyterko, you write: 'now it is the year 1969– a year that is not very heroic, a year of widespread extreme conservatism.' Do you really think that there was an extreme conservatism in our country at that time?

Answer: When I used that expression, I believed that, at the time of writing this letter, we were experiencing the process of Stalinization in our country. It referred not only to modern literature, but also to democratic human freedoms, the crackdown on them, and the suppression of certain decisions of the 20th and 22nd Party Congresses.

Question: Do you think that the process of Stalinization is still going on?

Answer: In my opinion, there is a great threat of Stalinization and the tendency to restore Stalinism is dangerous for the cause of communism."[13]

Loginov was not in a hurry.

He retrieved the draft of another letter to the republican leadership starting with the words: *"According to statistical calculations ..."*

"You are presented with a document 'which slanders the Soviet state system and states that our country is allegedly pursuing a policy of genocide against young writers.'"[14]

---

[13] Criminal case N 47. Volume 1, Sheets 117-118.
[14] Ibid., Sheet 120.

This interpretation demanded a refutation from Stus, and, refusing to explain anything to the investigator, wrote down his objection to such an interpretation:
"*First of all, I reject the characterization of this letter as one that slanders the Soviet system. The purpose of the letter was to inform the Government and the Writers' Union of Ukraine about the complexity of the negative phenomena in literary and public life, and the need to remediate existing deficiencies so that Ukrainian Soviet literature, especially young writers, can work for the people, serve the ideals of humanism and justice with high coefficient of efficiency.*

Since the coefficient of artistic and aesthetic return is in many cases unacceptably low and sometimes equals zero, I started discussing the policy of genocide. In writing this, I did not mean that such a policy of genocide was planned. I meant that the general system of publication of manuscripts, their censorship without proper or no grounds, KGB protection, the system of discrediting honest names, dismissals from work, psychological terror, confiscation of manuscripts – up to the destruction of books – this system leads to the loss of creative work, creative years, creative lives. I fully assume that the expression 'policy of genocide' is too categorical, and arose from a state of pain and indignation at the negative phenomena of artistic life…

I looked through and read the document starting with the words 'According to statistical calculations made…,'[15] *and read it again. I am the author of this document, it was written by me. With this letter, I addressed the Secretary of the Central Committee of the Communist Party of Ukraine, F. D. Ovcharenko, and the Presidium of the Writers' Union of Ukraine. I sent it to these addressees in November 1971, after the October holidays…*

This letter was preceded by my repeated appeals to the Writers' Union of Ukraine, to the Central Committee of the Young Communist League, to the Central Committee of the Communist Party of Ukraine…"[16]

---

[15] This document—the letter "To the Secretary of the Central Committee of the Communist Party of Ukraine, F. D. Ovcharenko"—in the final version begins with the words: "Good people, you are doing the wrong things…" See Vasyl Stus. Tvory. Volume 4,409-411. In his Tvory it is erroneously dated January 23, 1972.

[16] Criminal Case N 47. Volume 1, Sheets 120-124.

The investigator was especially interested in who among Vasyl's friends encouraged him to write such a letter.

Stus snapped:

"*I am personally responsible for the letter, and therefore... I consider it immoral to mention other people's names.*"[17]

After leaving the investigator's office, from which, unlike his premises in the internal prison, he could see the other side of Volodymyrska Street and even the domes St. Sophia's Cathedral, Vasyl decided to write a letter to the governing bodies of the republic and try to explain the reasons for his actions in a humane way. They were people too and they must understand him.

The letter was finished before "lockdown," but he dated it the next day.

"TO P[etro] Yu[khymovych] SHELEST
Dear Petro Yukhymovych!
Situations in life happen when there is a desire to speak as if confessing. Today, sitting in the KGB remand prison, I feel precisely this.
Shevchenko once wrote:

I love my poor Ukraine so much,
that I curse holy God,
I will destroy my soul for her.

I would repeat these words, replacing the word 'Ukraine' with the word 'truth,' meaning 'justice.'

I have a strong, maybe even painful sense of justice, which I have always wanted to see complete, perfect. I believe that such justice should exist in our country, which must set an example for the people of the world. We are bound by the 50-year experience of the practice of the pathfinders of socialism and communism. The fate of world socialism and communism depends a lot on what kind of socialism and communism we establish.

So, I have always been concerned that justice in our country be the highest, that the socialism we build be more socialist, and that communism we build be more communist.

---

[17] Ibid., Sheet 126.

And yet I saw the facts of injustice, especially the situation of an honest, principled and nice person living worse than a dishonest, unprincipled, unkind one. And because he lived worse precisely due to his best human qualities, I then came to understand that this is a very dangerous practice, which can lead to a wider decomposition of the most valuable human substance. And then I came to understand that by building communism in this way, we were making it difficult for us to achieve it.

I think that the experience of condemnation by the Party of the cult years has greatly encouraged the non-Party communists of other countries to develop an independent mode of socialism – to avoid many of our losses, mistakes, and injustices. Because Stalin, though he did a lot of good for our country, also did many things that history will never forgive him for. In building socialism, he committed many sins against it.

Following this sense of enhanced justice, I have repeatedly tried to discover in the official institutions the paradoxes of our time, which are incomprehensible to me. I addressed the Central Committee of the Young Communist League of Ukraine, the Party Committee of the Writers' Union, and the officials of the Central Committee of the Communist Party of Ukraine. And none of them gave sincere answer to my sincere inquiries.

I am not a nationalist. On the contrary, I considered it necessary to do my best to dispel the toxin of narcissism, anti-Semitism, and backyard narrow-mindedness among a certain number of Ukrainians. I also thought it necessary to do my best to dispel the toxin of disrespect for the Ukrainian language, culture, history, disrespect for the work of the peasant, who kindly gives us all bread and salt from his calloused hands, among a certain number of Russians, Jews, etc.

I always tried to side with the weaker, more honest, more principled, more courageous people, even if I did not completely share their position ...

I believe that my only sin is that I have sought too much absolute justice, which today may not yet be entirely possible. This is, so to say, a non-legal characterization of my 'crime' (the legal one will be given to You by more competent persons).

So, I do not plead pardon. I can only say that some phrases, lines, words were dropped by me impulsively, in a fit of anger, and anger is a bad adviser. I was trying 'to get rid of it like filth,' but I could not always get rid of it: too often I was treated, not in a non-Soviet way, but simply not in a human way. Here is just one case. In May 1966, thanks to the efforts of S. D. Zubkov, Deputy Director of the Institute of Literature of

the *Academy of Sciences of Ukrainian SSR, I was dismissed from the archives. I was left on my own, my wife pregnant with my son and us being in need of something to eat. I worked on the construction of the metro, drove trolleys, but they fired me because I had higher education. When I got a work injury, I was informed about my dismissal by the personnel department officer. In such moments, I could be evil and unjust in my poems or articles, although, of course, I should not have responded to injustice with injustice. I am just explaining, not making excuses. And there were a lot of such cases.*
 Sincerely Yours,
 Vasyl STUS
 January 18, 1972"[18]

It is probably worth explaining the contextual meaning of some of the words and expressions. "Non-Party communists" does not, of course, mean people prejudiced against communist interests. Stus uses this expression, which was common at the time, to describe persons committed to the good and justice but not members of the Communist Party. This was a formula, and its use at the time made it "beneficial" in his situation. It should also be borne in mind that the pathos of this rather frank letter derives from the game with "open cards" that Vasyl Stus was conducting with the investigation, rather than from his sincerity.

It is unlikely that the poet believed that his letter would find its way into Shelest's hands (although this cannot be completely excluded because, as the investigator would say, the case was monitored directly by the Central Committee) but it was an important component of the behavior chosen by Vasyl Stus for himself. Having sent the letter, he no longer behaved as an accused man but like a writer: he demanded from the investigator that a literary critic be present during the interrogation (because how can a lawyer professionally evaluate literary works?) and refused to answer questions until he was allowed to write and translate Goethe's poems (his guilt had not yet been proven, therefore no one was allowed to steal his time).

---

[18] Vasyl Stus. Tvory. Volume 4, 406-409.

This letter was even more important for the poet's inner state. Having frankly stated his position, Vasyl Stus seemed to draw a limit: this I can give in, but no farther. However, the investigator seemed to have taken this as a sign of the prisoner's first weakness. He would press a little more and the prisoner will "break." How could he know that this was the limit, and more pressure would be hopeless?

Vasyl seemed to brighten up. After writing the letter, he felt such relief, such a state of high calm, that the next morning all the pain and gnawing uncertainty, which had afflicted him for four days, began to melt into verse. The "time of creativity" began, a time he would sacrifice everything for ...

A star was shining on me this morning,
stuck in the window. And grace d —
so clear fell on my soul
humble, that I understood blissfully:
this star is just a fragment of the pain,
soaked with eternity like fire.
That star is the herald of your path,
cross and destiny — like an eternal mother,
elevated to heaven (from the earth
at a distance of justice), forgives
you a moment of despair, gives
inspiration of faith that the distant universe
heard your faint cry, but answered
with hidden desire for compassion
and a spark of high disagreement:
for to live is not overcoming a limit,
but conformation and self-exploration.
Only a mother knows how to live,
to shine like a star.
January 18, 1972[19]

---

[19] Vasyl Stus. Works. Volume 2, 12. The same day Stus wrote the poems: "Iake blazhenstvo — radisno sebe..." [What a blessing — joyfully to set feet...], "Otse tvoie narodzhennia nove..." [This your new birthday...], "Nu y son — napadaty ne khoche..." [What a sleep — It does not want to attack me...], "Taka khruska,

This poem marked the beginning of a new period of Vasyl Stus' work—the period of "Palimpsesty" [Palimplsests], a time when, according to Kostya Moskalets, on a mystical-sensual level Stus managed to synthesize in his work two contradictory directions: "fate," or the obedience to fate inherent in the East and *"the spirit of ascetic activity and kshtaltuvannia [forming]"*[20] inherent in the West.

The poet finds himself at the intersection of many directions: East and West, life and death, liberty and captivity, despair and hope, honor and dishonor, love and hate ... And in the fictional rather than the deliberately and consciously discovered poetic space of a new book, Chas tvorchosti [The Time of Creativity], it is suddenly revealed that opposites fuse into one thing: East and West merge into humanity, life and death grow into the lifespan of one's king, liberty and captivity into free circulation in the spirit space, love and hate in the strict necessity of the way.

But this logic is valid only at a crossroads: what to choose. Beyond, you have just a new road.

The collection forms a kind of chronograph of Stus' experiences of human states and phenomena both in the micro- and macrocosm, a kind of diary of memories of past life and a record of the soul's movements, which the winds of Fate have thrown on the a hillside and is now "forming" itself into a new state, because, theoretically, it is impossible to prepare for life at the very heights of the spirit.

Once Yevhen Sverstyuk told me in conversation:

---

taka huchna..." [Such crunchy, such noisy...]. See Vasyl Stus. Tvory. Volume 2, 13-15.

[20] Kostiantyn Moskalets. Liudyna na kryzhyni. Literaturna krytyka ta eseistyka. [A man on an ice floe. Literary criticism and essay theory].—K.: Krytyka. [Criticism]—1999, 227. Moskalets explains the contradictory, but no resonant term "forming" as follows: *"Kshtaltuvannia* [forming] represents a humanistic direction ... it depends on human efforts and actions, unfolding as the implementation of a rational project and declaring that there is no irrational fate" that can influence human choice and behavior, just as "there are no magical means of influencing the success of a project, whatever it may be (the soul's salvation, entrepreneurial activity, scientific research ...).."

"There, in prison, I tried to suppress all memories of home. Because to remember meant to torture oneself. After all, it was possible to regain your liberty with just one statement, but you could not write it without losing your human dignity. So I tried to have no recollections, 'no remembrance of anything'..."

Vasyl Stus, on the contrary, remembered.

Being confined in a kind of creative reclusion, he not only tortured himself every day with memories of the past, but using them constructed a new, and not only poetic, world, filled the space, drew inspiration and harrowed his soul with a constant sense of loss. It gave rise to the extreme sensuality and emotionality of the "time of creativity."

In the first days, weeks, months of imprisonment, Vasyl still almost physically remembered the warmth of his wife's hands and the tenderness of her looks, he saw the faces of friends and relatives as large as life, felt the warmth of conversations. However, everything was perceived from the perspective of separation.

"*But – unbearable – innocent punishment,*
even if you get angry, even if you go crazy."[21]

And although it was difficult to get rid of this thought, he hoped that his wife would continue to understand, his friends to support, his parents to believe and that his son would not forget and grow angry ... Arrest, trial and separation frighten and distress unprepared people: Are they ready or is she, Valia, at least ready to understand that this is the way to go? That I was chosen? That I have to endure ...

His extreme acuteness of perception and the desire to suppress insidious doubts motivated him to systematic work. Writing or translating spares you, at least during the day, from being torn by doubts. They came only before going to bed, filling with ghosts the emptiness of the cell exhausted by Stus' predecessors:

What a sleep – It does not want to attack me,

---

[21] Vasyl Stus. Tvory. Volume 2, 13.

Is haunting about a place!
Dad has tearful eyes,
and mom is pale and sad.
And looking down at my mother,
my dad begs – save.
Oh, let me cover with my hands
My son's severe loneliness.[22]

This was written on January 18, on the fifth day after his arrest. This day appeared to mark the beginning of a powerful burst of creativity that lasted until the court hearing. It is clearly defined chronologically: January 18 – September 30, 1972. The period of the investigation, the time when the spiritual work of the prisoner seems to require all his vital energy. Stus obviously did not lack any. To a large extent, his spirit was nourished by his own work, which comforted him with the successfully rendered lines of the radiant Goethe or his own poems, opened the closed layers of consciousness and the sources of self-energy, nourished by faith, gave unexpected answers to the most sensitive questions. Creativity became a *samosoboiuzhyvlennia* [self-nutrition] and *samosoboiunapovnennia* [self-filling]. In creativity, he unexpectedly and almost suddenly felt himself on the same plane with the great figures, those whom, until 1972, he could see only from below. Now, in a space of *"Six and a half steps in one direction / four steps in the other"*[23] (the area of Vasyl Stus' first prison cell), he could talk to them – Goethe, Rilke, Pasternak – as if on equal terms: because both they and he were already on the other side, beyond the everyday life of a man.

The "compensation" for the suffering was a truly royal one. A new – nonlinear – dimension of time was opening, a dimension that accelerated the appearance of new texts: completely different in form, milder, so to say, more acceptable to the Ukrainian reader.

The creative pursuits of recent years exploded with the shift of time planes, the crystallization of content and experiences, the ruthless rejection of self-conscious writing and philological water,

---

[22] Ibid., 14.
[23] Ibid.

an almost inhuman emotional completeness in every moment. And could it be differently, when every life moment is felt to be the last? Stus not only escaped from the intertemporal state but established his — Stus' — time. He felt it and was not afraid of this sweet feeling. And having trusted, already without any fear, he declared:

> *How good it is that I've no fear of dying*
> *Nor ask me how ponderous my toil*
> *Now bow to cunning magistrates, decrying*
> *Presentiments of unfamiliar soil,*
> *That I have lived and loved, yet never burdening*
> *My soul with hatred, curses or regret.*
> *My people! It is to you I am returning.*
> *In death I somehow find my fate.*
> *I turn my pained but goodly face to living*
> *And in filial prostration I begin.*
> *I meet your eyes in fair thanksgiving*
> *And join my kindred earth as closes kin*

January 20, 1972[24]

This was no longer a blank declaration. The right to pathos was obtained in exchange for a decision: even at the cost of losing your freedom, you, Vasyl Stus, must not betray yourself if you do not want to repeat the sad fate of Tychyna, so painfully and desperately portrayed by you in "Fenomen doby" [The Phenomenon of Our Time].

But no matter how deep the personal experiences, they are only an impulse, the humus, the soil from which those sufferings sprouted with poems of universal content, was formed before the arrest. And here, in the KGB cell, Vasyl worried that the streams nourishing this humus had become painfully shallow. It was his sense of context and the ability to contextually exist-create-breathe in the circle of the elect that saved him. His closest friends that year were Hölderlin and Goethe, Rilke and Pasternak, the early Tychyna

---

[24] Ibid., 15.

and Shevchenko, Svidzinsky and Ortega y Gasset, Camus and Sartre, Jung and Plato, Skovoroda ... He joined the high tragedy of the Ukrainian people of the twentieth century, which made him feel like one of the last warriors, on whose conduct defeat or victory depends, which will be the memory of the people of your nation.

Even Vasyl Stus himself was amazed at the triviality of this realization, nourished by thousands of his predecessors, who at different times found themselves alone with history and found the strength, like Petro Kalnyshevsky, not to lose their dignity and preserve a good conscience.

"*Be worthy of your ancestors, Vasyl! You are one of the last people in a culture that is more and more becoming a provincial one.*"

Sometime during those days, the Stus' persona became not only a man, a personality, but also bore the burden representing the whole nation, as he will remind himself in all his subsequent work.

The poet does not limit himself by the comprehension of human existence in the Soviet empire, but considers it in a much broader dimension: the atomization of humanity becomes global — to continue feeling yourself as part of your kin at the end of the twentieth century you have to overreach yourself, live to the maximum, get out of your own problems for the sake of generally valid ones. To get out, even though you know very well that it hurt to almost no one anymore:

*This your new birth —
in the renewed body and spirit.
And having recognized the new sight and hearing
I felt that someone was living
in my body. He is secretly outliving
me from myself. Attracting all the time,
for my gaze faded,
like a candle...*[25]

Thus, out of the conscious need to remain faithful to the idea for which (according to Stus) the greatest predecessors laid down their

---

[25] Ibid., 13.

lives, the creation of a kind of diary of a human being who comprehends his own existence as a small part of something bigger and more significant started.

Flashback-sketch-reflection-impression—this is the plot sequence on which, like beads, the images of Stus' inner visions and dream-experiences are strung, composing a picture from several structurally interconnected poetic texts in the collection-diary. Later, already in "Palimpsesty," when the pain of loss has deadened, the forming of the spirit embodied in the text will become even more crystallized, and the texts will be carefully cleansed of obvious biographical motives. But neither the language nor the style of the poet will change. That is why the key to the hermetically closed "Palimpsesty," as Yu. Shevelyov described it, is here, in *Chas tvorchosti*.

However, *Chas tvorchosti* is more than a diary of existence. The collection is an anthem. the exaltation of a human being over circumstances, the liberation of the spirit from the decay of the flesh, the maturing to a c o n s c i o u s choice. It is for these reasons that sometimes the author allows himself minor adjustments and assembles several poems not in their chronological order but subordinates them to a hierarchy of maturation.[26]

But poetry is in "the realm of psychiatry, not art," and therefore "the establishment of being through words" involves understanding all the stages of existence: birth—development—maturity—twilight—the pressure of culture. In this he was almost following Heidegger, who claimed that "poetry is the inaugural naming of being and of the essence of all things."[27] Poetry illuminates

---

[26] Specifically, the collection opens with the poem "Napevne tak i treba..." [Certainly it should like this...], written on September 30, 1972; "Otsei svitanok—niby rivnyi spalakh..." [This dawn is like an equal flare...], written on February 23, is placed between the poems "Bietsia sertse, yak ptasha nime..." [The heart beats like a dumb bird ...] and "Zahorodyly bilyi svit..." [The world is blocked...], written in January. There are a few more such cases.

[27] Martin Heidegger, "Hölderlin and the Essence of Poetry," trans. Douglass Scott, in *Existence and Being*, ed. Werner Brock (Indiana: Gateway, 1949), 270

the shaded and backwoods things that suddenly become the essential core, the most important things, which restore the lost sacred meaning, the seemingly long-dead senses.

And it is in this sense that poetry ceases to be a thing, but becomes sacred, the most important source capable of filling with vital energy the dead spirit of a vegetating language, elevating the poet to the level of watcher-creator, who fills the ocean of language with his own creativity.

And the sacrifice of the creator is not in vain, because it attracts new believers, who, picking up his style and his faith, move farther in the indicated direction, even when they seemingly deny his achievements. They no longer fan the faintly smoldering embers but support the small tongues of flame with their own sacrifices.

Thus, in the pre-trial detention cell of the Kyiv KGB, the process of creation of the poet's own language finished, which was decisive for the poet, because it was the language that established the invisible but real relationships between the parts that confirmed the birth of a new poetic world and a new poetry.

But Stus' true poetry begins beyond the bounds of senses, where the personal folk become part of the world, where the boundaries between good and evil, optimism and pessimism, between life and decay are blurred. It is impossible to comprehend it. It is an object of conscious faith. In this crucible of the intolerable, Stus completed a kind of initiation, after which not only a new person but also a new language would be born. Vasyl realized with horror and joy that on this path worldly joys and wisdom are unimportant, and only the presence of power in the lines of the time matters.

"Palimpsesty" was being born — a symbol-icon pendant of fate, writing something new over the erased autographs of previous impressions. It should be noted that an important component in this process was Goethe's poetry, translated by the poet during the investigation.

With a defiant kind of perseverance, proving to himself every day that no circumstances could force him to surrender, the poet on the shores of the German edition of Goethe every day planned to translate some lines the following day.

Strictly speaking, work on translating Goethe's poems began in the late 1960s, but it was a period of study and material accumulation rather than of active translation. The vast majority of the translation work was done by Vasyl Stus in 1972, in the pre-trial detention cell of the Kyiv KGB.

But under these unfavorable conditions, Stus surprisingly revealed not only the secret world of the great poet and sublime master mason, but also parallels with his — Vasyl's — "experience" of the world through him:

I am sneaking through the wilderness,
With prepared flintlock.
Your sweet image
Emerged from the darkness to me...[28]

In this way one of the most original collections of Ukrainian poetry of the last century was born. It is a book where poetry echoes in translations, as if enriched by their context, so as to have the strength to perceive the foreign spirit and recreate it as its own, in modern times and in another culture.

While working on the book, whose outline the poet saw more and more clearly, he became really furious when, on January 19, Loginov again summoned him for questioning and immediately started a conversation about anti-Soviet statements in the draft autograph of the poem "Bezpashportnyi zakripachenyi v seli" [Having no passport enslaved in the village].

"This draft poem," Vasyl snapped, "*was written seven or ten years ago. I consider it unfair, moreover, a violation of the law to charge me on the basis of a draft.*"[29]

They parted after this remark. Vasyl Stus had emphasized again that he had no desire to talk about literature with an investigator who was not a specialist and therefore could not speak professionally on this topic.

---

[28] Vasyl Stus. Tvory. Volume 2, 270.
[29] Criminal Case N 47. Volume 1, Sheet 128.

Of course, Loginov was impressed by the detainee's aggressive behavior. The one whom he had thought the day before a "weakling" who would be easily broken displayed a steel temper. However, he was ready to bring a charge.

And at 6:15 p.m. on January 22, 1972, Stus had the chance to familiarize himself with it.

"DECISION
on status as defendant
Kyiv
January 22, 1972
The investigator of the KGB Department under the Council of Ministers of the Ukrainian SSR of Kyiv region, senior lieutenant LOGINOV, having considered the materials of the criminal case concerning STUS Vasily Semenovych, d —
HAS ESTABLISHED:
Sufficient evidence has been collected regarding the case to bring charges against STUS V.S. that during 1969-1971 he systematically produced, reproduced, and distributed documents in which he slandered the Soviet state and social order.

In 1969 he wrote an article, "Mistse v boiu chy v rozpravi," containing defamatory statements, which he reproduced, and distributed to others. This article was published in the illegal anti-Soviet "Ukrainsky Visnyk" magazine, published abroad.

In 1971, he wrote and distributed a letter to the Presidium of the Writers' Union of Ukraine and Party bodies, which contained slanderous fabrications that disgraced the Soviet state system. By his actions, he committed a crime stipulated by Art. 187-1 of the Criminal Code of the USSR.

Based on the above and guided by Articles. 131 and 132 of the CPC of the USSR —
HAS DECIDED AS FOLLOWS:
STUS Vasyl Semenovych, born on January 6,[30] 1938 is to be named as a defendant in the case and charged with committing a crime stipulated by Art. 187-1 of the Criminal Code of the USSR... "[31]

---

[30] In the decision the wrong date of January 8 was given.
[31] Criminal Case N 47. Volume 1, Sheet 131.

Instead of a signature that would indicate acknowledgment with the document, the writer left in the minutes his emotional reaction to the information he read:

"I reviewed the content of Article 187 of the Criminal Code of the Ukrainian SSR and I understand it. I do not plead guilty to the charges. As for the charge, I can explain that during 1969-1971 I neither distributed, nor produced, nor reproduced any documents slandering the Soviet state and social order.

The article "Mistse v boiu chy v rozpravi" was addressed to L. Dmyterko, who slandered the honest Soviet writer I. Dziuba. Since I observed a recurrence of the cult massacre in Dmyterko's stance, I defended the honest, open I. Dziuba's stance against the attacks of Dmyterko, a man who, until 1956, was not distinguished by having high human principles.

I typed this article and sent it seemingly to two addresses: to Literaturna Ukraina and to L. Dmyterko himself. Thus, I neither "produced" it, nor reproduced it, nor distributed it, although, perhaps, I did show it to someone I knew (but I did not give it to anybody).

The same applies to the letter to the Presidium of the Writers' Union of Ukraine and F. D. Ovcharenko.

I typed 3 copies of each article (two for the official bodies and one for myself). These copies for myself, or rather, the last and only copy, I put into a drawer of my desk. I did not acquaint anybody with them, but I may not remember it well, as I did not see any sedition in the articles. My only wish was to remedy the abnormal situation in the literature..."[32]

A draft of another letter by Vasyl Stus to Shelest, written at the turn of 1965-1966,[33] remained in the case file. The poet did not send the letter, but its manner only strengthened the investigator's belief that he was dealing with an enemy.

"Dear Petro Yukhimovich!

You did not answer my first letter. You are exercising the right of the gun, which seems to excuse human rudeness. Being the representatives of democracy, you despise the opinion of the people. It is not obligatory for

---

[32] Ibid., Sheet 132-135.
[33] Ibid., Sheet 187-188.

you to answer ordinary people, people having deputy's seats or world-renowned inventors. The power of the people pays attention only to the people, not to individuals.

On my behalf, I reject the right of the weak and do not ask for anything. I do not want to offend myself by feeling my own weakness just because there is no organized force behind me that made me be your obedient performer. In the end, you promise the people the coming of communism, and you probably think it will be a realm of obedient robots.

I'm not a robot. I know that the right to think and express one's thoughts freely is *a b i o l o g i c a l* ability that cannot be controlled and limited by any decrees. This is my biological right, which is not determined by the area of the chair that each of us occupies. I have almost completely given this right into your hands, leaving myself the highest right – to ecstatically approve everything that comes out of the wise heads of geniuses according to their position.

As a member of society, I have given you my lifelong right to determine my life by myself. In the end, you voluntarily took it from me referring to the unanimity of the ancestors, who, going the whole hog, won power for one person. They did not know that the dictatorship of the proletariat would become someone's personal pension, that the age-old despotism, crushed in February and October 1917, would still laugh bitterly at the victors.

So, your power consists of millions of circumcised human wills. Therefore, being a servant of the people, you are partly my servant. However, I will say otherwise: you are my debtor. I 'passed' the right to choose one's own way of life, future, etc. to you even before birth, hoping that you would not abuse it, that being clamped in a single brain pan, the people's thinking would bring good results ...

* * *

Socialism by its nature arose from a great desire of humans to achieve their own freedom. Thus, the socialism of the future, as the ideal of a socially secured human will, must have been especially dear to the peoples of a country like Russia, with its age-old regime of arbitrary power.

The dictatorship of the proletariat, desperately needed at the time of the overthrow of tsarism and the strengthening of Soviet power was based on slave psychology, even if it was perceived as a temporary necessity...

They have extended the system of dictatorship into our country. Extended it for an indefinite period. In so doing they preserved that conditional human captivity which should be fought by socialism and be "removed" by it...

As a child, swollen with hunger in the postwar years, I was obliged to shout, 'Thank you, comrade Stalin, for our happy childhood.' That was the first social trauma. The number of the following injuries is a million. Imagine the vulnerable soul of a Soviet schoolboy who has to skin himself several times during 10 years of study. On one day he accepts in good faith what he will give up the next day, or more precisely, what he will curse the next day. That happened to my generation. The great leader and teacher turned out to be the nations' executioner, a state criminal and, in fact, an enemy of socialism. You will say that thanks to him our industrial and economic potential increased (we like to give figures and percentages). Answer: Hitler forced the Germans to do no less in seven years. So this is not a merit of socialism. The Institution's tutors, systematically 'overthrowing' the Stalin cult, repeated in reverse order the things that prostituted Parisian journalists performed in the early days of Napoleon's Hundred Days War. These mentors-tutors were like those journalists, the prostitutes. It pains me to say this: a teacher is always a teacher, and it is difficult to say the bitter truth about even the worst.

But there are too many bitter things. We survived the disgrace of the 'Hungarian events.'[34] We survived the disgrace connected with the enriching of Marxism by Khrushchev. We survived the disgrace of his overthrow. The hypocrisy did not stop. It is continuing.

It cannot be so!

... the faith's traumas, a great deal of what has been done, are much more severe than individual economic shortcomings. The faith's traumas lead to insanity, to meanness, they decompose the most honest people, they decompose them from inside, cultivating cunning, petty calculation and supreme unscrupulousness. 'You cannot be honest! Who needs your stupid honesty?' shout the conditions. You must love as long as ordered, believe so deeply that tomorrow you will painlessly renounce your faith, hate so passionately that tomorrow you will be indifferent when you do not love, and so on.

---

[34] The reference is to the 1956 uprising in Hungary against Soviet dictatorship.

Let's take an "ordinary" Soviet man. He has damaged age-related reactions to the world. He has learned to laugh when he is very distressed (in this way the order is received – Rejoice! Sing!). He 'voluntarily' does what he is forced to (say, join those 'voluntary' societies by which they want to camouflage the lack of the right to create mass organizations), praises what is not worth any attention (say, Khrushchev's famous 'instructions' to artists, made in 1962-1963), condemns what he secretly admires. The man is besotted. He allegedly lost the ability to understand such simple words as love, hate, goodwill, freedom, democracy, justice, humanism, and so on. He does not know anymore what these words mean...

Today man is driven deep underground and he feels himself like a state criminal there. In the public eye, he has his counterpart, a version 'for everyone,' as respectable as a robot that is reprogrammed daily with new thoughts and new formulations of the old question. This man, taken in the version 'for everyone' resembles a prostitute, who is tired of taking on more and more new clients, but, accepting them, makes a profit. This is the way that a human being is gradually demoralized. He seems to have lost himself, forgotten the deep meaning of the words 'a human being.' Today he is unlikely to answer what he has to do to be 'a human being'...

We still remedy the atrophy of bodies (the grain problem is an eternal one like 'the Lord's prayer'), but we do not care about the progressive atrophy of souls.

It seems that the master of our country is a great philistine, who is produced by all the sections of society – from the worker to the academician. The summit of degradation is our so-called intelligentsia, which, however, is saved from complete shame by the afterlife halos of martyred, obsessed, tortured people, such as the Mayakovskys Dovzhenkos, Pasternaks, Charents, Zabolotskys, Vertovys, Kurbas, and Meyerholds. Let's take the history of our writing. Almost all the classics of socialist realism consist of victims. Let's take Ukrainian literature. Ellan (Blakytny), Vyshnia, Golovko, Sosura, Kulyk, Tychyna, Yanovsky, Slisarenko, Kulish, Kurbas, Kosynka, Rylsky, Johansen, Petrytsky, Pluzhnyk, Yanovsky, Bazhan, Zerov, Dry-Khmara, Filipovych, Pidmokhylny, Polishchuk, Semenko etc. – which of them was not a 'fierce nationalist,' which of them lived his life safely? For a show we have a permanent staff of happy mock suns, now filled with dmyterkos of various grades, they are given prizes – state and republican, they are read now and then, but do not get read.

Name at least one significant Ukrainian writer, for whom our always sinless pastors would not grant the remission of their sins — for some, at the price of heads, for the others with a life of penance in a modern cell, and for others still with great moral torment.

Name at least one great Russian writer! Remember Mayakovsky, Pasternak, Sholokhov, Platonov, Zoshchenko, Ehrenburg, Paustovsky, Koltsov, Olesha, Babel, Martynov, Mandelstam, Zabolotsky, Akhmatova — which of them enjoyed the greatest freedom in the world?

Who, say, except the always agreeable comrade Philistine believed in the recent trial of Synyavsky and Daniel?[35] *The 'fair' critics (Yeromin, A. Vasiliev, Kedrina) cite almost the same passages from their 'fascist' works, and doing it so badly that they even burned their own fingers. As is well known, 'the entire Soviet people' unanimously condemned the 'turncoats.' But why not Jacobson not have the right to defend himself? Why didn't any of the outstanding writers speak up for him? Why can a person be judged for a work of art? Why, unanimously agreeing with the philological conclusions of justice, are 'the entire Soviet people' forced to take it all for granted (perhaps, having read the works of 'fascists,' a person would draw his own conclusions: he would 'unanimously' support the verdict or lose such unanimity)? Why is it possible to judge works by subjecting them to life imprisonment in special camps, etc.? They were put on trial for slandering the Soviet reality. Although the word 'slander' in the Soviet reality loses its exact characteristics: N. Korzhavin, anticipating by some decades the decision of the 20th Congress of the Party, 'slandered' Stalin; the things that Lenin said about Stalin in the 1930s were slander, then, under Khrushchev, it became true; and it is still undecided what it is now (there is no indication). Khrushchev's 'genius Marxist-Leninist provisions,' approved by the entire Soviet people, have become anti-Marxist today. The word 'slander' has grown faded, it has become as 'slippery' as the classic term 'enemy of the people.' No one will believe the quotes drawn like cards when they play Witch.*[36] *Does all this remind you of the medieval witch*

---

[35] On February 10, 1966, the trial against Synyavsky and Daniel began, and appeared to mark the beginning of mass persecution of the intelligentsia in the USSR, or, more precisely, of people who did not want to remain silent that the world, depicted by Stus in this letter, was insufficient for human life.

[36] "Witch" is a children's card game in which each player blindly draws one card from a partner, discarding pairs: two jacks, two kings, etc. The goal is not to be the one holding the queen of spades at the end of the game.

trials? Everyone unanimously believes in fear, in the slave morality sanctioned by centuries– 'not in my backyard,' 'keep it shut,' 'he that talks much, errs much,' 'he knows much who knows how to hold his tongue' – this is the most accurate foundation of our ethics.

The trials that have already taken place in Ukraine (in Ivano-Frankivsk, Ternopil, Lutsk, Odesa, Kyiv) clearly showed the judge's ethics. Tell me, was the condemnation of Karavansky[37] also unanimously supported by the entire Soviet people? Did the trial really take place or was he simply arrested as 'incorrectly rehabilitated'? Is his greatest crime a personal appeal to the communist parties of the world about the persecution started against the young Ukrainian intelligentsia?

As for the incident at the Ukraina cinema on September 4, 1965, I. Dziuba's greatest sin was that he mentioned the arrests. Mentioning is forbidden! The people who made the arrests were sure that everyone would prostrate themselves on the ground and lie like that. But Dziuba was not frightened and so 'failed' greatly the initiators of the arrests: they were out in their reckoning on the animal sense of self-preservation.

I was indignant that some informant blatantly shouted: 'This is a lie! There were no arrests! This is a provocation!' I was indignant that some 'activists' shouted: 'This is not the place to discuss such issues' and began to draw my first conclusions from all this. Indeed, the cinema is not a place for such conversations, but where is the place? I simply could not bear such a mockery of the truth of facts, of the truth of human ethics. And it **is my fault that I did not have the strength to endure this shame, it is my fault that I wasn't scared when I had to be scared, that I was indignant at what I could not help but be indignant about.** *Then comrade Usenko shouted at me: 'Yes! Svitlychny is the enemy!' He knew even then that Svitlychny was the enemy. How did he know? Did he see Svitlychny with his own eyes? So why is this 'enemy' kept in prison for 7 months now? Now it is clear even to the blind that* **everything is far from**

---

[37] Sviatoslav Karavansky, a human rights activist and linguist, the author of *Slovnyk rym* [The Dictionary of Rhymes], produced publicistic articles against the Russification of schooling. In 1945, he was sentenced to 25 years in prison for ties with a group of Ukrainian youth close to the Organization of Ukrainian Nationalists (OUN). In 1960 he was amnestied. In November 1965, he was arrested again and forced "to stay in prison" for 8 years and 7 months. While serving his sentence in Mordovia in 1969 for writing articles in prison, including the one on the Katyn Forest tragedy, a new criminal case was initiated against him. After his release in 1979, he emigrated to the United States.

what Usenko thought at that time. And Usenko is an old man and in his life has seen, or at least heard of the universal devices, the cells of the 1930s, which perfectly mastered the technology of the mass production of 'criminals' and 'enemies.' To who will you now prove, comrade Usenko, that the people arrested today are enemies? To whom will you prove that Gevrych (one of them) was the enemy when his trial was c l o s e d ? You will not manage it in any way, convince anyone or prove it to anyone. A closed court means a false court.

But let's return to the issue of the 'disclosure of secrets.' Let's talk about censorship again.

As is well known, all the best from the golden fund of socialist realism used to experience birth pains. The great Soviet prose writer M. Sholokhov had a hard time with his G. Melekhov.[38] The same happened to Fadeev, Dovzhenko, Twardowski, Mayakovsky and Platonov. Almost everything was perceived at first as very unfriendly and was canonized afterward, often after the death of the writer. Remember the dead crowds of the great. Don't you see that a significant half of them are headless riders? They were dug out of the grave and put on a horse.

Of course, we are shouting that here as well we are leading the world. Take a pencil and count the number of artists killed by Stalin and Hitler. Find the proportion. And then you will see which of them was a communist, and which was a fascist, which of them was a bandit, and which was a leader. You are materialists and believe in statistics, not the delusion of what merely seems.

In art we are decades behind, we have been pushed back. We are regressing further. And our genius artists, such as Pasternak, Tsvetaeva, Mandelstam, are better known abroad than in their motherland. The whole world knows the ingenious Archipenko, Krushelnytska, Myshuga, and Koshit but not the native people.

All this is a consequence of a huge spiritual dictatorship, which loves only the usual, the clear, the unambiguous, the ordinary. It needs everything to be 'in the spirit of,' i.e., repetition, comment. Every 'spirit' is a 'spirit' only when the heart beats. And a heart beating is irreversible. 'To speed up' by force means to give up on the fact that this 'spirit' is alive.

---

[38] Grygory Melekhov is a character in M. Sholokhov's novel "Tykhyi Don" [Quiet Flows the Don].

Our time is a time of the dictatorship of the aesthetics of the Khrushchevs, the Stalins, the Zhdanovs, dishonest people who did not and do not understand anything in art. They do not know why it is needed, but treat it as an outdated etiquette ...

The dozens of arrests made in Ukraine have whetted the appetite of people deprived of conscience and honor. Maybe [it is] some kind of business for them? Many people were fired, others were expelled from the Party. The apartments of many of them were made subject to secret or official 'legal' briefs. Many were monitored or subject to official 'legal' searches. Many poets and critics are not published. There is one goal: to intimidate every person, make him tremble alone, make him see in every neighbor a state criminal. There is one goal: to engrave fear in everyone's soul. The goal is to arouse the animal instincts of each person, exercising the mass hypnosis and mental trauma that was brilliantly carried out by Stalin and his guardsmen.

These 'campaigns' resulted in the growth of mistrust between fraternal peoples ('those Ukrainians who always speak their mova [language] are potential or real enemies of the Russian people!'). This is being hammered diligently into the philistine's head. And he believes in everything! Having heard from comrade N the Ukrainian language, so unusual in 'gorod Kiyev' [city of Kyiv], comrade Philistine asks: I wonder, are you a nationalist?

Comrade N was surprised: Sorry, what? And what is a nationalist?
Comrade Philistine: One who wants an independent Ukraine.
Comrade N: But Ukraine is independent. Don't you know?

Already the 'inconsistencies' emerge. Now comrade Philistine has blushed, frightened by the topic he raised.

The connections here are made as an unconditioned reflex. The 'Ukrainian bourgeois nationalist' is a mortar, more powerful than 'enemy of the people.'. Once you are called that, it says it all. There is nothing more to talk about. When you speak Ukrainian, it means that you hate the Russian people and Russian culture, so you need to be 'clammed up.' And a person is 'clammed up.' For many years, we used to 'clam up' about the fact that in the Ukrainian SSR the vast majority of the urban population ignores s Ukrainian books. During an hour in any bookstore in Kyiv you can hear several times: 'And in Russian – no?'; 'Ah, it is in Ukrainian,' etc. Outs is a situation in which the consumers of Ukrainian books are the writers themselves, peasants, a meager part of the urban population and ... waste paper piles ...

Working for some time as a literary editor of the Ukrainian twin of Sotsialisticheskiy Donbass [Socialist Donbas] and looking for non-existent Ukrainian equivalents for Russian mining terminology (Ukrainian mining terminology is not really mastered at the Institute of Linguistics of the USSR Academy of Sciences, which is the only place where some of these terms can be heard), I felt myself at a minimum as a criminal. Especially when I approached the kiosks and saw people cursing this Ukrainian twin. I remember being 'taken care of' by employees who never spoke Ukrainian, but tried to teach me. I remember such a case. One of the regional committee officials died. He died abruptly, as we can say, by a sudden death. I tried to write like this: he died abruptly, he died an abrupt death. I was denied. I insisted. Then I was told: tomorrow there would be a reprimand to the editor I. Domanov about both of us. 'How can you be so disrespectful when talking about the dead?'...

All this leads some Ukrainians with their inherent national inferiority complex openly boasting about their ignorance of their native language! All these are traces of the accursed imperial past, which morally crippled the Ukrainian nation, declaring national consciousness and pride to be a crime. And now it is proceeding on its own. This has become the norm. Because we will not convert people to the old faith! The denationalized element resembles the declassed one. There is nothing sacred left in their souls. And this leads to even greater moral degradation. This is also one of the ways to mass produce comrade Philistine, who has a brilliant ability to change everything. From his own 'I believe' he can make a checkbook, he knows how to change conscience into money and in the sense of patriotism he can find 'unused reserves' of his own income.

The Philistine, being the ideal "human material" for the construction of s u c h 'communism' as appears in our country will agree to anything, as long as it brings him profit. But the country where the philistine is elevated to the rank of an exemplary citizen is anything but socialist.

* * *

And reflecting on all of this, I am becoming increasingly convinced that s u c h socialism is not socialism. And s u c h political freedoms are not freedoms. S u c h a 'paradise' is not paradise. S u c h 'truth' is not truth.

S u c h enslavement of the human soul, of human conscience, and *s u c h* dehumanization of man is almost intolerable. Then the greatest freedom opens up – the freedom of the slave, who does not care if he has to be silent, to praise the boss, to lie – about himself, about the environment, about life.

Such a deprivation of souls destroys any value of human existence. The shots that cut off the lives of the Mayakovskys, Skrypniks, Ordzhonikidzes, Fadeevs, Khvylovs, and the nooses around the Yesenins and Tsvetaevs were signs of an equation between the benefits of life and the fears of hell. This is the path they are running away from, remaining unconquered and gaining the personal freedom that is not given by your socialism. Here is the reason for that daring courage, examples of which will further be given to you more often...

I know that no Jesuits, no executioners will be able to break the human soul completely. It, like the Phoenix, is self-born. I see human spines starting to straighten, real proletarian internationalism growing, where no one calls nationalism the pain you feel for your people and their spiritual nature. Where Lithuanians, Georgians, Ukrainians, Jews, Russians and all other peoples of the Soviet Union are starting to realize the need for democracy, see clearly the damage of modern absolutism, which spreads chauvinism, hypocrisy, treachery, multi-level bureaucracy and many other 'satellites' brought by the totalitarian dictatorship into its orbit.

Socialism is the most honest human system. And it grows on the pure, natural human basis of honesty, justice and mutual respect but is supported by a gang of paid spies, policemen, informers, careerists, whose name is human impersonality.

And such socialism should be struggled against to the last breath."[39]

Vasyl Stus successfully "earned" his term of imprisonment. Having read this letter, written five or six years earlier, Loginov fully realized his wrong initial impressions of the arrested Stus. The investigation still lacked evidence of the poet's anti-Soviet activities, but if, initially, a satisfactory result would have been a "repentant" poet's letter in the press condemning his own "bourgeois-nationalist" activity and casting aspersions on one of the more famous figures of the "movement," there was no longer talk about it. Global

---

[39] Vasyl Stus. Tvory. Volume 4. – P.411-432.

appeals, accusations against the first person of the republic and strong criticism of KGB policy towards Ukrainian patriots and the youth national-cultural movement, in which the ideologues of the CPSU saw a threat to the integrity of the USSR, and which the poet supported in his 1965 letter to Shelest, did not leave the investigator any choice: Stus must be isolated, otherwise it could threaten his — Loginov's — career.

Not merely an investigator but "comrade Philistine" in person came to the fore, clearly understanding what he needed to do and what he needed to achieve because a "defeat" (there was undoubtedly insufficient proof of the detainee's guilt) did not threaten mythical state interests, but the well-being and career of the investigator himself. Comrade Philistine could not allow this and therefore with even greater diligence began to "dig" to find "evidence" of Stus' guilt.

On January 25, he summoned Vasyl Stus to his office with this very intention. But the first question of the investigator, concerning the draft version of the letter, starting with the words "A specter is haunting Europe ..." was met with Stus' harsh answer: *"I will not provide testimony regarding the case until I receive answers to my statements from the competent authorities. I clarify my answer: since I am accused on the basis of letters sent to official institutions more competent on matters concerning the Ukrainian literary process than the KGB, I would like to continue my conversation with the KGB investigator upon receiving an assessment of my literary works from the Central Committee of the Communist Party of Ukraine, the ideological department in particular, and from the Writers' Union of Ukraine. Until then, I will not answer the investigator's questions."* [40]

The relationship grew contentious. Several of Vasyl's subsequent sessions with the investigator did not give Loginov anything special, unless information about the reasons for the non-release of *Zymovi dereva* in Ukraine could be considered a "success."

The investigator paused, looking for ways to get the prisoner to provide the necessary information and answers.

---

[40] Criminal case N 47. Volume 1, Sheet 137-138.

On February 12, and for the next few days, he asked the poet about his relationship with the informal leaders of the sixties, trying through Stus' testimony about them to gather information against him. Some accounts given by Vasyl Stus regarded the "formal" sixtiers (arrested on the Dobosh case) targeted in the same investigation:

"*Ivan Svitlychny is one of the most honest and clearest heads in modern Ukrainian Soviet literature. And I am happy to be among his acquaintances. I was connected with him by my involvement in literary criticism (with an emphasis on research), literary work; my relationship with him is a relationship between two writers. I love him just like a man. I have known him since he studied at the postgraduate program at the Institute of Literature of the Academy of Sciences of the USSR, i.e., sometime since 1963-1964.*"[41]

About Yevhen Sverstyuk: "*I have known Sverstyuk since 1965-1966... He is a man of bright intellect and extremely high ethics. For me, he is an exemplary writer who has served the good and justice despite everything.*"[42]

When asked by the investigator what he knew "*about the production and distribution of anti-Soviet and defamatory documents by Zinovia Franko,*" Stus replied:

- "*I don't know anything about it. I think this is slander against Zinovia Franko's good name. In any case, I absolutely do not believe that there are any grounds for such a charge.*"[43]

About Viacheslav Chornovil: "*I respect him as a principled, brave, even courageous man. But, at the same time, I have no close relations with him, although I have nothing against him as a person and a citizen; moreover, I respect him.*"[44]

About Mykola Kholodny: "*I have known Mykola Kholodny since 1964-1965. I met him in the literary society at the Molod [Youth] publishing house, before that society was disbanded. I highly value him as a talented Ukrainian Soviet poet, one of the most socially significant modern Ukrainian artists in words. I rate highly his poems on rural themes. There*

---

[41] Ibid., Sheet 155.
[42] Ibid., Sheet 159.
[43] Ibid., Sheet 162.
[44] Ibid., Sheet 166.

is a lot of gloomy humor in his poems, but that is not surprising for a man who has been so ruthlessly mocked for many years. Because this may be his natural vision of a world that is unjust to him. He is a complicated man. I know that before university he was full of pure Komsomol faith in goodness and justice; however, later, affected by severe and unjust suspicions, scolding, persecution, his faith diminished a little. At least I, being a man who has never belonged to his close friends, got this feeling. I may be wrong when speaking of the diminishment of his faith."[45]

The last interrogation took place on February 24. However hard Loginov tried to "drag out" from Stus at least some criticism of the other detainees, he did not succeed.

Then the investigator took a month's break, assigning a for Stus, who every day poisoned his life with various provocations.

Loginov decided to change tactics. In late February and early March, he met with Vasyl Stus' relatives, wanting them to influence their husband-son-son-in-law: either he started cooperating with the investigation, or the court's sentence for "his crimes" could be very severe. However, he did not succeed in this area either.

Yet the month-long stay in the cell, during which Vasyl Stus was not summoned to the investigator, put pressure on the prisoner's psyche.

Completely isolated from the outside world, deprived of any information about the investigation of the other detainees and not knowing anything about the health of his relatives (although, as if incidentally, the guards from occasionally hinted that, for instance, although he had only been a month and a half away from home, problems had already begun… They did not specify the kind of problems—let him worry about it). Vasyl Stus could not stand it. Conflicts with the supervisors started, planned in some cases and forced others.

The only salvation during this time was Goethe. The pages "planned" for translation each day forced the poet to focus. Stus used to drop into the poetic world of the great German, searching for and taking delight in a successful line, an image found or a finished poem.

---

[45] Ibid., Sheets 171-172.

After the obligatory work on the translations, falling under the power of memories and reflecting on fate, in a constantly lit cell (the light in the cells was on all night) he always had a pencil at hand to write down a successful line or the finished text of a new poem:
*Do not indulge in sorrows. Because it is useless —
to indulge your sorrows in vain.
That is how your mother birthed you,
To get to know what a prison is.
And maybe there is no better way,
As to cut yourself short by the stars...*[46]

Finally, on the morning of March 24, an extremely nervous Stus was summoned to Loginov. On the way — again the snapping of fingers, again the deliberate isolation, which Vasil often and provocatively violated with loud announcements: "*Stus is being taken for interrogation,*" "*good morning, friends,*" or some other. As Ye. Sverstyuk observed, Vasyl was the only one in the Kyiv KGB prison noted for such a pronounced violation of prison rules.

Of course, sometimes there were beatings with batons or fists. However, this happened only once or twice, because the loud declaration of this fact to the whole prison was not in the plans of the guards at all — they were simply confused by such provocative behavior.

The morning conversation lasted 35 minutes. Vasyl demanded to be informed about the health of his wife and relatives, and the investigator began to ask questions. Neither got answers.[47]

The evening conversation lasted longer, but the only reply the investigator got in response to a question about Valentin Moroz was: "*When writers become criminals, it is a very dangerous sign for society. And when it comes to the culprit — this is mutual guilt: both man and society. It is in such situations that understanding is needed, an honest, open discussion, not a massacre behind closed doors.*"[48]

---

[46] Vasyl Stus. Tvory. Volume 2, 73.
[47] Criminal case N 47. Volume 1, Sheets 175-176.
[48] Ibid., Sheet 182.

To influence the prisoner, Loginov included senior KGB officials (Senior Lieutenant Parkhomenko,[49] the Head of the Division of the Investigation Department of the KGB of the Ukrainian SSR, was present at the interrogation on March 28) and even Makarenko,[50] the Assistant Prosecutor of the Ukrainian SSR, the Senior Counselor of Justice. However, this had little effect on Vasyl Stus.

On March 31, 1972, the interrogation did not last long again. The investigator's poking around in fragments of the draft letter to P. Yu. Shelest provoked a new outburst of indignation: *"the quote mentioned by the investigator from my draft letter, which is neither defamatory nor anti-Soviet (it may simply contain certain erroneous statements by a man who fights for socialism, not against it), corresponds to my text. I do not consider this quote defamatory. Because socialism without guaranteed individual freedom is not real socialism. Contrary to the right to freedom of conscience and belief guaranteed by the Constitution of the USSR, the investigator attaches a manuscript to the case, which I did not give to anyone and, in the end, did not finish. To accuse me on the basis of drafts of my thoughts and blame me for holding them as convictions is not only obscene but also illegal: it contradicts my constitutional rights, which the investigator wants to violate.*

In protest against such arbitrariness, I refuse to testify about my draft recordings and unfinished works.

Because I do not want to be an ally in the violation of the Constitution."[51]

On April 4, Loginov decided to talk about *Vesely Tsyntar* [The Merry Cemetery] and but Stus hammered back: *"I believe that the question of* Vesely Tsvyntar *does not concern the investigation."*[52] When Loginov came to the poem "Kolesa hlukho stukotiat..." [The Wheels are Thumping...] (in memory of M. K. Zerov) and the line *"Rad-sots-konts-taboriv soiuz"* [of Soviet-socialist-concentration-

---

[49] Ibid., Sheet 184.
[50] Protokol dodatkovoho dopytu obvynuvachenoho vid 29 bereznia 1972 r [Record of additional interrogation of the defendant of March 29. 1972] // Ibid., Sheets 186-188.
[51] Ibid.—Sheets 190-191.
[52] Ibid.—Sheet 193.

camps union], which the investigator interpreted as slanderous, Stus told him:

"*This is not fiction or slander on the Soviet state and social order. These lines refer to concentration camps, not to the country as a whole.*"[53]

The poet opted not to discuss the poem "Marko Bezsmertny" with the investigator at all.

On April 11, the "accused" told the investigator that the *Postat golosu*[54] [The Figure of the Voice] collection presented to him "*would not be looked at by him because it had been 'dishonestly' confiscated. Who was the author of the collection's poems, who published it and who had given it to him, he refused to answer, saying that it would do 'you too much honor.*"[55]

The same happened with the *Pidsumovuiuchy movchannia*[56] [The Summing-up of Silence] collection of poems. When Loginov started questioning the poet about a poem dedicated to V. Moroz, Vasyl "*called the investigator a state criminal.*"[57] He repeated the same when asked about Kordun's collection of poems *Tykhyi maister dytiachykh ihrashok* [The Quiet Master of Children's Toys], which contained Stus' preface.

In April, Loginov tried unsuccessfully to draw out Vasyl in the investigation, asking questions about the "history" of the transfer of the *Zymovi dereva* manuscript abroad and its publication in Brussels, but was constantly exposed to Vasyl Stus' audacity and unwillingness to heed the copies presented to him of testimonies from L. Seleznenko, G. Kotsurova, I. Svitlychny. Stus read them carefully and ... demanded a face-to-face encounter because you can fabricate anything.

Something had to be done. And Loginov found a way out.

On April 29, 1972, he managed to obtain a resolution "on providing an expert forensic psychiatric examination in the case of STUS Vasyl Semenovych."[58]

---

[53] Ibid. – Sheet 194.
[54] *Postat Golosu* was a collection of poems by Hrigory Chubay.
[55] Criminal Case N 47. Volume 1, Sheet 196.
[56] *Pidsumovuiuchy movchannia* was a collection of poems by Ihor Kalynets.
[57] Criminal Case N 47. Volume 1, Sheet 197.
[58] Criminal Case N 47. Volume 2, Sheet 171.

On May 6, 1972, Vasyl Stus was forcibly taken to the 13th Department of the Kyiv City Clinical Hospital named after the academician Pavlov.

"*They are taking Stus to the insane asylum.*" — This was repeated behind the silent walls of the KGB internal prison, it was heard in the corridors of the internal prison when he was taken out to the *voronok* for the compulsory examination.

Loginov's submission particularly emphasized that "*Stus did not plead guilty, explaining that the documents he had produced ("Mistse v boiu chy v rozpravi" and the letter to the Presidium of the CPU and Party bodies) were not defamatory.*

Throughout the investigation, Stus, refusing to give truthful testimony in his case, behaved defiantly, unnecessarily insulting witnesses and other participants in the process. In addition, he shows signs of persecution mania and an uncritical attitude to his actions and behavior.

In addition, Stus was registered at the 5th hospital of the Zhovtnevy district of Kyiv with some other diseases.

... the above-mentioned signs in the behavior of the accused Stus raise doubts about his mental state... "[59]

After announcing to Vasyl the "Resolution on the assignment of an expert forensic psychiatric examination," between 1 p.m. and 2:20 p.m. on May 6, 1972 in Loginov's office, the poet stated:

"*1. I consider the examination unjustified, because for the past 34 years I have never been informed by a psychiatrist about the presence of any mental anomalies.*

2. I believe that this examination is the KGB's attempt to massacre me in a new and inhuman way.

3. I strongly protest against such an examination.

4. The explanation for the need of such an examination is false. I was not the first to offer insults to any of the witnesses or other KGB agents. I insulted them only when I had to defend myself against insults.

5. The alleged signs of persecution mania are purely a KGB fabrication.

6. The reference to my being registered at the 5th hospital of the Zhovtnevy district is a futile attempt to support the fabrication, because,

---

[59] Ibid., Sheets 173-175.

despite suffering from a chronic stomach ulcer, I was never registered at the hospital."[60]

Vasyl Stus refused to sign the resolution.

One of his most difficult trials began—a seventeen-day attempt to break his will with the help of psychotropic drugs and other psychiatric means.

In the hospital, Vasyl had to radically change his behavior immediately. "Doctors in uniform" made it clear to him that any "hard" statement would automatically entail an additional dose of medication, something the psyche would not be able to handle.

He had to become a little more compliant, because—as he was told openly—here, in the hospital, you can do anything to a person with impunity: everything would be written off as mental illness.

It is safe to say that Act No. 643, which concluded that Stus Vasyl Semenovych was mentally fit, marked a small victory for his compliance:

"ACT № 643
Regarding Inpatient for forensic psychiatric examination
Stus[61] Vasiliy Semenovych

On May 23, 1972, the expert forensic psychiatric examination of the Kyiv City Clinical Hospital № 21 named after the Academician Pavlov (psychoneurological) examined Stus Vasiliy Semenovych, born in 1938, accused under Art. 187-1 of the Criminal Code of the USSR.

Stus has been in the hospital's forensic department since May 6, 1972.

Information received about the person under examination is as follows:

... Since his service in the army has suffered from a peptic ulcer ...

Believes that the above-mentioned works ["Mistse v boiu chy v rozpravi," "Vidkrytyi lyst", the Zymovi dereva collection] *should not be considered a crime, that he could be wrong in something, may have been somewhat sharp in style, but wrote in the pursuit "of the good, not evil." His practice is "purely ethical." Given all this, he does not consider himself guilty of anything.*

---

[60] Ibid., Sheets 177-178.
[61] This is the spelling used in the document.

"As can be seen from the character reference ... of the Institute (of Literature), Stus violated the norms of behavior of the scientific institution's staff, did not want to register with the Komsomol, refused public assignments. In 1964 he was fined for indecent behavior in the club of the Bolshevik plant. In 1965 he tried to organize, without authorization, a literary evening at one of the Kyiv plants ...

During the investigation, Stus understood the substance of the charge, pleaded not guilty, stating that the above documents were not defamatory. During interrogations, Stus behaved arrogantly, insulting witnesses and other participants in the process, sometimes refusing to testify, sometimes expressing unfounded suspicions, which provided the grounds to commission this examination.

PSYCHIC STATE

He is fully oriented. He behaves naturally. He is polite. He answers the questions to the point... His attention is steady. He understands the purpose of the examination, is outraged to be referred to a psychiatric hospital, as he does not consider himself mentally ill. He reports valid complaints of a somatic nature. Regarding the suspicions expressed during the investigation, he said that once, when he was very tired after the interrogation, the doctor gave him a purgative, but after taking it slept for a very long time. He got the idea that he had been given a sedative without being informed, and that they did this with the aim 'of possibly influencing my will in some way.'

... While administering the experimental-pathopsychological examination ... by Eyusenck, a predominance of introversion was noted.

... In conversations he persistently asserts his view on this or that issue, making references to literature, public and social events and facts. He recognizes that he is highly irritable, sensitive. He believes that this is a consequence of 'abnormal living conditions.'

Typical of Stus are irritability, excessive straightforwardness and sharpness, a tendency to suspicion. Introversion is exhibited in his psychopathic traits but no mental illness.

... he should be considered mentally competent."[62]

---

[62] Ibid., Sheets 179-180.

Stus' next meeting with Loginov took place on June 13. Although the detainee's position softened, he did not make any fundamental concessions.

In particular, when asked by the investigator the name of the author of the confiscated draft letter "Skilky molodykh avtoriv pobuvalo..." [How many young authors visited...] (the forensic examination of May 11, 1972, established that it was Ivan Dziuba), he explained:

"[Stus'] answer: I doubt that this draft letter was written by Ivan. I know that it I did not write it. I do not know how this draft happened to be among my papers. For this reason, I cannot give an exact answer to the rest of the questions...

Question [Loginov]: The content of the manuscript presented to you shows that it relates to the issues you wrote about in a letter addressed to the Secretary of the Central Committee of the Communist Party of Ukraine and the Presidium of the Writers' Union of Ukraine. Did you consult with Dziuba about writing a letter to the Secretary of the Central Committee of the Communist Party of Ukraine and the Presidium of the Writers' Union of Ukraine? If so, what were Dziuba's ideas about writing such a letter and when did you discuss the matter?

Answer [Stus]: The content of the mentioned draft can refer to anything. I do not object to such an interpretation, as the range of issues raised in the draft is on the agenda. These are questions that dozens and dozens of writers are writing and thinking about today, aware of their duty to the time, to people, to art and to communism.

I do not remember consulting with I. M. Dziuba about the last letter to the Government.

Question [Loginov]: Dziuba's manuscript presented to you is a plan for writing a letter on the position of young writers, including suggestions that you partly used when you wrote the letter to the Secretary of the Central Committee of the Communist Party of Ukraine and the Presidium of the Writers' Union of Ukraine ... Did you use Dzyuba's above-mentioned manuscript when writing your letter?

Answer [Stus]: I doubt that this manuscript is by Dziuba and that is is a plan for a letter about the position of young writers. Any thematic coincidences between my letter and the present draft are possible, just as the same rain cloud coming from the the Kyiv Sea can be seen by a person who lives in Bilychi and another who lives in Korchuvate. I do not remember using any of Dziuba's advice when writing my letter to the Government. I can say that I did not use the draft presented to me."[63]

The next day the interrogation lasted from 11:35 a.m. till 7:15 p.m.

The game went on: the investigator tried to mount accusations based on unbalanced judgments contained in Vasyl Stus drafts, which were not included in the final texts of his various appeals to the government. The poet resisted, emphasizing that accusations can only be based only on published materials, the "slanderous" nature of which was extremely difficult to prove.

The prisoner's insolence and fearlessness, which contrasted so greatly with the fear of the "majority" of witnesses, particularly irritated the investigator, forcing him to search for the smallest details and to interrogate and even humiliate those who did not conceal their respect for Vasyl Stus. During the few months that he was investigating the case, the poet became Investigator Loginov's personal enemy.

But if the investigator was not able to get any useful information from the poet himself, various institutions and casual acquaintances helped him to achieve what he wanted.

The accusation had a new basis. At the instruction of the Directorate of the Taras Shevchenko Institute of Literature of the USSR Academy of Sciences, a senior researcher, a Ph.D. in the philological sciences, a member of the Writers' Union, A. A. Kaspruk, wrote reviews of Stus' materials. His conclusions counted as an expert official evaluation and were indisputable evidence of Vasyl Stus' guilt in the court. The reviewer certainly did his best.

In his review of the *Zymovi dereva* collection, Kaspruk wrote:

"The Zymovi dereva *collection of poems by V. Stus was published abroad, in London, in 1970.*

The foreword included by the Literatura i mystetstvo *[Literature and Art] publishing house states that this collection was "struck off" by the* Radianskyi pysmennyk *[Soviet Writer] publishing house in 1965.*

---

[63] Criminal Case N 47. Volume 1, Sheets 213-216.

What provoked this reaction to this collection of poetry by the Soviet publishing house and the Soviet literary community?
I must say at once – its anti-Soviet content.
... it is the poetics of decadence, the poetics of ideological decline, which derives from the poetics of Western European decadence, as well as from the Ukrainian kind (Pachovsky, Karmansky, Filyansky, Chuprynka, etc.).

V. Stus sees only black, twilight colors, curses, death in the world around him. People around him are monkeys, mannequins, monsters ('Otak zhyvu: yak mavpa sered mavp' [*Here's how I live: like an ape among apes* ...], 'Spravliaiu v lisi samotu...' [*I celebrate loneliness in the forest* ...], 'Vyidu v nich. Pid sosnamy proidu...' [*I'll go out at night. I'll walk under the pines* ..., etc.).

And even the images themselves in V. Stus's poems are of a decadent character: 'kolir bozhevillia i sudnoi doby' [*the color of madness and Doomsday*], 'pekelnyi nimb' [*devil's nimbus*], 'liudstvo dushytsia' [*humanity is suffocating*], 'zhyvi – u domovyni' [*alive – in the coffin*], and so on.

However, the content of V. Stus' collection is not limited to decadent poems of decline.

The collection contains some poems that are clearly anti-social and anti-Soviet. He describes life in Soviet Ukraine as 'pravo – nadryvatysia v yarmi' [*the right to overstrain under the yoke*], as life in the 'prokliatomu kraiu, vitchyzni boiahuziv i ubyvts' ('Ne mozhu ya bez posmishky Ivana...') [*cursed land, the homeland of cowards and murderers* ('I can't do without Ivan's smile')].

The poems 'Zvirom vyty, horilku pyty – i ne charkoiu, postavtsem...' [*Howl like an animal, drink* horilka *and not from glass but a jug*...], 'Dazhd Nam, Bozhe, dnes...' [*Give us, O Lord, this day our daily bread*], 'Ostannii lyst Dovzhenka' [*Dovzhenko's Last Letter*], 'Rozmova' [*Conversation*], 'Balukhati mystetstvoznavtsi...' [*Goggle-eyed Art Critics*], 'Iakyi tse chas?' [*What Time Is It?*], 'Idut try tsyhanky roztsiatskovani...' [*There are three gypsies walking all with bells and whistles* ...], 'U Marintsi stoiat kukurudzy...' [*Maryinka has corn growing*...] are also imbued with a hatred of Soviet reality.

And V. Stus lived, studied, was brought up, worked among the Soviet people. Where did this so-called 'poet' get so much bile and hatred from?

It is not necessary to prove that V. Stus' book is harmful in the whole of its ideological direction, in its essence.

A normal unprejudiced person can only read it with abhorrence, with disdain for the 'poet' who so defames his land and his people."[64]

This was already a kind of "proof." Such expert evidence could be used to confirm the anti-Soviet nature of Vasyl Stus' published works.

The same "expert" reviewer also wrote about the *Vesely Tsvyntar* [The Merry Cemetery] collection:

"V. Stus' typewritten collection Vesely Tsvyntar is, actually, not a collection of poems, but a collection of poetic lampoons of Soviet reality.

V. Stus depicts the whole life of our people, their work, their daily routine, their leisure, their art in black, distorting colors. According to Stus, the Soviet people are soulless vending machines, people without heads, mannequins that mechanically play a silly performance set by some scheme.

The anti-Soviet nature of most of the poems in the collection is quite clear. For example, 'Os vam sontse, skazav cholovik z kokardoiu na kashketi...' [Here is the sun for you, said the man with the cockade on his cap ...]. In this so-called poem a concentrated defamation of Soviet life is presented. V. Stus imagines our life as regulated by a 'man with a cockade.' Here, instead of the sun, there is a copper penny, instead of space, there is an area of just a few feet, measured by the toe of a boot.

To write such a lampoon, you need to really be filled with hatred and malice for the land where you grew up, for the people among whom you live ...

As to their literary character, the poems of V. Stus' Vesely Tsvyntar collection are stupid, malicious muttering; and, seen from the political side, they are a conscious slander, denigration and deception of our Soviet modernity."[65]

---

[64] Criminal Case N 47. Volume 1, Sheets 335-336. In the court judgment, the reviewer's passages were quoted almost verbatim.
[65] Ibid., Sheet 333-334.

The last sentence is further proof of "denigration and deception." It was especially important that this evidence was provided by a representative of an official literary state institution. Stus could now say anything he liked. The defamatory nature of his work was obvious not only to the KGB's representatives and to his fellow writers.

Do not be surprised by the superficiality of these reviews. Such were the "rules of the game": for the investigator, the main thing was that an official "independent" literary critic introduced the key words—"anti-Soviet character," "slander of Soviet reality," and on the rest.

Kaspruk wrote about "Fenomen doby" [A Phenomenon of Our Time]:

"It must be said at once that when covering the great historical period studied by V. Stus (1917-1967) and assessing P. G. Tychyna's work, V. Stus favors anti-Soviet, nationalist positions.

V. Stus, in common with Ukrainian nationalist critics, acknowledges only the early Tychyna, the author of Soniashni klarnety *[Solar Clarinets], a collection in which, according to V. Stus, the poet 'became the most notable singer of the Ukrainian revolution ... of March 1917 ...'*

... imposing on P. G. Tychyna the glorification of the Ukrainian counter-revolution ('Bard Tsentralnoi Rady' [Bard of the Central Rada]) in the first collection and allegedly mourning the defeat of this counter-revolution in the second collection, **Zamist** *sonetiv i oktav [Instead of Sonnets and Octaves] ... V. Stus tries to present Tychyna's later work as poetic decline, as degeneration.*

V. Stus depicts Tychyna's natural evolution from generally abstract ideas, abstract humanism, and some national illusions to the assertion of the ideas of Soviet power's and Communist Party membership as 'frustrated optimism' and 'nationalization,' the transformation of the poet into a closet prophet and agitator ...

... In his blasphemy, V. Stus even reaches a point where he speaks about Tychyna's poetic death of from the 1930s to the end of his life ...

It is quite clear that V. Stus slanders P. Tychyna ...

It is in this defamation of P. Tychyna's work that V. Stus' 'patriotism,' and all his scientific objectivity lies."[66]

About the article "Znykome roztsvitannia" [Disappearing Blossoming], devoted to an analysis of Volodymyr Svidzinsky's work, Kaspruk wrote:

"V. Stus' initial position in this article is an idealistic interpretation of poetry in general and of V. Svidzinsky's poetry in particular.

For V. Stus, as a creative act, poetic creativity is 'a kind of otherness,' a 'clinical situation.' 'Social art constructions are at the very least meaningless'...

Poetry and creativity for V. Stus are not a reflection of real life, they do not serve the interests of Soviet society, but are a retreat into a range of personal, individual, subjective impressions and ideas. This is how idealistic bourgeois aesthetics understands creativity and interprets poetry.

But V. Stus does not only adhere to the position of an individualistic, idealistic interpretation of art and poetic creativity. He also gives his political assessment of V. Svidzinsky's poetry ... he speaks of V. Svidzinsky's poetry not only as 'sealing one's own spirit,' but also as "an elixir against the gangrenous era of Stalinist cultism.'

V. Stus is also fascinated by the mystical, unreal motives of V. Svidzinsky's poetry. Its poetic world is "subject to its own laws, open not to comprehension, but to sensory recollections, insight and intuitive discoveries'... This world includes 'otherworldly shadows,' where 'invisible hands touch, long-frozen voices are heard.'

Thus, V. Stus' article is typical of bourgeois-idealist writing, and alien to Soviet criticism and literary studies."[67]

However, not all of the blame should be placed on this "reviewer." Firstly, the staff of the Institute of Literature, as a state-funded ideological institution, were required to write "commissioned by the KGB," so it was impossible to avoid doing so without damaging one's career. And secondly, many literary critics really thought this way on both the political and — more importantly — cultural planes. Without a proper education, and having established a career executing "state" orders regarding literature, they could not help but recognize that the contextual interpretation of

---

[66] Ibid., Sheets 335-336.
[67] Ibid., Sheet 337.

the works proposed by Stus would mean their inevitable scientific death. And the latter meant the end of their financial well-being. Vasily Stus was again treading on the corns of "comrade Philistine."

The investigation record was also complemented by individuals who crossed his life and performed no worse than the "official" reviewers:

"I stayed with him [Stus] at the Rassvet [Dawn] sanatorium in Morshyn. I stayed in this sanatorium from December 18, 1971, to January 12, 1972. I arrived at the sanatorium a week after Stus, and I was lodged in room №23, building №10, where Stus and Victor Kislinsky were already staying.

... Stus seemed to be selfish and bad at mixing.

I got the impression that Stus was hostile to the Soviet system. I came to this conclusion after repeated arguments with him. In the course of these disputes and conversations, Stus delivered judgments alien to a Soviet man ...

Stus expressed the opinion that the Bandera people shown in the film [Bilyi ptakh z chornoiu oznakoiu *(The White Bird with a Black Mark)] were Ukrainian national heroes ... it was a mass movement. Stus said that if this film had been 'set correctly,' it could have been an anthem for the Bandera people.*

Stus told me that the Ukrainian language is in a worse position than any other foreign language taught in Ukraine."[68] This was the testimony of Pyotr Matskevych, a Belarusian with whom Vasyl Stus shared a room during his stay in the Morshyn sanatorium.

He also testified in court that the poet had once told an anecdote which included a cynical remark about Lenin, but that, after his reprimand concerning this, Stus stopped telling such anecdotes.

"Sometimes in conversation with Kislinsky,[69] *Stus compared the situation of workers in our country and the capitalist countries,"* Matskevich's testimony continued. *"When he did so, Stus said that the unemployed abroad are better off financially than our workers. Stus also said that there is more freedom and democracy abroad than in our country..."*

---

[68] Criminal Case N 47. Volume 2, Sheets 2-3.
[69] Stus' roommate in a *Svitanok* sanatorium in Morshyn.

Stus mentioned Solzhenitsyn, describing him as a true writer."[70]
Similar "information" about Stus' anti-Soviet activities was provided by two other neighbors in the Morshyn sanatorium, Vasyl Sidorov and Viktor Kislinsky:

Sidorov testified: *"During my stay with Stus, I had conversations and disputes with him of an ideological and political nature, on the basis of which I got the impression that he was an avid nationalist with beliefs alien to our Soviet reality and dangerous to those around him.*

He struck me as a very unpleasant man ... he was dissatisfied with everything, nothing satisfied him here."[71]

The main "evidence" of anti-Soviet agitation was collected. The face-to-face confrontations began, in which Vasyl Stus mostly kept a low profile. He broke down only once, in a face-to-face meeting with a close friend of recent years — Leonid Seleznenko.

At first denying the facts of Vasyl's "anti-Soviet" influence, Seleznenko later admitted them, under extreme psychological pressure, and — in a state of psychological shock — said everything that the investigator and later the judge wanted to hear from him.

"What did you do to the man!?" exclaimed Vasyl Stus.

Mykola Kholodny gave an interesting description of the writer:

"Stus should not be here. Stus was brought here by despair. No sooner had Stus got up from his chair in the Ukraina cinema (during the famous excesses of 1965) than he deprived himself of all the 'chairs' he could sit on in the future. For the same reason, he was fired three or more times, for the same reason he was not published. Only one way was left to him — samvydav. And Stus chose this way about a year ago. As a poet, he did not write acute social things, at least such poems were not in his line. He said that the politicization of art is a forced thing ... But, beating his head against a closed door (he closed it, of course, himself), Stus, against his will, went into publicism. That was his option 'A.' The so-called "Committee for the Defense of Karavanska"[72] *became his option 'B.' It was necessary to put an end to it. I still feel sorry for Vasyl. Although it does not*

---

[70] Criminal Case N 47. Volume 2, Sheets 4-5.
[71] Ibid., Sheets 8-11.
[72] After the December 8, 1971 arrest by the Odesa KGB of microbiologist Nina Antonovna Strokata-Karavanska, whose only "crime" was that she *"did not give*

make me feel better or worse, Seleznenko or Stus will go to the camps. They both have something greater than a horse thief, a rapist, or an alcoholic..."[73]

Actually, the fact that "Stus should not be here" was clear to everyone. However, he was already held by the KGB and not only did he not show any fear when interrogated, he also adopted a rather aggressive position towards the "investigation," not wanting to lose his dignity even if it meant the threat of imprisonment.

This was the main reason why, on June 30, 1972, Vasyl Stus was presented with an indictment made by Senior Lieutenant Loginov. He found that Stus *"on the basis of anti-Soviet beliefs and a dissatisfaction with the existing state and social order of the USSR, to undermine and weaken Soviet power, starting in 1963 and until the day of his arrest, i.e., until January 1972, systematically produced, stored and distributed anti-Soviet and defamatory documents discrediting the state and social order, and was engaged in anti-Soviet oral agitation."*[74]

The investigator gathered the following evidence:

- between 1963 and 1972, Stus wrote and kept in his apartment until the day of his arrest 14 poems: *"Dovoli! Sytyi vzhe..."* [It is enough! I am full...], *"Bezpashportnyi..."* [Passportless ...], *"Opuskaius – niby pidnimaius ..."* [I am going down—as if I am going up ...], *"Rozmova z druhom ..."* [Conversation with a friend ...], *"Koly bahrianila..."* [When it turned crimson ...], *"Komunisty—vpered!"* [Communists—forward!], *" "* [Director of cannibals ...], *"Kublo bandytiv..."* [The band of the bandits...], *"Try S. – nenache zhart..."* [Three S's—like a joke], *"Nasha natsiia – naiperedovisha..."* [Our nation—the most advanced one...], *"Na istorychnomu etapi..."* [At the historical stage...], *"Mizh bozhevilliam i samohubstvom..."* [Between

---

up her husband, who was sentenced to a long term," even under considerable pressure from the KGB, the Public Committee for the Protection of Nina Strokata was established based on the "guarantees of the USSR Constitution, the Declaration of Human Rights, and the Covenant on Civil and Political Rights." The members of the committee included the Moscow economist Viktor Krasin, the Kyiv pensioner Oksana Meshko, the Lviv poet Iryna Stasiv-Kalinets, the Odesa sailor Leonid Tymchuk, Vyacheslav Chornovil, the Moscow historian Petro Yakir, and Vasyl Stus. Criminal Case № 47. Volume 2, Sheets. 209—211.

[73] Criminal Case N 47. Volume 5, Sheets 133-134.
[74] Criminal Case N 47. Volume 1, Sheet 272.

madness and suicide..."], "Vid radosti—u step..." [*Feeling joy — to the steppe...*], "*Vy khodyly do Petliury...*"[75] [You went to Petliura...]. In these poems, "*the Soviet state and social order are denigrated and the living conditions of the Soviet people, the CPSU and the USSR Constitution are slandered* |;

— between 1965 and 1972 Stus wrote 10 anti-Soviet and libelous documents, including "Shanovnyi Petre Yukhymovychu!" [Dear Petro Yuknymovych!], the manuscripts "Pryvyd brodyt po Yevropi..." [A specter is haunting Europe...], "My zhyvemo v duzhe tsikavu epokhu ... [We live in a very interesting era ...], "My zhyvemo v chas paradoksiv ..." [We live in a time of paradoxes ...], «Frantsiia—tse ya ...» [France is me ...], "Vidvidyny. Lektsiia na zavodi ..." [Visits: Lecture at the factory ...], "Tse isnuvannia ye zlochynom ..." [This existence is a crime ...], "Isnuie tilky dvi formy ..." [There are only two forms ...], "Iakyis kyianyn ..." [some Kyivan ...][76]. "*In these works, STUS denigrates the socialist attainments of our country, identifies the Soviet system with the Hitlerite regime, alleges national oppression in Ukraine and the violation of socialist legality, seeks to prove 'the impossibility of building a communist society in the Soviet Union'*";

— On July 28, 1970, STUS wrote a letter with hostile content, using the manuscript of the article "Pryvyd brodyt po Yevropi ..." [A specter is haunting Europe ...] to the Central Committee of the Communist Party of Ukraine and the KGB of the USSR, which was later published in the so-called *samvydav* magazine Ukrainian Herald, issue 3 of 1970;

— wrote a letter "Nyni zrozumilo kozhnomu ..." [Now everyone understands ...] (confiscated from Dziuba I. M. on January 13, 1972), which is "*imbued with slanderous fabrications about the Soviet reality, in particular about the material and spiritual life of our people. The*

---

[75] All the poems are unfinished and have not been published anywhere, even in the samvydav. Even the poet himself did not remember about them before the search.

[76] Initial drafts of statements and letters to top party and state institutions, which were written "hot on the trail" of an event, and then either substantially revised, or simply kept in the archives.

letter also attempts to clear the name of V. Moroz and contains appeals to defend him";

- wrote an article "Kozhne normalno orhanizovane suspilstvo ..." [Every normally organized society...] (based on "Frantsiia – tse ya..." [France is me...]), published in Ukrainian Herald, issue 3 of 1970. In these documents, *"Stus slanders the national policy of the CPSU, defends those engaged in hostile activities and considers the measures taken against them by the Soviet authorities as arbitrary power exercised against man and his conscience"*;

- wrote a letter in defense of Karavansky S. Y. *"In April 1969 the letter was published in* Suchasnist *[Modernity] magazine in Munich, and in May 1969 in the* Ukrinske slovo *[The Ukrainian Word] newspaper in Paris, and in May 1969 and December 1970 in the* Shliakh peremohy *[The Way of Victory] newspaper with the tendentious headlines: 'Cowardice – the second name of meanness' and 'Literature surrendered to Poltoratskys'"*;

- wrote a letter "Mistse v boiu ..." [A place in the battle ...] (shown to Seleznenko), published in Ukrainian Herald, issue 1, January 1970; the text was confiscated from Meshko O.Ya.;

- in the Zymovi dereva collection, published abroad, there were "slanderous" poems: "Ne mozhu ya" [I cannot], "Zvirom vyty ..." [Howl like an animal ...], "Dazhd nam ..." [Give us, Oh Lord ...], "Rozmova" [Conversation], "Balukhati mystetstvoznavtsi" [Goggle-eyed Art Critics], "Iakyi tse chas?" [What time is it?], "Idut try tsyhanky ..." [There are three gypsies walking ...], "U Marintsi ..." [In Maryinka ...]. These are also imbued with hatred for the Soviet reality. If you believe Stus, *"our state ... is the "Fatherland of cowards and murderers"*. He presented two copies of Zymovi dereva to Seleznenko, one each to Dziuba, Svitlychny, and Iryna Kalynets. *"In 1970, Seleznenko handed over to the citizen of Czechoslovakia Kotsurova Hanna one copy of the* Zymovi dereva *collection received from Stus, which she took abroad and handed over to LEVYTSKY, who lives in England."* The book was published in London;

- the poem "Ne mozhu ya bez posmishky Ivana..." [I can't do without Ivan's smile] was published in Suchasnost [Modernity], issue 12 of 1971;

- In the poems "Os vam sontse" [Here is the sun for you], "Kolesa hlukho stukotiat ..." [The Wheels are Thumping ...], "Riatuiuchys od sumniviv ..." [Escaping doubts ...], "Marko Bezsmertnyi," "Ikh bulo dvoie ..." [There were two of them], "Naperedodni sviata ..." [On the eve of the holiday ...], "Sohodni sviato" [Today is a holiday], "V period rozghornutoho ..." [In the period of developed ...] from the *Vesely Tsvyntar* [The Merry Cemetery] collection: "*The USSR is compared to a concentration camp, the assertion is included that socialism in our country is allegedly built 'on blood and bones.'* He presented the collection to Svitlychny and Shabatura;

- recited the poem "Kolesa hlukho stukotiat ..." to Seleznenko and Kalynychenko, and after latter requested permission, allowed him to copy this poem;

- wrote the hostile articles "Fenomen doby" [A Phenomenon of Our Time] and "Znykome roztsvitannia" [Disappearing Blossoming],

- acquainted Z. Franko, I. Svitlychny, L. Seleznenko, S. Telnyuk with the work "Fenomen doby" and gave one copy to Iryna Kalynets. Another was confiscated from Ye.S verstyuk [77] together with a few more pages ...

"*In this way,*" Loginov concluded, "*STUS committed a crime stipulated by Article 62, Part 1 of the Criminal Code of the Ukrainian SSR.*

Based on the above, and guided by Articles 131-132 and the Criminal Procedural Code of the Ukrainian SSR of the USSR,

ORDERED

To abandon the earlier accusation made against STUS Vasyl Semenovych under Article 187 of the Criminal Code of the Ukrainian SSR and charge him in this case of committing a crime under Article 62, Part 1 of the Criminal Code of the Ukrainian SSR regarding the above-mentioned, the new charge to be announced to him.

Investigator of the KGB in the Cabinet of Ministers of the Ukrainian SSR in the Kyiv region Senior Lieutenant LOGINOV

"AGREED" Head of the KGB Investigation Department under the Council of Ministers of the Ukrainian SSR, Lieutenant Colonel TURKIN

---

[77] Ibid., Sheets 272-282.

Stus *refused to sign the order."*[78]

The situation grew more complicated. Where the original charge carried the threat of three years in prison, now it would be possible to get seven.

It became increasingly clear to Vasyl that the investigation and trial were a banal farce, with a predetermined finale. And the only consolation was the flow of poems that almost every day filled his homemade notebook. One of them was born on July 1:

And I feel the mystery of life,
aware that I will lose it.
I seem to mean more by silence,
Than by conversation. It is useless
To wait for my going back...[79]

All that remained was to acquire what he did not inherit, to live in the "time of creativity" and to maintain a sense of dignity. He had chosen a line of action and had to follow it to the end:

"My 'criminal activity' was invented by the KGB investigators, who attached extraneous qualities to certain literary and artistic works or publicistic articles," he told Loginov immediately after reviewing the text of the indictment, which stipulated the change of the article of the Criminal Code to be applied. *"I had no, have no and cannot have anti-Soviet beliefs. Similarly, I have never had and could not have the goal of 'undermining and weakening Soviet power.' I had a natural ethical reaction against what was committed on our land in the past by criminals like Yezhov, Yagoda, Beria, etc. Here are my remarks.*

The investigation calls my 14 texts 'poems,' though they are actually just drafts and even ill-considered drafts. They appeared when I was treated in a bandit-like way by certain people, on whom I was dependent for my destiny, my daily bread, my creativity and my desire to do good for the native people. It is evident that to consider drafts as poems – moreover, drafts whose moods are far from my stable, calm convictions – means consciously bringing the author to the condition required by the KGB, making something out of nothing and an enemy out of Stus Vasyl. It is shameful

---

[78] Ibid., Sheet 282,
[79] Vasyl Stus. Tvory. Volume 2, 142.

that in 1972 such a practice of 'fashioning' a crime (and a crime in quotation marks!) is still possible. This indicates that the KGB is going to carry out a new massacre of the young Ukrainian creative intelligentsia.

This massacre seems even more brutal than the massacre of 1965. None of this should have even started and the KGB should simply stay out of my drafts, which could not play any social role. Because this is a violation of the most basic human rights.

Recorded in my own hand

V. Stus"[80]

In the poet's other rebuttal of Loginov's charges, which was read by the prosecutor during the court hearing almost unchanged, and which Stus was not allowed to express, his objections are as follows:

Interrogation of July 1, 1972 (12:15 p.m. – 2:00 p.m.)

"I will personally continue to comment on the order presented to me on June 30.

The order mentioned 10 'documents' containing anti-Soviet and defamatory content, which I allegedly wrote in 1965-1972. The investigation undertook a specific kind of presentation to present fabricated details as real ones. In fact, these '10 documents' are just unfinished, densely underlined drafts that did not play any social role, that were written in a state of indignation, i.e., they presented my immediate, ill-considered, impetuous thoughts. The fact that some of these drafts were left for 5-7 years without any attempt to complete or finalize them indicates that they had no part in my further interests. Thus, to include in the 'case' drafts rejected by the author himself is to impose on the author something that he himself had refused. I did not 'save' them as stated in the indictment. I simply did not always have the time to put my papers in order. When I came across such random drafts, I burned them or tore them up. And the drafts we are talking about were only waiting for their natural end, i.e., destruction. In addition, if a sheet was not completely covered, I saved it, not wanting to waste the paper.

I also oppose the interpretation of their content. I never identified the Soviet system with the Hitlerite regime, but only, with pain in my heart,

---

[80] Criminal Case N 47. Volume 1, Sheets 287-288.

sometimes noted that certain related features (especially between the period of the cult of personality and Hitlerism) existed and that this phenomenon is unacceptable for a socialist country (for example, mass repression).

The order further states that the author of these 10 'documents' 'claims that there is alleged national oppression in Ukraine.' As far as I remember, I could never have written that, because the truth is that some facts of nihilism regarding Ukrainian culture are not facts of oppression, but, so to say, facts of chauvinism (and chauvinism of the unconscious type, chauvinism in tradition of the tsarist time, which more than once or twice made itself known contrary to theoretical guidelines). Thus, the reference was to the facts of the retreat from Leninism or its distortion in Stalin's time or later. And simply saying 'oppression' means to object to this distortion of theoretical postulates and, of course, first of all Lenin's own.

Given that I asked to clarify this context, referring to the above-mentioned 10 'documents,' and the investigator refused; and, in addition, did not allow me to review my texts to discover one or another draft opinion; given, finally, my doubts that this is a fabrication of the investigation itself, and that I am not allowed to confirm the fact, I cannot give my explanations about these drafts-'documents' written and rejected long ago.

Since investigator Loginov deprives me of the opportunity to respond to the charges specifically, in detail, concerning one or another completed or unfinished draft, I must declare the following. Each of the charges in the indictment is presented in an untrue form, devoid of factual confirmation. Each of the charges of the accusation gives a false interpretation of my literary work. Under such conditions I do not want to take part in the massacre of myself, defending myself against the statements, thoughts, views, attitudes, and so on, imposed on me."[81]

During the interrogation of July 7, 1972 (4:40 p.m. — 7:10 p.m.) Vasyl Stus was allowed to read the text of his two letters to Shelest as well as drafts of letters, which were offered by the investigation as evidence of his "anti-Soviet activities."

Stus: *"Since my previous request (to be able to look through my drafts with a fresh eye) has been satisfied, I agree to continue the explanation.*

---

[81] The same. Volume 1. — Sheets 290-294.

Having reviewed my manuscript drafts, I am convinced that the opinion of the investigation, that the author of the drafts 'alleges existing national oppression in Ukraine,' is unjustified. As I assumed, there are no such statements (even in the drafts). Similarly, there is no identification of the Soviet system with the Hitlerite regime. Only repressions in general and repressions against writers in particular are mentioned. I think that these similarities, unfortunately, existed. And it is good that all these repressions were condemned at the 20th and the 22nd Party Congresses.

The investigation's assertion that the author of these drafts 'seeks' to prove 'the impossibility of building a communist society in the Soviet Union' is also unjustified. In fact, I was talking about certain phenomena of the moral order, which — even if sometimes proclaimed by one or another ideological mentor — objectively harm the creation of a high moral atmosphere, which can adversely affect (and is adversely affecting!) the moral life of a person. For example, the fact that yesterday everyone loved Khrushchev as a faithful Leninist, and today, on October 16, 1964,[82] everyone blames him, shows the weakness, instability and, perhaps, even the lack of principles in certain moral structures. It was these (and similar facts) that allowed me to make the polemical statement (but a draft statement!) that you could not build communism with such an ethic. And let's recall that sometimes a man, very respectable and conscious of his position, allows himself things unworthy of any honest decent man — robs the state, gives away or squanders public property, secretly builds villas, cottages, etc....

The allegations that I am 'slandering the Soviet reality' and claiming that the intelligentsia is being persecuted in Ukraine are at the very least inaccurate. I wrote about the arrests of members of the young creative Ukrainian intelligentsia, not about the Ukrainian intelligentsia in general. I wrote that the supporters of Stalin's style of work ... were starting again (the 'fairest articles' written by Poltoratsky, and writers like O. Honchar, Y. Smolych, M. Bazhan, B. Oliynyk and E. Gutsalo are wrong). And on these questions I requested clarification from the government, hoping for an answer. Because the truth cannot be on the side of the Poltoratskys. Because the Poltoratskys, given their past, have no moral right to be

---

[82] On October 16, 1964 N. S. Khrushchev was removed from the post of General Secretary of the CPSU Central Committee. His place was taken by L. I. Brezhnev.

spokesmen for socialist justice and humanism. I believe that this also applies to the letter «Mistse v boiu chy v rozpravi» [A Place in a Massacre or a Battle or a Massacre]. I categorically protest against the investigation's imposing 'anti-Soviet positions' on me ...

My attitude to things is always the attitude of a person who is primarily concerned about ethics. That is why I could not help but express my opinion when I saw that the generation of Ivan Dziuba – people who grew up and gained a moral, civil life during the 20th and 22nd Congresses of the CPSU, started being harassed by people like Poltoratsky and Dmiterko, these typical representatives of cult of "civic" service. When young people, brought up on the ideals of the 20th and 22nd Congresses, started being harassed by people whose biographies have been stained since Stalin's time; when moreover, the latter resort to fabrications and direct insinuations (like Poltoratsky's "attributing" a fictional phrase to V. Chornovil), this cannot be progress. This shows that people like Poltoratsky are dragging public opinion back to the times when unjust things were done, to the times condemned for their leadership practices, with the help of Stalin's iron order, with the help of 'voluntarist' logic.

... Defending Dziuba, I defended moral behavior from immoral behavior. Being one and a half is always easy. Being Poltoratsky is always easy, being Dziuba is always difficult, since it is always difficult for an honest, principled, decent and highly talented person ...

The greatest fabrications are the investigation charges that I describe the life of the people in Soviet Ukraine as a 'voluntary DOPR' [House of Correctional Public Labor]. This is a misrepresentation of words twisted to a bad purpose: the expression is taken from a poem about the hard life of collective farmers in the post-war period. 'Barlig' [Den] is a place where a person works all day and earns 200 grams per working day or even ends up owing a debt.

The same misrepresentation is found the investigation's statement that 'our state according to Stus is the 'Fatherland of cowards and murderers.' The phrase is taken from a poem written in 1965, under the influence of the arrests of August-September 1965. The era of Stalinism and its incomprehensible mass vertigo was in the past. The 22nd Congress of the CPSU happened four years earlier. And then we had the arrests. This inevitably provoked my reaction to the anachronistic measures taken – arrests, secret investigations, organized slanders, and, later, closed courts.

However, I admit that my statement was too categorical, although it should be understood contextually. 'The right to overstrain under the yoke' was my personal conclusion regarding my very unjust, criminally unjust fate when I was fired both from my manual and professional jobs and left to my own devices.

I may have given my collection to one or another acquaintance or fellow writer. But I don't remember to whom specifically. I do not remember giving L. two collections, i.e., two copies to Seleznenko.

The Vesely Tsvyntar *[The Merry Cemetery] collection was an experimental and ill-considered one. It does not include a single anti-Soviet or defamatory poem. It is grotesque and desperate to some extent. My position was the position of one condemning human ethical anomalies, primarily ethical. There was no insult to the measures taken by the Party to commemorate the 100th anniversary of Lenin's birth there at all.*

And the statement that the USSR was compared to a concentration camp there is completely unfounded.

Actually, the concentration camp there was a concentration camp, to which people get accustomed, planting flowers around the barbed wire ...

It is a lie that I claimed that socialism in our country was built on blood and bones. In the poem in memory of the repressed M. K. Zerov, there are the following lines:

Moscow – Chibyu, Moscow – Chibyu,
Pechora concentruck *[concentration camp]*
Creates a new time
on blood and bones.

Thus, Pechora concentruck, *and only Pechora* concentruck, *is named, which the investigation for some reason ... identifies with the USSR ...*

The investigation statement that, in my opinion, the principle of partisanship in Soviet literature is a negative phenomenon, 'governmentalization' and 'optimism of lost faith,' is a kind of logical abracadabra, which it is difficult to answer, because it is impossible to understand. The fact is that I did not adapt certain moments – the repressions of the 1930s, the famine of 1933, the tendentious criticism of Tychyna in the late 1920s, the suppression of his early work, all happened in the 1930s. The investigation, blaming me, dares to say that the famine of 1933 was normal, that the repression of writers in the 1930s was fair, that the selection of Tychyna's work, produced in the late 1930s, was all but commissioned by the poet himself at an early age.

As for the article about V. Svidzinsky's work, it does not include slander or defamation, as the investigation states, nor anything that would be of interest to the KGB. The fact is that Svidzinsky's fate in the 1930s is shared by certain poets after 1963 – he was almost never published. Being a high intellectual by education, he could not find his place in a time when the Ukrainian (and not only the Ukrainian!) intelligentsia had to either 'be restructured' or else go to explore the White Sea Canal or Komsomolsk-on-Amur. I certainly wrote about this – in other words, the specifics of the 'gangrenous era of Stalinist cultism.' But, in my opinion, this is a fact. Such a great loss of the substance of intelligence and intellectualism experienced by Russian or Ukrainian culture in the 1930s, this they do not seem to have known before and have not known since.

I may have given both articles to my literary acquaintances, but I do not remember to whom specifically. I wanted to clarify my position, to avoid unjust and inaccurate thoughts, statements, attitudes.

I will add that both articles were confiscated when they were still unfinished. In fact, the KGB interrupted my work on them...

Actually, I did agree to sign the appeal regarding the arrest of N. A. Strokata, not seeing in this petition anything that would contradict my views on the circumstances of the case, as always, carefully hidden from the public. Neither did I see in the appeal either defamatory allegations or false information about the reasons for the conviction of N. A. Strokata's husband.

The atmosphere of secret investigations and closed courts, the attempt to interfere in family relations and break them apart, the harassment of a woman scientist – all this gave me the grounds to sign the appeal ..."[83]

The passage about the Morshyn witnesses, which certainly further enraged both the investigator and the KGB leadership is of interest as well:

"In conversations with the so-called witnesses from Morshyn, I did not make any anti-Soviet or slanderous allegations. I believe that some of these 'witnesses' were instigated by the KGB and they 'testify' that I said

---

[83] Criminal Case N 47. Volume 1, Sheets 308-315.

things that I did not tell them. The content of our conversations that they submitted is one big lie.

Finally, I must point out that in opposing both Art. 187 and Art. 62 part 1 of the Criminal Code of the Ukrainian SSR, under which I have been charged, I have the following grounds:

Raised in an atmosphere created by the 20th and 22nd Congresses of the CPSU, I always tried to defend truth, honesty and justice.

Criticism of certain aspects of our lives or individual facts has always been ethical. Yezhovtsi, Beriivtsi, Yahodyntsi killed people. I said it was ugly. I was deprived of the opportunity to work for my native authorship, fired, harassed, slandered, not published. I just said it was ugly.

I believed and still believe that all my deeds and actions were dictated by the single desire to ensure that in our socialist country there was more good and that the people who act unjustly, in an ugly way, were at least morally condemned. And, in fact, only morally condemned. I am not a supporter of massacres — even of bandits, the Berias or Yezhovs. I sought justice, socialist justice.

I did not discuss anything with the Soviet authorities, far less did I agitate against them. This is a big lie. I defended the Soviet government and the Soviet principles of human relationship in spite of temporary anomalies, which I firmly believe will be condemned in the near future."[84]

Vasyl Stus was not consistently allowed to deliver all his thoughts either at the court hearing or even during his last plea. It is likely that Loginov, who decided to take the case to court, did not attach any importance to them.

However, something else became obvious to Loginov: he was wrong about the man from the very beginning. Stus would not repent. He would not confirm the obvious facts regarding anyone's "anti-Soviet activities," even when they themselves confessed to involvement in such "activities," and would insist on his opinion to the end.

According to great-power logic, such persons should be isolated.

On July 11, the accused V. Stus was informed of the end of the preliminary investigation and the transfer of the case for trial. The

---

[84] Ibid., Sheets 317-320.

poet carefully studied the text of the resolution, but refused to sign it, telling the investigator that he would defend himself in court, without the help of an official attorney.[85]

In a statement on this occasion, addressed to the investigator Loginov and the Prosecutor's Office of the USSR, Vasyl Stus wrote:
"*Having read the case materials, I must say the following:*

1. My arrest and the search held on January 12, 1972 were based on "unfounded" "grounds": I did not meet the Belgian citizen [Dobosh], yet the decision to conduct a search was made by the Lviv Prosecutor's Office. This is the first violation and the first arbitrary act against me.

2. During the search, no anti-Soviet works were confiscated from my apartment, so attaching my literary work to the 'case' ... is an illegal act.

3. During the search on January 12, 1972, I was not informed about the confiscated manuscripts, notebooks, books, letters...

7. I protest against the very offensive and very unfair reviews by A. A. Kaspruk ...

11. I protest against the entering into the record of my notebooks, draft notebooks with poems, private letters, photographs ...

13. I protest against the whole case, written in 11 volumes ...

15. I protest against the arbitrariness of my literary destiny, the destiny of many of my fellow writers, offended either inside or outside the KGB.

16. I protest against the accusation, which, I believe, is completely unfounded."[86]

In fact, protesting was the only thing a person in Stus' situation could do, left one on one with a repressive system and with no help within reach (of course, not that there was hope of success, but simply not to give up). The scholars from the Institute where he once worked gave the investigator and the future court unfair and extremely harsh criticisms of his literary works from a political point of view. His appeals to the Writers' Union[87] and Deputy

---

[85] Criminal Case N 47. Volume 5, Sheets 182-183.
[86] Ibid., Sheet 192-197.
[87] The sixth volume of Criminal Case N 47 (Sheets 18-19) contains a statement or, rather, a cry of despair from the "prisoner" Vasyl Stus to the Chairman of the Writers' Union of Ukraine, Yu. Smolych:
"*Dear Yuri Korniyovych!*
Today I feel the same way as Kafka's clerk felt in the novel Protses *[The Trial].*

Chairman of the Council of Ministers of the Ukrainian SSR, P. T. Tronko,[88] went unanswered and there was no powerful official who

---

My present is incomprehensible to me. I do not know for what sins I am being kept under guard. I do not know what I have to done to deserve the KGB's great attention. I have been living in conditions impossible for creativity for 7 years now. It seems to me that many of my fellow writers are in a similar condition — unhappy only because, in addition to talent, they have a great **desire to work honestly for their people, to give the gifts of their minds and hearts to the people** *— with their honest hands. To have a conversation about this, I visited you twice on Zolotovoritska St. The first time you were not available, the second time you were hosting a foreign delegation and, your secretary told me, there was no way to reach you.*
It was the same when I tried in vain to meet O. T. Honchar ...
In 13-15 years of literary work I have written about 200-300 poems, only 30-50 of which were published; I have more than 30 articles on Ukrainian literature, only 5-10 of which were published; translated poems by various poets from around the world — Blok and Bunin, Pushkin and Pasternak, Zabolotsky and Brecht, Lorca and Enzensberger, M. Valek and Borodulin, Ruzhevich and Bobrovsky, Goethe and Günther, Celan and Bachmann, Kestner, Heine, Hesse and German poets of the Middle Ages. As early as 1966, I submitted to the Dnipro publishing house more than one printer's sheet of Maupassant's poetry, but my translations had recently been rejected, thus delaying the publication of the eighth volume of the French classic.
I am sure that there are a good hundred of my own poems that will be read by our descendants ...
For a year or two, I felt that I had reached a certain level when it was possible **to accomplish and finish everything that I had nurtured for years.** *Among my plans were the completion of my dissertation, a study of the problem of aesthetic consciousness in Ukrainian poetry of the 20th century, a study of the poetics of M. Rylsky and M. Bazhan, the existentialist elaboration of Svidzinsky's topics, the ethics of Skovoroda, and the philosophy of Ukrainian song folklore. I would work on scripts, prose, a cycle of elegies, etc.*
As a poet, I became more and more attracted to psychological poetry — my generalized world- and self-perception and awareness. The world of Rilke, Eliot, Zabolotsky, Bazhan, the Italian 'hermeticists' — this is what, perhaps, determined 95% of the main direction of my poetry ...
I admit that there were some mistakes — both artistic and ideological — but they could be addressed in a creative discussion, not in the office of an investigator, who gives a legal character to every artistic trope.
Understand me and believe that, feeling strong, I am sure that I can do a lot for my native culture. I am 34 years old and I feel I could climb the hill
Let me work. I want to work. I **have to** *work. Work like hell.*
I do not feel sorry for myself. I feel sorry for my talent.
02.02.1972
Sincerely Yours, Vasyl Stus".

[88] Ibid.,—Sheets 20-21. The letter is very similar in content. Its conclusion was even more eloquent: "I do not feel sorry for myself. I regret that I cannot do everything I was born to do. I feel sorry for my talent, this curse of holy fortune."

would protect the poet from reprisal. Instead, the investigator did his best to transform "tiny" faults into the gravest charges. How then could Stus continue to believe in "justice," or hope that an attorney appointed and paid by the government would defend his interests in court?

Stus was refused this request as well.

In fact, the poet was immediately forbidden to defend himself even in a closed session. So, he had to prepare himself for the inevitable.

Hope, however, lingered in the poet's soul, despite the farce that began on August 31, 1972, presided over by Judge Dyshlya G.A., with the participation of the people's assessors Voitenko G.P., Samchenko I.S., Secretary Kukharsky S.G., prosecutor Pogorily V.P. and "assigned" attorney Krzhepitsky S.M.[89]

The defendant's request to invite members of the literary community to court was denied as was the remark that the investigation had gathered "unilateral" evidence. Thus, Vasyl Stus' fate was determined by a photo that was confiscated from a Belgian citizen, an ethnic Ukrainian Dobosh, while his crossing the Soviet border. It was the photo that caused the search and later brought Vasyl Stus to the prisoners' dock.

The nature of the guilty verdict left no doubt that there was a farce with a predetermined end. Improvisation was possible only in the behavior of minor characters—witnesses Mykhailyna Kotsyubynska, Ivan Svitlychny, Ivan Kalynychenko (according to eyewitnesses, the judge even shouted and stomped on him, threatening that he could turn from a witness into an accused), Oleg Orach, Anatoly Lazarenko and even the defendant Stus—but not in the agenda of the "directors" and the main executants of the "performance"—the judge, prosecutor and people's assessors.

In search of some compromises—because, as you know, hope springs eternal—Vasyl Stus even said that he regretted that "not being able to publish "Zymovi dereva" in local publishing houses, I made a homemade collection **to create the limits of my creativity**...

---

[89] Ibid., Sheet 79.

I do not know in what way one of the copies of the self-made "Zymovi dereva" collection got abroad.

The fact that my collection was published abroad did not make me happy, I was even indignant about it. But I could not deliver an open letter in our press for ethical reasons. Because I had to apply to those officials who kept refusing to publish my works.

And I did not want this statement to be the first of my works to be published. This is probably my mistake, – said Vasyl Stus during the session and denied the whole previous pathos with the next sentence. – *But now I cannot do it for ethical reasons."*[90]

The only consolation throughout the court session was the faces of those who did not lose their human dignity. It was Ivan Svitlychny whom Vasyl saw at the session for the last time. From those whose will could not withstand the pressure, he simply turned away, not wanting to watch the death of human nature in a human being.

The farce ended on September 7.

He was sentenced to five years in the special regime labour camp and three years internal exile.

The same day, Stus was allowed to see his wife and father[91], whom the poet was trying hard to calm down[92]. His wife somehow

---

[90] Ibid., Sheets 100-102.
[91] Ibid., Sheet 314.
[92] It is probably worth quoting Semyon Demyanovich Stus' letter, appealing his son's sentence:"
To the Chairman of the Supreme Court under the Council of Ministers of the USSR in Kyiv citizen Stus Semyon Demyanovich registered at Donetsk-26, 19 Chuvashska Str.
Statement
On January 13, 1972, KGB officers arrested my son, Stus Vasyl Semenovych, who is still under guard and until now is imprisoned and I do not why. I know that our son grew up with and was raised by his parents until he became an adult, studied at school for 10 years and also studied at the university for 5 years. After graduation he was called up for military service. While in service he behaved honestly and his superiors sent us a letter acknowledging this fact. From his early age to the time of his military service no one complained to us about him and people were happy with him wherever he was. After military service everybody was happy working with him and what has happened to him now? He languishes in prison, wrecks his young age, loses his mental capacity, and tears his nerves which are perhaps severely ragged. He is serving a sentence for reasons unknown to us. We think of him every minute, enduring

stood firm and he tried to avoid his father's hard look because he could not explain anything to him.

"*The trial is a plastic surgery operation on me,*" Vasyl Stus wrote in his statement to V. V. Shcherbytsky on September 12, 1972. "*They plan to destroy me—with this ugly image imposed on me, full of the smell of corpses, simply unbearable for me.*
But why? For what reason?
It is incomprehensible.
It is creepy.
It is scary."[93]

It is scary, because having finished *Chas tvorchosti* [The Time of Time] on the eve of the trial, the poet did not doubt that the verdict of the court would pose, first of all, a terrible threat to his dearest children—the poems. Would he be able to save at least some of what he created during the six months of the investigation? At one point it even seemed to him that to preserve his talent, he would sacrifice everything.

The tears of his father and Valia, who succumbed to the attorney's seemingly convincing arguments, persuaded him, especially his father, to file a cassation appeal and write a letter "of the type

---

sorrow and grief, sadness. His mother cannot walk because of tears, she is nothing but skin and bones, and in old age there will be no one to care for us and we are old. I am 82 years old and my wife is 71 years old. What will we do next? Given the above-mentioned, I ask you to carefully consider his case, and if he violated the law of the Soviet government, it may have been in error. And it also happens that people who have made denunciations against him mostly try to build their own happiness on someone else's misfortune. Things like that happen in the world quite often. It is possible that Stus Vasyl fell under such a wrong choice. I brought him up as an honest and conscientious man, and I believe in his honesty, that he has never done anything bad to anyone, and that he would not do anything bad to the end of his life.

Given the above-mentioned I ask you, as head of the court and all the commission members, to consider his case carefully and take into account his young age. At this age a person can make mistakes, just as at the advanced age of me and my wife. And to forgive him his sins, to set him free from custody.

I hope that the Soviet government does not punish but teaches us and after that he will become a more humane person and will work for the benefit of our Motherland.

Sincerely Yours, Stus S.

10.11.72 ». —Criminal case N 47, Sheets 322−329.

[93] Ibid., Sheet 312.

they wanted." Vasyl knew that under no circumstances would he ever blame his friends for anything. He was ready for everything else. Vasyl Stus' open letter still exists. Shortly after the poet's reburial in Kyiv, a communist newspaper even published it as proof of Stus' inconsistency.

"Open letter

I am sorry that some of my works are being used by reactionary bourgeois propaganda. Although I did not send my works abroad, the fact that they are used by the enemies of my homeland in their dirty political game offends me as a writer and as a citizen.

Since the collection of my poems was published by the Brussels Bandera publishing house, I must categorically declare to my uninvited publishers: with the gentlemen from the yellow-blue huts, with the holdovers of the Bandera lap-dogs — we part ways!

Such has it always been. And such will it always be.

Because my Ukraine is red, Soviet. Because my people are Ukrainian and Soviet. Because my homeland is the USSR. Because the feeling of a united family of the peoples of my Motherland is also my sacred feeling.

Publication of a work without the desire, consent and knowledge of the author[94] *is an immoral act, at the very least immoral. A writer who is*

---

[94] In this letter and cassation appeal, Vasyl Stus twice violates his own ethical conviction to save what is "higher than me," as he later wrote. The newly discovered aesthetics of *Chas tvorchosti* [The Time of Creativity], which later, when emotion subsided and it became possible to look at everything detachedly, gave birth to "Palimpsesty" [Palimpsets], was such a great achievement for him that he rose above situational ethics, political games, and even renounced *Zymovi dereva* — a collection, which Stus, according to Ivan Kalynychenko, "rejoiced over like a child." However, that collection was already a thing of the past, and the new poems and new horizons that opened up to him seemed so significant that, struck by the cruelty of an unjust trial, he accepted the imposed rules of someone else's game: if you need it, I will spurn the book published abroad (published indeed!) to create a new one. It is probable that it was easier for Stus to renounce the collection than to write about certain "disagreements" with the convicts V. Moroz and S. Karavansky, as stated in the cassation appeal (it did not matter that, in private conversations, the poet condemned the use of art for political purposes). However, Vasyl Stus did not mention V. Chornovil even once, something obviously required of him, because no matter how different their views were at that time, testifying against a person under investigation was a shame to which he could be forced neither by the tears of a father, nor the illness of his wife and son, nor the fear of losing the poems, which, in 1972, the

deprived of the opportunity to control his publication, make the necessary amendments, clarifications and corrections, finds himself in the situation of a mother who cannot recognize her children as her own. Because the social existence of the book imposes on the author a number of responsibilities that do not face the individual, private collection of the author's work or his manuscript.

That is why I cannot acknowledge as my own many poems in the published book. This applies, first of all, to poems that lack the necessary concretization in time and space, which create a fertile ground for misinterpretation. This ground is the better, the greater the desire to give a biased interpretation of the author's text.

I am very sorry that among the poems in the collection there are those in which I, succumbing to the inertia of a personal mood, gave a false picture of certain facts of our reality.

This was facilitated by certain color blindness of vision, a misunderstanding of some historical situations and a reassessment of the significance of certain facts as well as an unhistorical and timeless view of the world.

This refers to an even greater extent to my articles and letters, where I made a number of too categorical ... affirmations, drew erroneous parallels and offered some definitions that were as sharp as they were unjust.

Looking back, I must admit that these mistakes were caused by the loss of a proper worldview control over my own actions, which, unnoticed by me, started to be infected by the bacillus of nationalism and certain ideological perversions.

Without my knowledge and permission, these articles were published abroad and appeared in the pages of the reactionary nationalist press and were broadcast on hostile anti-Soviet radio stations. At the same time, the troubadours of anti-communism seized, first of all, on certain hyperbolic expressions, giving them a favorable interpretation.

What do they care that these are just embarrassing signs of my individual mistakes, traces of subjective shifts in real scale and proportions?

---

poet valued much higher than his own life. It is not known for certain, but it is very plausible that before his arrest in 1972, Vasyl Stus did not consent to the publication of his publicistic statements in *Ukrainskyi visnyk* [Ukrainian Herald] and other emigré periodicals, considering those letters only as personal reactions to specific cases of injustice.

What does it matter to people who are always sad about our successes and always happy about our troubles?

What do they care about our Great Justice? They do not want to hear about it. What do they have compared to our faults? They are just looking for an opportunity to mock or to pour their long-standing rage on our country.

When addressing young writers, I must say: beware of uninvited publishers! This is one of the biggest dangers that awaits your creativity.

Their criticism is not terrible, but their praise is deadly. Redrawing the features of the author's face, anatomizing his soul, they are ready to dissect the artist and then torture him with notoriety.

Therefore, I cannot recognize as my own any foreign publications of my works, which are offensive to my people, to my Motherland, and to me personally.

Because my successes belong only to my Motherland, and my mistakes belong only to me.

The deadly hostile praise helped me to understand these mistakes.

And I would say to my earlier self: get real! Not a step further! Because tomorrow you will put your foot over the abyss, and it will be your worst suicide.

So, it's time to get back on the road, leaving behind the wrong turning. Because the wrong turnings are taken by wondering individuals and the road is paved by your people, within whom you exist like a grain in an ear.

I know for certain that I will find the strength to remove the coating of certain nationalist non-Soviet sentiments, I will be able to reconsider my creative position's stand in line with those who are undertaking a great campaign.

I know for certain that I will find the strength to fully condemn my wrong doings as politically blind, socially erroneous and objectively harmful.

I condemn them today.
Vasyl Stus

20.09.72

*Finally, I want to tell You: I am not a criminal, although I have overstepped the bounds more than once. But I overstepped them not to harm anyone, but as a writer who has **a boundless** desire to serve my native* *people, my native literature, my Fatherland. My other sins are grimaces of pain, temporary frustration and despair both temporary and fleeting.*

*I understood these grimace-sins as flaws and mistakes even before my arrest. Today I understand them more deeply, more precisely, more clearly, and therefore I know for sure that there will **be no more of them. I am sure of it!***

Alexander Blok once wrote:

*Forgive his gloominess: it isn't
A hidden motor of his might:
In the triumph of freedom over prisons,
He is a child of good and light.*

I like these lines very much.

I would like you to believe me as a person who has already understood his annoying mistakes and faults and condemned them forever is the court of his own conscience, in the court of his civic duty.

22.09.72

Vasyl Stus"[95]

The writing of these terrible lines, so contrary to himself, distressed Vasyl for several days. He had made incredible compromises– he rejected a collection published abroad, some poems, condemned his reckless behavior. And all this was done for the opportunity to work in literature, for the completion of a new—his best— book of poems, which began with *Chas Tvorshosti* [The Time of Creativity]. However, despite the inhuman pressure visited on him, he did not renounce his friends, lose his self-respect or (leaving aside some of his socio-political convictions) betray his poetic gift and the nature of his talent. It was a kind of catharsis, which allowed us to survive the greatest fall, but knowing certainly: everything possible was done to somehow appease the authorities. However, his sacrifice was in vain. Politicians, attorneys and judges spoke and thought quite differently than Stus. They were not satisfied with his self-criticism of certain actions and refusal of any further social activity. The poet was required to crush everything human in himself

---

[95] Ibid., Sheets 328-329.

so that his destiny would become an example to others. But Vasyl Stus, who weighed every word since his childhood, equating each to an action, could not do it. He even regretted that, in a state of emotional shock caused by meeting his father, he wrote the cassation appeal and the open letter.

The hearing of the case of Stus Vasyl Semenovych under the cassational procedure of the Supreme Court of the Ukrainian SSR took place on November 16, 1972. The court's verdict was unchanged. The poet felt relieved: fate was merciful to him, and his momentary weakness had no terrible consequences.

Vasyl Stus' attempt to reach an understanding with the rulers of the country he loved even more than himself ended in complete failure. And this love was a high excuse for his momentary weakness ... but why the weakness? Genius is a terrible curse, and Vasyl Stus could not bury it with his own hands. The gravediggers turned out to be the state and faceless representatives of its omnipotent punitive services, which were unable to perceive anything bright and incomprehensible.

Stus was too bright and completely incomprehensible. So, for the sake of bureaucratic calm, he had to be isolated ...

Thus, in November 1972, the patriot of his country Vasyl Stus became not just an enemy of the state that existed in that country and at that time, but became an enemy who had to redeem the unaccepted victim, and therefore there could be no compromise with the official representatives of that state.

In the camp, he wrote his own commentary on the court's verdict and very deliberately sent it for publication abroad:

"I say that I did not admit my guilt in the last plea. Thus, sincere remorse concerned only hot lines in the drafts such as: 'a band of KGB bandits, thieves and rapists settled in the capital as a party of Bolsheviks.' Of course, there were no promises to serve the Fatherland honestly. I had to admit that lines like the one mentioned above have a certain touch of non-Soviet sentiment because I insisted that I was not a nationalist and did not agree that my work should be called anti-Soviet agitation and propaganda. At that time I still called this country my Motherland and could not decide on a great refusal: if in your native land you are crucified for

love of it – then you have to accept that you have a native land, but no native country ...

Beyond hundreds of fences and barbed wire lies my land, Ukraine, appearing only in painful dreams. It shines like a distant star in the Mordovian evening sky. And your path of enslavement leads even farther from my land – beyond the gray ridges of the Urals, into the Siberian horizon. For tortures test you: will your heart endure? Will it break under stress?

... During the investigation I wrote many poems and translated more than 100 poems by Goethe. Having refused an attorney, I demanded legal literature to prepare for my defense. I was not given anything, not even a copy of the code. At the court hearing, I protested against the closed trial, demanded literary experts ... the chief interrogator at the pre-trial detention center, Sapozhnikov, cursed and beat me with his fists because I shouted 'They are taking Vasyl Stus to the Pavlivsky Insane Asylum!' as they dragged me through the prison corridor on May 5. The reason for this was that I refused to give any testimony and called the KGB interrogators 'Stalin's dogs.' It is exactly Beria's atmosphere of imprisonment, except that they do not beat. As for the court, it is a case of brutal vigilante justice, where you do not want to open your mouth to the torturers. 'Please give a scientific definition of the term 'anti-Soviet,'' I demanded in court. The judge smiled and was silent. Because what could he say."[96]

After the trial, the mental pressure eased considerably, and Vasyl Stus spent 20 days before prison transportation in a cell with Slavko Gluzman, previously unknown to him, a Russian-speaking Kyivan who got penal sentence for providing an independent psychological examination to General Grygorenko, who had been declared mentally ill by Soviet doctors.

In talking with Stus, the Russian-speaking Gluzman discovered the unknown continent of Ukrainian culture, and started to realize that. among the "Ukrainian bourgeois nationalists" whom

---

[96] Vasyl Stus v zhytti, tvorchosti, spohadakh ta otsinkakh suchasnykiv / Uporiadkuvaly i zredaguvaly Osyp Zinkevych i Mykola Frantsuzhenko [Vasyl Stus in the life, work, memories, and assessments of contemporaries / Edited and compiled by Osyp Zinkevych and Mykola Frantsuzhenko]. – Baltimore and Toronto: Ukr.Vyd-vo "Smoloskyp" [Ukrainian publishing house "Torch"], 1987, 143,146, 147.

he considered to be narrow-minded people, there were real Europeans who felt *"an unbearable pain for their people whose culture was under threat of elimination, but without small-town, rural problems."*[97]

"He [Stus] was well aware," Semen Gluzman recalled, *"that these problems were much more complex and serious ... Stus was the first person to tell me that the land in which I was born and raised had a history. I had not even guessed about it. I was not told this at school. My parents could not give it to me either, because they simply did not know it. But Stus used to tell me. Naturally, eventually we touched on the topic of Jewish-Ukrainian relations. And Stus told me a lot of interesting things ... I knew about the bloodshed, but only as it concerned the Jews. And I did not understand the preconditions, partly connected with the Polish influence, partly with some inter-religious problems and partly simply with the mentality of the population. He told it all very interestingly. It was a wonderful feeling when he told and at the same time illustrated it by singing an ancient Ukrainian song ... When they go to some Itzyk to ask for the keys to the church."*[98]

After a few days, they both felt that they had known each other for a long time. Vasyl even recited his poems to Semen, patiently explaining certain images, words, and even some unknown plots. Having recited "Tserkva sviatoi Iryny" [Church of St. Irene...], Stus even had to deliver a mini-lecture on the history of the KGB courtyard: once there was a temple of the Furies, the deities of revenge, on the territory of the inner prison, later there was a church, then the NKVD-Gestapo-KGB ...[99]

Stus' camp universities began, where he was both a student and a teacher at the same time. And new arrivals felt frustration and disappointment when they learned that they would have to go by different prison transportation.

Having caught an unspoken question in the eyes of Semen Gluzman, asking if they will be together in one camp, the KGB officer did not hold back:

"Do not hope."

---

[97] Ibid., 215.
[98] Ibid., 215-216.
[99] Ibid., 212.

Bibliography

Kryminalna sprava № 47 po obvynuvachenniu Stusa Vasylia Semenovycha u vchynenni zlochynu, peredbachenoho st. 62. ch. 1 Karnoho kodeksu URSR. V 12 tomakh. [Criminal Case N 47 on accusations against Stus Vasyl Semenovych in committing a crime stipulated by the article N 62, part 1 of Criminal Code of Ukrainian SSR in 12 volumes].—Zberihaietsia v arkhivi SBU [Deposited in the Archive of the Security Service of Ukraine]: N 67298 fp. [archival uni]

Netsenzurnyi Stus. Knyha u 2-kh chastynakh. Uporiadkuvannia Bohdana Pidhirnoho.—Ternopil: Pidruchnyky i posibnyky, [Uncensored Stus. Book in 2 chapters. Compiled by Bogdan Pilhirny.—Ternopil: Textbooks and manuals], 2002, 2003, 336+320 p.

Rogachev P., Sverdlln M. Natsii—narod—chelovechestvo.[Nations-people-mankind].—Moscow, 1967.

Malanchuk V. Torzhestvo leninskoi natsionalnoi polityky. [Triumph of Lenin's national policy].—L., 1963.

Ukrainskyi istorychnyi zhurnal [Ukrainian historical magazine], 1966.—N 11.

Yevdokymenko V. Krytyka ideinykh osnov ukrainskoho burzhuaznoho natsionalizmu [Critique of the ideological foundations of Ukrainian bourgeois nationalism].—K., 1967.

Solzhenitsyin A. Miniatyuryi. Ozero Segden. [Miniatures. The Lake of Segden].—Typewriting.

Chubai Hryhorii. Postat holosu. [The Voice Figure].—Samvydav collection.

Kholodnyi Mykola. Kryk z mohyly. [Scream from the Grave].—Samvydav collection.

Kostenko Lina. Poezii.—Smoloskyp. [Poetry.—Torch]

Vybranyi Kazimir Edshmidt. [Selected Kazimir Edshmidt[.—Munich, 1960.

Krutoi marshrut. Khronyka vremen kulta lychnosty. [Steep route. Chronicle of the cult of personality times].—Typewritten text.

Braichevskyi M.Iu. Pryiednannia chy voziednannia? (Krytychni zamitky z pryvodu odniiei kontseptsii). [Joining or reuniting? (Critical notes on one concept).—Typewritten text.

Dziuba Ivan. Internatsionalizm chy rusyfikatsiia. [Internationalism or Russification].—Book photocopy.

Kostenko Lina. Zorianyi intehral. [Star integral].—Typewritten collection.

Andiievska Emma. Bazar. [Market].—Munich, 1967.

Kalynets Iryna. Pidsumovuiuchy movchannia [Summing up the silence]: [Handmade poetry collection].—L., 1970.

Vovk Vira. Kappa Khresta.—Suchasnist [The Christ's mouthguard.—Modernity], 1969.

Yunh K.H. Arkhetyp v symvolyke snovydenyi. [Dream symbol archetypes].—Photocopy of the book's fragment.

Stus Vasyl. Tvory u 4-kh tomakh (shesty knyhakh). Z dodatkovymy 5 i 6 (u dvokh knyhakh) tomamy.[Works in 4 volumes (6 books). Additional the 5th and the 6th (in 2 books) volumes.]—L.: Vydavnycha spilka "Prosvita" [Publishing Union "Education], 1994—1999.

Moskalets Kostiantyn. Liudyna na kryzhyni. Literaturna krytyka ta eseistyka [A man on ice floe. Literary critics and essay studies].—K.: Krytyka. [Criticism]—1999, 256 p.

Vasyl Stus u zhytti, tvorchosti, spohadakh ta otsinkakh suchasnykiv / Uporiadkuvaly i zredaguvaly Osyp Zinkevych i Mykola Frantsuzhenko. [Vasyl Stus in the life, work, memories, and assessments of contemporaries / Edited and compiled by Osyp Zinkevych and Mykola Frantsuzhenko].—Baltimore—Toronto: Ukrainian publishing house "Smoloskyp" ["Torch"], 1987, 463 pp.

Epilogue:
A Chronicle of Resistance

> Throughout history, 99% of artists have been servants of those in power: they have carried out their whims while being able to live well (i.e., parasitize). Artists used to lose their adherence to principles, and produced as a daily assignment what later became known as the law of art. And the downtrodden people created their own culture, sometimes — as if culture ... losing on one side, won on another (the spirit that opened to the primitive and fled the academic cold).
>
> Vasyl Stus

It is still unclear why in 1972 Soviet government officials wanted to make Vasyl Stus an enemy. He spent his whole life searching for a sphere in which he could serve the people with the greatest benefit, but he never got the opportunity. Therefore, willingly or not, he had to follow the path of irreconcilable confrontation, where on one side there was the state apparatus of coercion, and on the other side, the will of a man who determined — come what may — to save his good name.

And how to forgive (not to reconcile or forget, but to forgive) the tears of father and mother, the despair of his wife, the inability during the most fruitful period of life to engage in his favorite work. When you have to do something for long, in hostile circumstances, it turns out that you get used to it and either break or develop the ability to go against the flow.

"When life is taken away, I do not need crumbs," Vasyl Stus said to the face of the KGB agents and supervisors who, until the last days of my father's life, kept a close eye on the enemy they had molded.

In 1973, the period of my, so to say, unconscious communication with the man whom I have the honor to call father began.

I remember my mother hiding from me, for several years, the fact that my father was in prison. It was too difficult for her to find the right words to explain to the little boy why his father, who had harmed anyone, suddenly had found himself next to rapists, thugs, swindlers, and bandits; why he traveled with them in the same car, ate the same thin broth, wore the same clothes and breathed the same air.

After my father's arrest, *Dedia*, Vasyl Karpovych Popeliukh, my mother's father, was very ill. My mother was under treatment for a long time too and for some reason I was very afraid to stay in the apartment alone, screaming and terribly frightened that those "evil guys" who took my father would come back. At the end of 1973, the illness that afflicted grandmother Olya, my mother's mom, aggravated and in early 1974 she died.

The mother at once changed from a very attractive young woman to a grieving one who kept her eyes peeled for her husband. She went to Mordovia for the first visit alone. To my questions — when will my dad come back? — she replied that he was on a long business trip. However, probably when I was in the second or third grade, she sometimes used to read fragments from my father's letters and I could not understand why his "business trip" lasted so long.

In the summer of 1974, I learned the truth from the neighbor Misha Sytnytsky: my father was "an enemy of the people." Mishka, a Jew by nationality, was my closest friend at the time.

One day, while we were playing at home, he snatched three or four metal rubles, which I bragged about carelessly, from my money box, and hid them in the firewood, at the other end of the large yard, near the sheds. He was ashamed that he had stolen the money, so he ran to me the next day with childlike spontaneity and, perspiring all over, blurted out: "*Dimka, ya tam rubl nashol. V drovah. Pashli, tam esche shto-to blestelo*" [Dimka, I found a ruble there. In the firewood. Let's go, there is something else shiny]. We ran there, chasing each other, but he knew where to look and I did not.

All this could have remained an annoying episode, but the same day I found out (I needed to show Misha that I had rubles of my own!) that rubles with the same pictures as he found had disappeared from my money box. For some reason, I really valued these five or six iron pieces, and even refused to give them to my mother, when she had no money to go to the store.

At first, I was very angry. I even cried, but then decided that such coincidences do not happen. Of course, we had a fight. I do not remember who won, but when his parents found out about it (his grandmother even returned some paper rubles to me, but who the hell needed them?), Misha, apparently repeating their words, blurted out to me:

"You are the son of an 'enemy of the people.'"

I cried then and my mother explained to me for a very long time why my father was in prison. Of course, I stopped being friends with Misha. At least our communication became much more limited. Instead, I sometimes started writing letters to my dad. I was writing in large, awkward letters: "Dear dad...," informing him about my modest academic achievements. Father was annoyed with my grades, but for a long time did not attach much importance to them, or, more likely, extinguished the irritation in himself, believing that he could not demand anything from his son.

In 1976, I went to see my dad for the first time. There were three of us: me, mom, and aunt Marusya, dad's sister.

From Saransk, our diesel drove into a seemingly endless compound, crossed by a railroad track separated from the black and white striped jumpsuits of the prisoners by several rows of barbed wire. I remember asking my mom and aunt, "Is it true that these wires are electrified?" "Of course they are not," they replied uncertainly ...

Finally, we had our visit. I was searched, though quite "moderately," although in such a way that my mother and aunt could see everything, other people's hands searching whether women had hidden something forbidden in their children's clothes to carry into the zone. Mom and Aunt Marusya were searched behind a screen. I heard only a tense whisper and saw the white, almost bloodless, faces of my aunt and then my mother. For some reason, they came out looking utterly depressed.

"What did they do to you?" I asked.

"It is all right, son," my mother answered.

Finally, the first meeting since 1972 with the estranged man ("call father 'Dad,'" Mom told me). His hands smelled of tobacco. There was a corridor and two rooms stuffed with microphones and invisible spying devices.

When my father wanted to say something important, he did not speak but wrote on a piece of paper, which was then burned in the trash bucket. We played a game with him, making words with matches. But it was not possible to overcome the alienation that created by years of living apart.

After the meeting, we were not searched.

This may not have been necessary because the KGB already had the technical ability to keep such a close eye on the prisoners during visits that it knew very well who was trying to get something out of the camp and who was not. However, perhaps they were simply convinced that the women, frightened by the first search, would simply not risk taking something out of the camp.

The road back sank in the mist. I only remember that a Georgian sneaked the conductor a hundred rubles just not to be put in a sitting carriage, how we had to flounder to Moscow (at the Potma station most of the passengers were prisoners or their relatives. So why should they have a reserved seat? Let them go in a sitting carriage).

After the visit I was interested in only one thing:

Huddled on the second level all the way to Moscow, I thought about which was better, to serve a sentence for stealing something or, like my father, for nothing. That time I decided that it was better to steal because it would be too infuriating and annoying otherwise. The trip did not shake the children's faith in the justice of the Soviet system: innocent people were not thrown into prison there.

I did not go to the Magadan region to see my father. There was already a wall of alienation between us, built by distance, time and mutual misunderstanding. And the plane ticket was "pricey." My mother's trip alone cost two and a half times her monthly salary. And my resentment towards my father was growing: for the sake of mythical inventions, he left me and my mother alone ... I started doing badly at school, getting one or two satisfactory grades every quarter as if deliberately.

Father was annoyed by such "successes."

In 1978, we met at the funeral of grandfather Semen. To be able to say goodbye to his father, my dad had to go on a hunger strike in the Ust-Omchug KGB, because the medical certificate meant nothing to the the KGB. Supported by the Kalyntsi couple and Vyacheslav Chornovil, the Stus' hunger strike drew attention in foreign media and he was allowed to leave.

My father arrived in Donetsk earlier than we did; and, before him, the local KGB had visited the apartment, bringing my cousin, who had been very scared of them, to tears.

When we got off the train and went to the house lost in the settlement behind the Donetsk railway station, my father was still in the hospital. Grandfather Semen's last words were depressing:

"Son, what a deep shame it is for me..."

He passed with these words without betraying the rural and Christian philosophy, which gave any bandit an unlimited benefit of the doubt, sincerely believing that all power was given by God ...

When my darkened father entered the yard, he did not notice anyone except his mother, my grandmother Yilynka.

"Dad died."

"I know."

I hid from him. He noticed my mother after about 10-15 minutes.

The incredible efforts he had to make to obtain permission for this trip finally convinced him that he would not be allowed to return to Kyiv and the second round would begin in the village of Matrosov, where he was in exile. My mother did not believe that he would return either.

The funeral turned into a meeting of fellows. For some reason, I remember mostly Leonida Svitlychna and Rita Dovgan, who already at that time almost worshiped my father.

A rather large funeral procession followed the coffin almost to the railway station, where police forced people to get on buses.

The funeral feast lasted all night, slowly and imperceptibly transforming into talks about the generation of the sixtiers, most of whom, after serving seven years in prison, were scattered throughout the vast territories of the Union.

The political prisoners' wives, who had recently learned where their husbands had been exiled, were hesitant whether to go there or not. After a night of conversation, many of them made their decision because my father's words that exile under Soviet conditions was much harder than camp convinced them.

Svitlana Kyrychenko, Yurii Badzio's wife, was already condemning my mother for not going to my father in the village of Matrosov, but raising me and maintaining the family instead.

In fact, the conditions of my father's exile did not give her the opportunity. Unlike the vast majority of exiles, he not only could not rent an apartment, he could not even choose a room in a workers' dormitory to his liking. And he was forced to work not anywhere, but only in the mine, where he was to be "re-educated" by a communist brigade of workers mining gold.

Realizing that Vasyl was holding on with his last strength, my mother, having weighed all the pros and cons (there were incomparably more of the latter), even started a conversation about the possibility of traveling to the ends of the earth. The young egoist, without hesitation, replied:

"*Go. I will stay with Dedia.*"

My resentment towards my father skillfully inflated by the ideology instilled in school was too painful.

I remember the surprise on the face of a Donetsk photographer who made a portrait of my father after a group photo.

"*Ya dumal vy rebionka khotitie sniat*" ["I thought you wanted to take a picture of the child..." (Russian)] Today that photo of my grief-stricken dad photo is probably the best of all his photos.

After returning from Donetsk, I was more and more attracted to the street. School entertainment "on the verge" of and "beyond" breaking the rules dragged me down but saved me from the unfortunate fate of some other children of political prisoners, who started to retreat into themselves and turned into "mother's darlings" growing up outside of social realities.

It was not interesting with them. I tried at all costs to avoid such meetings since I recited the poem *Fate* at one of the Taras Shevchenko evenings organized in Yuri Badzio's apartment in the mid-1970s. For some reason, after I read the poem—learned in a hurry—by heart, almost all the women began to cry, and, amazed by this reaction, I ran away from there and decided to avoid such gatherings.

A few months before his return to Kyiv, dissatisfied with my "successes" (soccer instead of school, the street instead of an intellectual environment, sports instead of theater), my father wrote me a cutting letter, to which I replied with an even more cutting one.

When at the end of August 1979, we met the plane from Moscow, on which my father was to arrive, I could not imagine how I could hug a man who was almost unknown to me, who would step forward to meet me.

Besides me, there was my mother, her sister Oleksandra, Margarita Dovhan, maybe someone else. I approached my dad last. I offered my hand and we hugged reluctantly.

We went home by taxi — an incredible luxury for that time.

Dad was very worried that we had to return not to Lvivska but to Chernobylska Street, where we had been moved to a multi-story warren six months before his return. And although it came close, for me and him, that apartment did not really become truly home, although for the nine months of his conditional Kyiv "freedom" he brought some order to it.

Hopes for a few months of vacation (he had not taken them while working in the mine) were not realized. A week after his return, a militiaman started visiting us:

"*Zdrastvuitie, Vasilii Siemionovich. Kogda nachniotie rabotat'? Nie zabyvaitie, vy pod nadzorom, potomu sho tak i nie ispravilis'* ["Hello, Vasily Semyonovich" [When will you start working? Do not forget, you are under surveillance because you haven't improved" (Russian)].

Father was annoyed by the crippled Russian-Ukrainian *surzhyk* of a dwarf in a police uniform. And on the second or third visit, he stopped letting him into the apartment, and I watched with interest as the policeman tried to enter at least the corridor, and my father demanded the prosecutor's orders from him.

Within a few weeks, my father was forced to start working at the Paris Commune Plant, where he pulled heavy iron casting boxes. After the shift, the swollen veins of his legs became menacingly dark red, sometimes transforming into rather wide ugly ranges. Even I was scared to look at them.

After the shift, he used to rest in bed for three or four hours because he could not even sit. In the evenings, having switched on his favorite Chopin, Mozart, Beethoven, Bach or Pergolesi, he was completing the work of his life—the *Palimpsests* collection. It was the book for which the Chairman of the Nobel Committee Heinrich Böll nominated Vasyl Stus for the Nobel Prize in literature in 1985. In fact, not even for the whole book, but only fifty of its poems, translated by Anna-Halia Horbach, and published as a separate book: disengaged images of existence, already deprived, unlike *The Time of Creativity*, of direct sensory experience. The *Palimpsests* are dense in content, the somewhat dry emotional text of a man who has long left behind the need to melt into his text excessively individual impressions or emotions.

It is almost close to the outside, a hermetic book of poems, which could be called a metaphysical book of the human spirit's existence, doomed to grow inward.

> *This is how I live, deprived of time,*
> *and I do not call out and invite my native Ukraine.*
> *In the slavery ways I stopped dreaming gradually,*
> *the poplars no longer rustle in my head.*
> *And my native Kyiv will neither strike respectfully the loud gold*
> *nor lend wings to dreams,*
> *the brazen sounds of the old St. Sophia's domes*
> *will not revive hope and the magic of returns.*
> *This is how I live, like a fallen leaf,*
> *only a sharp-pointed moon frowns.*
> *This is your life, both simple and straightforward,*
> *Like a dandelion in the wind under the bluster.*
> *And my son is running away – he started from the steep slope*
> *for joy and punishment – the whole earth trembling.*
> *This is you, my wife and homeland,*
> *and potion and poison and the death current.*

Yurii Shevelov, the author of the preface to the first edition of *Palimpsests*, drew attention to a certain hermetic quality of Stus' poems. However, the incomprehensibility of the poems cannot be explained only by this. Often the texts of *Palimpsests* are so chimerically created from stale and almost forgotten images that, on a first reading, the perception of the content should be forgotten, perceiving instead the melody, the mood and the work's sound pattern. Only after the fourth or fifth reading, some verses start to "open" ... But *Palimpsests* can be understood only in this way. Modern formal research methods will shed little light on the content of Stus' poems, which become transparent and understandable only when they correlate with a real episode of his life or mood.

In particular, here is how the memory of a "long" (full day!) visit by his wife in the camp has been embodied in Stus' poetry:

* * *

You are here. You are here. All white as a candle –
you are burning so timidly and subtly
and with broken sincerity you are predicting,
gulping down sobs from behind the shoulder.
You are here. You are here. As in a long-awaited dream –
You are crumpling a handkerchief with thin fingers
and with your glances, passionate movements
seems ghostly to me.
And suddenly – the river! From the age-old separations
rushed, found and captured.
And a terrible wave was hurrying
in the hasty like horses' shores.
Wait! Let the rain of pure
Svyatoshin memories fall on us.
Oh, stay with me! Do not you dare go to the city
Of boring maidans, streets and squares.
You escaped, moved – a mountain
slow landslide, a floodgate, a continent disintegration
sudden shift and lingering,
and the trembling of hands and the eyelids' dumb vibration.
She has gone along a long tunnel further into the night -
into the darkness – snow – into the blizzard heather,
Your white lips swelled with tears.
Farewell. Do not look around. And do not call.
Farewell. Do not look around. Good news
informs about that world meetings

> *with the green star of the evening. Fragile*
> *spring cried. Tell me – my son*
> *may live the ages without me.*
> *Farewell. Do not look around. Look around!!!*

The same happens in every verse, in which every image or detail conceals unread information about a man who forced the world to reckon with the fact of his presence on this earth. However, those who prefer to indulge in the charms of Stus' sound pattern, behind which the deeper, sensual knowledge arises are certainly right to do.

> *Share with me your death,*
> *I will share with you my life,*
> *and the two of us will avoid loneliness like traps,*
> *and we will not need to come back*
> *to the past, that became the future,*
> *in the majestic endless dream of the steppes.*
> *And the sky blazed up behind you*
> *lit by a thunderstorm of Pleiades.*

Taking a break, father multiplied the autographs and contents of the collection every day, not finding the final version, and maybe deliberately leaving different versions not only of individual poems (there are at least five or seven versions of the main text of "The Evening's Broken Branch Is Swaying"), but also of the collection itself. It varies depending on the time: there is the "Magadan" version of *Palimpsests*, the "Kyiv" version, the "full corpus of poems," the regular poetry cycles (the order of poems in such cycles is always the same), which the poet composed differently. Two parts of the *Palimpsest* collection corpus were mostly completed by him. He did not have time to make the third, not even in draft.

Between the two terms, he was most often visited by Ivan Kalynychenko, the only person with whom my father often sat in the smoky kitchen, discussing various topics, from politics to literature. And although their artistic tastes differed considerably, they both enjoyed the conversation so much that Ivan used not to leave until long after midnight.

Shortly after his return, my father, accompanied by Svitlana Kyrychenko, went to Moscow for a few days to meet with leaders of the Soviet Union's human rights movement. Upon her return, Oksana Meshko visited us and suggested that he should head the second Ukrainian Helsinki Group, because, after the arrest of all its members, someone had to "show the world that the Ukrainians kept up their spirits after the repression." Dad agreed, though not immediately.

After Oksana's visit, a lot of different people came, most of them trying to persuade my dad not to "put his head in a noose." "As soon as they get to know that you are heading the Helsinki Group, you will be arrested": this is "a setup, a trap"; "a guarantee of a new arrest"; "complete madness"; and "you are a poet and must guard your talent." They used to repeat the same song in different voices.

One of these visitors received the following answer from my father:

"All right, you have convinced me. The Helsinki Group can really be headed by someone 'simpler,' as you say, than me. But I must know for sure that when I give it up, there will be someone else who will head the Group instead of me. Will you lead it?"

"No, Vasyl... To head the Helsinki Group in Ukraine today is madness!"

"Then why did you start this conversation?" Dad asked, rising from the table and making it clear that there was nothing to talk about anymore. The man left with the bottle of cognac, which he brought with him and which was emphatically put by father in his hands before sending him out of the apartment.

He never came to us again.

At the end of the autumn, Stus was informed about administrative supervision, the perlustration of his correspondence and the requirement to always stay at his place of residence from 8 p.m. to 8 a.m.

All this time, from August to December, my dad and I were on opposite ends and lived, so to say, a dog-and-cat life...

Sometimes there were almost absurd situations. Having earned good money while working in the mines of the Magadan region, my father wanted to buy some furniture to set up home. One day my mother and father decided to replace the thirty or forty-year-old bookstand in my room with a modern bookcase. But when I came home and saw that my parents were cleaning out the bookstand, a fight erupted, which ended with me banning my parents from entering my room.

I slammed the door and left the apartment.

When I returned at midnight, I saw that my parents (my mother) had arranged my books on the bookstand. The conflicts (Margarita Dovhan, Mykhailyna Kotsyubynska, and others came to reconcile us) between us lasted until almost mid-December, causing indescribable pain to my father. Nobody knew what this ever-growing conflict would entail, but the KGB helped us.

It happened this way.

Sometime in late January, I, skipping another boring Ukrainian lesson, was found somewhere outside the school and summoned to the director.

There was a man wearing a leather cloak waiting for me. The director introduced him as an official of the State Security Committee. He spoke of "the enemy of the Soviet homeland, Vasyl Stus." As though to say: he receives parcels from insidious imperialists and wishes misfortune to all people, and, taking advantage of the humane Soviet legislation, continues hostile anti-Soviet activity.

I do not know why, but I did not like those words very much. I was never an exemplary boy. After saying a bunch of brutal and boorish things to the stranger and the director (my mother later even had to promise that after the 8th grade I would leave school), I ran out and wandered through the Svyatoshinsky forest until almost midnight.

I was shocked greatly and the hatred for the people who had slandered (I was absolutely sure!) my dad was so strong that it opened the way to our understanding. Since then, our relationship became much warmer, and even an element of trust began to appear. However, our relationship could still hardly be called ideal.

Nevertheless, the five months left before his second arrest not only made me look at myself differently, but also considerably shaped my consciousness. I do not know if Vasyl Stus was familiar with the elements of the Masson upbringing, but during our conversations, which took place two or three times a week, he imperceptibly laid the foundations not only of my education but also instilled in me the knowledge that would develop at a certain stage of my education. It happened almost invisibly and quite naturally. He offered to analyze the works of Tsvetaeva, Akhmatova, Pasternak, Tolstoy, Bunin, Hemingway, Mark Twain, or Jack London and turned the conversation in such a way that, strangely, always concerned various aspects of man's search for his place in the world.

What should a man be like? How can I find (feel) my own vocation? Why do you need the hygiene of education? How can I get up after defeats? How can I withstand the pressure of circumstances? Why is losing oneself, i.e., not finding the strength to actualize oneself as a person, the greatest "sin"?

I remember this the most.

We referred to Ortega y Gasset, Berdyaev, Skovoroda, Shevchenko, Lesya Ukrainka (my father was the first to provoke me to think about the positives of Kylyna and Mavka's limitations), Vynnychenko, Khvylovy, Kurbas, Shestov, Platonov, Jung, Camus, Sartre, Beckett, Borges and many other thinkers and writers. It was a great stimulus for growth because the world opened by my dad was so attractive and so different from the one I was used to and with which I had got bored.

Paradoxically, even today, I am convinced that I primarily owed my education to the short conversations and disputes we had in that smoky kitchen, in his room, or during our rare walks in the Sviatoshyn forest.

I learned to feel time as the fullness of life, and he explained its "nonlinear," non-chronological nature to me.

"*The more actively and densely we fill our time,*" he said, "*the more intensive and interesting our life is. There are moments worth centuries, and there is a gelatinous senselessness of existence that lasts for hundreds of years. Nothing happens, nothing is created and time 'slips through the fingers.' The same is true of a man. One lives only when one makes time meaningful. Jeanne d'Arc's life is fuller, bigger and more interesting than a so-and-so person who just sat before the TV or played dominoes. A minute of d'Arc's life is worth dozens of the so-and-so's lives. Do you understand?"*

I wanted to understand. But I lacked knowledge and courage. However, conditional shelves were laid out as parts of something more complete and it was up to me whether they would ever be filled.

"Listen to the conversations of interesting people, even when you do not understand what is being said. Although it is better, of course, to understand. In such a case, you are enriched with the emotions, moods, attitudes of those people to a particular phenomenon, thus preparing an emotional background for the perception of something by the mind. However, it is still probably too difficult for you..."

On January 11, father, unable to continue to carry heavy casting boxes, resigned from the Paris Commune Plant. His health deteriorated, and the visits of the local militia officer became more frequent:

"Kagda nakanets vy perestanete tuneyadnichat'?" ["When will you finally stop parasitizing?" (Russian)], he asked, once again staying outside the apartment. *"You must let me into the house!"*

"Tell your KGB that I agree to any job but the KGB's note is everywhere: do not accept. So you've come to the wrong address," Dad finished the conversation, closing the door in the militia officer's face.

On February 1, he was finally employed as "a trainee at a lasting edge glue spreader on the assembly line of the 'Sport' Kyiv Shoe Production Association." He spread glue on sneakers five days a week up until the time of his arrest.

Physically it became easier. But father's psychological state had significantly deteriorated. The monotonous work annoyed him, but he quickly found a way to diversify it: he learned English words, studied poetry, and searched for variants of lines that he did not like.

In the spring, my father was already awaiting arrest. It annoyed me a lot and even made me laugh: what threat was there from a person working on a conveyor belt? Why should you be arrested, I thought, when you are home all the time? Well, he had written a letter in defense of the unknown Mykola Horbal. So what if there were a lot of unjustly arrested people being beaten in militia departments nearby!

I did not understand my father's absolute conviction that he was one of the greatest Ukrainian poets of the twentieth century.

"Dad," I dared ask him, "*what kind of a great poet are you if you are not studied at school and not a single book of yours has been published in Ukraine?*"

"*I am writing for people, for the world, for those like myself. And the power only publishes the books of its minions ... However, we won't talk about it, God willing (for some reason he always said Gid, not God), you will learn to understand poetry, then you will understand that a poet should not be recognized in his lifetime.*"

We did not touch on this topic again. I even decided that my dad was suffering from a common delusion of grandeur and genius. Well, "a poet" — let him be a poet.

That is how we lived until the middle of May 1980.

The tension I did not understand was growing stronger, and I began to linger more and more often on the forest soccer field, which I built together with my classmates near Petropavlivska Borshchahivka.

The Soviet Union was getting prepared for the Olympics. A group soccer tournament was to take place in Kyiv, and more and more I heard rumors that the city was being cleansed of "undesirable elements." My mother became very nervous and reacted strangely to every doorbell.

On May 15, after passing some missed assignments in Russian literature, I came home in a great hurry to get my uniform go play soccer in the woods.

No one was supposed to be home, but when I opened the door, I was gently but firly pressed by strong hands against the bathroom door, searched, and the canvas bag I carried to school instead of my briefcase was torn from my hands. I did not even have time to get scared, because I immediately saw my dad's face.

"*Well, it finally happened... what I warned you about,*" he said, after a pause, to relieve the tension.

However, the effect was the opposite.

I writhed out only one phrase:
"*Who are these people?*"
"*It is a search,*" Dad said calmly.
I went to my room to somehow get control of myself.

My few notebooks and summaries of the books I read (although diligently hidden from my father, I learned to write down the most interesting impressions from my reading and any spontaneous thoughts arising while reading books), in a pile with soccer statistics tables, were scattered on the table and floor. The scattered school textbooks were dumped in a pile by the bed, and for some reason one of my favorite books happened to be under the cover ... I was driven mad that the visitors had brazenly looked through my diary (the next morning I burned it so that no monster could rummage through my records without permission).

Tears of helplessness, anger and unbearable resentment blinded my eyes. I found my sports uniform and gym shoes and rushed to the front door. They seemed to be waiting for me there.

"*Today you will have to do without soccer,*" the man said, almost sympathetically.

"*Why?*"

"*Because it is forbidden to leave the apartment during a search.*"

"*Bitches,*" I hissed, trying not to burst into helpless tears. I hid in the room, slamming the door behind me.

"*I'm sorry, father,*" I was speaking to myself, "*that I did not believe you when you spoke of the imminent arrest ...*" Tears streamed down my cheeks, and I wiped them from my face, worrying so much that my dad or one of those scoundrels would come into the room. "*No, bastards, you will not see my tears,*" I decided. "*No one will see my tears anymore. Nobody, never!*"

They were talking loudly behind the wall.

Well, you cannot even behave yourself in someone else's apartment. Work like this now.

I turned on the TV at full volume, and since there was a break on both the TV channels, the apartment was immediately filled with a very unpleasant shrill sound: "*y-mmmm...*"

In an instant, a loud conversation broke out and a red-faced man ran into the room and pulled the plug from the socket.

"What are you doing?"
"And you, what do you want?"
"*Sidi molcha, a to budiet plokho!*" ["Sit quietly or it will be bad for you!" (Russian)].
"I insist that you be polite to my son. Anyway, do and look for whatever you want. I will neither get in your way nor talk to you. Everything has been decided beforehand!" Dad finished, offering the red-faced KGB agent to leave the room.

He did not answer but just returned to the corridor that led to the room, when the whole house filled with "*y-mmmmm...*" again.

This time he pushed me roughly and pulled the plug out of the socket. I seethed with anger. But before he could say anything, I pulled the cord away from him and turned on the TV again. A terrible unpleasant sound filled the apartment again. The red-faced agent was even confused for a moment. Several pairs of eyes looked at us from the door.

This time my dad interrupted the unpleasant howl of the TV.

"*Don't do that, son.*" And then he spoke to them: "*Go and look for what you need, I will sit with my son.*"

The KGB agents left. We were sitting in silence, and I squeezed my father's shoulder with all my might, looking for salvation from such brute physical force, against which I did not know what to oppose, and so felt completely humiliated.

"*...learn to stand up,*" I heard the end of the phrase before realizing that I was listening only to myself. "*No person can avoid falling. But you should learn to stand up. After you have fallen, stand up, you fall and stand up again like a tin soldier. And go on, trying to avoid falling into the potholes where you fell before.*"

We were sitting in the room for two hours and talking about something. For some reason, I almost did not understand the meaning of the words, being captivated by his voice, intonations, mood. Simultaneously my father wrote something on sheets of paper and threw them behind the bed without comment.

"*Mom is coming soon,*" I interrupted his endless monologue. "*Shall I peel the potatoes?*"

"*In a few minutes. I am finishing right now.*"

In the kitchen, we were even joking about something, knowing well that this was the last chance to be together.

"*I will fry the potatoes. Do you mind?*" he asked me, habitually expecting me to want something else.

I did not object. That day I could not contradict any of his wishes or even orders.

When my mother came, the potatoes were ready, but my father put too much pepper into the dish and it was impossible to eat them.

"*Valia, I put too much pepper because of them.*" Mom just leaned on Dad's shoulder.

To allow my parents to be alone, I went out into the corridor.

"*Vso budit kharasho*" ["It is going to be alright" (Russian)], a KGB agent who looked more like a human than the others told me.

"*Vasyl, dear, beloved Vasyl...,*" my mother cried her eyes out while the three of us pushed dinner into our mouths.

Around midnight, father was said to be getting ready for a trip.

At first, he said goodbye to me.

"*Today, son, you have suffered, perhaps, the greatest humiliation and disappointment in your not so long life. I know how annoying it is for a man to realize his helplessness. I feel sad that while seeing injustice you cannot change anything. But we have to be patient ... I do not know whether we will see each other again, that is why all I am asking you is to forgive this day these people who caused you, me, and your mother so much pain. Forgive them but remember it as an experience, never to do anything like it to others. Promise me ... Because ... if you grow angry, if you believe that the world is cruel and to live in it you have to become evil, the world will close itself to you, your cruelty will turn your eyes, wide open to the world, into embrasures of hatred through which it will flow to the world. Then you will receive the same from the world. Despite all the injustice, we should be able to love, believe, and stay hopeful, because our world is good, only the limitations of human views have distorted it in our perception. Know this, or, for now, believe. Unfortunately, I cannot forgive anymore for being tired or something like that...*"

Then my father said goodbye to my mother. I still could not comprehend what I heard, and only a few decades later, having come across this idea in Umberto Eco's works, I realized that on May 15, I got the most important lesson in my life: the lesson of love.

After the door closed, I saw only my mother's dry, black eyes. And in the eerie silence that reigned in the apartment, I could not get rid of the thought that those eyes were the worst payment for the right to be yourself.

The trial was fast and wrong. During the investigation and trial, Vasyl Stus did not even answer questions about his name and surname. He did not recognize the right of the authorities to judge him — and he actually did not need to since everything was already decided: 10 years of special regime camps (that is, a cell-type camp) and 5 years of exile.

Clearly aware that within the Soviet system of justice (is it only the Soviet one?), the defense lawyer was the prosecutor's closest assistant, Vasyl Stus flatly refused to familiarize himself with the case materials in the presence of the "court-appointed" attorney. Lyudmila Korytchenko, who was first appointed as Vasyl Stus' lawyer, realized that the defendant, having no personal claims against her, considered her a personal enemy and she rejected the assignment. But her successor, Viktor Medvedchuk, then a lawyer for the Shevchenkivsky District Legal Advice Bureau, did not. Certainly, they did not manage to communicate but only irritated each other. The state-paid attorney did not even inform my mother about the beginning of a "closed court hearing."

I would like to emphasize that there is not even a hint in the court materials that would confirm the report in the *Chronicle of Current Events* that Stus' attorney asked for the maximum term for his client (what good would it do him?). But my father's phrase for the man — "*little son of a bitch*" –became the reason for our hourly meetings with father, allowed to each prisoner immediately after the trial, to be stopped.

My mom and I last saw my dad in 1981. The late Ural spring greeted us with dirty wet snow, broken roads and the drunken workers of the town of Chusove, where that classic of Russian literature, Viktor Astafyev, lived for almost twenty years.

We were waiting for the bus to Kuchino for a whole day in the dirty café located in the bus station. When in the afternoon students from the local vocational school filled the square, I heard gunshots from nearby. My terrified mother ran to me, and I had to go into that dirty room to calm her down.

Finally the bus appeared. In the evening, we had a meeting with the camp authorities.

"Daiom vam svidaniie na adni sutki, tol'ka vam nada budit niemnozhka patarapitstsa, patamushta vy dalzhny uspiet' na viechiernii rieis. Nachievat' u nas niegdie" ["You will have a visit for one day but you will have to get a move on, because you will have to make the evening flight. We have no accommodation here" (Russian)].

The administration stole several hours here as well.

On our way back from the visit, it seemed to both of us that we had seen each other for the last time, so we hardly talked on the way to Chusove.

In 1984, father rejected a visit. Judging by his letters, he had to go through five or six humiliating search procedures, a "ritual" in the camp language. He could not stand even one of them. They say he did not even know that we were waiting for him.

My mother cried all the way home, and I was so angry because of her tears. The resentment was so strong that in six months I wrote only one letter to my father.

In 1985, Vasyl Stus' grandson Yaroslav was born. Neither the telegram announcing the birth nor letters were given to him. He was just informed through teeth. And although Leonid Borodin, Stus' last cellmate, calmed him down for a while, no one could prevent his angry outburst at the administration's actions.

A few days before his death, one of the guards looking through the cell's spyhole remarked to Stus that he could not read a book as he was doing, putting it on a pillow with his elbows resting on the bed, because this allegedly violated the "bed making order."

Stus took the book in his hands and asked:

"Can I read this way?"

"You can."

On the same day, a report appeared in which Vasyl Stus was accused of violating the prison regime. When my father read this report, he exploded with another outburst of rage.

For this, he was given 10 days in solitary confinement.

On leaving the cell, Vasyl Stus told Borodin:

"*I declare a dry [i.e., without drinking water] hunger strike.*"

"*For how long?*" Borodin asked, frightened.

"*To the end.*"

Ukrainian political prisoners claimed in their memoirs that Leonid Borodin did not provide them with this information (this is quite possible because Stus and Borodin's cell was located away from all the other "residential" cells). Leonid Borodin claimed that he informed others about Vasyl Stus' decision but the "Ukrainians" did not attach much importance to it. That is very probable because the camp, having lost Yurii Lytvyn and Oleksa Tykhy a year earlier, lived in anticipation of a new victim, and people held on with all their might. Under such conditions, only the instinct for self-preservation worked.

I am inclined to believe Borodin.

It was the so-called "off-season time."

They wore summer clothes: striped cotton, which has long been wiped on gauze. In the stone hole the solitary confinement, there were iron upholstered bunks and a stool screwed to the floor. During the day the temperature reached fifteen degrees. At night, the water froze in the urinal. There was no blanket. You had to warm up the whole night with physical exercises, falling into a half-sleep for a maximum of 20–30 minutes. Then you had to warm up again.

It was impossible to warm yourself during the day as well.

To make it more "comfortable," inventors from Leningrad made a circle with ice, located under the cell's floor.

On a limited solitary confinement ration, a person became so physically exhausted after 10 days that it took several weeks to regain strength. How you could stand it there for a few days without water, I do not know.

There are many hypotheses about Stus' death. According to one, warrant officer Novitsky, the cruelest guard of the camp, without warning pulled out the rod that fastened the bunks (connecting the upper and lower to each other), weighing about 90 kilograms, to the wall in the daytime. And Vasyl Stus was knocked dead.

Another version seems more probable to me. Absolutely exhausted physically, father simply did not have the strength to lower the bunks, and they fell on him. The guard was in a hurry and did not pay attention to the dull thud. He hurried to watch TV, or play dominoes, or play cards.

It is known that on September 1 and 2, 1985, Vasyl Stus asked the warden for validol: his heart hurt a lot. It was not given to him.

When the four of us: my mother, her sister Oleksandra, Margarita Dovhan, and I, then a construction soldier, reached Kuchino, we were greeted by a freshly grave.

"*Sho zh vy tak dolga yekhali?*" ["Why did you go so long?" (Russian)], the local officer answered our question with his own question, explaining in his own way why relatives were not allowed to say goodbye to the body and perform simple church rites.

Only one hour later we lifted my mother from the mound of dry earth, which had become the first place of rest for Vasyl Stus.

A CHRONICLE OF RESISTANCE
1972

December. Vasyl Stus was convoyed to camp no. ZhKh-385/3-5 in the village of Barashevo (Mordovian Autonomous Soviet Socialist Republic). Stus was assigned badge no. 200.

1973

May 15. Vasyl Stus was reprimanded for refusing to wear his badge.

May 17. For refusing to wear his badge and failure to comply with the norm of production, he was deprived of the right to purchase food for one month.

May 21. He was deprived of regular visits for refusing to appear for the morning check-up.

May 24. For refusing to wear a badge, for smoking in the ranks, and for failure to comply with the requirements of the inspector, he was transferred to a special housing unit for 7 days.

August 22. The administration called him for a talk regarding his non-compliance with production standards and his tactless behavior.

December 27. For refusing to comply with the request of the duty inspector and failure to appear when called, he was reprimanded.

December 30. *"Annual" internal character reference of the convicted Vasyl Stus: "...Full of anger against the administration, the judiciary and CPSU policy. He makes slanderous fabrications against these bodies as follows: he is exploited and the money is taken away to fatten KGB, ITK-3, the officials of correctional labor colony no. 3, etc. He supports anti-Soviet convicts and Zionists. He himself announced several hunger strikes, which lasted from one to five days. He refuses to participate in an individual labor competition. He does not take part in the work of amateur organizations ... He does not regularly attend political and mass events. He pleads not guilty. He considers himself a victim of the Soviet state's repression of the Soviet intelligentsia. He constantly expresses dissatisfaction with the correctional labor policy in the USSR."*

1974

January 8. For non-compliance with the requirements of the administration, constant violation of internal regulations and unauthorized speech before the ranks of convicts at check-up, he was transferred to detention in a cell-type facility for six months.

January 13. For violating orders, he was deprived of the right to purchase food for one month.

February. Character reference of Vasyl Stus signed by Major Alexandrov and the colony commandant, Boykov: *"Upon arrival at ITU [correctional labor institution] ZhKh-385/3, he was determined to work as a motorist in sewing gloves. He mastered this specialty quickly and from January 1973, he started to meet monthly production standards by 102–111% until June 1973. Since August, his attitude towards work has worsened ... He refuses to participate in labor competitions and does not attend production meetings on a regular basis. He did participate in*

All-Union Sunday work on April 22, 1973. He considers labor competition to be worthless. He constantly violated the requirements of the internal order and regime – in May 1973, he tore off all the badges sewn earlier from his clothes and refused to wear them until July 1973. He was punished for this violation: he was reprimanded, deprived of regular visits and forbidden to buy food in the prisoners' commissary for one month and was placed in SHIZO [punishment isolation cell] for seven days ... He treated ITU employees arrogantly, insolently and did not hide his hatred for them ... He called the employees of the administration sadists as though they were exploiting him, taking money from his earnings to fatten the KGB and the administration officials. He was reprimanded on December 28, 1973, for failing to appear when called to the inspectors' room. On January 11, 1974, he was transferred to a cell-type facility for unauthorized speech in front of ranks of convicts during an evening check-up with a defamatory speech on the correctional labor policy and on the death of the convicted Klemanskis in the hospital. He did not regularly attend the politico-mass events and when attending them tried to ask provocative questions, accompanied by personal comments, turning them into an attempt to defend his anti-Soviet views. Instead of the issued clothes of the camp kind, he wore overalls thrown away by other convicts. He held three hunger strikes, as follows. On May 20, 1973, he went on a three-day hunger strike in dissatisfaction with the detention of convicts in the ITU... From September 4 to 6, 1973, he went on a hunger strike to celebrate the anniversary of his conviction and to protest against the correctional-labor policy of the USSR, allegedly repressing the Soviet intelligentsia. From December 5 to 10, 1973, he went on a hunger strike in connection with the anniversary of the "Declaration of Human Rights" and the alleged violation of these rights in the USSR. In personal conversations, he behaves arrogantly, insolently, pleads not guilty, tries to justify himself by slandering the CPSU, the Soviet state and the correctional labor policy of the USSR."

March 25. For refusing to go to work, he was deprived of the right to purchase food for one month.

August 6. The administration called him to a talk because of his refusal to work.

1975

February 11. For violating the internal regulations, he was reprimanded.

March 3. He wrote a letter to the Supreme Court of the Russian Soviet Federative Socialist Republic in defense of Viacheslav Chornovil.

April 4. He held a one-day hunger strike to protest the ill-treatment of prisoners in solitary confinement.

April 14. For failing to appear for the morning check-up, was reprimanded.

April 30. He was deprived of regular visitation upon refusing to work.

June. An open letter to Ivan Dziuba was published in *samvydav*.

July 4. A conversation was conducted for uniform violation.

July 16. The criminal Sidelnikov attacked Stus and wounded him with a self-made knife in response to the poet saying that Friedrich and Malyshevsky (Sidelnikov's friends) were stealing food and medicine from the prisoners. Marked aggravation of Stus' ulcer occurred. Sidelnikov was sentenced to 15 days in solitary confinement. Throughout the imprisonment, the writer was not given vicalin and when the necessary medication was sent by his wife upon the administration's prior permission, the parcel was returned.

July 22. He was reprimanded for refusing to appear at the evening roll call.

July. He signed the appeal by political prisoners to the Commission of Legislative Proposals of the Supreme Soviet of the USSR, in which four principles concerning the legislative registration of a political prisoner's status were formulated.

August 2. He lost consciousness due to gastric ulcer aggravation and internal hemorrhage. A hunger strike declared by women political prisoners of the neighboring camp (Nadiya Svitlychna, Iryna Stasiv-Kalynets, Nijolė Sadūnaitė, etc.) saved him from death. In the morning, help was provided by a camp doctor, who thanked the women for going on a hunger strike, because otherwise he "would not have been saved." Instead of a hospital, he was transported by a special convoy to Kyiv for a "talk": KGB representatives hoped that a sick Stus would sign a repentance in the hopes of surviving. A visit by his wife was not allowed.

December 10. He was operated on at the Leningrad Hospital for Prisoners named after Gaaz. During the operation, Vasyl Stus was in a state of clinical death for a short time. Approximately 2/3 of his stomach was removed

December. For 10 days, he was transported to Mordovia, camp ZhKh-385/17. The only food during the transportation was herring and water.

1976

February. The parcel sent to Stus with medicines and food was returned to his wife. Stus was deprived of dietary food due to strong criticism of the administration.

June 4. For violation of an order deprived of the right to purchase food for one month and of the right to receive a parcel.

June 14. He was transferred to a punishment isolation cell for 14 days without being taken to work for systematically writing complaints in which he "slandered and insulted the VTK ["improving labor colony"] administration."

June 19. For insulting the VTK administration during the transportation to the punishment isolation cell, he was deprived of the right to regular visits.

Beginning of July. The manuscript of the *Palimpsests* collection was confiscated from Vasyl Stus for inspection.

July 15. Vasyl Stus renounced his Soviet citizenship:

"To the Presidium of the Supreme Soviet of the USSR.

I am a Ukrainian writer who was politically repressed in January 1972.

In fact, I was convicted of striving for social justice, because there were forces that at first were acutely hostile to this desire, and later called it a criminal tendency leading to anti-state activities.

I was supportive of democratization, but it was seen as an attempt to slander the Soviet system; my love for the native people, my concern for the crisis of Ukrainian culture were characterized as nationalism; my rejection of the practice which laid the basis for Stalinism, Berievism, and other similar phenomena was perceived as a particularly vicious slander.

My poems, literary-critical articles, official appeals to the Central Committee of the Communist Party of Ukraine, the Writers' Union of Ukraine and other bodies were recognized to be acts of propaganda and agitation.

The investigation and the trial, in fact, dashed all my hopes for any participation in the literary process and deprived me of human rights for a long time. All my writings as a poet, critic, translator, prose writer were outlawed, and my work, 15 years in the making, was confiscated and perhaps largely destroyed.

In captivity, I experienced even greater humiliation, outraging my sense of human dignity.

For a long time, with a hard heart, I refrained from the fatal step of renouncing my citizenship (I consider myself unjustly convicted). I hoped that soon my legal position, like that of my comrades, would be restored, and that the course taken to intensify the domestic political climate would be reconsidered, at least given its obvious futility.

I appeared to be wrong.

The 1972 repressions showed that, in discussions with Ukrainian "dissidents," the authorities found no more convincing arguments than the use of force. And the camp conditions convinced us that the range of the application this force has no bounds. A year ago I was on the verge of death.

Most recently, on May 14, 1976, due to my refusal to go to the hospital without books, I was handcuffed, scolded and kicked. My body has been aching for two months now but the moral distress caused is much more sensible. I sued the offenders, and in revenge, I was subjected to new punishments, thus demonstrating my complete helplessness before the local law. They did not hesitate to throw a person who had recently undergone major surgery (gastrectomy) into a punishment isolation cell for two weeks — for slander allegedly contained in the complaints. This so exceeded the usual practice and camp punishments that it led to a two-week hunger strike by eight prisoners in the zone, which was actually provoked by the administration's actions.

I would add to this the brutal confiscation of letters sent to me, the systematic confiscation of poems that I rewrite in letters to relatives, the real threat of losing the manuscripts of my camp poems upon release, factual non-treatment, complete lack of political prisoner status, and so on and so forth.

It goes without saying that these facts are in sharp contrast to the principles of humanity and legal order declared in the USSR, that they contradict the law and the provisions of the Helsinki Accords.

Today I have concluded I have been deliberately reduced to the status of a chattel registered at the KGB property department.

Analyzing the reaction of the local authorities to my appeal to you dated April 15, 1976, I became convinced that the repressive bodies represented by the KGB under the Council of Ministers of the USSR were directly pushing me to decide to renounce Soviet citizenship. This is understandable: I am a Ukrainian patriot, for this reason, I am guaranteed lifelong KGB surveillance.

Therefore, I declare that I do not consider it possible to remain a citizen of the USSR any longer and request that I be expelled from the country in which my human rights are violated in such an unceremonious way.

It is extremely difficult to make such a decision, but it appears even harder to refrain from it under current conditions.

Vasyl Stus"

August. The ZhKh-385/17 camp was disbanded. The poet remained in a camp hospital. During the disbanding of the camp, the manuscript of *The Time of Creativity* was confiscated from Stus' belongings.

August 15-20. The poet was brought to the ZhKh-385/19 camp where he was informed of the destruction of the poems confiscated from him — in fact, of all the poet's works written in prison.

August 20. For insulting the inspectors during the search, he was deprived of the right to regular visitation.

August 25. For insulting the administration of VTK and failure to comply with the requirements of inspectors, he was deprived of the right to purchase products.

August 30. For refusing to attend the evening roll call, he was placed in a punishment isolation cell for 13 days without being taken to work.

Autumn. The notebook with *Palimpsests* was returned to the poet (of the 50 notebooks with poems confiscated from Stus, fewer than 10 were returned).

EPILOGUE 359

November 10. For violation of the internal regime, he was placed in a punishment isolation cell for 13 days with the ability to work.

December 5. Vasyl Stus supported the Armenian political prisoners Paruyr Airikyan, Azat Arshakyan, and Razmik Markosyan, who sent statements to the Presidium of the Verkhovna Rada of the Armenian SSR demanding the legalization of the National United Party of Armenia and and a referendum on self-determination in the republic.

December 10. Nadiya Svitlychna sent a letter to the Central Committee of the CPSU (later distributed in self-published form) with the information that *"the poet Vasyl Stus had an eavesdropping device sewn into his pea coat's flap before being sent for a complicated stomach operation, and then about 800 verses and translations were taken from him. This detective vaudeville was led by the chief of the ZhKh-385/3 operating department, Captain Shalin ... with the participation of Major Shorin."*

1977

January 11. One day before the end of Vasyl Stus' imprisonment, he was transported to the place of exile.

January. A characteristic reference of the convict Vasyl Stus was signed by the ZhKh-385/19 camp commandant Nikulin and the detachment chief, Khlevin: *"Stus undertook actions insulting to the representatives of the administration of the places of imprisonment (systematically wrote defamatory complaints) resulting in the prohibition, from March 25, 1974, of product purchases for one month. On April 14, 1975, he was reprimanded; on April 30, 1975, he was deprived of regular visitation; on July 21, 1975, he was reprimanded; on July 8, 1976, he was deprived of the right to purchase products for one month; on July 14, 1976, he was sent to a pre-trial detention center for 14 days; on July 19, 1976, he was deprived of regular visitation; on August 28, 1976, he was deprived of regular visitation; on August 23, 1976, he was deprived of the right to purchase products for one month; on August 30, 1976, he was placed in the punishment isolation cell for 13 days; on November 10, 1976, he was placed in the punishment isolation cell for 13 days ... He systematically writes complaints to various institutions, which contain slanderous fabrications against the policy of the Party and the Government of the USSR, and he does not hide his anger and hatred for the Soviet reality."*

March 5. The poet arrived in Matrosov village in the Magadan region.

March 6. Vasyl Stus was enrolled as a trainee "shaft man of the underground mining section at the Matrosov mine of the *Severovostokzoloto* All-Union Production Association of the Ministry of Non-Ferrous Metal Industry of the USSR."

June 15. The poet was transferred to work as a shaft man of the 3rd category of the underground mining section.

August 20. An accident occurred. The poet's roommate had left for his shift without leaving the key to the room at the dormitory and the poet could not get in after work. He tried to climb in through a small window and fell from the second floor, which resulted in his breaking both heel bones. He spent two months at the hospital.

1978

February 10. There was a 10-hour search of the room in connection with the case of Levko Lukyanenko. The poet was interrogated for three days in the Ust-Omchug KGB district department. He was threatened with 15 days' detention because, during the search, Vasyl Stus called the militiamen and KGB agents rummaging in his private belongings and papers *Polizei* [alluding to the Nazi occupation police]. He was threatened with a new term of imprisonment.

February 16. Vasyl Stus sent a telegram to Andrei Sakharov: "In protest against the conviction of Vasyl Ovsiyenko, to demand his release and the punishment of the originators of the court fabrication, I am starting a political hunger strike."

August. He started a three-day hunger strike demanding permission to fly to Donetsk to see his terminally ill father. Ihor and Iryna Kalynets and Viacheslav Chornovil also went on a hunger strike in support of these demands.

Vasyl Stus became an honorary member of the London PEN Club.

1979

August. He returned from exile to Kyiv.

Vasyl Stus joined the Ukrainian Helsinki Group.

October 22. Vasyl Stus started to work as a former of the 2nd category in the casting shop of the Kyiv Paris Commune Plant for the repair and manufacture of construction machinery.

December 7. Vasyl Stus was placed under administrative supervision for a year.

1980

January 11. V. Stus resigned "at his own request" from the Paris Commune Plant due to extreme physical exertion,

February 1. Stus was employed as a trainee lasting edge glue spreader on the assembly line of the Sport Kyiv Shoe Production Association.

October 2. The Kyiv City Court sentenced the "particularly dangerous recidivist" Vasyl Stus to 10 years in a special regime camp and 5 years of exile. The defendant was not allowed to have the last word. *"Executioners! You did not even give me the last word!"* the poet exclaimed as a special squad dragged him out of the courtroom, twisting his arms behind him. The last words his wife heard were: "And you will not wash off with all your bloody poison/The Poet's righteous blood!" [the last lines of Mikhail Lermontov's poem written in response to the death of Alexander Pushkin in 1837; translated by Yevgeny Bonver].

October 12. The academician Andrei Sakharov sent an appeal to the participants of the Madrid conference to ratify the Helsinki Accords and to the leaders of the countries participating in the Helsinki Act: *"1980 was marked in our country by many unjust sentences and by the persecution of human rights activists. Even against this tragic background, however, the sentence passed on Ukrainian poet Vasily Stus is distinguished by its inhumanity ... A man's life has been irretrievably broken in reprisal for his elementary decency and nonconformism, for loyalty to his convictions and his own personality. Stus's conviction is a disgrace to the Soviet system of coercion.... I appeal to Vasily Stus's colleagues, to the writers and poets of the entire world, his academic colleagues, Amnesty International, to everyone who values human dignity* and justice: speak out in Stus's defence! ... Stus's sentence must be repealed"

1981
Spring. Vasyl Stus' last meeting with his relatives.

1982
The notes by Vasyl Stus entitled *From the Camp Notebook* were published in Russian translation in no. 65 of the *Chronicle of Current Events*, in the section "News of Samizdat."
Vasyl Stus was awarded the Amnesty International Literary Prize.

1983
January 6. At Christmas, Stus was thrown into solitary confinement.
January 10. For the transfer and publication of the notes *From the Camp Notebook*, Vasyl Stus was additionally punished by one year of solitary confinement with a reduction of ration.

FROM THE CAMP NOTEBOOK
RECORD I

Thus, on March 5, I arrived at Kolyma. Behind me were 53 days, almost two full months of transportation. I remember the cell of the Chelyabinsk prison with swarms of cockroaches on the walls. As I looked at them for a long time, I felt my whole body itch. Then there was the Novosibirsk transit prison, where I was together with V[iktor] Khaustov, and the terrible Irkutsk jail, where I was thrown into a cell with alimony defaulters. Being lousy, dirty, stupefied, they exuded a spirit of such asphyxiating provincial freedom that I wanted to howl like a wolf. It turns out that this sort of life is also possible, this prison misery is also endurable. The drunken Irkutsk guards seemed to have been snatched from a cohort of despotic gendarmes of the time of Nicholas I or Alexander II. One of them almost beat me because I spoke up about his brutal behavior. Eventually, it was Khabarovsk and then a passenger plane, in which the free and imprisoned were separated by rows of seats. There was no need to be ashamed here. I was handcuffed to a recidivist for the 2 hours of flying time.

And then, suddenly, Kolyma: a cold low sky, a small prison located on a pasture, relatively good food and warm dark solitary confinement. Once they had been deloused, even my clothes were tolerable. The commandant summoned me: he had supposedly never seen a political prisoner before.

Several days later, I was driven in a *voronok* [a popular name for a black car used by Soviet security agencies to transport prisoners; literally: "little raven"] with a small cast-iron stove inside to Ust-Omchug, 400 kilometers from Magadan. After being held in KPZ [a preliminary detention cell] for several days, I was summoned by Pereverzev, a militia commandant, who told me that I would be working as a miner at the Matrosov mine and living in room N 6 at the dormitory. Since I had complained about my health, he promised to have me examined. The doctors looked me over in about 20 minutes and all of them declared that I was fit.

On the evening of March 5, I was brought to the village. In the room that I was to share, several young men were drinking vodka sitting as if expecting me. No one was surprised to see me. The radio was roaring and a tape recorder and the radio transistor were blasting. Gaiety filled the room.

My work began. It was a Communist shock brigade. Almost half the workers were Party members. A model brigade. They were to rehabilitate me. There was really bad dust at the mine because there was no ventilation. They were drilling blind vertical shafts. The hammer weighed about 50 kilograms and the rock bolt up to 85 kilograms. When "windows" were being drilled, you had to shovel. The respirator (a gauze face mask) was useless as it got soaked and covered with a layer of dust within half an hour. Then you had to take it off and work without protection.

They say that young men (who have just finished their army service) develop silicosis after six months of this hellish work. You cannot see the shovel you are working with because of the dust. When you finish work, there isn't a dry thread left on you, and you step out into the icy air of the unheated cage. Pneumonia, myositis and radiculitis are the scourge of every miner. And in addition, there are vibrations and silicosis. But for 500 to 700 rubles per month people are afraid of nothing. In 5 years if he does not go to drink or become a cripple, a miner can save enough money to buy a car.

The accident rate at the mine is quite high. Things happen: one day the ceilings caved in, resulting in miners being choked with "cutter break"; another day, a driller fell down the slopes or under a minecart, almost every second man had his arms, legs, or ribs crushed. But the Kolyma people are strong. They know that reaching prosperity is not an easy thing. You have to pay for it with your youth, health and even life. Life can be cruel and you cannot do anything with it. And Kolyma does offer meat, although you cannot always get it. But then, where can you?

RECORD 2

I would come back to my room and collapse with exhaustion. There was only work and sleep—nothing in between. I endured this for three months and then had to state that, with the condition of my health, I was not up to this kind of work. The militia was angry, and the first persecution began. In addition, I changed my room. That was a new violation of the rules: How dare I do so when (contrary to the regulations dealing with exile) I had been ordered to live in this room and these people and no others. But their constant drinking left me no peace.

In May, I was summoned to the district center and warned that if I disobeyed any other rules I would be brought to trial again. I cited the rules of exile, which allowed me to decide where I wanted to live within the district. Pereverzev only smiled maliciously and swore. I had to put him in his place. "No one used such language to me even in the concentration camp, so stop swearing, otherwise I will leave. You were the one who summoned me, so you had better speak decently."

Soon my wife came to visit and we were given a room at the so-called hotel, accommodating at the same time two KGB agents who were listening to everything we said. Once they broke into our room, sat down at the table, and one of them took out a knife and began to test my nerves. I refused to fall for this cheap trick. One of my roommates wanted to give me a knife. I turned down the gift even though I did not know that this was a provocation which could lead to a conviction (possession of a weapon)!

When my wife left, I had an accident: my roommate had taken off for a few days without leaving me the key, and when I tried to get in through the window, I fell and broke both heels. I was taken to the hospital; my feet were placed in casts, and a new occupant was placed in my room. Having become used to total surveillance, I had no doubt where this occupant came from. After two months in the hospital, I went back to my room. I had plaster casts with metal arches on both feet. Outside there was frost and snow. The outhouse was 200 meters away. I had crutches and cast shoes from which my toes protruded. This time, the room was empty. Going for water, down to the canteen, or outside to answer nature's call became a very difficult problem. I would come back from these voyages with my forehead covered in a cold sweat. It wasn't funny at all.

RECORD 3

Having solved the transportation problem simply by cutting off the casts which I was supposed to wear for another two months, I worked on my poems. Occasionally I went to the post office, which in the life of an exile provides a semi-existence and makes human contact possible. The post united us, exiles, brought back the voices of Chornovil, Shabatura, Sadunaite and Kotsyubynska, and also brought news from abroad.

I had to fight a real war with the KGB over my letters. Dozens of letters simply disappeared. My complaints were answered in a very peculiar way: "*The mailbag at the Magadan airport had a hole.*" Several times, I whipped off telegrams to Andropov: "*Your agency has been stealing my letters.*" Telegrams went off but they brought no results. This became apparent during my monthly visits to the militia (for the so-called registration). It was a trip of more than 30 kilometers, to the village of Gastello. I sensed that a storm was brewing.

On November 10, 1978, when I was hardly able to walk but was already back at work in the mine, I was called to the personnel department. It turned out that a squad had been flown in to search me. The group was headed by Major Hrushetsky from Ukraine. The search regarded Lukianenko's case. It did not matter that I did not know Lukianenko and I had only exchanged one or two letters with him. They took drafts of my letters to [Rasul] Gamzatov, [Petro] Hryhorenko, some letters from other friends and a notebook of poems. Then they interrogated me for three days in Ust-Omchug. I did not give any evidence and only expressed my indignation.

Now the persecution took a new turn. Several drunkards were put in my room (they would be witnesses at my next trial). They drank in my room and one of them even urinated in my tea pot. When I protested, they said: "*Keep quiet, or you will find out where you are.*" I demanded that they be moved—in vain. I tried to find another room—and was forbidden to do so.

I got to know that the KGB, the militia and the Party committee were assiduously setting people against me. One man, for example, was offered to plant a rifle or a knife among my things, another to get me drunk. They were promised a reward—1500 rubles (twice the monthly wages in Kolyma). And to what degree? Just enough for there to be a scent, they answered. But I did not know this yet. Every evening someone visited me—a Komsomol patrol or the militia. The conversation was malevolent, provocative. Captain Lubavin was especially annoying. I decided simply not to react whenever he appeared.

Just then I got a telegram that my father was on his deathbed. But the militia would not let me go home and I had to declare a hunger strike in protest. They allowed me to go in a week, but before they did so they held me overnight in a preliminary detention cell for posting a sign on my door: "*Do not disturb. I am on a hunger strike demanding the right to bury my father.*" All the way—from Ust-Omchug to Donetsk—I was accompanied by a squad of KGB spies. So it was at the airport and in Donetsk. After burying my father, I returned to Kolyma, as if to a prison. I sensed that I could be locked up again at any time.

RECORD 4

When I returned to Magadan, a summons to the regional KGB was waiting for me. I had to spend the night in a hotel. On Monday I went to the city (it is 60 kilometers by road). I was received by Deputy Commandant Safonov. He read me a second warning with a threat to put me on trial. In Ust-Omchug, when I went to the militia Commandant Pereverzev, a new surprise was awaiting me. The deputy editor of the district newspaper *Leninskoe znamia* (Lenin's Banner) said that she was going to write an article about me and asked some provocative questions. I told her that I was familiar with her genre and preferred not to answer.

Sure enough, in a little while, there appeared a long article entitled "The Friends and Enemies of Vasyl Stus." It mentioned everything: I was receiving parcels from abroad; I had torn up my trade union membership card when I learned that the trade unions were objecting to my receiving medical treatment; and "testimony" against me, given by many workers at the mine. As it turned out, Supryaga had not wasted time: she had been making expeditions to the mine and preparing her article while I was in Donetsk. Many people later told me that they had said nothing of the sort but Supryaga, fortified by her KGB shield, understood her journalistic duties in her own way. "Stus is ready to rob and kill," a nurse from the transportation department testified. "He looks like a fascist who killed children in my presence." Others played the game.

I felt sorry because of this. I had once refused to work because there were no respirators. I was promised one for myself. I rejected it saying that every miner had to have a respirator. I was defending a general principle [of protest] against the violation of industrial safety rules. So respirators were finally found and everyone was given one. But I was punished for "striking." Supryaga did not fail to mention this incident, but distorted the facts beyond recognition.

Just then my wife arrived. The article had its effect. People avoided me like the plague. I realized how easy it was to manipulate public opinion, especially when there is no community and people have no opinions. Seeing that it was useless to sue Supryaga (no Soviet court would agree to take such a case), I insisted that I be allowed to reply to her publicly. The authorities agreed. They summoned an open meeting of the mine committee and invited select public members. There was even a reporter from the newspaper (Supryaga did not come). When I started to strongly correct misinformation in a well-argued manner, the stage managers saw that their show might flop and refused to let me speak. There was nothing left to do but to accuse the public of cowardice and leave the meeting hall with my wife.

The storm in the press did not die down: in the usual Soviet way, dozens of readers expressed indignation about my behavior. Now my situation became even more dramatic. Saying goodbye to my wife, I told her: "*I feel that we will probably meet again in a camp.*" She tearfully agreed. But I was prepared not to bow my head no matter what happened. Behind me stood Ukraine and my oppressed people, whose honor I had to defend to the death.

RECORD 5

All this time I was not receiving any medical treatment. Upon coming home from work, not feeling my feet, I heated water in a basin with an electrical heater and soaked my feet in a salt bath. My left foot was crippled: the surgeon had simply not noticed it. I had to put on the paraffin applications by myself.

But the number of provocations increased. Once, after a heavy cold, when my roommate had come back from the "continent," I drank with others 100–150g of cognac, not knowing that I was not allowed to drink. The militia immediately got to know about it and was on the watch for me. When I went outside of the dormitory for a moment that evening, they pounced on me and took me to a sobering station. I told them that I would go on a political hunger strike if they did not stop playing the game. The doctor who was summoned by the militia diagnosed light intoxication. I sat down to write a protest to the prosecutor. During this time the attackers changed their plan and took me back to the dormitory. Later I learned that the militia had decided to sign me up for compulsory alcoholism treatment and needed any small pretext. That was when they offered 1500 krb. to get me drunk. But the trick did not work. I had to check my belongings in my room to make sure that no rifle, knife, or pornography, etc. had been planted. I often found the door broken when I came home from work. So I submitted a special declaration to the prosecutor's office: if weapons, explosives, gold dust, etc. were found among my belongings, it would be as a result of a provocation.

Pushed over the edge, I sent a declaration to the Supreme Soviet of the USSR in which I again renounced my Soviet citizenship. It was in late 1978. I wrote that the ban on creative work, the constant denigration of my human and national dignity, the conditions under which I was made to feel like an object, a property of the KGB, and the situation in which my Ukrainian patriotism was regarded as a crime against the state, the national and cultural pogrom in Ukraine—all these compelled me to declare that holding Soviet citizenship was quite impossible for me. To be a Soviet citizen means to be a slave. I am not fit for such a role. The more I am tortured and abused, the greater is my resistance to the system of abuse against a man and his elementary rights, and to my slavery. I am doing it out of a political motivation.

This declaration of October 18, 1978, being already the second one on this subject (the first one I wrote in the camp) did not get a response. Later, in March 1979, I was summoned to see Voitovich, the mine director. About 20 people were sitting in his office, so-called "representatives of the public," several unknown persons and the militia commandant Pereverzev. The latter announced that he had been instructed by the Presidium of the Supreme Soviet to reply to my declaration. He started to read it, repeatedly saying that it was slander for which I had to be brought to trial.

RECORD 6

He threatened to send me to Omchak (a village six kilometers from Matrosov, where there was a strict-regime labor camp). I considered the situation to be critical and that I would have to answer him appropriately. When the director tried to relieve the tension, I stopped him: *"What are you talking about? He had an arrest warrant in one pocket and handcuffs in the other!"* This office trial lasted about an hour. This was the end of the KGB's attempts to take me by storm. There were no more unpleasant incidents until the end of my term of exile. Only during the court hearing did I get to know that the first court interrogations of the so-called witnesses dated back to April 1979. Mainly those were people mentioned by Supryaga in her article: only the tone of the lie became even more outrageous and frightening. It was funny for me to read this testimony. Apparently, I did not show enough humor in court when I took exception to one such false witness, a camp criminal accused of domestic assault, Sirik (he was released before the end of his term from the 19th camp for cooperating with the KGB); and, like an attorney, I started asking him tricky questions. It cannot be called a mistake, but I did feel a little sorry: let the devil arrange a trial for himself, arranging it as a comedy of probability, what is all that to *me*? So I came back to Kyiv. A surprise was waiting for me there. It turned out that a week before my arrival, KGB agents had broken into my apartment, seized my wife when she was on her way home, seized her in the street, forced her into a car and were driving her around Kyiv for two hours until the invaders left our apartment.

In Kyiv, I learned that the people close to the Helsinki Group were being brutally repressed. At least this was the case in the trials of Ovsienko, Horbal and Lytvyn and would soon happen with Chornovil and Rozumny. I did not want to see *this kind* of Kyiv. Realizing that the Group had been forsaken, I joined it, because I could not do otherwise. When my life was taken away, I did not need crumbs. I had to set about rescuing my poems and contributing to the information work of the group. The work at the Paris Commune Plant (I was employed as a former) happened to be too hard for me; it was not my specialty. Standing on the assembly line I slapped glue with a brush on shoe soles. For this, I was paid between 80 and 120 rubles per month.

Psychologically, I understood that the prison gate had already been opened for me and, in a few days, it would close behind me again for a long time. But what was I supposed to do? Ukrainians are not allowed to go abroad, and I was not very keen to go. Who would remain here in Great Ukraine to be the voice of indignation and protest? This was my fate, and fate cannot be chosen. You accept it, whatever that fate may be. And if you do not accept it, it takes you by force.

On May 14, the KGB agent came to the factory where I was working. That night I was driven to the main KGB building, where I saw that a warrant for my arrest had been signed on Monday. Thus, I was given two days' grace. The warrant was signed by Prosecutor Glukh and Fedorchuk. There was nothing to be done. A trial was unavoidable. The investigation was a redundant and unnecessary procedure. In the USSR you have to go to jail a second time. Then everything is clear and simple. There are no surprises.

RECORD 7

The attempt to keep a diary under these conditions is a desperate one: the present conditions are worse than those people remember in Mordovia, the black zones, or Sosnovka. The regime established in Kuchino has reached the peak of police power. All appeals to supreme authorities remain unanswered and are frequently punished. Three times within six months I was denied visitations, a month later I was forbidden access to the prison shop, and I spent three weeks in solitary confinement. Nowhere else was one punished for a hunger strike by the withdrawal of visitation rights. But there hunger strikes were an infraction of the rules. I was twice punished for hunger strikes: on January 13, 1982, and on the anniversary of the death of Jü[ri] Kukk, Mart Niklus' co-defendant. It had never happened before that a guard beat a prisoner, as was the case with Niklus. Mart was in an isolation cell, writing complaints. The drunken guard Kukushkin opened the cell, struck him in the face with his fist and then began kicking him with his boots. Niklus raised a roar. We all began to shout and ring the bells. This stopped the drunken boor, who became alarmed. But the administration took him under its wing and in response to our demands to punish Kukushkin, punished Niklus, accusing him of slandering a vigilant guard.

In other words, Moscow had given the authorities here carte blanche, and anyone who has any illusions that laws govern our relations with the administration is profoundly mistaken. A law of complete lawlessness is what governs our so-called relations.

In the camps, we were never forbidden to take off our shirts during the recreation period, but here it is forbidden, and we are punished when we try to catch a bit of sunshine. Searches are conducted in the most arbitrary fashion: they seize anything they like without any notice or official record. We have lost every right to be ourselves, not to mention the right to have books, notebooks and notes. There is a saying that those whom God wishes to destroy he first drives mad. It cannot go on *like this* much longer. Pressure such as this is possible only before death. I do not know when death will come for the others, but I personally feel it approaching. I seem to have done everything that I could in my lifetime. Writing is absolutely impossible here: every poem is confiscated when there is a search. I am forced to study languages. It will be at least a small benefit if I master French and English during this ordeal. In fact, there is nothing to read. We get some books to read in the cell (V[asily] Belov, Ch[ingiz] Aitmatov, etc.) but there is absolutely nothing in Ukrainian. Today we have the cult of talentless Yavorivskys. It is their time now. The gifted writers are either silent (like [Roman] Andriyashyk), or are doing God knows what (for example, Drozd or Shevchuk). Lina Kostenko was enthusiastic about several talented books but still remained on the margins of the present stagnation. Because it is not her time. It is not Vinhranovsky's time. It is not the time of [Ivan] Drach, the poetry defeatist. The times test every artist for strong patience and resistance. When they started torturing, the first to be broken were the talented ones. Every year Drach exhibits increasing femality. Today he is like a talkative aunty. [Ivan] Dziuba appears to be a similar talkative aunt. He wants his old style but in light of the new conditions. It comes out as lot of chatter, but ineffective. His article about [Mykola] Vinhranovsky's *Kyiv* is both good and sinful. Because your time, Ivan, has passed. Because it is impossible to write today about Vinhranovsky, a poet of the early 1960s. After all, Dziuba himself is a critic of the early 1960s. And they feel uncomfortable in the atmosphere of the 1980s. They are thrown out of their times to their fate. They are gifted writers (what a master Drozd is!), but where can he apply his talent? And so he decorates public toilets — because this is the only form allowed to Ukrainian artists in their public service.

RECORD 8

I recollect the letter [Dmytro] Pavlychko's wrote to Yurii Badzio. It was a letter-response to Badzio's remark that Pavlychko was wrong when, in one of his public speeches, he spoke of [Ivan] Franko as a fighter against Ukrainian bourgeois nationalism—perhaps the most important feature (in the Soviet way) of Franko's genius. Pavlychko was extremely indignant at the remark: he was sincerely angry at this deceptive philosophy to which Dziuba contributed (according to Pavlychko) as well. *"Never praise me,"* Pavlychko finished his letter, demonstrating his polar opposition to Badzio. This was around 1978. Badzio was later repressed as the author of the nationalist work *The Right to Live*. It was nationalist because, according to Badzio, every nation must breathe and not kennel under an imperial yoke. I wonder how Pavlychko feels now that Yu. Badzio has been imprisoned.

Isn't the so-called Ukrainian intelligentsia tired of threshing the old straw—between Mazepa's patriotism and Kochubey's Russian-style internationalism, i.e., professing a philosophy of greater or lesser national betrayal? Isn't there enough for them, this intelligentsia, in what we already have—when we are deprived of history, culture, the whole of our spirit, and are only allowed to create the soul of a younger brother? How can such servility lead to anything good?

Only a madman can believe that the official form of national life can lead to anything. Everything that was created in Ukraine in the last 60 years has been infected by the bacillus of disease. How can the national tree grow when half of its crown has been cut down? What is Ukrainian history—without historians, when it is left without the Cossak chronicles, the history of Kyivan Rus, [Mykola] Kostomarov, [Mykola] Markevych, [Dmytro] Bantysh-Kamensky, [Volodymyr] Antonovych, and [Mykhailo] Hrushevsky? What kind of literature can there be if it is missing more than half of its writers? And those are first-rate writers, including [Volodymyr] Vynnychenko, [Mykola] Khvylyovy, [Valerian] Pidmohylny. And so we have prose by collective farm teenagers, all singsong and sweet. They are writing in the language of a village granny who cannot say a word without *-enka* [a pet form suffix], i.e., a typically colonial literature. *"Kyiv has such beautiful flora but what one can say about its fauna!"* said Viktor Nekrasov. And I cannot disagree with him, seeing this set of lick-spittle literati, the carriage sutlers of aesthetics, who sew themselves the painted *sharovary* [traditional Ukrainian trousers] of clown-dancers at the national tragedy, and dance a dashing *hopak* on the corpse of Ukraine. Really, it is easier to lose your mind than to be oneself, because you have nothing.

One's own impotence in the face of injustice is insulting. How can you remain silent when you know that somewhere behind bars Oleksa [Tykny] is in critical condition and is being tortured? But your voice is impotent likewise when you address complaints to the prosecutor (they will find "disallowed expressions" in every complaint and punish the author: I think they punish us for the form of the complaint-appeal itself). It is insulting when they forbid you to strip to the waist during the recreation period and sickly Semen Skalych is forced to wear a quilted jacket in the terrible heat. It is insulting to talk to a prosecutor and commandant who cynically and automatically replies "it is not allowed" to every complaint and then your voice breaks and you either stop talking to Captain Dolmatov (a unit head) or call him a hangman, murderer, etc.

The form of existence is not to be found here (I would not call any individual behavior ideal, because it is simply impossible to behave ideally here). Mart Niklus, for example, has made a practice of writing long, frequent complaints: he believes they can be useful. Others refuse to go on mass hunger strikes (usually they take place on 30 October and 10 December, but this year we commemorated the 10th anniversary of repressions in Ukraine and the anniversary of Kukk's death) because they believe they are ineffective. Each position has its good argument. So, everyone behaves as his mind and conscience dictate.

The work is very hard: to fulfill the quota, you need to work all 8 hours nonstop. But you can get used to anything. It is insulting when guards break into the cell and take away all records and books, leaving only 5 books (including magazines). Confiscation of letters is insulting as well. Almost no one gets letters from indirect relatives or friends. Everyone has only one permitted addressee, but even his letters do not arrive easily. In one word, the government has allowed everything to be done to us.

There is no hospital or medical treatment. People wait to see the dentist for 2-3 months or even longer. And even when he appears he does nothing more than pull teeth. And yet almost all the prisoners are ill. Semen Skalych, Yuryi Fedorov, Vasyk Kurylo and Oleksa Tykhy are in especially poor condition. But the rest do not feel much better.

The zone has not changed quantitatively over the last year. Some military prisoners (*Polizei* [from the period of the Nazi occupation]) went to the black zone, others joined us (I[van] Kandyba, Vasyl] Ovsienko, the criminal Ostroglyad). M[ykhailo] Horyn and prison convicts (among them I[van] Sokulsky) are to arrive. And the zone is held by 30 people: 20 of them are behind bars. i.e., only one-third in the open section [without cells]. So far there are nly three [prisoners]: O[les] Berdnyk, [Henrikas] Jaškūnas, and Yevgrafov (a former domestic criminal). I wonder if the KGB will offer a second cohort of domestic criminals to be transferred to this zone, in which the admixture of the *Polizei* is declining in number every year (now there are about 10–12 people but, in a year, there may be no one left behind bars). So far, apart from the military, our lives are poisoned by two of them: V. Fedorenko and the domestic criminal Ostroglyad. What will happen next?

RECORDS 9-10
Kyiv is celebrating its 1500th anniversary. The Golden Gate through which no one enters or exits has been restored. The Zaborovsky Gate was a symbol of Kyiv for me. Now it is bricked up. Because this Kyiv has been sealed off. The more beautiful Kyiv becomes, the more terrible it is. Instead of a living city, it has been turned into a masquerade, a vampire mask that grows more beautiful as it drinks the blood of its sons and daughters. I recollect a woman from *The Sun Machine* [a science fiction novel by Volodymyr Vynnychenko] with a snake-like head. Golden-domed Kyiv has a snake's head. I cannot shake off the feeling that Ivan Svitlychny's coffin (is he still alive?) hangs over Kyiv like the statue of Christ over Rome. The boasting of Kyiv' jubilee is proud with

intruders and toadies. Because they cannot be proud who have self-serving love. Only the bureaucracy's multitude, so-called Soviet style intelligentsia has the official right to love Kyiv.

Does a Ukrainian intelligentsia in fact exist? I think that either it does not exist or it is young and immature. It has lost its character or has never attained it. A Ukrainian intellectual is 95% bureaucrat and 5% patriot. Thus, he tries to express his patriotism in bureaucratic clauses, and his patriotism is neither deep nor binding. Because patriotic gravity has still not been created in Ukraine. Introduced into the state system, this intelligentsia does not feel any duty to the people, who have also not acquired an individual face. The Soviet Worldview is a two-faced Janus too. This official intelligentsia striving to live is headed for an inglorious death, and we, history's prisoners, are heading into life (if only it will accept us after many generations).

I think about the millennium of Christianity in Ukraine. I suppose, the first mistake was accepting the Byzantine-Muscovite rite, which connected the most easterly part of the West to the East. Our individualistic Western spirit, locked up by despotic Byzantine Orthodox Christianity, could not free itself from this spiritual duality, which later created a hypocrisy complex. It seems that the backward-looking spirit of Orthodox Christianity fell like a heavy stone on the young and immature soul of our people and made femininity an attribute of our spirituality. The iron discipline of the Tatars and Mongols impregnated the Russian spirit completing it with aggressiveness and a pyramid-like structure. The Ukrainian spirit could not break out from under the heavy rock of this backward-looking faith. Perhaps this is one of the causes of our national tragedy. No, I do not like Christianity.

RECORD 11

Perhaps it is also true that a huge block of spiritual Christianity fell on the too young soul, on its not yet strong shoulders. In any case, we are the biggest victims of Orthodox Christianity. We could not get out from under its eastern charms. It destroyed our vital, life energy.

It seems that the negative impact of Christianization on language could be disjunction. But there was already a current, the flow of national history.

Perhaps these thoughts are too unprepared, provisional ones. But my life is such that negativism towards backward-looking Orthodox Christianity cannot but develop.

I think about the worldview: in my opinion, this concept is very metaphysical. A more effective feeling is the ratio of duty and desire, will and logic, will and duty. Worldview is largely a matter of temperament and conscience, our vital activity. Sometimes the worldview is determined by the chances for survival, or social influence, or size. But life circumstances undergo changes, and these are followed the changes in the components of the worldview. In my current state, any selfish-calculated considerations cannot define it. What should be done then? A look of eternity or despair? I am bored with the fragments of destinies, broken lines of desires and accomplishments, grimaces of consequences.

It is scary to feel that you are without your land, without the people you have to create for from your aching heart. Maybe it lived in the between-times period, and maybe, when historical conditions change (but will they change for the better?), it will be possible to identify this life flow of the people, its life impulse. It is not visible yet. Hence our overwhelming despair, the devouring of souls, which can happen even among the best. But so far I see — nothing and no one. No sign of hope.

In the summer of 1981, Oleksa Tykhy was thrown into a punishment isolation cell — three times in a row for 15 days at a time. It was very cold and he was troubled by his bad stomach. He could not even get up during those 45 days. Noticing his catastrophic condition, a doctor granted permission for him to be given a hot water bottle at night. Oleksa was transferred from the punishment isolation cell to the hospital, where he spent three months more, in a hellish condition, then returned to his cell.

How painful it is that under our conditions ordinary human solidarity — a general hunger strike and protest — is impossible. It is one thing that people are exhausted by the long struggle, it is another that any kind of resistance under these completely closed conditions is completely ineffectivene. How the soul is crippled when you see but remain silent.

Vitaly Kalynychenko made a few attempts to get in touch with the outside—and all in vain. He is not lucky. The KGB got hold of his sharply worded protest. On October 15, 1981, he was placed in solitary confinement for a year. Half a year later, on April 8, 1982, Mart Niklus got a year of solitary confinement. I was next –three refusals to allow visitations and three weeks in a punishment isolation cell. The latter I got because I lost my temper and called the KGB agent Cherkasov a fascist and a Gestapo agent. I have stopped writing statements, as they have no results.

RECORD 12

I have been following events in Poland since my time in Kyiv. Long live the volunteers of freedom! I am impressed by their, the Poles', opposition to Soviet despotism, their nationwide tremors, the workers, the intelligentsia, the students—everyone except the army and the police. If these events continue, the flames will spread to the military tomorrow. What will the Brezhnevs and Jaruzelskis do then? No other nation within the totalitarian world is defending its human and national rights with such dedication. Poland is an example to Ukraine (psychologically, we Ukrainians are closer, perhaps the closest, to the Polish nature, but we lack the most important thing—the sacred patriotism that unites the Poles). What a pity that Ukraine is not ready to learn from the Polish teacher.

But the Soviet and Polish regimes, having resolved to fight their people with brutal police pressure, have once again revealed their despotic nature. After Poland, it seems to me, only a complete fool or a scoundrel can believe in Moscow's ideals. Unfortunately, I do not know what impression Poland has made on the people of the USSR and the entire camp.

Trade union liberation would be very effective in the USSR as well. If the first steps made by the engineer Klebanov were supported across the country, the Soviet government would encounter, perhaps, its most modern antagonist. Because the Helsinki Group is like advanced mathematics for this country, just like the national-patriotic movement. But a movement for housing and bread, proper wages for a worker—this is a common acceptable language.

I admire the Polish spiritual victors and regret that I am not a Pole. Poland is a landmark in the totalitarian world and prepares for its collapse. But will the Polish example become ours? That is the question. Poland set Russia on fire throughout the nineteenth century. Now it is trying again. I wish the Polish insurgents success, and I hope that on December 13 the police regime will not smother the sacred flame of freedom. I hope that forces will be found in the occupied countries to support the liberation mission of the Polish freedom volunteers.

Given the Polish events, the faults of the cowardly and respectable Helsinki Group became even more apparent. If it were a mass movement with a popular initiative, with a broad program of social and political demands, if it were a movement with the idea of holding future power, then it would have some hope of success. But, now, the Helsinki Group is like a baby trying to speak in a deep voice. Certainly, it has to be defeated, because with mournful intonations it foresaw this pogrom. Perhaps the next change of power in the USSR will alter the chances for the better, but so far the social pessimism of Soviet dissidence really is justified.

Finally, please keep in mind that a number of local prisoners here need material and financial support, at least to subscribe to literature. So, possibly, at least 50–100 rubles annually would significantly help such prisoners as M[art] Niklus, I[van] Kandyba, V[asyl] Ovsienko, V[asyl] Stus, V[italy] Kalynychenko, and O[leksa] Tykhy.

The Bolsheviks, stultifying the people with their repressive propaganda, developed a method based on exceptional hypocrisy. The facts are never verified, the arguments are presented with Bolshevik versions of the facts. An example of this is Kuroyedov's article in the *Literaturnaya gazeta* (Literary Newspaper) (July 1982). It mentions S[emen] F[edorovych] Skalych, a Ukrainian Repentant, a martyr of the [pre-World War II] Polish Sanacja policy and the Bolshevik liberation.

In 1936, at the age of 16, he came down with a severe infection in his leg and became a cripple. In 1945, the Bolsheviks found a partisan pamphlet that he kept and sent him to Balkhash. The torments he endured for 10 years of imprisonment would be enough for any great martyr. Since 1953, he has linked his life with Repentance, an interesting folk version of Ukrainian messianism. And what Kuroyedov writes is a 100% lie. For example, Skalych was not in the OUN [Organization of Ukrainian Nationalists]. He is a man of God, very conscientious by nature, who believes in the new coming of Christ with fanatical devotion. Maria Kuts, whom Kuroyedov mentions, had nothing to do with Repentance, her disability resulted from madness. But the Bolsheviks used this fact to discredit Repentance. What was Skalych on trial for? For his religious beliefs, for a nationalist version of Christianity, which is dangerous to Moscow. The 700 poems taken from Skalych are the fruit of his reflections on the world, faith, and Christianity. Could Skalych be on trial? For what? I have not seen a greater crime in the camp than the one committed against Skalych. I believe that all honest people of the world should care about the fate of this Ukrainian confessor. He needs special support from the world's confessional organizations. A person who has neither letters nor money (even to buy food for 4 rubles a month), he retains an exceptional dignity. Trusting results to God's will, he is sure that here, on this cross, he will die. But he does not complain about fate: it is beautiful for him because he is a martyr for the faith.

Recently, O[leksa] Tykhy was deprived of a visit. Ukrainians are the first to suffer pressure. This prison is anti-Ukrainian in its purpose. Thus, the threat of Ukrainian revolt to the authorities is appalling.

Please do not abandon my mother, Stus Olena Yakivna, born in 1900. Her address: 19 Chevashska St., Donetsk-26, 340026. She lives with her daughter, Maria Semenivna (born in 1935, a math teacher). The mother needs, first of all, moral support, crying her eyes out for her son. Good people, write to her, let her not be alone in her grief — support her spirit!

Vasyl Stus [1982]

1984

September. Statement by Vasyl Stus to the Soviet government: *"On August 23, being unable to withstand the inhumane conditions in the VS-389/36 concentration camp, Ukrainian political prisoner Yurii Lytvyn attempted suicide. He opened his stomach with a blade, pouring his entrails into a bloody bed. He was taken away unconscious. He may have already died.*

Before that, Lytvyn, a prominent Ukrainian human rights activist, was regularly deprived of visits. On one occasion, because he was hit by a criminal provocateur (!), and, on another, because the local authorities, Lieutenant Colonel Fedorov, did not like his looks.

Lytvyn is seriously ill, but he has been given almost no medical care. He waited for 9 months for prosthetic teeth, living without his teeth (he could not eat anything almost all this time). Lytvyn is almost completely blind, and he is fed in such a way that his body could atrophy. Yu. Shukhevych lost his sight due to malnutrition – that is, due to concentration camp rations. And Lytvyn was brought to that point as well: at the age of 50 he weighed only 46–48 kg. It was these conditions of inhuman abuse that led to the death of another Ukrainian human rights activist, Oleksa Tykhy, who was actually murdered – by cold, hunger and lack of treatment three and a half months ago!

Other political prisoners – M[ykhailo] Horyn, V[alery] Marchenko, V[asyl] Kurylo, L[evko] Lukyanenko, S[emen] Skalych and V[asyl] Ovsienko – i.e., almost the entire Ukrainian contingent of local political prisoners also live in situations that could result in a new death every day!

This situation reminds one of the darkest years of Stalinism when the best sons of the Ukrainian people – M[ykola] Zerov, L[es] Kurbas, M[ykhailo] Dry-Khmara, and M[ykola] – were dying and going made in Stalin's murder sites.

I ask: what is the point of such executions? The hopes that any of us will break are futile and absolutely useless. We are all ready to die for the future of our people, for justice and progress. And our sacrificial blood, shed in the Kuchino concentration camp, will forever remain our glory, and your black shame. Think on it well. Know that we are under the care of the people's memory. We are. Not you.

I know that there is no one to write to. Ukrainian werewolves, janissaries, will not let this letter be sent to its destination. After all, did they not usher the Ukrainian youth of the 1950s – 1980s under the knife of the newest followers of Stalin and Beria? So why am I writing?

I am doing this to remind you: after today, there will be tomorrow. Find your wits, people! [an allusion to Taras Shavchenko's poem To My Fellow-Countrymen, in Ukraine and Not in Ukraine, Living, Dead and As Yet Unborn...]."

Autumn. A notebook with poems and translations—the last collection of poems entitled *The Bird of the Soul*—was confiscated from Stus.

1985

Heinrich Böll nominated Vasyl Stus for the the Nobel Prize.

Beginning of August. Stus was thrown into solitary confinement on the false accusation that he was "bothering other convicts": his cellmate Leonid Borodin requested the guards to tell a soldier on the tower to stop singing.

August 30-31. Upon the false denunciation of the guard, Vasyl Stus was thrown into solitary confinement in the VS-389/36 camp for 15 days.

Night of September 3-4. In solitary confinement, during his "dry" hunger strike, Vasyl Stus' heart stopped beating.

VASYL STUS' LAST POEM
rewritten in the letter of June 12, 1983

We are circling around the trunk.
Will you try to catch me up?
(We know that this will not happen anymore,
however — you live).
Your laughter is so rolling,
That bursts into tears.
I am sorry for I will not send you
a message. I am sorry.
That's impatient! Not in vain
pine bark is being tanned.
"Up the hill — I want to!" — "Down — along a steep bank!"
"And shall we wander more?" — "It's time!"

* * *

To come to mind and part
forever, for-not-for...
"Don't become a Vendee, you worwalking girl"
She's silent, lamenting and secret.
And here is our house — a stork's nest
in the swaying branches of the floors,
and the memory is chippering by the nightingale
up to cuckoo' augury.
That memory can be useful to us,
when the time is right.
"Isn't it really forever?" The tray is dancing,
The face is growing pale.

"Is the tree swirling in a whirlwind?"
The wedding fire bursts into a blaze!
Three-musicians' group's melody is heard,
It finally happened!
We are circling tightly,
and keep falling out of step.
The world is growing dark. We are brightening
when there is neither strength nor force.

UKRAINIAN VOICES

Collected by Andreas Umland

1 *Mychailo Wynnyckyj*
Ukraine's Maidan, Russia's War
A Chronicle and Analysis of the Revolution of Dignity
With a foreword by Serhii Plokhy
ISBN 978-3-8382-1327-9

2 *Olexander Hryb*
Understanding Contemporary Ukrainian and Russian Nationalism
The Post-Soviet Cossack Revival and Ukraine's National Security
With a foreword by Vitali Vitaliev
ISBN 978-3-8382-1377-4

3 *Marko Bojcun*
Towards a Political Economy of Ukraine
Selected Essays 1990–2015
With a foreword by John-Paul Himka
ISBN 978-3-8382-1368-2

4 *Volodymyr Yermolenko (Ed.)*
Ukraine in Histories and Stories
Essays by Ukrainian Intellectuals
With a preface by Peter Pomerantsev
ISBN 978-3-8382-1456-6

5 *Mykola Riabchuk*
At the Fence of Metternich's Garden
Essays on Europe, Ukraine, and Europeanization
ISBN 978-3-8382-1484-9

6 *Marta Dyczok*
Ukraine Calling
A Kaleidoscope from Hromadske Radio 2016–2019
With a foreword by Andriy Kulykov
ISBN 978-3-8382-1472-6

7   *Olexander Scherba*
    Ukraine vs. Darkness
    Undiplomatic Thoughts
    With a foreword by Adrian Karatnycky
    ISBN 978-3-8382-1501-3

8   *Olesya Yaremchuk*
    Our Others
    Stories of Ukrainian Diversity
    With a foreword by Ostap Slyvynsky
    Translated from the Ukrainian by Zenia Tompkins and Hanna Leliv
    ISBN 978-3-8382-1475-7

9   *Nataliya Gumenyuk*
    Die verlorene Insel
    Geschichten von der besetzten Krim
    Mit einem Vorwort von Alice Bota
    Aus dem Ukrainischen übersetzt von Johann Zajaczkowski
    ISBN 978-3-8382-1499-3

10 *Olena Stiazhkina*
    Zero Point Ukraine
    Four Essays on World War II
    Translated from the Ukrainian by Svitlana Kulinska
    ISBN 978-3-8382-1550-1

11 *Oleksii Sinchenko, Dmytro Stus, Leonid Finberg (compilers)*
    Ukrainian Dissidents
    An Anthology of Texts
    ISBN 978-3-8382-1551-8

12 *John-Paul Himka*
    Ukrainian Nationalists and the Holocaust
    OUN and UPA's Participation in the Destruction of Ukrainian Jewry, 1941–1944
    ISBN 978-3-8382-1548-8

13 *Andrey Demartino*
    False Mirrors
    The Weaponization of Social Media in Russia's Operation to Annex Crimea
    With a foreword by Oleksiy Danilov
    ISBN 978-3-8382-1533-4

14 *Svitlana Biedarieva (Ed.)*
Contemporary Ukrainian and Baltic Art
Political and Social Perspectives, 1991–2021
ISBN 978-3-8382-1526-6

15 *Olesya Khromeychuk*
A Loss
The Story of a Dead Soldier Told by His Sister
With a foreword by Andrey Kurkov
ISBN 978-3-8382-1570-9

16 *Marieluise Beck (Hg.)*
Ukraine verstehen
Auf den Spuren von Terror und Gewalt
Mit einem Vorwort von Dmytro Kuleba
ISBN 978-3-8382-1653-9

17 *Stanislav Aseyev*
Heller Weg
Geschichte eines Konzentrationslagers im Donbass 2017–2019
Aus dem Russischen übersetzt von
Martina Steis und Charis Haska
ISBN 978-3-8382-1620-1

18 *Mykola Davydiuk*
Wie funktioniert Putins Propaganda?
Anmerkungen zum Informationskrieg des Kremls
Aus dem Ukrainischen übersetzt von Christian Weise
ISBN 978-3-8382-1628-7

19 *Olesya Yaremchuk*
Unsere Anderen
Geschichten ukrainischer Vielfalt
Aus dem Ukrainischen übersetzt von Christian Weise
ISBN 978-3-8382-1635-5

20 *Oleksandr Mykhed*
„Dein Blut wird die Kohle tränken"
Über die Ostukraine
Aus dem Ukrainischen übersetzt von Simon Muschick
und Dario Planert
ISBN 978-3-8382-1648-5

21   *Vakhtang Kipiani (Hg.)*
     Der Zweite Weltkrieg in der Ukraine
     Geschichte und Lebensgeschichten
     Aus dem Ukrainischen übersetzt von Margarita Grinko
     ISBN 978-3-8382-1622-5

22   *Vakhtang Kipiani (ed.)*
     World War II, Uncontrived and Unredacted
     Testimonies from Ukraine
     Translated from the Ukrainian by Zenia Tompkins and Daisy Gibbons
     ISBN 978-3-8382-1621-8

23   *Dmytro Stus*
     Vasyl Stus
     Life in Creativity
     Translated from the Ukrainian by Ludmila Bachurina
     ISBN 978-3-8382-1631-7

***ibidem**.eu*